College Student Mental Health
Counseling

Suzanne Degges-White, PhD, LPC, LMHC, NCC, is professor and chair of the counseling, adult and higher education department at Northern Illinois University, DeKalb, Illinois. Her research interests include adult wellness over the life span from adolescence through older adulthood, the use of the expressive arts in counseling, and sexual identity development. She enjoys working with adolescents and adults in her private practice and integrating expressive arts interventions to encourage clients to explore multiple methods of communication and self-exploration. She is the author of the book *Friends Forever: How Girls and Women Forge Lasting Relationships* (2011) and coeditor of *Counseling Boys and Young Men* (2012) and *Integrating the Expressive Arts Into Counseling Practice* (2011).

Christine Borzumato-Gainey, PhD, LPC, is a counselor and instructor at Elon University in Elon, North Carolina. She received her doctoral degree in counseling and counseling supervision from the University of North Carolina at Greensboro. She is currently a mental health counselor at the Elon University Counseling Center as well as director of the BASICS program, which addresses substance abuse concerns of students. She has over a decade of experience working within the college setting, is the author of several publications and presentations addressing this population, and is coauthor of *Friends Forever: How Girls and Women Forge Lasting Relationships* (2011).

College Student Mental Health Counseling

Counseling

A Developmental Approach

Suzanne Degges-White, PhD, LPC, LMHC, NCC

Christine Borzumato-Gainey, PhD, LPC

Editors

SPRINGER PUBLISHING COMPANY

NEW YORK

Springer Publishing Company, LLC
11 West 42nd Street
New York, NY 10036
www.springerpub.com

Acquisitions Editor: Nancy S. Hale
Composition: Amnet

ISBN: 978-0-8261-9971-3
E-book ISBN: 978-0-8261-9972-0

13 14 15 16 17 / 5 4 3 2 1

The author and the publisher of this Work have made every effort to use sources believed to be reliable to provide information that is accurate and compatible with the standards generally accepted at the time of publication. The author and publisher shall not be liable for any special, consequential, or exemplary damages resulting, in whole or in part, from the readers' use of, or reliance on, the information contained in this book. The publisher has no responsibility for the persistence or accuracy of URLs for external or third-party Internet websites referred to in this publication and does not guarantee that any content on such websites is, or will remain, accurate or appropriate.

Library of Congress Cataloging-in-Publication Data

College student mental health counseling : a developmental approach / edited by Suzanne Degges-White, PhD, Christine Borzumato-Gainey, PhD.
    pages cm
  Includes bibliographical references and index.
  ISBN 978-0-8261-9971-3 (print edition : alk. paper)—ISBN 978-0-8261-9972-0 (e-book) 1. College students—Mental health. 2. College students—Mental health services. I. Degges-White, Suzanne, editor of compilation. II. Borzumato-Gainey, Christine, editor of compilation.
  RC451.4.S7C672 2014
  616.8900835—dc23

                                                    2013019652

Printed in the United States of America by Edwards Brothers.

*We dedicate this book to all of the emerging adults that
follow a path that leads to campus.*

Contents

Contributors

Susan R. Barclay, PhD, LPC, NCC, ACS
Department of Leadership Studies
University of Central Arkansas
Conway, AR

Stephanie C. Bell, MA
Department of Leadership and Counselor Education
The University of Mississippi
University, MS

Esther Nicole Benoit, PhD, LPC, NCC
College of Social and Behavioral Sciences
Walden University
Minneapolis, MN

Caroline S. Booth, PhD, LPC, NCC
Department of Human Development and Services
North Carolina A&T State University
Greensboro, NC

Nathan R. Booth, MEd
Department of Leadership and Counselor Education
The University of Mississippi
University, MS

Megan M. Buning, PhD
Department of Leadership and Counselor Education
The University of Mississippi
University, MS

Emily Franklin, MEd
Department of Leadership and Counselor Education
The University of Mississippi
University, MS

Katherine M. Hermann, PhD
Department of Counselor Education
University of Louisiana at Lafayette
Lafayette, LA

Edward F. Hudspeth, PhD, NCC, LPC, RPh, RPT-S, ACS
Assistant Professor, Counselor Education
Henderson State University
Arkadelphia, AR

Marcela Kepicova, MA, EdS, LPC, NCC
Doctoral Fellow, Counselor Education
Montclair State University
Montclair, NJ

Wendy Killam, PhD, NCC, CRC, LPC
Director, Clinical Mental Health Counseling Program
Stephen F. Austin State University
Nacogdoches, TX

Leslie Kooyman, PhD
Montclair State University
Montclair, NJ

Jeane B. Lee, PhD
Associate Professor, Counselor Education
Alabama State University
Montgomery, AL

Joshua Magruder, PhD, LPC, NCC
The University of Mississippi Counseling Center
University, MS

Kimberly Matthews, MEd
Department of Leadership and Counselor Education
The University of Mississippi
University, MS

Tony Michael, MA, LPC
Department of Leadership and Counselor Education
The University of Mississippi
University, MS

Rebecca Earhart Michel, PhD, LCPC, NCC
Division of Psychology and Counseling
Governors State University
University Park, IL

Kattrina Miller-Roach, MA
Department of Leadership and Counselor Education
The University of Mississippi
University, MS

Elise Noyes
Elon University
Elon, NC

Gregory S. Phipps, BS
Doctoral Student, Department of Human Development and Services
North Carolina A&T State University
Greensboro, NC

Ricardo M. Phipps, MA
Department of Leadership and Counselor Education
The University of Mississippi
University, MS

Nicole M. Randick, MAT, ATR-BC, LPC
Counselor Education and Supervision
Division of Psychology and Counseling
Governors State University
University Park, IL

Meghan Lynwood Reppert, MA
Department of Counseling and Educational Leadership
Montclair State University
Montclair, NJ

Catherine B. Roland, PhD
Department of Educational Leadership, Counseling, and Special Education
Georgia Regents University
Augusta, GA

Laura McShane Schulenberg, BA, MAT
Department of Leadership and Counselor Education
The University of Mississippi
University, MS

Carrie V. Smith, MEd
Department of Counseling and Human Development Services
University of Georgia
Athens, GA

Kevin B. Stoltz, PhD, NCC, ACS, LPC
Department of Leadership and Counselor Education
The University of Mississippi
University, MS

Sterling P. Travis, MEd
Doctoral Student
Counselor Education
The College of William and Mary
Williamsburg, VA

Ian Turnage-Butterbaugh, MS
Department of Leadership and Counselor Education
The University of Mississippi
University, MS

Lori A. Wolff, PhD, JD
Department of Leadership and Counselor Education
The University of Mississippi
University, MS

Amy Zavadil, MA, NCC
Community Conduct Director
Barnard College
New York, NY

Preface

An increasing number of students arriving on college campuses are struggling with mental health disorders in addition to managing the typical college transition challenges. According to the National Alliance on Mental Illness (Gruttadaro & Crudo, 2012), depressive disorders and anxiety disorders are just two of the many significant self-reported presenting issues college counselors might be called on to address. It is well known that the stigma attached to mental health concerns results in a lower reporting of incidences than is actually experienced, so there are likely many more students who have neither acknowledged nor sought help for their mental health distress. Newspapers and television news shows continue to highlight the mental health crisis on the nation's college campuses, and it is clear that college counselors must be prepared to assist this population. We hope this book will provide useful information that will allow counselors to gain a deeper understanding of how college students may be affected by mental health issues, as well as how best to work with these students within the campus counseling office confines. Further, we provide a developmental framework for understanding this population— a great deal happens to young adults from the ages of 17 to 22, and we emphasize the importance of viewing each member of this population as a "work in progress."

THE SCOPE OF THE BOOK

This book offers an in-depth look at the ways in which contemporary undergraduate students may differ from past generations, as well as noting how some things never change, such as needs related to finding social support, romantic intimacy, and academic achievement. The first chapter of this book, "The Myriad Faces of College Student Development," provides a brief overview of the various developmental transformations that are taking place within the many levels of cognitive, affective, and physiological development of emerging adults.

Next, we lay out the typical counseling concerns that counselors can expect to meet across the academic year. Rather than provide a clinical and empirical review of the literature, however, this chapter is written from the perspective of a well-seasoned counselor who has witnessed the tide of presenting issues over the year in the college counseling center. Because the experiences of each class differ markedly from one another, we have divided this chapter according to class year: freshmen, sophomores, juniors, and seniors. We then provide a closer look at the obstacles and transitions that are faced by underclassmen (freshmen and sophomores) and by upperclassmen (juniors and seniors). These first four chapters offer a holistic perspective on how the inner development of students influences their responses to the external transitions they face.

The next two chapters of the book address the social concerns of students as they seek to find the best way to fit in on campus. We address the growing diversity of college campuses as well as provide counselors with guidance on helping their clients connect into the campus community. Following these two chapters, we move into ways to assist clients who are facing unexpected hurdles, including grief over the loss of significant others; difficulties with self-esteem and self-image presented by the competitive culture of college-age females; and navigational challenges in romantic relationships that may be more intense and sexually tinged than prior high school relationships had been.

In Chapters 11 through 18, we address specific mental health disorders that frequently appear in the college-age population. We provide information about how relevant symptoms may manifest in a college student population, as well as provide a framework for understanding the challenges each disorder presents within an academic and social setting. The chapters also provide guidelines for treatment and intervention that are relevant to college counselors working within a brief counseling framework. Topics include eating disorders, substance abuse, depression, anxiety, self-injury, suicidal students, obsessive-compulsive disorder, and impulse-control disorders. Finally, the last chapter provides readers with ideas for promoting student well-being beyond the counseling office.

WHO WILL BENEFIT FROM THIS BOOK?

While this book's primary audience is college counselors or students in higher education counseling programs, it is an excellent resource for anyone working with the college-aged population, whether through students affairs, admissions, or other areas. Although the focus of the book is on undergraduates, much of the information is relevant to those who work with graduate students or young adults in other settings. By taking a closer look at the social, academic, and professional transitions of young adults, we have created a guide that can benefit anyone who is committed to facilitating the development of these individuals.

OVERALL VALUE OF THIS BOOK

There are many treatment planners available to mental health counselors, but we wanted to provide a resource that went beyond a broad "cook-book approach" to meeting mental health needs. We believe that helpers must be highly cognizant of the inner development that emerging adult clients are experiencing as they face the novel challenges met on campus. In order for readers to gain the best understanding possible, we've not only used a developmental lens to frame the mental health problems of students, but have simultaneously considered and applied the concepts to students within the college environment. The case studies and symptom presentation descriptions provided are actual composites of the college student clients we have treated. A lot has to happen in the years students are on campus, and the inherent stress experienced when they are faced with new challenges frequently encourages students to seek help. We believe this book will provide a very useful breadth and depth of knowledge to our readers.

REFERENCE

Gruttadaro, D., & Crudo, D. (2012). *College students speak: A survey report on mental illness.* Arlington, VA: National Alliance on Mental Illness.

Acknowledgments

The development of this book was dependent upon the labor and commitment of a group of individuals who are dedicated to meeting the needs of the contemporary college student population as effectively as possible. We are indebted to our collaborators and contributors who shared expertise that can be gained only through firsthand experience with this unique population. We also would like to acknowledge the strong support and insightful assistance provided by our Springer Publishing Company copilots Nancy Hale and Katie Corasaniti. This book springs from a desire to better meet client needs as well as offer readers a contemporary and very timely perspective on the experiences and counseling needs of this "emerging adult" population, and we acknowledge that this is best accomplished through teamwork and sharing knowledge. Thank you to all of the members of our team—we share the collective knowledge within the covers of this book.

S.E.D. & C.J.B.

To my coeditor, Christine; thank you for being the spark that ignited the enthusiasm that brought this project from just a "good idea" into a robust resource for college personnel—I appreciate the energy and passion you bring to every collaborative project. I am also grateful to my partner, Ellen, and our three children, Georgia, Andrew, and David. All of the kids are "emerging adults" at this moment in time and they have provided me with what seems to be a more than generous number of firsthand learning opportunities about the challenges young adults face during this developmental stage. However, watching each of them follow their winding paths to adulthood—challenges and all—brings immeasurable joy that overshadows those few moments of terror!

S.E.D.

I am indebted to my coeditor, Suzanne, for including me on this wild book ride. My academic life would not have the same zest without your support or your adventures. I would also like to acknowledge Chris Troxler, the "Superman of Counseling," for sharing his wisdom that helped guide the framework of this book. And a special thanks to my little family, Howard, Brooke, and Drew, for their love, patience, and the efforts they made to be self-sufficient while I was engrossed in the creation of this book.

C.J.B.

Section I: Developmental Issues

1

The Myriad Faces of College Student Development

KATHERINE M. HERMANN, ESTHER NICOLE BENOIT, AMY ZAVADIL, AND LESLIE KOOYMAN

The secret of eternal youth is arrested development.
—Alice Roosevelt Longworth

For counselors working in higher education and with increasingly diverse populations, it is essential to understand the worldview of the client. The years in which a student is traditionally engaged in higher education are a time of great personal development and reflect changes in many aspects of a student's functioning. The duration of this transitional period, now termed *emerging adulthood*, is increasing, and for a large number of individuals, this development is fostered during the college years (Arnett, Ramos, & Jensen, 2001). As access to education has evolved, moving on to college is expected for more than half of all graduating American high school students (Bureau of Labor Statistics, 2012; National Center for Higher Education Management Systems, 2008). It is important to recognize, however, that students represent a diverse range of experiences, skills, and abilities, approaching this life transition from a variety of perspectives.

Tinto (2006), writing about college retention, asserted the importance of "the concept of integration and the patterns of interaction between the student and other members of the institution especially during the critical first year of college and the stages of transition that marked that year" (p. 3). During the 1960s and 1970s, theories of college student development emerged, and have continued to evolve and develop as demographics have changed (Gardner, 2009). Gardner (2009) summarized the series of student development theories that build upon the work of Erikson's

1

life span development theory, focusing specifically on the college years. Many models exist, with a common expectation of the need to resolve an issue or develop a skill to progress in the developmental process (Gardner, 2009). Practitioners have also recognized the need for awareness of the ever-changing demographics, and corresponding needs, of college students (Astin, 1998; Bishop, Lacour, Nutt, Yamada, & Lee, 2004). As the population of individuals entering college increases in diversity and numbers, it is important to consider the range of developmental needs that may impact, as well as be a result of, the transition to college as part of this stage of the life span. For some, the transition to college may be a relatively quick settling in during the first semester of a student's first year, but this time of transition is more likely to span the first years of the college as students navigate their own complexity within a diverse community.

Developmentally, the college years are a time for developing oneself including self-sufficiency and personal responsibility (Arnett, 2003). College campuses strive to provide a supportive environment geared toward challenging students to grow and develop. Look to the mission statement of most colleges, and words like *growth, citizenship, development*, and *responsibility* are anticipated outcomes of the college or university experience. The evolving demographic of college students is well documented, specifically through 40 years of data collection with the Cooperative Institutional Research Program Freshman Survey (Pryor, Hurtado, Saenz, Santos, & Korn, 2007), as well as discussion of the impact of changing demographics through the scholarly literature (Astin, 1998; Bishop et al., 2004). Thus, when conceptualizing college students, there are many developmental models through which we can view this population. College students are still very much adolescents and the developmental path of this group moves through many different landscapes, including cognitive, psychosocial, neurological, and emotional realms. The following models provide a lens through which we may be able to better understand students' adaptive or maladaptive methods of approaching the many challenges of the college years. Each of these descriptions can be isolated to explain specific actions and conflicts, or they can be reflected upon collectively to expound on college students' experiences and reactions to events. We will begin with one of the more recently developed perspectives on this group, through the lens of understanding the emerging adult.

EMERGING ADULTHOOD

Jeffrey Jensen Arnett (2000, 2012) presents one avenue for understanding the college years in current literature. He identified *emerging adulthood* as the transition period from adolescence to young adulthood and used the ages of 18 and 25 as boundary points. During this time most individuals have not yet experienced many of the developmental tasks indicative of a transition into adulthood such as marriage, parenting, or occupational stability, yet these topics are the focus areas for the transitions that will occur during this period.

Emerging adulthood is a time when goals that focus largely on exploration of identity and life course, including career, education, and relationships, unfold (Salmela-Aro, Aunola, & Nurmi, 2007). Arnett (2000) described this as a period of role hiatus in which burgeoning autonomy, coupled with a lack of persistent adult responsibilities, allows individuals to experiment and explore. This extended period of exploration and learning acts as a bridge between childhood dependence and adult roles and responsibilities (Roisman, Masten, Coatsworth, & Tellegen, 2004).

Overall, well-being tends to be stable over time; however, emerging adulthood is one period of the life span when well-being can shift dramatically (Schulenberg, Bryant, & O'Malley, 2004). While the transition from college to work can be disorienting, the smoothness of this shift is not necessarily associated with overall satisfaction (Murphy, Blustein, Bohlig, & Platt, 2010). This finding may suggest that the struggles experienced by college upperclassmen are a normative, and even an additive, component of emerging adulthood. It should be noted that although the concepts of emerging and young adulthood are supported in the research literature, these are culturally bound constructs and not immutable developmental truths.

AN ECOLOGICAL DEVELOPMENTAL MODEL

An ecological developmental framework offers a perspective of this time of identity exploration, as well as physiological, physical, social, and emotional change. Pascarella and Terenzini (2005) identify areas of student change, such as psychosocial and cognitive-structural, that occur within the transition to college. Particularly with traditional-aged first- and second-year college students, the individual college student transitions from his or her familiar adolescent environment to a college environment marked by both opportunity and expectation of individual responsibility. Students bring to this transitional experience a vast range of life experiences. Student persistence and retention, staying in school to achieve the desired goal (often a diploma), are complex issues. Engagement, students' connection within their educational community, particularly in the first years of college, supports retention and requires recognizing the diversity of students and their environments (Tinto, 2006).

Bronfenbrenner (1977) provides an ecological development framework for considering the development of the individual within the context of his or her environment. This includes considering not only the current environment, but also the many systems that can shape an individual. Bronfenbrenner defined microsystems as the person–environment relationship related to a setting, taking into account elements such as place, time, activity, and role of the individual (p. 514). Students who are classmates in their first year of college provide an example of a microsystem. Each student, though sharing this microsystem as a member of an incoming class at a specific institution, is influenced by the mesosystem, that is, interaction with other specific current influences such as family, peers, work, or other school experiences. This in turn is influenced by an exosystem, which is defined as broader societal institutions, such as government, school, media, or neighborhood influences, which impact the individual, but are not directly controlled by the individual. The exosystem includes college policies and practices that are defined by others, yet will influence students. Finally, the macrosystem in which these systems all are encompassed can be described as the cultural influences that underlie and inform each of the other environments. Taylor (2008) describes student's involvement in the micro-, meso-, and eco-systems as "important variables that play a part in the developmental process" (p. 220). In addition to individual characteristics and personal experiences, the salient environmental influences of an individual can vary at any given time. This framework can be visualized as a Venn diagram showing both overlap and unique influence among the various ecological factors (Bronfenbrenner, pp. 514–515).

Although we may first envision students as categories, that is, freshmen, sophomores, and so forth, it is essential to recognize the heterogeneity of each group's population. In preparation for work with college students, a broad ecological view of the variety of possible factors, experiences, and environments that can impact individual development is helpful to effectively support a client as well as encourage a campus community conducive to individual and community growth. Adjustment to college includes adjustment to academic, emotional, and social realms. Considering the individual student's characteristics and life experiences can inform responses to both identified and anticipated needs, as well as support development within each realm. We must remember that while the college experience brings together groups of students facing similar transitions and challenges, students will also face their own personal challenges that reflect their identities and personal path.

PSYCHOSOCIAL DEVELOPMENT

Erik Erikson, one of the pioneers of developmental stage models, designed a theory describing individuals' progression through eight developmental stages from birth into adulthood. In this model, Erikson offers insight into the typical interpersonal conflicts and important life events during each period. According to this framework, the sixth stage of development, Young Adulthood, marks a period when individuals, between the ages of 19 and 40, focus on forming close, loving relationships. During this stage, individuals battle isolation as they search for intimacy and meaningful connections with others. For many, this transition is reflected in the commitment to another individual and/or the desire to form a family of one's own.

Negotiating the interpersonal conflicts surrounding the resolution between intimacy and isolation can be a unique struggle during the later years of college. As students strive to become adults—establishing secure identities, becoming independent, and conforming to social standards (Barry, Madsen, Nelson, Carroll, & Badger, 2009)—they must negotiate the coexistence of meaningful relationships with their postgraduation goals and current obligations. For many individuals, this growth process requires a balance of forming meaningful romantic relationships while cultivating the self-understanding necessary for individual identity formation. While this can be a valuable period for exploration and formation of building meaningful lifelong connections, conflict can arise when students are unable to concurrently balance their connection to their social network and their romantic partner or when they seek to find stability during this period of transition by coupling. Erikson's model provides valuable insight into a natural area of conflict that many college students experience—the link between identity and intimacy. This issue will be discussed in further detail in chapters addressing sexuality and romantic relationships.

PERRY'S INTELLECTUAL SCHEMA

Like Erikson, William Perry created a structure for understanding developmental growth. Perry's research, a reaction to his observation of "increase[ed] relativism in society and diversity on campus" following World War II (Love & Guthrie, 1999, p. 5), provides a developmental epistemology for investigating the lifetime evolution of individuals' knowledge (McAuliffe & Lovell, 2006). Through his longitudinal research on over 500 students at Harvard and Radcliffe, Perry created a nine-position, four-stage developmental sequence to describe undergraduate students' process of making meaning during their academic and personal college experience (Granello, 2002; Love & Guthrie, 1999; West, 2004).

Perry's model provides a "map" of adult intellectual and moral development/ethical changes. Students begin at the most basic stage of dualistic thinking; in this stage, individuals perceive a simple "right or wrong" answer to every question or challenge. Thus, students are eager to gain facts, which they believe will provide the knowledge necessary to succeed. The next stage is multiplicity in which there is the realization that there is no real single truth and that knowledge is much more subjective than once believed. As students begin to recognize that answers still need to be found, they begin to move into the third stage, relativism. In this stage, ambiguity in knowledge and answers is recognized as an unavoidable circumstance, and students may be discombobulated by the recognition that all answers must be evaluated and that all answers may have merit. This disequilibrium may move a student forcefully into the final stage, commitment. This may reflect a commitment to a vocational path or moral ideals and marks the ability of the student to hold conflicting viewpoints and accept ambiguity from a point of personal commitment (Granello, 2002; Love & Guthrie, 1999; McAuliffe & Lovell, 2006). These hallmarks of higher development and stronger identity formation are more frequently characteristic of the behaviors observed within students during the end of their college experience. Advanced reasoning capabilities enable students to manage additional stressors and developmental challenges. As a result, students are not paralyzed by a search for a single truth and definitive result, but are comfortable navigating through unclear experiences.

Ideally, college students progress through the early dualistic developmental positions during their first year in college, and acquire relativistic reasoning capabilities before graduation. Nevertheless, research presents conflicting evidence about the average student position at the time of graduation (Love & Guthrie, 1999), with some evidence suggesting students can graduate from a university without reaching a relativistic level of reasoning. In addition, in times of high uncertainty and unbalanced levels of challenge and support, students may regress to earlier developmental positions in search of comfort and security. This notion of seeking security and operating within an established support system is closely related to the challenges described by Erikson during this period of life. If individuals are capable of negotiating the need for connection away from isolation, they may be better equipped with peer and/or romantic support that will encourage their success as they embark from an environment of familiarity into an uncertain milieu.

The demonstration of dualistic reasoning—whether the byproduct of external factors, life circumstances, situational regression, or other variables—may result in students who are less capable of operating within an environment of high uncertainty. For these students, the many transitions during the later college years may be particularly challenging.

MORAL DEVELOPMENT

The transition to college coincides with development in moral reasoning, as an individual's process of response to a moral dilemma evolves over time. Lawrence Kohlberg describes development across three levels of moral reasoning related to ethical behavior (Power, Higgins, & Kohlberg, 1991; Terenzini, 1987). The work of Kohlberg focused on an ethic of justice or fairness, whereas Carol Gilligan expanded on this notion with the perspective of an ethic of care or responsiveness to others (Gilligan, 1988). Gilligan's work introduced gender differences in how one approaches moral reasoning.

As students operate from different stages or levels of moral development, as well as an individual place on the spectrum of the ethic of justice or care, managing student conflict is increasingly complex. Students at different stages of moral development will react differently to similar social, academic, and cocurricular experiences; conversely, exposure to a variety of such experiences can serve to support moral development (Mayhew, Seifert, & Pascarella, 2010). As with other aspects of student growth, providing opportunity for student engagement, as well as sufficient challenge, can support moral development and enhance ethical decision making to benefit the individual and their current community.

EGO DEVELOPMENT

Jane Loevinger's (1966) theory of ego development offers yet another valuable developmental framework for understanding the experiences of this population. In the 1960s, Loevinger formulated the theory of ego development as "the way individuals make meaning of their personal life experience and the world at large" (Krumpe, 2002, p. 1). Since her original research, ego development has been described as "the organizing aspect of personality, or as the 'master trait' [since] it organizes and governs how a person perceives and thinks about a problem, and thus determines how a person behaves" (Clements & Swensen, 2000, p. 1; Sheaffer, Sias, Toriello, & Cubero, 2008; Swensen, Eskew, & Kohlhepp, 1981).

Loevinger organized the developmental process into nine stages, which begin during infancy and continue throughout the lifetime. Like many stage models, ego development unfolds as a linear process whereby each new stage builds upon mastery of the previous. These stages are not associated with age, and advancement to a subsequent stage is not predicted based on an established interval; rather, individuals advance at unique rates as they experience various milestones. Ego development is dependent upon an individual's potential and environment; nevertheless, one's preexisting, intrinsic, and intellectual capacity may restrict growth potential. As described with Perry's developmental schema, individuals can regress to previous stages of development during periods of increased stress.

Current literature links an array of positive characteristics to higher ego development levels, such as "increased nurturance, trust, interpersonal sensitivity, valuing of individuality, psychological mindedness, responsibility, and inner control" (Hauser, Gerber, & Allen, 1998, p. 209), characteristics that are ideally cultivated in students prior to leaving college. However, data on the developmental progression of college students have been rather inconclusive. While scholars often assume college students experience a consistent advancement during their academic careers as a result of increased stressors, some data indicate that college seniors experience a decline in their developmental level (Loevinger et al., 1985). Some speculate this decline may be the result of increased stressors prior to graduation when testing has been administered. Regardless, this organizing principle of personality provides a structure for understanding the growth demonstrated by many students as they accept a greater sense of personal responsibility and ability to self-reflect, and begin to exhibit greater tolerance and acceptance of others. Developmental growth along this continuum may be especially meaningful as college students prepare for employment, where personal responsibility and the ability to understand and tolerate divergent perspectives are of great benefit.

BRAIN DEVELOPMENT

The ramifications of students' ongoing physical development are a final developmental transition with explanatory power. Because all individuals do not progress along a uniform timeline physically, college students, especially males, are likely to continue to experience physical changes. One area of consequence is the brain's developmental course. The prefrontal cortex, one of three areas of the frontal lobe, is the last area of the brain to finish developing, usually around the mid-20s. This area of the brain, described as having neuropsychological functions, is strongly related to behavior (Miller, 2007). When the prefrontal cortex is fully formed, individuals typically have acquired the advanced reasoning skills associated with adult maturity such as the recognition of consequences to actions, avoidance of socially unacceptable behaviors, foresight, reduced impulsivity, and increased organization (Giedd, 2008; Miller, 2007).

In many instances, this advanced stage of brain development closely coincides with the completion of an undergraduate program, so as students prepare for greater levels of responsibility, they simultaneously recognize the ramifications of their actions and the importance of their decisions. The combination of actual and recognized responsibility can be overwhelming for some students, yet the balance of ability and opportunity is one of the unique markers of this life stage.

REFERENCES

Arnett, J. J. (2000). Emerging adulthood: A theory of development from the late teens through the twenties. *American Psychologist, 55*(5), 469–480.

Arnett, J. J. (2003). Conceptions of the transition to adulthood among emerging adults in American ethnic groups. *New Directions for Child and Adolescent Development, 2003*(100), 63–76.

Arnett, J. J. (2012). New horizons in research on emerging and young adulthood. In A. Booth, S. L. Brown, N. S. Landale, W. D. Manning, & S. McHale (Eds.), *Early adulthood in a family context* (Vol. 2, pp. 231–244). New York, NY: Springer Publishing Company.

Arnett, J. J., Ramos, K. D., & Jensen, L. A. (2001). Ideological views in emerging adulthood: Balancing autonomy and community. *Journal of Adult Development, 8*(2), 69–79.

Astin, A. W. (1998). The changing American college student: Thirty-year trends, 1966–96. *Review of Higher Education, 21*(2), 115–135.

Barry, C. M., Madsen, S. D., Nelson, L. J., Carroll, J. S., & Badger, S. (2009). Friendship and romantic relationship qualities in emerging adulthood: Differential associations with identity development and achieved adulthood criteria. *Journal of Adult Development, 16*, 209–222.

Bishop, J. B., Lacour, M. A. M., Nutt, N. J., Yamada, V. A., & Lee, J. Y. (2004). Reviewing a decade of change in the student culture. *Journal of College Student Psychotherapy, 18*(3), 3–30.

Bronfenbrenner, U. (1977). Toward an experimental ecology of human development. *American Psychologist, 32*, 513.

Bureau of Labor Statistics. (2013). *College enrollment and work activity of 2012 high school graduates.* Retrieved from http://www.bls.gov/news.release/hsgec.nr0.htm

Clements, R. H., & Swensen, C. H. (2000). Commitment to one's spouse as a predictor of marital quality among older couples. *Current Psychology, 19*(2), 110–119.

Gardner, S. K. (2009). Student development theory: A primer. *ASHE Higher Education Report, 34*(6), 15–28.

Giedd, J. N. (2008). The teen brain: Insights from neuroimaging. *Journal of Adolescent Health, 42*(4), 335–343.

Gilligan, C. (1988). *Mapping the moral domain: A contribution of women's thinking to psychological theory and education* (Vol. 2). Cambridge, MA: Harvard University Press.

Granello, D. H. (2002). Assessing the cognitive development of counseling students: Changes in epistemological assumptions. *Counselor Education and Supervision, 41*(4), 279–293.

Hauser, S. T., Gerber, E. B., & Allen, J. P. (1998). Ego development and attachment: Converging platforms for understanding close relationships. In M. P. Westenberg & A. Blasi (Eds.), *Personality development: Theoretical, empirical, and clinical implications of Loevinger's conception of ego development* (pp. 203–217). Mahwah, NJ: Lawrence Erlbaum Associates.

Krumpe, S. (2002). *A phenomenological investigation of women's experiences in family therapy: Interviews with ten mothers.* Doctoral dissertation, The College of William & Mary, Williamsburg, VA.

Loevinger, J. (1966). The meaning and measurement of ego development. *American Psychologist, 21*(3), 195–206. doi:10.1037/h0023376

Loevinger, J., Cohn, L. D., Bonneville, L. P., Redmore, C. D., Streich, D. D., & Sargent, M. (1985). Ego development in college. *Journal of Personality and Social Psychology, 48*(4), 947–962. doi:10.1037/0022-3514.48.4.947

Love, P. G., & Guthrie, V. L. (1999). Perry's intellectual scheme. *New Directions for Student Services, 8*, 5–15.

Mayhew, M., Seifert, T., & Pascarella, E. (2010). A multi-institutional assessment of moral reasoning development among first-year students. *The Review of Higher Education, 33*(3), 357–390. doi: 10.1353/rhe.0.0153

McAuliffe, G. & Lovell, C. (2006). The influence of counselor epistemology on the helping interview: A qualitative study. *Journal of Counseling & Development, 84*, 308–317.

Miller, B. L. (2007). The human frontal lobe: An introduction. In B. L. Miller & J. L. Cummings (Eds.), *The human frontal lobes: Functions and disorders* (2nd ed.). New York, NY: The Guilford Press.

Murphy, K. A., Blustein, D. L., Bohlig, A. J., & Platt, M. G. (2010). The college-to-career transition: An exploration of emerging adulthood. *Journal of Counseling & Development, 88*, 174–181.

National Center for Higher Education Management Systems (NCHEMS). (2008). *College participation rates: College-going rates of high school graduates.* Retrieved from http://www.higheredinfo.org/dbrowser/index.php?submeasure=63&year=2008&level=nation&mode=data&state=0

Power, F. C., Higgins, A., & Kohlberg, L. (1991). *Lawrence Kohlberg's approach to moral education.* New York, NY: Columbia University Press.

Pryor, J. H., Hurtado, S., Saenz, V. B., Santos, J. L., & Korn, W. S. (2007). *The American freshman: Forty year trends.* Los Angeles, CA: Higher Education Research Institute.

Roisman, G. I., Masten, A. S., Coatsworth, J. D., & Tellegen, A. (2004). Salient and emerging develntal tasks in the transition to adulthood. *Child Development, 75*(1), 123–133.

Salmela-Aro, K., Aunola, K., & Nurmi, J. (2007). Personal goals during emerging adulthood: A 10-year follow up. *Journal of Adolescent Research, 22*(6), 690–715.

Schulenberg, J. E., Bryant, A. L., & O'Malley, P. M. (2004). Taking hold of some kind of life: How developmental tasks relate to trajectories of well-being during the transition to adulthood. *Development and Psychopathology, 16*, 1119–1140.

Sheaffer, B., Sias, S., Toriello, P., & Cubero, C. (2008). Ego development and preferred social distance from persons with disabilities. *Rehabilitation Education, 22*(2), 147–158.

Swensen, C. H., Eskew, R., & Kohlhepp, K. (1981). Stage of family life cycle, ego development, and the marriage relationship. *Journal of Marriage & the Family, 43*(4), 841–853.

Taylor, K. B. (2008). Mapping the intricacies of young adults' developmental journey from socially prescribed to internally defined identities, relationships, and beliefs. *Journal of College Student Development, 49*(3), 215–234.

Terenzini, P. T. (1987). *A review of selected theoretical models of student development and collegiate impact.* Paper presented at the annual meeting of the Association for the Study of Higher Education.

Tinto, V. (2006). Research and practice of student retention: What next? *Journal of College Student Retention: Research, Theory and Practice, 8*(1), 1–19.

West, E. J. (2004). Perry's legacy: Models of epistemological development. *Journal of Adult Development, 11*(2), 61–70.

2

Counseling Concerns Over the College Academic Year

JOSHUA MAGRUDER AND
SUZANNE DEGGES-WHITE

The transition from secondary school to college is marked with the significant and empowering rite of passage, high school graduation. A young person's achievement of this milestone requires the investment of a large amount of effort from the family of origin, social support groups, and, especially, parents or guardians. Rightly termed *commencement*, this moment is the beginning of a young person's entry into emerging adulthood and, for many, the college experience. As college counselors, we are firsthand witnesses to their continued development as we work with them in the counseling office. Following are brief descriptions of the typical issues a college counselor might encounter during the development of these emerging adults (Table 2.1).

FRESHMAN YEAR

Entering college for the first time, freshmen typically bring much energy and anxiety to this experience. Usually excited to be away from home, perhaps for the first time, they learn that there are many times in which the family of origin is the best support system they can access. Obviously, homesickness can play a role, but once a peer group is established, homesickness tends to lessen and eventually evaporate. For others, it may take just a day or two of exploration and making new connections to become comfortable in their new soundings. The struggle for independence is constant and most students experience great pressure from home to succeed.

TABLE 2.1

Counseling Concerns Over the Academic Year

Time of Year	Freshmen	Sophomores	Juniors	Seniors
Start of Fall Semester	Anxiety, stress from new academic environment; homesickness, adjustment from high school to college; struggle for independence	Noticeable growth and development from freshmen year; freedom expands as most move off campus; peer group creation or loss of peer group concerns	Decision about majors must be finalized; most of time spent off campus; more established relationships and peer groups with growth and further development of interpersonal skills	Noticeable changes in the counseling room; balancing fun during final year vs. finishing strong academically; natural duality between college and real world
Fall Midterm	Stress from new academic environment and test format; focus on finding peer groups	Most still cramming for test and papers; with more freedom, more responsibility—actualizing into role of college student	Career/graduate school options become a concern; tests and papers are less of an issue vs. life planning	Active participation in counseling; more career focused than exam focused
Fall Break	Desire to be with family of origin vs. growing independence; managing peer group from home vs. college peer group	Family of origin still a concern in the room	Family of origin may be influencing career decisions; expect more responsibility for counseling work from juniors	Stress from family of origin; being pulled to find job/ensure plans for graduate school
Final Exams	Pressure from home; internal pressure to do well results in a lack of self-care	Pressure of exams continues; large reports of using study drugs and cramming; increased maturity visible	Career, graduate school, GRE, GMAT, LSAT concerns; relationship issues arise with the end of semester	Cramming vs. self-care and preparation; overly ready for break

Time of Year	Freshmen	Sophomores	Juniors	Seniors
Start of Spring Semester	Feels like a fresh start; expect a change in client roster; seeking closer relationships with peers	More constant client roster as clients mature; roommate/living off campus concerns	Internships and co-op concerns; more autonomous decision making	Focused on peer/partner relationships; school is a second thought to short time left in college
Spring Break	Vacationing with peers vs. family of origin; exploration of limits/choices	More mature attitudes toward traveling with friends, many more experience study abroad, though some stay with stereotypical party mentality	Midsemester begins planning senior year	Seniors spend many hours planning the "last spring break"; may overindulge and have consequences to address; maintaining relationships is a critical issue
Post Spring Break	Clients may return from break with legal, medical, or family issues; some need help to readjust to academics	Some clients begin to take responsibility for grades and work to improve study habits	Relationships are deepening for juniors; also address academic issues as they prepare for interviewing/career activities	May view academics as a third or fourth shot to succeed vs. students who focus on finishing as well as they started; may express sentimentality at end of college career
Spring Finals	More prepared than before; stress still present with internal and external pressure; trying to schedule social life and study time	May discuss study habits, but as sophomores seek deeper relationships, more focus on how school affects time with peers or significant others	More prepared for exams and exam format, less anxiety; pressure of decision making still present	Commencement ceremonies, parties, aware of relationship junctures; also focused on leaving college for job/graduate school

Fall Semester

Family and campus-based pressures are visible early on, often felt by students the moment they arrive on campus. Counselors and clients can build strong therapeutic bonds now, and relying on client-centered practice will help keep clients focused on their issues related to independence and interdependence. This can allow the student to better develop the appropriate balance of these two needs for the family of origin. Relaxation training for new students is always useful, especially because the move to a college or university can usher in new stressors related to re-creating a strong support system. This can often generate a high stress environment for freshmen.

Socially, freshmen may struggle through roommate issues that can range from slight disagreements to all-out battles. Students who are only children tend to have more issues with roommates than students who have siblings. Conflict between roommates can emerge over any number of topics from posters on the wall, sexual behavior, study habits, to even sleeping and eating arrangements. Some may seem minor to novice counselors who are hoping to sink their counseling teeth into a more meaty issue. However, these seemingly *minor* incidents are of the utmost importance in helping students adjust to college as well as to perform well academically, and each must be met with honest respect and genuine empathy.

Homebound Romance

The freshman's adjustment to college does not just end with roommate issues; relationship issues from home often are the focus of counseling sessions. Some freshmen cling to high school relationships, romantic or platonic. Others may feel abandoned by their old peer group, and seek help to cope with the sadness that accompanies the loss of old friends and the work required to make new friends. Year after year, in my experience as a college counselor, there has never been a fall semester that has not included at least a handful of freshman clients struggling with high school relationships, generally those of a romantic nature. Often, it involves one partner being younger than the other and the associated challenges that result from attempts to make a long-distance relationship work.

Freshmen couples counseling may also be required of a college counselor. If a high school couple decides to attend the same college, they may seek assistance dealing with the new campus environment. Couples counseling for freshmen often focuses on independence, trust, jealously, and breakups. Although these issues are common to couples of all ages, college counselors should be prepared to work with less mature couples and to meet these couples at their developmental level.

Whether it is a high school couple now on campus or a freshman trying to navigate new romances, relationships will always be an area of focus for freshmen in a counselor's office. While peer groups quickly become one of the most necessary and influential support systems early on, many freshmen are often eager to find a romantic partner and this effort—whether fruitful or unsuccessful—can greatly affect a student's acclimation to college life. While freshmen ostensibly come to college for an education, their educational experiences extend beyond the classroom in many ways.

In the Classroom and at the Books

Academically, most freshmen enter college with the expectation that it will be different from high school, but they are unaware just how greatly the environments can differ. Stress can become almost unbearable for some freshmen who have high expectations placed on them by others or by themselves. They often turn first to the residence assistants and hall directors for assistance and these individuals ideally refer these students to the campus counseling center. Overachievement stress is becoming an increasingly large problem as students face new academic expectations and competition in the classrooms. Counselors can help students combat this issue by training students in relaxation techniques. Oftentimes, group relaxation training and weekly practice sessions can show a profound effect on students' ability to manage stress. Some counseling centers run 6- to 8-week psychoeducational groups that promote healthy coping mechanisms such as meditation, guided imagery, and progressive muscle relaxation. At the university counseling center at which I work, we have implemented this type of program and students give it high marks for effectiveness in helping them manage stress and succeed academically.

Midsemester Stressors

As the fall semester continues, the stress level begins to decrease as peer groups start to form. Those individuals who have been held back by homesickness or other issues may visit counselors just to be able to have some form of relationship in which they are heard. Counseling centers may have success in helping clients who feel isolated find connections through the use of interpersonal groups; these can jump-start a student's ability to get connected to the community. By midsemester, roommate issues have either reached a level of homeostasis or, at the opposite end of the spectrum, may have escalated. During the middle of the semester, college counselors should expect to be brought in to floor meetings in residence halls or perhaps even to provide mediation. Also by midsemester, if a college or university has a Greek system, then counselors should expect to be called in to assist there as well. Most counseling centers attempt to keep a direct link with the Greek Life office. This creates a thread between the two departments so that response can be quick and easy. Greek Life and other social issues are huge distractions from academics to freshmen students. However, many Greek organizations have raised their academic standards and now enforce attendance at "study halls," which has contributed to improved academic performance.

Academically, during midterm season, freshmen tend to pay little attention to the first major exam of their college career. Students who seek counseling for academic reasons typically will be in one of two states: not caring at all or caring too much. Students that act as if they do not care pretend to know the system and know how to easily succeed on tests. Often they find that they have not prepared enough and their attitudes will have changed by the time final exams come around. The overachieving student will present with high levels of stress, low levels of self-care, and typically a low ability to function. College counselors should promote healthy lifestyles: good sleeping patterns and a healthy diet. However, for students suffering significant and potentially clinical levels of anxiety, referral to medical doctors and more intensive counseling may be needed. Test anxiety maintains a pervasive presence on college campuses, but there are many tools to help students find ways to cope and manage their stress. A basic breathing exercise can do wonders for a student who experiences panic before an exam. This extra anxiety creates thoughts of home, and freshmen can then re-present with homesickness.

Fall Break—Return to the Nest

Most freshmen hate to admit that they miss home because they relish their new freedom so dearly. However, by fall break, most if not all freshmen are ready to return home for a time-out. A few students, however, may express a desire to stay on campus and avoid a visit home. In the counseling office, this can create some interesting situations. Students may speak with bravado about preferring campus life to a week at home, but their behavior may remove the veil and reveal that they are tired and ready for a break. The majority of students do have concerns about school breaks and the relationships they have formed on campus. They express anxiety about whether the relationships can maintain their normal functioning during and after the break or if they will be changed because of the time at home. This concern appears at semester breaks as well. Students' anxiety can be controlled by encouraging them to develop a plan to stay in touch. Providing students with empathy, understanding, and encouragement are all powerful interventions for freshmen leaving for their first break.

Returning from fall break, students immediately feel the pressure of final exams and final papers. Although freshmen may have had cumulative finals in high school, they are still inexperienced in prepping for college finals. Counselors can expect a split in clients who present in their offices at this time. Half of them worry too little and hardly study knowing they have had these types of exams before. The other half is anxious, paranoid, and overall generally stressed out. Building on self-efficacy from midterms and positive encouragement become a counselor's best tools during finals. While relaxation exercises would be helpful, if freshmen are not already practicing these techniques they may already be too anxious to learn these methods. Setting up a plan of action can be very effective at this time of year, and the more the student is involved in the creation of the plan, the more effective it will be.

Final Exams Before the Lull
Socially, freshmen typically try to attend every social function possible. They cram late at night so they can spend time with friends. In the counseling office, students reveal significant deficits in sleep and self-care. Again, it's important to revisit self-care and healthy living, but often students just need a place to vent around this time of year. They are under pressure, and peer groups help relieve some of that pressure. Counselors can expect to hear tales of late night parties and the possible use of "study drugs." Most freshmen come to college with a preexisting knowledge of study drugs and how to get them legally and illegally, and counselors must be aware of the potential risks students face and encourage healthy choices by their clients. As exams end, students pack up and head to their hometowns for a few weeks. During this time, they may plan visits with college friends and romantic partners and work at part-time jobs. Most freshmen enjoy their time away from college stressors but are ready to come back in January.

Spring Semester

The holidays soon pass, and the spring semester begins before any counselor or student is completely ready. For freshmen, there is a different feel to this semester. There are breaks that are more evenly distributed, which create a sometimes calmer semester than the fall. Freshmen have already had a semester's worth of experience at college and are eager to start the spring in a better place. A phrase often heard in the counseling room is "This semester is going to be different. . . ."

Seeking a Fresh Start Academically and Socially
Some freshmen are able to live up to this aspiration and make changes to adjust and mature to their new environments. However, many freshmen that had been active and steady clients in the fall may not return for

the spring; counselors should not be surprised if they face an entirely new client list. Freshmen that do appear in the counseling center at the beginning of the spring semester typically are ready for a new start. Their grades might not have been as good as hoped or they might be looking for assistance in seeking out new peer groups. In the case of campuses with Greek systems in place, you may find freshmen sorority or fraternity members as new clients. These organizations often initiate right before the fall semester is over, or at the beginning of the spring semester, but this will vary from school to school. In the counseling office, these clients frequently express a need to either become closer with this new peer group, or alternatively, they may be seeking assistance in finding a way out of the organization. Some family of origin issues may keep them involved with the Greek chapter, while students might be searching for other peer groups or social outlets. Campus and community resources are essential pieces of information to have available to share with these students.

Academic resources are also needed. Some freshmen are not overly concerned with the start of the new semester unless their fall grades were poor. Others come to counseling seeking assistance with building study skills, enhancing their grade point average (GPA), and getting a handle on academics. These students are the students who did not come in during the fall and need time management resources and support to focus on class work. As counselors, we can provide resources, study techniques, or even administer personality assessments to help clients find the best way to complete their tasks.

Spring Break Initiation

Eventually, all academic tasks get pushed to the background as spring break approaches. For freshmen, this, too, is a rite of passage. It may be the first vacation they have taken without family. It may be something that these students have been dreaming about since middle school. In the counseling office, there is much excitement, but we as counselors need to reflect their feelings while helping them stay in touch with realistic expectations, potential consequences of overboard behavior, and plans for making safe decisions. Counselors can encourage safety and sound decision making as some students may disclose plans for experimentation with alcohol and drugs. Harm reduction becomes an extremely important topic for discussion leading up to spring break. Although counselors cannot control their clients' choices, it is important to bear in mind that the counseling office should be perceived as a safe place to return and seek help, if needed. Harm-reduction models are the most logical for a student's self-control. Also, these models help to strengthen the therapeutic relationship with freshmen and all classifications of students. Most students are surprised to learn that college officials do not always advocate for an abstinence model for all stereotypical spring break activities.

Counselors are privy to students' revelations about their experiences during that "magical" week of spring break. And counselors are often called upon by students to provide triage in the event of negative experiences. The potential fallout from a spring break trip gone awry can affect students on multiple levels. These can include legal issues, family issues, medical issues, or academic issues. College counselors should be fully prepared with resources and referrals to a wide variety of professionals, if needed. Counselors should be prepared to have students sign releases should discussions with parents be required as well as any consultations with other relevant professionals. Although most freshman spring breakers seeking counseling will only need the core conditions of counseling— empathy, unconditional positive regard, and authenticity—it is helpful to expect the unexpected and be prepared to offer assistance in a variety of ways.

Final Exams

As spring break excitement, memories, and regrets start to fade, freshmen then turn their attention to final exams. Since freshmen have experienced final exams during their first semester, they are generally better equipped to juggle a social life with an academic life. The pull of social and peer groups is stronger in the spring due to the impending long summer break. Again, freshmen like to use as much of the 24 hours of the day as they can. While study drugs are never totally out of the picture, their use becomes more visible and widespread during finals.

"Goodbye for the Summer"

Counselors can expect to hear more romantic relationship issues as summer approaches. Many freshmen develop intense attachments to their girlfriends or boyfriends during the year and because this may be their first serious relationship, they may want to focus on these relationships extensively in the counseling office. Both partners must discuss and plan for the long months apart. Freshmen know they have little time with finals, and they know they have less time in counseling, so they often seek direct answers. Students may be frustrated as counselors continue to encourage the client to work through the issue to find their own best answer. But the counselor's encouragement and belief in the client typically support the client's ability to come to some sort of resolution that works for the client. Counselors should bear in mind that although freshmen have a year of college under their belts, they are not yet fully cognitively mature and decisions are still made with a still-developing brain.

SOPHOMORE YEAR

The sophomore year of college marks further development and growth in students. Most have moved off campus and are now living with their friends. Freedom has been extended concurrently with the responsibility of living in a house or an apartment.

Domestic Situations

Now that they are living on their own, sophomores must now actively participate in negotiating rent, utilities, and other bills with their room-mates. These negotiations can result in conflict and counselors frequently hear about these issues in counseling sessions. Friends that now live together have many issues to discuss and negotiate, such as purchasing and accounting for groceries, friends coming over, partner issues, among others. Counselors can expect to hear a great deal about these issues during the first few months of sophomore year.

Shifting Circles of Friends

On the other end of the spectrum, sophomore year always brings in a number of clients who have lost their connection to a peer group from the prior year. Students may have been removed from a fraternity or sorority, or summer break may have created relationship breaks. Regardless of causation, these students will likely feel isolated and will need encouragement to find a new peer group. Luckily, most college campuses provide many resources for finding and building new peer group networks through such means as interest clubs or intramural sports. Emotional and financial support from home is still very important during sophomore year. Most students are still dependent on their family of origin for money, tuition, and other needs. In the counseling office, counselors will hear students express a strong need for that support, although they may try to veil it through the expression of negative feelings toward their families.

Hitting the Books

Academically, the start of sophomore year brings many nervous students into our offices. After the first year, some students have been put on academic probation and have been recommended to counseling. On the other end of the spectrum are high-achieving students. They may have had a 4.0 GPA freshmen year, and now the pressure to maintain those grades is there, as well as pressure from home and internal pressure. These high-achieving students need perspective-taking exercises and continued relaxation exercises. Encouraging good self-care from the start of the semester is a good idea as well. If counselors can get these students into some healthy habits, these habits could continue into midterm and finals season.

Midterm Exams

Midterms for sophomores are still a time of high stress and pressure. With two semesters behind them, some begin to learn how they best study. However, most still prefer to cram and use study drugs to keep their energy levels up. For sophomores in the Greek community, there are more responsibilities with social, philanthropic, or administrative positions. Even more than freshman year, students try and use every hour possible. For the high achievers, student government, honor societies, or other extracurricular activities are high on the priority list. In the counseling room this manifest itself as extreme stress and anxiety. It can lead to interpersonal issues with family and friends as students learn to balance so many different priorities. Sophomores are given much more responsibility, and the stress of that responsibility is clearly seen in the college counseling office.

Fall Break

Sophomores adjust better to midterm breaks such as fall break or Thanksgiving break than freshmen do. They have experience with the emotional stressors that going home and returning to campus can create. They are better able to handle these transitions their second year than their first. In counseling sessions, sophomores are more likely to discuss family of origin issues when breaks are approaching, but they exhibit a better understanding of the situation and better perspectives of their parents. Thus, counselors can rely on these clients to be more open to honest and logical explorations of these issues, and can challenge their clients' behaviors if relevant to discussions about family of origin issues.

Final Exams

When sophomores return from midterm break, their next focus is final exams. As in prior semesters, sophomores are more likely to rely on cramming methods as preparation than other methods. Counselors can still use this period to address more effective methods of time management, study habits, and so forth. High-achieving students are beginning to learn and use coping mechanisms to relax by this point in their academic careers, but as they are only sophomores, this final exam period might instigate their first visit to the college counseling center. Stereotypically, sophomores still maintain a level of immaturity that contributes to problems with cumulative exams.

The last part of the first semester of sophomore year does bring some positive attributes to the counseling process. Because of their increased sense of responsibility, sophomore clients can take more responsibility for their productivity in the counseling process. Typically, they become more involved with their personal growth work and generally will complete counseling homework, if given. Sophomores are by no means fully mature adult clients, but their development since freshman year is noticeable and may be a focus of acknowledgment and positive reinforcement by counselors.

Spring Semester

When the increasingly mature sophomores return from the holiday break, counseling centers see many more returning clients. New clients will appear as well. However, due to the higher volume of extracurricular responsibilities held by sophomores, these clients may not return to the counseling center immediately after a break.

The Social Life of Sophomores

Sophomores seeking relationship help have a higher return rate than those working through other issues as the extended winter breaks seem to stress college relationships. Socially, sophomores have more "house parties." These create new issues in the counseling room as many unexpected and unplanned events can occur at a house party. Sophomores are exposed to different drugs and new ways of drinking that can cause problems with academics, friends, relationships, and family. Counselors can expect to see the difficulties of house parties be overshadowed by spring break events for sophomores.

Spring Break

For sophomores, spring break is still a very important event in their lives, but fewer students are looking for that over-the-top, glamorized experience that they have seen in a movie. Counselors can still expect to hear about wild antics and unsafe behaviors, but during sophomore year, students may decide to travel abroad or take some type of job for school credit. This is another sign of their growing development through college; making the choice of school over vacations becomes a focus and sophomores begin to realize the value of long-term planning and creating a vision for the future. Spring break can still affect the family of origin, and counselors will certainly face that in the counseling room after the break is over. Also, with sophomores, counselors will hear some inspiring stories of service and excitement over students' experiences in addition to the revelations and regrets typical of freshmen.

Final Exams

Spring finals remain a very stressful time for sophomore students. Because the spring semester typically offers more breaks for students, some sophomores have been able to develop stronger study skills. As sophomores begin to take more responsibility for their academics, they begin to communicate less with their family of origin about grades. By the end of their second year, counselors can expect to hear phrases such as, "I know my bad grades are my fault, but how do I fix it now?" However, when things go poorly, most sophomores will call home for help. Counselors tend to receive fewer phone calls from parents during a student's sophomore year than the previous year. This is another sign of growth and development from year to year in college; when sophomores become juniors, a very noticeable developmental shift occurs.

JUNIOR YEAR

The junior year of college is one that really highlights the emotional and cognitive development of college students. They are typically ready to choose their major course of study and move out of campus housing. Most have successfully navigated the typical friend/roommate relationship conundrums. Juniors generally have a well-established peer group. Romantic relationships usually grow more intense as the end of college nears. Interpersonal skills have been growing and deepening as well. The junior year of college is certainly an interesting one for most students.

Social Life

Socially, juniors have a defined group of friends that often will shrink in number. Fewer and closer relationships are preferred over a mass of superficial acquaintanceships. Some juniors may seek the means to live alone, if possible, as academic success becomes increasingly important. It may be helpful to remind clients without roommates to refrain from isolating themselves from others and to find opportunities to network and socialize with their support network members. Established romantic relationships tend to become more serious during junior year and, in the counseling office, conversations about commitment are much more frequent.

Academics Matter

Academically, the start of the junior year is hectic. Students must choose and commit to a major. There is pressure from administration and home to begin the job search. Graduate school becomes a real option and with that comes the pressure of preparing for exams like the GRE, GMAT, or the LSAT. Internships and co-op programs become options as well. Juniors face many significant life decisions and they come to counseling seeking assistance with these issues. Counselors, of course, cannot give these clients answers even if they did have them, but can help students learn the best way to make good decisions. Working with juniors usually involves giving them tools to cope with new sources of stress and to build cognitive decision-making skills. During their junior year, however, students are faced with a large number of people who are trying to influence the many decisions that should be left solely to the student. The family of origin has expectations for career or graduate school, mentors have their opinions, and even friends try and influence what should happen in a junior's life.

Midterms and finals are less stressful for juniors. Their stress comes from thoughts of the future. In the counseling room, this is often manifested with high anxiety and maybe even panic. Counselors should be prepared for high levels of intensity when working with juniors. Generally, they have become more autonomous and take counseling quite seriously. Juniors typically come to the counseling center with a clear purpose and work eagerly toward their goals. The added maturity makes counseling enjoyable at times, but it also can create an atmosphere of intense effort in the counseling office.

By spring semester, most juniors have calmed down. They are less stressed about the final decision for their future, but are still concerned with internship or co-op programs to build their resume. They come to the counseling center seeking guidance in life rather than basic career concerns for a short while. But career issues reappear throughout the junior and senior years. Spring can be an interesting semester for juniors; they have just returned from break where some of the pressure from the family of origin may be increased or decreased depending on the family's priorities and understanding of their students. Either way, juniors at this stage seem more autonomous in their decision making and are typically ready to plan their senior year and possibly make plans for further into the future. Other juniors, however, still carry that high anxiety and intensity into the spring, especially those high-achieving students who are intently focused on academic performance. For them, junior year is full of pressure, but even for them the spring semester lowers their anxiety.

SENIOR YEAR

As juniors become seniors, the content of counseling sessions shows a noticeable change. Seniors are on the cusp of "the real world" and counseling work tends to focus on making plans for the future.

Social Life on Track

Socially, seniors are torn between having fun and finishing their education academically strong. The peer groups of seniors are often small, and closer relationships are more important. Intimate relationships often become more serious than ever before, and seniors bring these relationship issues into the room. Many seniors often get sentimental about their time at college or university, and their activities often reflect that. The majority of seniors have learned the limits they need to set for themselves regarding substance use and either enforce these themselves or have become involved in campus-based substance programs. Working with seniors is very different from working with underclassmen and their sessions often have a very different flavor, although the general topics may be similar to that of underclassmen.

Academic Fine-Tuning

Academically, there seems to be a duality of choices from seniors. Some desire to finish strong so their GPA will be higher as they look for jobs or enter graduate school. Others go into a "senioritis" place where they just want to coast through classes. With either type of student, in the counseling office there is generally a feeling of calmness that is noticeably absent from the typical stress- and anxiety-infused sessions from prior years. As a rule, seniors are focused on their goals and are active participants in counseling.

Couples Counseling and Family Issues for Seniors

Couples work with seniors is more similar to adult couples work. This group's maturity can lead to highly productive couples counseling. Clients may be stressed by the increasing depth and complexity of their relationships and seek to understand how to make relationships work as they face academic and professional tasks not encountered during their first 3 years of school. Stress may also arise from the clients' families of origin as they wrestle with job and graduate school decisions as well as additional geographic transitions.

Moving Forward Beyond Graduation

As seniors wind down their final year, they will be finalizing plans for the next step on their journey. If graduate school is the next step, there is less of a transition component in the counseling work. If a new job is in the future, the transition can be much more important to focus on in counseling, as can any geographic relocation that might be on the horizon.

By spring, most seniors are ready to "let loose." In the counseling office, students seldom want to address academic issues and, instead, are very future oriented. Seniors tend to work to clarify or enhance relationships and address issues with friends. The idea of leaving, or their peer group dispersing, is a major topic of discussion. However, although virtually every senior has envisioned this transition, it is never perfect nor does it replicate what they had envisioned it to be. Counselors may be asked for guidance in ways to maintain friendships, while at the same time, clients are looking ahead to new personal and professional relationships.

CONCLUSION

This brief overview of college student development was designed to provide counselors with a broad perspective on how the counseling center traffic might appear based on student classification and season. While each group of students will bring in issues with similar themes in counseling, their depth and engagement with the topic may be quite different based on client age. In general, counselors will notice an increasing maturity that grows with each year of college experience. This developing cognitive and emotional maturity significantly influences the atmosphere in the counseling office and the work that will be accomplished. College counselors should be prepared to be creative and flexible. The transition from adolescent to adult is a fascinating period and college counselors are in a prime position to witness and positively affect this powerful transformation.

3

Underclassmen:
Making the Transition

WENDY KILLAM

Entering college is often one of life's major events. Though usually an exciting time, leaving home for the first time can be difficult. Students are expected to become self sufficient and responsible adults while meeting high academic standards and exploring a new identity, without their accustomed support system. The college environment is designed to inspire cognitive and moral growth; thus, challenge and personal change are foundational components of a student's new world. Adjustment to college includes development within academic, emotional, and social realms. Simultaneously, new environmental stressors can take a significant toll.

In this chapter, we provide a brief overview of several of the most common challenges that first- and second-year college students face, including balancing responsibilities, adjustment to roommates, homesickness, social pressures, Greek and other club memberships, and choosing a major.

PRACTICALITY MATTERS

Prior to college, parents often guided student decision making and managed the student's schedule. Students may find themselves overwhelmed with having to manage new tasks such as money management, laundry, food preparation, and time management. Students may present for counseling due to high levels of stress that can be remedied by lessons in time management. Others may have difficulty juggling their first job with their academic responsibilities and social lives. Presenting time management workshops for students can make a positive difference.

As students move toward becoming more independent, they may find that they need to take on new responsibilities (Robotham, 2008). Juggling new responsibilities with increased personal choice and freedom can create new problems such as deleterious changes in sleep patterns and chronic deficits of adequate sleep (Liguori, Schuna, & Mozumdar, 2011). For some, the freedom of being curfew-free can lead to overly late nights and inadequate rest. Lack of sleep can lead to issues with wellness and can compromise all aspects of a student's life. Missing classes and being late for jobs are just two examples of the negative impact of sleep deprivation. Students frequently enjoy social activities late into the night, thus any student who chooses an earlier (and healthier) bedtime may feel left out of the critical social bonding that occurs early in the college years. The academic and social adjustments of freshmen are tantamount in their decision to complete their education and degree (Tinto, 1994). Students may need to be reminded that it takes only one semester of "wild abandon" or irresponsible choices to negatively affect their grade point average (GPA), which can have college career-long implications. Some students may view a low semester GPA as a "wake-up call" and work to remedy the situation over subsequent semesters. Others may continue their downward slide and face academic probation or enrollment in mandatory retention programming. Depending on the level of "abandon," students also may be involved in conduct issues that result in the student being sent home.

Residence Halls and Roommate Issues

For many incoming students, living in a residence hall is a rite of passage, and a student's residential circumstances can significantly influence the new student's adjustment to college. For students who are not adequately prepared for the challenge of college, adjustment can be difficult on many levels, particularly residential life (Enochs & Roland, 2006). Sharing living space with friends or strangers can be challenging, and research shows that first impressions are important. When a pair of previously unacquainted roommates begins the relationship with positive interactions and a positive impression of one other, they are more likely to have a harmonious relationship and can address disagreements in a constructive manner (Marek, Wanzer, & Knapp, 2004). Because they are in close daily proximity to each other, college roommates may become confidants and lifelong friends (Degges-White & Borzumato-Gainey, 2011). When a roommate relationship is riddled with conflict, however, it can have highly destructive implications for a student.

The new unsupervised environment can lead to risk-taking behaviors such as casual sex, binge drinking, and use of other substances. Peer pressure can be strong in residence halls and research shows that risk-taking behaviors are even more frequent in co-ed residence halls

(Willoughby & Carroll, 2009). New social settings and the physiological drive toward independence that accompany this period in life can create personal conflict as students begin to explore the world and to determine and solidify their own values. In the past, universities and colleges took on more of a parental role in housing with dorm mothers and curfews, but most colleges today do not have curfews and students are free to come and go and have visitors as they please.

The more seemingly benign roommate conflicts can be disagreements about sleep/wake schedules, tidiness, music preferences and volume levels, and so forth. Issues that are clearly more significant might concern illegal drug usage and storage in the room, weapons, or sexual activity. But roommate conflict, regardless of topic, should be investigated for emotional or even physical abuse. Also, the residence hall may provide the first opportunity for some individuals to interact with those of a different background or ethnicity; unfortunately, current research predicts that interracial roommate dyads are less likely to last as long as same-ethnicity pairings (Towles-Schwen & Fazio, 2009). Thus, counselors, aware that this is a fairly common challenge, may want to be well-versed in conversations about respecting differences.

When significant conflicts of any type erupt, counselors should encourage students to practice assertiveness skills, but if this approach does not remedy the situation it is helpful for students to seek input and mediation from their residence hall assistants (RAs). Conflict resolution and mediation are typically the first step in deescalating roommate disagreements and there is strong evidence of the effectiveness of mediation by residence hall personnel or peer mediators who have completed campus mediation training programs. Although students typically wait until a "crisis point" before seeking assistance, developing outreach programming in residence halls can help develop proactive behaviors. Helping to enhance and support positive roommate interactions is important; according to Stern, Powers, Dhaene, Dix, and Shegog (2007), relationships with a roommate can be the most important factor in a college student's experience and can determine how a student views the entire university.

These transitions and challenges in living environment may lead a student to long for a time where there were fewer responsibilities, more home-cooked meals, and less freedom—and, for freshmen, this can often lead to feelings of homesickness.

Homesickness

Feelings of sadness and longing for home can be overwhelming for some students. They may miss the comfort of talking to mom after a long day of school or hanging with old friends on a Friday afternoon. Longing for home and old times, students may put more energy into maintaining their relationships at home, which makes adjusting to a new environment even more difficult. Homesickness can be surprisingly severe (Flett, Endler, & Besser, 2009). Leaving behind their social support networks, including immediate families, friends, and even their pets, for the unknown and challenging college environment is particularly difficult for students coping with feelings of anxiety. Perceived stress can influence the extent to which one feels homesick (Urani, Miller, Johnson, & Petzel, 2003); however, the degree of homesickness can be affected by other factors as well.

Family closeness and interdependence also influence the level of homesickness a student experiences as well as proximity to the family home. According to Tognoli (2003), the distance a student lives from family makes a significant difference in the degree to which homesickness is experienced. For students close enough for occasional visits home, the transition is easier than for those who can visit only a couple of times a year. Proximity to a student's hometown can be a source of comfort for some and can help ease the transition process. A student's distance from home can be important to assess and discuss, particularly with international students. Beck, Taylor, and Robbins (2003) found that students who lived farther from home had a more difficult time making friends and getting involved in campus activities. The lack of connection with others can then contribute to difficulties with adjusting to the college environment and increased feelings of loneliness and even depression. Additionally, these researchers found that students who were homesick had lower levels of self-esteem, which is likely to inhibit a student from reaching out to others and to resist the work inherent in establishing new relationships.

If students miss home too much, the significant problems in navigating the transitions inherent in college sometimes motivate them to transfer to schools closer to home or drop out of college altogether. This is especially true for first-generation college students (Woosley & Shepler, 2011) and for female students (Enochs & Roland, 2006). First-generation students face unique challenges such as lacking support or mentorship from families in navigating the university system. These challenges are detailed in the chapter on diverse populations. For all students, the need to connect with others is fundamental and if unmet, this appears to have major consequences. For some students, the need to connect might so far exceed their time management skills or academic motivation that their school enrollment could become endangered.

Balancing Work and School

The combination of working and going to school can present some major challenges. For freshmen, becoming acclimated to campus life can be stressful as students learn to manage class assignments and college expectations. Some students make the mistake of taking too many diffi-cult courses the first semester (Adams, 2011). Some studies have reported stress levels that are currently at an all-time high for college students (Pedersen, 2012), and for students who must earn money while in school, this stress is frequently exacerbated. A growing number of college stu-dents are working during the academic year out of necessity. This increase has been attributed to a number of factors, including the increasing costs of attending colleges along with a decrease in available funding options for students. Other contributing factors include more parents wanting stu-dents to become financially independent sooner (Lang, 2012). For some students a fear of debt is another reason for working while attending college (Humphrey, 2006). Although there has not yet been a conclusive finding as to whether or not working during college negatively affects grades, it has been determined that those who have jobs related to their majors tend to have higher grades than those who have not worked (Lang, 2012). These higher grades may be attributed, in part, to a student ben-efiting from real-world experience, as well as learning to manage time wisely due to the necessity of balancing multiple demands. Sharing the benefits of major-related work experience with clients is helpful, but it is also important to remind them to initiate open discussions with poten-tial employers regarding issues such as their academic responsibilities and weekly class schedules. Investing time in a job while in college can be financially advantageous, but it may also require a reorganization of students' social lives. Although a later chapter provides details regarding the value of social support and potential opportunities for developing a social network, the following section provides an overview of the poten-tial stressors of social relationships for first- and second-year students.

Social Pressures

The ability to establish connections with others and a sense of belonging at the university are necessary for success. While making connections on campus can be helpful for students, it can also increase feelings of stress. Oddly enough, if the support a student receives on campus is not meeting the student's needs, it can actually become a source of stress (Robotham, 2008). Stress results when students feel pulled into different directions. While trying to meet one's need to fit in with others and form healthy connections with others, some students may feel major pressure to fit in. Though it may have negative emotional or physical consequences, students sometimes compromise their own values or misrepresent them-selves in order to appear more like their peers and gain much desired acceptance. Students may engage in substance use, undesired sex, and other high-risk behaviors in order to feel connected. Other chapters of this book address the variety of ways that social pressure to conform impacts student well-being, but it is important to note that first-year students are particularly susceptible to these pressures and accompanying high-risk behaviors.

Counselors may help students make self-assessments of their newly developing support systems on campus. Students can be encouraged to evaluate the quality of the friendships and their contribution to feelings of stress or overall well-being. Positive relationships can help students to adjust to social pressures (Enochs & Roland, 2006). And ultimately, if a student can form a healthy social network, it increases the likelihood that the student will graduate (Hirsch & Barton, 2011).

HOOKING UP, HANGING OUT, AND DATING

Without curfews or parental regulations, college students often experience new-found dating freedom. The current dating "hook-up culture" will be discussed in more detail in a later chapter but it is important to note that college may be a student's introduction to this environment. Dating in college often leads to more intense sexual relationships than might have been experienced in high school. Not only is engaging in various romantic and sexual experiences not uncommon, it is an expected part of the college experience within American society (Vasilenko, Lefkowitz, & Maggs, 2012). But calling a romantic partner a "boyfriend" may be entering a zone perceived as quite risky and socially censured. Some students are deeply troubled as they try to learn the nuances of defining and publicly declaring their relationship status.

Even with the environmental pressures to stay single and be sexually active, young women still often face a double standard regarding their decisions related to sexual activity. Shaped by social intuitions and interpersonal relationships (Morgan, Thorne, & Zurbriggen, 2010), there is tacit approval of young men engaging in casual sex while young women receive mixed messages, encouraging sexual activity but emphasizing more discretion resulting in a single sexual partner. Perhaps these beliefs influence the different affective reactions of men and women to their early sexual experiences: Men view first sexual encounters as positive, but women view them as negative (Vasilenko et al., 2012). However, after the initial experience for women, they, too, begin to view sexual experiences as positive. It may be especially helpful to address boundary issues and healthy relationship guidelines with students who may be inexperienced in romantic relationships or with those who express discomfort or dissatisfaction with their relationships.

While most college romantic relationships tend to occur between geographically close partners, long-distance relationships do occur. In fact, long-distance dating relationships are estimated to account for approximately 25% to 50% of college student dating (Maguire & Kinney, 2010). Long-distance relationships can be challenging for college students to manage and in some cases romantic jealousy may develop. In any dating relationship jealousy can develop and though this may be counterintuitive to counselors and other adults, jealousy among young adults tends to increase as a relationship becomes more serious (Khanchandani & Durham, 2009). It is important to help students recognize the hazards of jealousy and the possible control issues found as a component of jealousy, as well as to help him or her build effective communication skills in order to have the healthiest relationships possible.

FRATERNITY AND SORORITY LIFE

Members of Greek organizations emphasize a relationship-orientation (Abowitz & Knox, 2003) and actively recruit members they perceive as desirable. For first-year students or other students who have yet to form social connections, Greek membership may hold great appeal. While the financial burden of membership can be prohibitive for many, membership in Greek organizations, among other organizations, can help students establish connections with others and create a sense of community (Elkins, Forrester, & Noel-Elking, 2011). The exclusive nature of Greek life has a strong effect on both students who are accepted into membership and those who are rejected. Being accepted may lead to a sense of accomplishment and belonging—students recognize that they are part of a select few, which increases self-esteem and loyalty to the organization. Rejection, however, may create feelings of frustration, rejection, depression, and anger. While rejection is painful for many of us, it is perhaps even more so for students who are trying to find their places in new environments. Involvement in any club can be both a coping mechanism and a means by which students can meet new peers with shared interests as well as to become connected to the university (Van Etten, Pressley, McInerney, & Liem, 2008). The chapter on social connections offers many ideas on how counselors can encourage students to get involved in other areas of campus life.

SECOND-YEAR STUDENTS

Once students feel connected to a strong social network, their vulnerability to emotional problems and environmental stressors tends to decrease. In addition to social connectedness, once students achieve sophomore status, they have often learned to somewhat effectively manage the multiple demands of the college academic environment. Sophomores have typically developed the ability to successfully balance social life, academic responsibilities, and part-time jobs, if they hold one. As this year progresses, young women become more interested in seeing their romantic relationships move into a more mature and adult level. They are thinking beyond the immediate social scene and looking toward long-term commitments. Socially, sophomores are less likely to cling to the past and are able to feel comfortable in their new social groups. They also feel more confident in their identities and are less interested in the need to conform in order to feel accepted by peers. They also acknowledge a greater feeling of comfort on campus and they also now have a handle on what professors expect in assignments. Where some sophomores may feel overwhelmed by the thought of "3 more years until I'm out," others are excited as they are letting go of the past and able to focus on their future with eager anticipation.

Once turning this corner, sophomores do not present for counseling related to transitions as frequently as they did as first-year students. However there is one college experience that tends to challenge students in the second year. Many colleges and universities expect sophomores to declare a major by the year's end and this task can be daunting.

CHOOSING A MAJOR—A LIFELONG COMMITMENT?

Students frequently perceive the declaration of a major as equating to a lifelong career decision and this can create a significant amount of anxiety for sophomores. Unfortunately, some students do not yet have an effective model or relevant experience for making major life decisions. Sometimes parents help students navigate the decision-making process but on occasion, parental guidance is either a hindrance or not available. For instance, students may be fearful of disappointing family members if they choose a major that reflects their personal interests over parents' preferences. Other factors greatly impact this decision-making process such as a student's level of self-knowledge and the ability to be comfortable with the unknown. Most colleges are putting significant financial resources into building career centers, which, along with academic advisors, may be a resource for students seeking help with choosing a major and a subsequent career. However, it is important for general counselors to also have some tools for helping students make this decision. Along with formal assessment instruments such as the Strong Interest Inventory and the Myers-Briggs Type Indicator, counselors can help students verbalize passions, goals, and potential personality–major fit. It is also helpful to examine student obstacles to choosing a major, especially if there is a major in which they express a good deal of interest.

CONCLUSION

In this chapter, we have addressed some of the common transitions and challenges faced by first- and second-year college students. The ability to adjust and adapt to a new environment is essential for a successful and satisfying college education experience. For many college students, having a roommate and interacting closely with those who are different from them is a new experience. For a growing number of students, holding a job during the academic year is not a luxury, but a necessity, if college is to be financially accessible. This additional time commitment can add an another layer of stress and can compromise adjustment. Students may face the task of balancing a bank account for the first time and missteps here can create distress both on campus and in family relationships. These challenges are compounded by a student's greater level of independence and freedom and the need to develop a strong sense of personal responsibility and solid decision-making skills. Students often come to campus with unreasonably high and unrealistic expectations of the college experience and they are unprepared to handle the pitfalls they find. Counselors should be ready to help students with time management skills, study skills, decision-making models, and support as students find their place in the new environment.

REFERENCES

Abowitz, D. A., & Knox, D. (2003). Life goals among Greek college students. *College Student Journal, 37,* 96–100.

Adams, C. (2011). Colleges try to unlock secrets to student retention. *Education Week, 1,* 16–17.

Beck, R., Taylor, C., & Robbins, M. (2003). Missing home: Sociotropy and autonomy and their relationship to psychosocial distress and homesickness in college freshmen. *Anxiety, Stress and Coping: An International Journal, 16,* 155–167.

Degges-White, S., & Borzumato-Gainey, C. (2011). *Friends forever: How girls and women forge lasting relationships.* Lanham, MD: Rowman & Littlefield.

Elkins, D. J., Forrester, S. A., & Noel-Elking, A. V. (2011). Students' perceived sense of campus community: The influence of out-of-class experiences. *College Student Journal, 45,* 105–121.

Enochs, W. K., & Roland, C. B. (2006). Social adjustment of college freshman: The importance of gender and living environment. *College Student Journal, 40,* 63–73.

Flett, G., Endler, N. S., & Besser, A. (2009). Separation anxiety, perceived controllability, and homesickness. *Journal of Applied Social Psychology, 39,* 265–282.

Hirsch, J. K., & Barton, A. L. (2011). Positive social support, negative social exchanges, and suicidal behavior in college students. *Journal of American College Health, 59,* 393–398.

Humphrey, R. (2006). Pulling structured inequality into higher education: The impact of part-time working on English university students. *Higher Education Quarterly, 60,* 270–286.

Khanchandani, L., & Durham, T. W. (2009). Jealousy during dating among female college students. *College Student Journal, 43,* 1272–1278.

Lang, K. B. (2012). The similarities and differences between working and non-working students at a mid-sized American public university. *College Student Journal, 46,* 243–255.

Liguori, G., Schuna Jr., J., & Mozumdar, A. (2011). Semester long changes in sleep duration for college students. *College Student Journal, 45,* 481–492.

Maguire, K. C., & Kinney, T. A. (2010). When distance is problematic: Communication, coping, and relational satisfaction in female college students' long-distance dating relationships. *Journal of Applied Communication Research, 38,* 27–46.

Marek, C., Wanzer, M. B., & Knapp, J. L. (2004). An exploratory investigation of the relationship between roommates' first impressions and subsequent communication patterns. *Communication Research Reports, 21,* 210–220.

Morgan, E. M., Thorne, A., & Zubriggen, E. L. (2010). A longitudinal study of conversations with parents about sex and dating during college. *Developmental Psychology, 46,* 139–150.

Pedersen, D. E. (2012). Stress carry-over and college student health outcomes. *College Student Journal, 46,* 620–627.

Quinn, P. D., & Fromme, K. (2012). Personal and contextual factors in the escalation of driving after drinking across the college year. *Psychology of Addictive Behaviors, 26,* 714–723.

Robotham, D. (2008). Stress among higher education students: Towards a research agenda. *Higher Education, 56,* 735–746.

Scott-Sheldon, L. A., Carey, K. B., & Carey, M. P. (2008). Health behavior and college students: Does Greek affiliation matter? *Journal of Behavioral Medicine, 31,* 61–70.

Stern, L. A., Powers, J., Dhaene, K., Dix, A., & Shegog, S. (2007). Liking cooperation and satisfaction between roommates. *Journal of College and University Student Housing, 34,* 53–60.

Tinto, V. (1994). *Leaving college: Rethinking the causes of student attrition* (2nd ed.). Chicago, IL: University of Chicago Press.

Tognoli, J. (2003). Leaving home: Homesickness, place attachment, transition among residential college students. *Journal of College Student Psychotherapy, 18,* 35–48.

Towles-Schwen, T., & Fazio, R. H. (2009). Automatically activated racial attitudes as predictors of the success of interracial roommate relationships. *Journal of Experimental Social Psychology, 42,* 698–705.

Urani, M. A., Miller, S. A., Johnson, J. E, & Petzel, T. P. (2003). Homesickness in socially anxious first year college students. *College Student Journal, 37,* 392–400.

Van Etten, S., Pressley, M., McInerney, D. M., & Liem, A. D. (2008). College seniors' theory of their academic motivation. *Journal of Educational Psychology, 100,* 812–828.

Vasilenko, S. A., Lefkowitz, E. S., & Maggs, J. L. (2012). Short-term positive and negative consequences of sex based on daily reports among college students. *Journal of Sex Research, 49,* 558–569.

Willoughby, B. J., & Carroll, J. S. (2009). The impact of living in co-ed resident halls on risk-taking among college students. *Journal of American College Health, 58,* 241–246.

Woosley, S. A., & Shepler, D. K. (2011). Understanding the early integration experiences of first-generation college students. *College Student Journal, 45,* 700–714.

4

College Upperclassmen: Preparing to Launch

KATHERINE M. HERMANN AND
ESTHER NICOLE BENOIT

It takes courage to grow up and become who you really are.
—e.e. cummings

Throughout the life span, individuals experience frequent shifts within their environments. The later years of college form a unique developmental period that takes a courageous commitment to personal growth, environmental understanding, and adaptation. As college upperclassmen often undergo the divergence from an often supportive environment into a period marked by new role-taking and responsibilities (Murphy, Blustein, Bohlig, & Platt, 2010), they frequently experience an unfamiliar range of stressors as well as physical (e.g., brain and neurological) and psychological changes. During this period, students may alter their perspectives on responsibility while simultaneously anticipating relocation, a transition from friend and family support, and a redefinition of their identity in an impending career.

Through this period of uncertainty, students often seek additional support from external resources, such as counselors. Nevertheless, individuals in the counseling profession may find themselves asking: How do college upperclassmen differ from their younger counterparts? What unique considerations do these young adults experience? What influences these students' views of themselves and others? Where do these students find meaning and personal value? How does the upcoming disconnection from familiar community affect their decisions, personality, and development?

In order to respond to questions such as these, counselors can benefit from becoming familiar with the many changes and challenges that occur during the later years of college. Just as the first years of college bring new challenges for older adolescents, the latter years also bring new challenges as these students plan their launch into new relational and professional realms. These years auger a period of marked physiological, physical, social, emotional, career, and identity transformations. We begin with an introduction to the many common transitions and stressors experienced by college students and conclude with a discussion of the implications for counseling professionals.

MULTILAYERED TRANSITIONS AND STRESSORS

Life is one big transition.—Willie Stargell

As college upperclassmen approach graduation, multilayered developmental shifts occur and interact across several domains (Roisman, Masten, Coatsworth, & Tellegen, 2004). A few of the major transitions for college upperclassmen include the solidification of future life goals such as the development of intimate adult relationships and navigating the transition from school to employment, while simultaneously moderating academic, social, and financial stress (Archer & Lamnin, 1985; Caspi, 2002). The junior year tends to be a relatively stable time for students as they are well acclimated to campus and community, but they begin to realize that they are halfway to the end of their college years. As graduation draws nearer, upperclassmen experience a tumultuous time characterized as a period of growth, change, and subsequently stress (Brougham, Zail, Mendoza, & Miller, 2009).

Relational Transitions

Love and work are prominent themes in the transition to young adulthood (Arnett, 2004). As college students make sense of their relationships outside of the context of their families of origin, new social rules and roles emerge. Establishing relationships with significant others and negotiating the process of creating and maintaining those relationships while simultaneously exploring one's own identity are commonly described as sources of stress by college students (Arnett, 2000). Relational tension, which may originate from social pressures, friendships, intimate relationships, and/or engagement with parental units (Archer & Lamnin, 1985), can greatly impact students' decisions and moods as they attempt to balance existing relationships, negotiate new relationships, and moderate the influence of these relationships on immediate and long-term actions. College upper-classmen are tasked with the complex balancing of increased autonomy and continued connection and support.

Romantic Relationships

Intimate relationships in particular may evolve as students experience greater levels of independence, reformulate the role of an intimate relationship within their lives, and evaluate the feasibility of the relationship after college. Typically beginning in sophomore year and intensifying in junior year, students long for and seek to establish more serious and committed romantic relationships. As upperclassmen experiment with emotional and physical intimacy, they often set about discovering relational preferences, and the result of these many coexisting dynamics can either provide a basis of social and relational support, buffering stress, or conversely become a compounding stressor as students negotiate future plans. Senior couples may seek counseling to address relational or communication difficulties as they prepare to make the leap from "college romance" to "committed couple." They also recognize the difficulty of locating new jobs in geographically proximal locations and this may create additional stress in their job searches. The complexity of these relationships can produce both interpersonal and intrapersonal conflicts as students mature and prepare for life after college.

Family of Origin Concerns

As students moderate the dissonance of establishing intimacy and long-term relationships, parents may offer college upperclassmen a thread of continuity during a time of great change (Brougham et al., 2009; Murphy et al., 2010), or they may be a prevalent source of stress (Archer & Lamnin, 1985; Brougham et al., 2009). Some students find that as they prepare for increasing levels of independence—financial, geographic, and emotional—and restructure their relationships with parents, they struggle with asserting their own independence. Nevertheless, according to some literature, the balance between autonomy and relatedness found in these relationships may be complementary rather than at odds (Arnett, 2000). As a result, the parents' role in the upperclassmen's environment should be considered an important element of their relational context.

Residential Shifts

The theme of experimentation and exploration is often paralleled in the living situations of college upperclassmen, which can be unstable (Arnett, 2000), as students live in a variety of settings with varying degrees of autonomy, including dormitories or fraternity houses, apartments, cohabitation with romantic partners, or with their families of origin. Changes in residential status are associated with transition points in development and illustrate the dynamic nature of this phase of life. During the junior year, the majority of students are making their homes off-campus, and they take on the new responsibilities of buying groceries, preparing their own meals, paying bills, and negotiating the thermostat temperature with roommates in order to stay in budget. Not until young adulthood (late 20s) does this period of relative instability end (Murphy et al., 2010). Each of these living situations represents examples of the varied experiences of college upperclassmen and should be considered when assessing and addressing the needs of students.

Crossing the Threshold Into Independence

As students move from their junior into their senior year, a major focus and goal is graduation. The influence of students' families of origin is still present and students fear disappointing these significant others. Van Etten, Pressley, McInerney, and Liem (2008) found that students feel a great amount both of external and internal pressure to graduate as the alternative outcome, an incomplete degree, is perceived to reflect both a waste of time and money. Factors that influence student success, including persistence and graduation rate, include gender, family support, levels of stress and depression, and first-year grade point average (GPA; Wintre & Bowers, 2007). For upperclassmen, their ability to successfully navigate their early college years will play a strong role in their ability to successfully transition into the next phase of adulthood.

A New Financial Perspective

Once students successfully complete their degree requirements, they may face the final "college crisis," the search for a job. The final semester can be a balancing act between passing courses and applying and interviewing for positions. Students view financial stability as a potential source of security, independence, and responsibility as well as an indication of their success. Conversely, students who feel high anxiety in the face of graduation are often deeply afraid that they will be failures, that a good job will be beyond their grasp, that their parents will be painfully disappointed in them, and that, despite years of hard work, success will elude them. Given the length of time employers may take to complete the hiring process, the anxiety seniors experience during spring semester may be hard to bear. While early adolescence was a time when work was recognized as an opportunity to earn extra money for recreational purposes, as students prepare for adulthood and seek employment, they begin to more seriously consider their individual strengths and the potential for job satisfaction (Arnett, 2000). Counselors should remind their graduating clients of any career services offered on campus. Referring them to the campus career center prior to their final semester will allow them to begin to build their job search more thoroughly and efficiently. Interview skills practice and resume review, in addition to job leads, are standard fare for career service centers. Counselors should remind graduating clients, too, that the skills they have learned in college go far beyond memorizing and basic information but also include social skills, problem solving, critical thinking, taking on additional responsibilities, and gaining insight into human nature. These skills will help them as they move forward and transition into their first jobs and the next chapter of their lives.

Future Focused

As upperclassmen and soon-to-be-graduates initiate occupational exploration based on career-related values and goals, refine their major, or seek information about graduate education programs, they begin to recognize the weight of their current and future decisions. As students explore career options, they frequently describe finances as an increasingly more prevalent source of stress (Archer & Lamnin, 1985). This increased stress can stem from a growing perception of responsibility related to biological and emotional developmental tasks, the anticipation of paying back student loans, difficulty finding employment, or the existential realization that maintaining financial stability will be a lifelong necessity as they emerge from the college setting. Regardless of the source of this stress, students are often preoccupied with the logistics of current and future financial obligations.

A final consideration, when addressing college upperclassmen, is the connection between academic achievement, stress, and self-efficacy. While some research states that upperclassmen tend to experience less academic stress than underclassmen (Baldwin, Chambliss & Towler, 2003), other literature cites continued academic pressure as one of these students' top stressors (Archer & Lamnin, 1985; Brougham et al., 2009; Ong & Cheong, 2009). Despite this debate, one can easily recognize the unique academic stressors salient to college upperclassmen. While these students continue to experience stress related to a heavy workload, professor characteristics, and competition (Ong & Cheong, 2009), they also often struggle with maintaining a high GPA in the face of burnout while preparing for and completing entrance exams for continuing education, and/or applying and interviewing for jobs. These new and challenging obligations and expectations apply another source of intellectual responsibility to students' current obligations as they adjust to a new emotional framework.

An undercurrent of many of these transitions and stressors is the ongoing uncertainty students experience as they prepare to shift from an undergraduate lifestyle into the next stage of their lives. Whether pursuing an advanced degree or entering the labor force, for many students, this period marks the first time their lives do not follow a predetermined developmental trajectory. This lack of certainty, while exhilarating for many students, can produce unfamiliar levels and forms of anxiety. As these students continually adjust to time demands, the renegotiation of relationships, identity exploration, financial concerns, and emerging levels of responsibility, they prepare to master the financial and geographical independence associated with successful postcollege adaptation (Murphy et al., 2010).

THE COUNSELING WAY

We do not grow absolutely, chronologically. We grow sometimes in one dimension, and not in another; unevenly. We grow partially. We are relative. We are mature in one realm, childish in another. The past, present, and future mingle and pull us backward, forward, or fix us in the present. We are made up of layers, cells, constellations.—Anaïs Nin

Counseling college upperclassmen can be an exciting yet challenging endeavor. As counselors work with this maturing population, they encounter unique and varied characteristics. While some students are "depressed ... in search of their identity" (Murphy et al., 2010, p. 174), and experiencing anxiety surrounding the transitions and stressors discussed, others may describe increased optimism "viewing the multitude of options as exciting and empowering" (Murphy et al., 2010, p. 174). Despite potential optimism, many students lack the skills necessary to navigate developmental transitions. Therefore, the unique aspects of each student's past and present experiences, environment, goals, and identity provide varying needs of support and vastly different therapeutic approaches.

Because every student is markedly different, we encourage counselors to integrate a phenomenological therapeutic perspective. By recognizing each student's subjective worldview, experiences, and complexity, and by tailoring interventions accordingly, therapists can ensure that every student feels heard, respected, and understood, increasing the student's receptivity to counseling services. In addition to this phenomenological outlook, we also recommend that counselors maintain a positive psychological perspective. As students approach this somewhat daunting period of their lives and the often unfamiliar counseling setting, the presence of an affirmative, supportive counselor has implications for a successful transition into the next life stage.

Consciously beginning the therapeutic process with a holistic assessment of emotional and environmental considerations will provide a more accurate understanding of the individual. Suggested areas of exploration include students' social support, family network, academic expectations, occupational endeavors, physical activity, alcohol consumption, spirituality, identity definition, and future goals. Each of these distinct areas can offer insight into current coping mechanisms or areas of maladaptive behaviors. Social support, which may consist of friendships, romantic relationships, and parental connection, is one area of particular importance in this population since these relationships can be a dominant source of stress or ease the stressors inherent in the transition from school to work (Murphy et al., 2010).

Depending upon students' needs, counselors can offer upperclassmen a spectrum of resources ranging from psychoeducation to personal growth facilitation. Psychoeducational programs focusing on occupational, cognitive, and emotional tasks may not only address immediate concerns but also may help students prepare for new role-taking experiences. For instance, with career exploration, the importance of realistic and flexible expectations in the move from college to career, and an understanding of the expectations of future employers (Murphy et al., 2010) may increase feelings of preparedness and reduce uncertainty. In addition, the introduction of concrete skills including ways to manage stress and time, prioritize tasks, communicate, and prepare for lifestyle changes may have both immediate and long-term effects. This combination of current and future-oriented skills may increase clients' perceived value of the counseling experience and thus help them incorporate the novel and effective skills more quickly.

In addition to providing psychoeducational content, addressing students' emotional tenor and current methods of managing stressors is important for immediate and long-term mental health. As students mature, existential life changes often facilitate deeper levels of reflection. As counselors, we can assist the navigation of these new experiences and feelings. It should be noted that while some literature points to the benefits of using students' existing emotionally focused skills as a catalyst to improve coping (Brougham et al., 2009), other findings point to problem-focused strategies as being more beneficial (Wang, Nyutu, & Tran, 2012). Nevertheless, because some stressors are more emotional and others more contextual, providing students with a means to tailor their coping strategies to their individual problems is optimal (Austenfeld & Stanton, 2004).

Finally, while the later years of college represent a new and engaging time of self-exploration and soul searching for students, the experiences are not necessarily growth inducing. Stevic and Ward (2008) explored the elements that contributed to personal growth experiences in college and highlighted the importance of a concept called personal growth initiative that is integral to students' successful navigation of the transition from college to the working world. Individuals who exhibit higher levels of personal growth initiative "have a strong sense of direction in their life, know their role in life, and have an action plan for accomplishing specific goals in the future" (2008, p. 525). Counselors would be well served to consider the concept of personal growth initiative as a resiliency factor when working with this population.

As college upperclassmen experience new transitional stressors and anticipate their shifting roles postgraduation, they may look to counseling professionals for support and guidance as they make sense of these changes. We are given a unique opportunity to nurture adaptations to improve well-being and impart valuable coping skills for ongoing personal growth throughout the life span.

CONCLUSION

College upperclassmen face a period of incredible opportunity, growth, and excitement as they move toward graduation. Yet, with these opportunities and transitions comes the inevitable ambiguity and uncertainty inherent in any major life transition. As counselors, we will benefit from ongoing attention to the varied, dynamic needs of college upperclassmen in order to provide them with the support and challenge needed to promote ongoing development as they embark on the next steps of their life journeys.

REFERENCES

Archer, J., & Lamnin, A. (1985). An investigation of personal and academic stressors on college campuses. *Journal of College Student Personnel, 26*(3), 210–215.

Arnett, J. J. (2000). Emerging adulthood: A theory of development from the late teens through the twenties. *American Psychologist, 55*(5), 469–480.

Arnett, J. J. (2004). *Emerging adulthood: The winding road from the late teens through the twenties.* New York, NY: Oxford University Press.

Austenfeld, J., & Stanton, A. L. (2004). Coping through emotional approach: A new look at emotion, coping, and health-related outcomes. *Journal of Personality, 72*(6), 1335–1364.

Baldwin, D. R., Chambliss, L. N., & Towler, K. (2003). Optimism and stress: An African-American college student perspective. *College Student Journal, 37*(2), 276–286.

Brougham, R. R., Zail, C. M., Mendoza, C. M., & Miller, J. R. (2009). Stress, sex differences, and coping strategies among college students. *Current Psychology, 28*(2), 85–97.

Caspi, A. (2002). Social selection, social causation and developmental pathways: Empirical strategies for better understanding how individuals and environments are linked across the life course. In L. Pulkkinen & A. Caspi (Eds.), *Paths to successful development: Personality in the life course* (pp. 281–301). Cambridge, UK: Cambridge University Press.

Murphy, K. A., Blustein, D. L., Bohlig, A. J., & Platt, M. G. (2010). The college-to-career transition: An exploration of emerging adulthood. *Journal of Counseling & Development, 88,* 174–181.

Ong, B., & Cheong, K. C. (2009). Sources of stress among college students: The case of a credit transfer program. *College Student Journal, 43*(4), 1279–1286.

Roisman, G. I., Masten, A. S., Coatsworth, J. D., & Tellegen, A. (2004). Salient and emerging developmental tasks in the transition to adulthood. *Child Development, 75*(1), 123–133.

Stevic, C. R., & Ward, R. (2008). Initiating personal growth: The role of recognition and life satisfaction on the development of college students. *Social Indicators Research, 89*(3), 523–534.

Van Etten, S., Pressley, M., McInerney, D. M., & Liem, A. D. (2008). College seniors' theory of their academic motivation. *Journal of Educational Psychology, 100,* 812–828.

Wang, M. K., Nyutu, P. N., & Tran, K. K. (2012). Coping, reasons for living, and suicide in black college students. *Journal of Counseling & Development, 90*(4), 459–466.

Wintre, M. G., & Bowers, C. D. (2007). Predictors of persistence to graduation: Extending a model and data on the transition to university model. *Canadian Journal of Behavioural Science, 39,* 220–234.

Section II: Social, Cultural, and Relational Challenges on Campus

5

Understanding Diverse Populations on the College Campus

AMY ZAVADIL AND LESLIE KOOYMAN

College is a time of identity development and exploration; however, students arrive with values and beliefs influenced by their precollege experiences. Prior family, community, religious, and educational experiences influence the ongoing development that is anticipated during the college years. While individuation is a crucial element of development in the late adolescent/early adulthood transition, this can be heavily influenced by individual, family, and cultural expectations (Arnett, Ramos, & Jensen, 2001; Gardner, 2009; Taylor, 2008). Historically, however, the administrative personnel and faculty of mainstream colleges and universities traditionally have reflected a White male patriarchal configuration, with the presence of female or minority members viewed by some as a necessary response to equal opportunity mandates. This high percentage of European American professors, staff, and students may limit an institution's awareness of and ability to meet the needs of its minority students and this limited perspective may interact with students' healthy individuation due to the lack of available role models and campus-based support for and understanding of their unique diverse culture.

Gusa (2010) asserted that overwhelmingly European American–populated campus cultures create environments with an inherent European American slant inside and outside of the classroom, and thus a "domination of one over others" in terms of cultural influence (p. 469). The use of the word *domination* does not entail complete control, but rather the ability to set the terms "by which other groups and classes must operate" in all aspects of college life (p. 469). Personnel must recognize the influence they hold over students and recognize that each student must be viewed in the context of background experiences and campus culture.

Social identity development is complex and encompasses an individual's view of racial, ethnic, socioeconomic, and sexual understanding of oneself (Gardner, 2009; Taylor, 2008). Students entering college may be at very different stages of this developmental process, though most will still be within an exploration stage on some level. This can be an awkward, stressful process amplified by the transition to college or supported through exposure to more peers like themselves. Identity development is complex, and can be further complicated when students experience growth in their transition to college that conflicts with their family or home community beliefs (Baber, 2012; Taylor, 2008). Assisting students in recognizing that development is not always linear and is influenced by one's environment is a step toward encouraging and growing coping skills during this time of transition.

In considering racial, ethnic, religious, or sexual minority populations, the challenge of understanding identity development of this age group becomes even more complex. These students are also experiencing identity development through the lens of color, ethnicity, and social class, to name just a few. Cross and Helms both delineate the identity development phases of these populations, which may include conformity to the majority culture norms, dissonance with identity (encountering racism or bias), and an immersion into one's own racial/ethnic group, followed by emersion from this phase into an internalization status of sorting out one's identity in relation to others. Finally, an identity of "integrative awareness" of racial/ethnic identity may be achieved (Cross, 1995; Helms, 1995). These stages are not linear and not reflective of every student, but are generalizable to a population that is adjusting to college life while discovering their own racial and ethnic identity.

ACKNOWLEDGING AND CHALLENGING DISCRIMINATION

Discrimination has long been a problem area on college campuses. D'Augelli and Hershberger (1993) reported results of a study in which they found that 89% of African American students reported having heard insulting racial remarks at least on occasion on campus, 59% had been insulted personally, and 35% reported having experienced threats or violence. Despite university efforts to diversify the campus and increase the level of support for students of color, racist incidents remain a problem. Students who feel they are being discriminated against are not likely to fit in at a college (Bean, 2005) and must learn to face both overt and covert prejudice. Although antidiscrimination and harassment policies are clear on the overwhelming majority of campuses, there can be subtle discriminatory practices that occur, as well as pockets of students who foster negative attitudes and behaviors toward those who are different. When these incidents of microaggression are tacitly accepted, it may "wear down the pride of minority and immigrant students and cause them to question if in fact they do belong in college" (Kadison & DiGeronimo, p. 51). A sense of belonging is crucial to healthy development as young adults face the task of building relationships to avoid self-isolation (Erikson, 1968). Thus, diverse students may decide to build relationships only with students who share their cultural identity; this choice can yield both protective and deleterious outcomes depending on ethnic identity (Levin, Van Laar, & Foote, 2006). And, unfortunately, students who have a sense of perceived discrimination can face consequences as significant as those of outright harassment.

Fitting in While Being Different

An important social concern for college students is to find a group with which they share values (Bean, 2005). Ultimately, at the root of social challenges for many minority students is the question of how to honor and adhere to one's own traditions in the midst of what can seem to be a foreign social and educational culture. Language, dress, social interaction, school traditions, campus organizations, and social events are often rooted in European American cultural and social norms (Gusa, 2010). Minority students may feel pressure, whether internally or externally, to fit in by adopting these majority norms.

On the other hand, pressure may also come from within a student's personal community to not stray from one's own cultural norms. Even if not victims of blatant discrimination, ethnic or religious minority students, particularly those from smaller minority groups, may struggle to find a place in the campus community. African Americans, in particular, may feel pressure from their own family, home community, or peers on campus to avoid "acting White"—which is construed as an insult that may refer to speech, dress, music preference, or social activities (Kadison & DiGeronimo, 2004, p. 51). Family, particularly parents, may add increased pressure both to be successful in school and to adhere to cultural traditions. Even if there is no external pressure, students may fear that they are surrendering their cultural identity or betraying their community as they adopt culturally divergent behaviors and values. Minority students who feel pressure—whether to adapt to or reject the dominant culture—are at risk of developing identity confusion.

Students may seek similar others as primary choices for association; for some students, including Latino students, this can lessen their sense of belonging on the college campus and, equally unsettling, their overall academic performance (Levin et al., 2006). However, African American students who primarily socialize with others who share their ethnicity actually felt a stronger sense of academic motivation and academic commitment at the end of their college years. College counselors should attend to the demographic makeup of their student bodies as well as learn about the ways in which diverse student groups relate to and perceive one another. Students must feel capable of developing and maintaining an individual, culturally relevant identity while still feeling a sense of belonging to the greater campus community.

The Influence of Religious and Spiritual Identities

There is a greater chance of isolation if the student belongs to a minority group with noticeable differences, such as appearance, traditions, dress, or values. A conservative Muslim female, for example, may suffer from exclusion by other females because she wears a hijab. Another very common example of values clashing are when alcohol-abstinent students feel left out of the college social scene not just at the bars and weekend parties, but also in campus residences. Bishop, Lacour, Nutt, Yamada, and Lee (2004) reported incoming student populations are becoming less likely to endorse a specific religious affiliation and are increasingly acknowledging that they may hold spiritual beliefs that are distinct from the construct of organized religion-bound beliefs. The CIRP Freshman Year survey reported a steady decline in religious affiliation among entering college freshman (Pryor, Hurtado, Seanz, Santos, & Korn, 2007), though there is a diversity of religious beliefs and practices among college students. Arnett, Ramos, and Jensen (2001) noted that during the college years, students are developing an individual ideological belief system that sometimes includes a component of religiosity. When students are moving toward a religious belief system that differs from their families' and friends' traditions, they may face strong opposition. This can create a significant and unexpected power struggle for young adults who may feel isolated and rejected by those who make up their primary social support networks. Individuation is difficult work, but when it includes developing a core value system dissimilar from long-held beliefs, it can be especially arduous. Counselors must be aware of the challenges this situation presents when students bring these struggles to their offices.

According to the director of multicultural affairs at a small liberal arts college (personal communication, 2012), the most important trait for minority college students to possess is confidence—in both their own cultural and personal identities. Such self-assuredness provides these students with a clear sense of who they are without feeling as though that identity is being threatened. Counselors, therefore, should take the time to help foster and strengthen clients' self-esteem and identity establishment. Counselor and client should collaborate to find ways of confronting or coping with external pressures that the student is facing. Given the central role of the family in many minority cultures, even if a family cannot join in the counseling process, the client can be encouraged to address familial values and expectations that he or she feels should be honored. While some students readily express their views and feelings outwardly and others are more reticent and remain silent, it is imperative that college campuses provide minority students with opportunities and an atmosphere in which they feel free to express their concerns. A recommended book for counselors is Claude M. Steele's *Whistling Vivaldi* (2010), which provides examples of ways in which our stereotypes may be getting in the way of understanding others, effectively communicating, and supporting our minority students in their pursuit of an education and fitting in.

International Students

In addition to being minority students in most cases, international students face unique challenges to successful social integration in college. In exploring the feelings of international students at one university, Sherry, Thomas, and Chui (2010) found that isolation, loneliness, rejection, and difficulties in communication were common themes. Language barriers served as a significant social obstacle and source of anxiety for international students, who reported that they were often unsure of how to communicate with American students. Their difficulty transcends classroom discussions to include social interactions as well. Combined with the unfamiliar social environment and language barrier, the lack of cultural familiarity—different food, different music, different television shows—may add to feelings of estrangement, loneliness, and homesickness (McClure, 2007). Financial difficulties, work restrictions, and lack of transportation can further isolate international students from the campus community (Sherry et al., 2010).

To succeed, international students must be well prepared and know what to expect prior to coming to campus. After arriving, many schools provide "buddy systems" that match international students with American students who can provide assistance with everyday needs, such as transportation. Campus organizations play an important role in helping international students adjust to life in a new country. In addition to multicultural organizations that are open to all students, organizations specifically for international students provide social opportunities and a chance to connect with students who are currently experiencing or have successfully navigated a similar transition. Educational classes—actual courses or informal classes—on language, currency, interacting with other students, American culture, and other similar topics may help with transitioning to life in America.

Lesbian, Gay, Bisexual, and Transgender (LGBT) Students

Although greater attention is provided to the experiences of this group in the chapter on sexuality, it is important to acknowledge that late adolescence can be the most difficult period in the coming-out process, which is the personal recognition and sharing of commitment to a sexual minority identity. In brief, Cass (1979) described sexual identity development as consisting of various stages. These include identity confusion (the questioning of one's difference in sexual orientation), identity comparison (the struggle of comparing oneself to majority heterosexual population), identity tolerance (learning to accept an LGBT identity while still denying or rejecting the identity as well), identity acceptance (self-acceptance with selective outness), identity pride (an immersion into LGBT culture to the exclusion at times of heterosexuals), and finally, identity synthesis (an integrative understanding of an LGBT identity). While these stages are also not linear or fixed, they do provide guidance in understanding the development of this vulnerable population in the early years of college. Also important is recognizing the differences among the varied groups that fall under the umbrella acronym, LGBT. Transgender and gender nonconforming students have experiences and support needs that may be quite distinct from LGB students. Differing definitions among gender nonconforming identities add to the challenges facing students and those who work with students (Scott, Belke, & Barfield, 2011), and counselors working with these clients should not allow popular media images or stereotypes to color their views.

College campuses often provide a diverse and accepting environment; however, this may depend on the overall climate of the campus, the community, and the geographical region in which the college is located. Although the nation's level of tolerance and acceptance of sexual minorities has increased overall, there are still many places in which intolerance and discrimination are the norm. In fact, in a recent study it was reported that the majority of students harbored moderately negative attitudes toward gay and lesbian people, with males holding a significantly more negative view than women (Chonody, Siebert, & Rutledge, 2009, p. 505).

Bullying—psychological and physical—toward LGBT students has been a major problem. These students are also more likely to experience or receive threats of violence, feel less safe on campus, and are more stressed than heterosexual students (Reed, Prado, Matsumoto, & Amaro, 2010). They also report greater feelings of fear and isolation (Waldo, 1998), harassment and violence from heterosexual students (Rankin 2005), and feelings of humiliation or "invisibility" in the classroom from a professor's comments or demeanor regarding LGBT individuals (Renn, 2000). In fact, about 36% of LGBT college students experience some form of harassment based on sexual orientation and close to one third of LGBT students consider transferring in their first year of college (Rankin, 2005; Rankin, Weber, Blumenfeld & Frazer, 2010).

In exploring solutions for the problems faced by LGBT students, a college counselor may first need to assess the campus community as a whole. Black, Oles, Cramer, and Bennett (1999) found positive changes in attitude toward and knowledge about LGBT students among heterosexual students after implementing a program that combined educational factors with exposure—in this case, a professor coming out to the class and discussing personal experiences as an out sexual minority. This method provides increased information to students, as well as personalizing issues related to sexual orientation with a speaker—perhaps one that the students already know. Campus-wide programs can also be very effective both in providing a supportive atmosphere to sexual minority students, and also in educating the heterosexual majority. Examples include "Safe Zone" and "Allies" training, with participating faculty and administrative personnel often provided with stickers or placards for their doors to show visible support for an often invisible minority.

For LGBT students themselves, campus organizations catering to them and their allies provide a place to meet other LGBT students, to discuss LGBT-identity–related concerns and issues, and to enjoy opportunities for leadership (Olive, 2010). In examining the factors that contribute to a successful college experience for LGBT students, Olive observed certain traits and themes among these students: self-confidence, autonomy, resilience, self-care, a strong relationship with at least one parent, and involvement in an LGBT organization on campus. Counselors should look to foster each of these traits in LGBT clients.

Students With Disabilities

The number of students with disabilities completing high school and continuing into higher education has steadily increased since the 1970s and the passage of disability legislation (Thomas, 2000). In a 2008 study, the U.S. Government Accountability Office (2009) found that students with disabilities accounted for 10.8% of enrollment in American postsecondary institutions surveyed. In addition to the same issues of transition to college as their peers, students with disabilities move into an environment where they must self-advocate for services and resources, an additional new responsibility that also requires "outing" themselves to college personnel. This need to self-identify can present hurdles for students and potentially hinder the sense of belonging in the new college community (Getzel & Thoma, 2008). In fact, self-advocacy and visibility are two factors that heavily contribute to how well a student with a disability is able to integrate into the college environment (Adams & Proctor, 2010).

Students who do not avail themselves of disability services are at greater risk of academic and social challenges. These students may need assistance in building skills or coping mechanisms for navigating this personal responsibility, or in understanding their own identity as inclusive of their abilities to support their persistence as they transition within the college experience. Raising awareness across the community, faculty, staff, and students about available resources can create a more inclusive community response to students with disabilities (Thomas, 2000).

It has been found that decreased visibility of the disability leads to a lower level of adaptation (Adams & Proctor, 2010). For these students, typically those with psychological or learning disabilities, the lack of visibility results in nondisclosure due to a fear of the social stigma attached to disabilities and, particularly, psychological disorders (Weiner & Weiner, 1996). These students often choose not to disclose their disabilities to their professors or their friends, as they "feel more pressure to adequately explain or 'justify' their disability, given that their disability is not readily apparent to the observer" (Adams & Proctor, 2010, p. 178). This is problematic for students because some of these disabilities result in academic difficulties and lower grades when not disclosed to professors, which could lead to low self-esteem, low self-efficacy, stress, or depression—all of which can negatively affect social life. Coupled with a lack of self-advocacy and self-determination skills, this can further limit the ability to build connections with other students and succeed academically. It should also be noted, however, that those with more visible disabilities—physical, sensory, or developmental—face their own unique challenges. Without the opportunity to manage others' awareness or knowledge of their disabilities, these students are more likely to be victims of the stigma attached by others to those with disabilities. They may face social exclusion and overt and covert discrimination from other students. Furthermore, for those with physical disorders, accessibility and transportation are also frequent obstacles to social involvement.

Although school disability services offices are there to advocate for student rights, it is necessary and highly advantageous for these students to learn self-advocacy skills to use in their classes, their social milieu, and throughout their lives after college (Adams & Proctor, 2010). Counselors should help foster self-determination and self-advocacy for students through training and workshops, as well as through working with faculty (Belch, 2004). In working one-on-one with students, counselors should focus on empowering the client. Providing information, assertiveness training, and role-playing exercises may provide the client with the knowledge and ability to self-advocate more effectively. Cognitive-behavioral techniques may also be beneficial if the student has developed self-defeating notions or has not come to terms with the disability.

Lower Socioeconomic Status (SES) and First-Generation Students

While there is certainly significant overlap between lower SES students and first-generation college students, there are also distinctions between the two groups. First-generation students do not necessarily come from lower SES families (National Center for Education Statistics, 2000), as a parent's economic health does not necessarily reflect a parent's educational attainment. Each student's experiences will be unique and his or her classification as "first gen" or "low SES" is only a part of the student's identity, but one that requires acknowledgment.

Lower-Income Students

Studies have found that college students from lower SES backgrounds experience more academic and social difficulties than their higher SES peers. According to data collected in 2002, almost 30% of students from families with incomes below $50,000 will drop out of college and 15% will have left after their second year (Pell Institute, 2004). The Pell Institute asserted that these figures could not be due solely to academic reasons, but that there is also a social factor involved. Students from lower SES backgrounds are less likely to become involved in student organizations than their wealthier peers and many spend less than an hour a week in social pursuits (Walpole, 2003). Because the vast majority of college students come from the middle and upper classes, the academic and social environments are geared toward those who have upper SES-related cultural and social worldviews and experiential backgrounds (Walpole, 2003). Not only may lower SES students feel culturally disadvantaged, they also frequently must limit involvement in campus activities due to longer hours at job sites or family commitments. They, like their first-generation peers, face diverse challenges to their educational success.

First-Generation College Students

The first-generation demographic is a group that has traditionally struggled in college—one study found that just 47% of first-generation students who enrolled at a 4-year college earned their undergraduate degree as compared to a 78% graduation rate among those students with at least one parent holding a college degree (Chen & Carroll, 2005). Thus, retention and academic success are two clear areas for college student service programming. In an unfamiliar situation, children naturally will look to their parents to provide advice on their experiences. A first-generation college student, however, is unable to draw upon his or her parents' experiences or suggestions for how to handle college life. Even more problematic, parents may see their child's entry into college as more of a departure from the family in which parents are left behind. This phenomenon has been given the name "breakaway guilt" (London, 1989, p. 153, as cited by Davis, 2010). As students accept the greater society's value system regarding higher education, their parents may feel resentment toward their academically successful and ambitious offspring and use this resentment to foster the development of guilt in their children. Thus, first-generation students are faced with the dilemma of succeeding academically to move forward versus sabotaging their success to mollify their parents.

First-generation college students can be expected to experience anxiety and feelings of eventual failure more often and at higher levels than other students (Martinez, Sher, Krull, & Wood, 2009). Davis (2010) attributed this to what he termed the *imposter phenomenon*, which for first-generation students is the feeling that they do not belong in college (p. 48). First-generation students may feel as though they are imposters on campus and that the "other" students are the true college students. The imposter phenomenon manifests itself in the classroom and in social life, and is characterized by a lack of self-esteem that leads these students to feel like their peers are above them. This can keep the students from attempts to build friendships or connections with other students as they feel that they will be seen as lesser than the others.

Counseling Implications for Lower SES and First-Generation Students

Due to the overlap between lower SES students and first-generation students, some of the same time management issues may be relevant for these groups, as many of them may also need to hold jobs to afford school. They may also need additional encouragement to join campus organizations and get involved in extracurricular activities. Dealing with the lack of time and the potentially lower self-esteem compared with other students, first-generation students may need additional encouragement and programming geared toward their specific needs. Also, because their families cannot provide experience-based wisdom and guidance in managing college life, it is important that first-generation students receive an in-depth orientation upon entering college. While this is frequently provided in first-year experience programs, it is often even more helpful to establish an organization or program specifically designed to meet the unique needs of first-generation students (Davis, 2010). Counselors working with these students in individual or group counseling settings may address the issues of low self-esteem and self-defeating thoughts through cognitive-behavioral techniques. Given the importance of family to these students and given the roadblocks that some parents may unwittingly put up, counselors may want to involve the parents as much as possible, if practical and if the student agrees.

Academic Pressure and Student–Faculty Communication
As student populations continue to diversify and access to higher education increases, there is an ongoing need to provide remedial support for preparation for college-level work—up to 25% of students report the need for such assistance, particularly in math (Bishop et al., 2004; Pryor et al., 2007). There are noted racial differences in this need for support and additional preparation. Managing the adjustment challenges of transitioning to college can have an adverse impact on academic success (Lee, Olson, Locke, Michelson, & Odes, 2009).

Many colleges have established first-year programs that address college adjustment issues in both the social and academic realms. According to the Pell Institute, these programs are structured to assist first-year students navigate the expectations related to college academic coursework as well as campus social interactions; they are often taught in learning communities by teams of teachers representing different disciplines. These programs are particularly helpful in the early part of the first semester, providing students with information and opportunities to meet fellow students who are also seeking to find their niche on campus.

Pryor et al. (2007) indicate first-year students report a reduction in the time spent with faculty. Much research supports the positive influence of contact with faculty as supportive of student learning and persistence (Astin, 1998; Astin, 1999; Tinto, 2006); therefore, encouraging students to seek assistance from faculty can be beneficial. However, Padgett, Johnson and Pascarella (2012) reported that first-generation students experience greater discomfort or anxiety, and lower well-being than other students when interacting with faculty. Students may benefit from workshops or outreach that encourages and normalizes such help seeking, as well as generates recognition of this individual responsibility of the student, while being aware that some students may not find the same benefit from faculty engagement.

Helping Students Get Connected

Gerdes and Mallinckrodt (1994) found that social adjustment during the transition to college is as important to persistence as academic adjustment. The importance of student engagement and social connectedness is well documented as an essential element for college retention (Astin, 1998; Gerdes & Mallinckrodt, 1994; Padgett, Johnson & Pascarella, 2012; Tinto, 2006). While social connectedness and student engagement in social activities have been shown to improve college retention, the college environment includes increased alcohol use and sexual risk-taking behaviors that can prove challenging to student's healthy identity development

(Kooyman, Pierce, & Zavadil, 2011). Therefore, it can be essential to help marginalized students find safe and supportive social outlets.

Many universities create virtual melting pots of diverse cultures as students are often recruited from across a state, region, the country, and the globe. Colleges should be prepared to help these students acclimate to the campus and the community by supporting campus-based organizations that engage diverse student groups. These groups can provide a community-within-the-community for students, as well as provide the opportunity for native students to learn more about diverse cultures and build relationships with students from other areas. Racism, prejudice, harassment, and general stereotyping may plague multicultural students, and campus organizations can offer them support and bring awareness to the university campus. Examples of these groups from a variety of schools include the African Student Organization, Asian Student Union, Black Student Alliance, Chinese Student Association, International Student Association, Korean Student Association, Latino Student Alliance, Cultural Dance Club, Multicultural Women for Change, NAACP, Students for Minority Outreach, Vietnamese Student Association, and Women of Color. There are even specific Greek organizations for cultural groups such as the National Pan-Hellenic Council (Divine Nine), which are historically African American Greek letter organizations, the National Association of Latino Fraternal Organizations, Inc., Greek letter organizations for students of Latino descent, and the National Asian Pacific Islander American Panhellenic Association for students of Asian descent. Whether a college counselor is working with a student who feels out of place due to cultural heritage or a student who is overly insulated in the majority culture, being aware of the diverse multicultural organizations on campus and in the wider community can provide excellent referral sources.

Be Prepared to Help Students Who Report Harassment of Any Type

A recent study showed that diverse college students are the targets both of inter- and intra-racial harassment (Smith & Jones, 2011). While campuses may try to develop diversity in student bodies and student activities, there are student-related obstacles that are difficult to minimize or eradicate. Specifically, students who openly cross racial borders in terms of romantic or platonic relationships are more likely to experience harassment. Thus, students of any ethnicity who choose to date those who are different from their own group are more likely to be harassed by their own ethnic groups. For African and European American students, friendships across racial lines multiplied the chances for harassment. Asian and Latino students who got involved in multiracial campus organizations were also more likely to be targeted by their own groups. Thus, counselors may be called upon to work with students who face hostilities and racially based discrimination from those who share an ethnic identity as well as those who are different.

Another form of harassment that is frequently perpetrated but less frequently addressed is sexual harassment. This form of harassment is prevalent in higher education settings, yet reporting of sexual harassment, including sexual assault, is extremely low (Bursik & Gefter, 2011; Fisher, Cullen, & Turner, 2000). Sexual harassment on college campuses takes many forms and is likely to have an adverse impact on individual well-being—personally, socially, and academically. Most college students indicate that sexual harassment occurs on campus, with two thirds of students indicating that they and/or their friends have been sexually harassed (Hill & Silva, 2005). Exposure to harassing behavior, frequently framed as "just joking," often makes it difficult for victims to name the behavior as harassment. In addition, revictimization is high for those who have already experienced sexual harassment (Berman, Izumi, & Arnold, 2002; Daigle, Fisher, & Stewart, 2009; Klem, Owens, Ross, Edwards, & Cobia, 2009). It is well documented that approximately one in four women will experience sexual harassment before graduating college, and between 10% and 15% of men report having experienced sexual harassment (American Association of University Women, 2001; Bursik & Gefter, 2011; Charney & Russell, 1994; Fisher, Cullen, & Turner, 2000; McCormack, 1995). Klem et al. (2009) report an incidence of college student experience of relationship violence ranging from 10% to 35%.

While the role of the counselor in a clinical setting is not to give advice or to pressure a client to report an incident of harassment or assault, it is important that counselors in higher education be familiar with their campus resources, including nondiscrimination policies and institutional grievance procedures for addressing reports of harassment to support students who experience sexual harassment or sexual violence. Institutional procedures include support and often interim measures designed to encourage persistence. In addition, familiarity with this policy and process is essential when working with an individual who has been accused of engaging in gender-based misconduct and may be facing disciplinary action.

CONCLUSION

Though the diversity of student populations is clear, incoming students bring different past experiences with diversity. Students acknowledge they will likely socialize with peers of different races or cultures, but do not always see the need to promote understanding of differences

(Bishop et al., 2004; Pryor et al., 2007). Pascarella, Edison, Nora, Hagedorn, and Terenzini (1996) described the need to support students as part of their psychosocial development in a diverse setting. Programmatic and policy decisions at any given institution will influence a student's experience, socially and academically (Astin, 1999; Kuh et al., 2008). Students who are struggling with their personal identity development and who lack social support are at risk of adverse impact on well-being and academics, including potential withdrawal from college—either voluntarily or as a result of academic or behavioral issues.

The complexity of student development given the diversity of individuals and communities requires flexibility and ongoing education. Recognizing the demographic constellation of the campus can assist in the development of relevant campus programming, as well as help counselors better understand the unique contextual experiences of all clients, regardless of cultural identity.

REFERENCES

Adams, K. S., & Proctor, B. C. (2010). Adaptation to college for students with and without disabilities: Group differences and predictors. *Journal of Postsecondary Education and Disability, 22*(3), 166–184.

American Association of University Women. (2001). *Hostile hallways: The AAUW survey on sexual harassment in America's schools.* (Research Rep. No. 923012). Washington, DC: Harris/Scholastic Research.

Arnett, J. J., Ramos, K. D., & Jensen, L. A. (2001). Ideological views in emerging adulthood: Balancing autonomy and community. *Journal of Adult Development, 8*(2), 69–79.

Astin, A. W. (1998). The changing American college student: Thirty-year trends, 1966–96. *Review of Higher Education, 21*(2), 115–135.

Astin, A. W. (1999). Student involvement: A developmental theory for higher education. *Journal of College Student Personnel, 25*, 297–308.

Baber, L. D. (2012). A qualitative inquiry on the multidimensional racial development among first-year African American college students attending a predominately white institution. *Journal of Negro Education, 81*(1), 67–81.

Bean, J. P. (2005). Nine themes of college student retention. In A. Seidman (Ed.), *College student retention: Formula for student success* (pp. 215–244). Westport, CT: Praeger.

Belch, H. A. (2004). Retention and students with disabilities. *Journal of College Student Retention: Research, Theory and Practice, 6*, 3–22.

Berman, H., Izumi, J., & Arnold, C. T. (2002). Sexual harassment and the developing sense of self among adolescent girls. *Canadian Journal of Counseling, 36*(4), 265–280.

Bishop, J. B., Lacour, M. A. M., Nutt, N. J., Yamada, V. A., & Lee, J. Y. (2004). Reviewing a decade of change in the student culture. *Journal of College Student Psychotherapy, 18*(3), 3–30.

Black, B., Oles, T. P., Cramer, E. P., & Bennett, C. K. (1999). Attitudes and behaviors of social work students toward lesbian and gay male clients. *Journal of Gay & Lesbian Social Services, 9*(4), 47–68. doi:10.1300/J041v09n04_03

Bursik, K., & Gefter, J. (2011). Still stable after all these years: Perceptions of sexual harassment in academic contexts. *The Journal of Social Psychology, 15*, 331–349.

Cass, V. C. (1979). Homosexuality identity formation. *Journal of Homosexuality, 4*(3), 219–235.

Charney, D. A., & Russell, R. C. (1994). An overview of sexual harassment. *The American Journal of Psychiatry, 151*(1), 10–17.

Chen, X., & Carroll, C. D. (2005). *First-generation students in postsecondary education: A look at their college transcripts* (NCES 2005–171). U.S. Department of Education, National Center for Education Statistics.

Chonody, J. M., Siebert, D., & Rutledge, S. (2009). College students' attitudes toward gays and lesbians. *Journal of Social Work Education, 45*(3), 499–512. doi:10.5175/JSWE.2009.200800002

Cross, W. E., Jr. (1995). The psychology of Nigrescence: Revising the Cross model. In J. M. Casas, L. A. Suzuki, & C. M. Alexander (Eds.), *Handbook of multicultural counseling* (pp. 93–122). Thousand Oaks, CA: Sage.

Daigle, L. E., Fisher, B. S., & Stewart, M. (2009). The effectiveness of sexual victimization prevention among college students: A summary of "what works." *Victims & Offenders, 4*(4), 398–404. doi:10.1080/15564880903227529

D'Augelli, A. R., & Hershberger, S. L. (1993). African-American undergraduates on a predominantly white campus: Academic factors, social networks, and campus climate. *Journal of Negro Education, 62*(1), 67–81. Retrieved October 24, 2012, from http://www.jstor.org/stable/2295400

Davis, J. (2010). *The first-generation student experience: Implications for campus practice and strategies for improving persistence and success.* Sterling, VA: Stylus.

Erikson, E. (1968). *Identity, youth and crisis.* New York, NY: Norton.

Fisher, B., Cullen, F., & Turner, M. (2000). *The sexual victimization of college women.* Washington, DC: U.S. Dept. of Justice, Office of Justice Programs, National Institute of Justice.

Gardner, S. K. (2009). Student development theory: A primer. *ASHE Higher Education Report, 34*(6), 15–28.

Gates, G. (2011). *How many people are lesbian, gay, bisexual, and transgender?* (Rep.). Retrieved October 24, 2012, from The Williams Institute, UCLA School of Law http://williamsinstitute.law.ucla.edu/wp-content/uploads/Gates-How-Many-People-LGBT-Apr-2011.pdf

Gerdes, H., & Mallinckrodt, B. (1994). Emotional, social, and academic adjustment of college students: A longitudinal study of retention. *Journal of Counseling & Development, 72*(3), 281–288.

Getzel, E. E., & Thoma, C. A. (2008). Experiences of college students with disabilities and the importance of self-determination in higher education settings. *Career Development for Exceptional Individuals, 31*(2), 77–84.

Gusa, D. (2010). White institutional presence: The impact of whiteness on campus climate. *Harvard Educational Review, 80*(4), 464–490.

Helms, J. E. (1995). An update of Helms' white and people of color racial identity. In J. G. Ponterotto, J. M. Casas, L. A. Suzuki, & C.M. Alexander (Eds.), *Handbook of multicultural counseling* (pp. 181–198). Thousand Oaks, CA: Sage.

Hill, C., & Silva, E. (2005). *Drawing the line: Sexual harassment on campus.* Washington, DC: AAUW Educational Foundation. Retrieved from http://www.bls. gov/news.release/hsgec.nr0.htm

Kadison, R., & DiGeronimo, T. F. (2004). *College of the overwhelmed: The campus mental health crisis and what to do about it.* San Francisco, CA: Jossey-Bass.

Klem, J., Owens, A., Ross, A., Edwards, L., & Cobia, D. C. (2009). Dating violence: Counseling adolescent females from an existential perspective. *Journal of Humanistic Counseling, Education & Development, 48*(1), 48–64.

Kooyman, L., Pierce, G., & Zavadil, A. (2011). Hooking up and identity development of female college students. *Adultspan Journal, 10*(1), 4–13.

Kuh, G. D., Cruce, T. M., Shoup, R., Kinzie, J., & Gonyea, R. M. (2008). Unmasking the effects of student engagement on first-year college grades and persistence. *The Journal of Higher Education, 79*(5), 540–563.

Lee, D., Olson, E. A., Locke, B., Michelson, S. T., & Odes, E. (2009). The effects of college counseling services on academic performance and retention. *Journal of College Student Development, 50*(3), 305–319.

Levin, S., Van Laar, C., & Foote, W. (2006). Ethnic segregation and perceived discrimination in college: Mutual influences and effects on social and academic life. *Journal of Applied Social Psychology, 36,* 1471–1501.

Martinez, J. A., Sher, K. J., Krull, J. L., & Wood, P. K. (2009). Blue-collar scholars?: Mediators and moderators of university attrition in first-generation college students. *Journal of College Student Development, 50*(1), 87–103. doi:10.1353/ csd.0.0053

McClure, J. W. (2007). International graduates' cross-cultural adjustment: Experiences, coping strategies, and suggested programmatic responses. *Teaching in Higher Education, 12*(2), 199–217. doi:10.1080/13562510701191976

McCormack, A. (1995). Revisiting sexual harassment of undergraduate women 1989 and 1993. *Violence against Women, 1*(3), 254–265.

National Center for Education Statistics, U.S. Department of Education. (2000). *The Condition of Education 2000* (NCES 2000–062). Washington, DC: U.S. Government Printing Office.

Olive, J. L. (2010). Relating developmental theories to postsecondary persistence: A multiple case study of gay, lesbian, and bisexual college students. *Journal of Ethnographic & Qualitative Research, 4,* 197–212.

Padgett, R., Johnson, M., & Pascarella, E. (2012). First-generation undergraduate students and the impacts of the first year of college: Additional evidence. *Journal of College Student Development, 53*(2), 243–266. doi: 10.1353/csd.2012.0032

Pascarella, E., Edison, M., Nora, A., Hagedorn, L., & Terenzini, P. (1996). Influences on students' openness to diversity and challenge in the first year of college. *The Journal of Higher Education,* 174–195.

Pell Institute for the Study of Opportunity in Higher Education, Muraskin, L., Lee, J., Wilner, A., & Swail, W. S. (2004, December). *Raising the graduation rates of low-income college students* (Rep.). Retrieved October 24, 2012, from http://www .luminafoundation.org/publications/PellDec2004.pdf

Pryor, J. H., Hurtado, S., Saenz, V. B., Santos, J. L., & Korn, W. S. (2007). *The American freshman: Forty year trends.* Los Angeles, CA: Higher Education Research Institute.

Rankin, S. (2005). Campus climates for sexual minorities. *New Directions for Student Services, 111,* 17–23.

Rankin, S., Weber, G., Blumenfeld, W., & Frazer, S. (2010). *2010 state of higher education for lesbian, gay, bisexual & transgender people.* Charlotte, NC: Campus Pride.

Reed, E., Prado, G., Matsumoto, A., & Amaro, H. (2010). Alcohol and drug use and related consequences among gay, lesbian and bisexual college students: Role of experiencing violence, feeling safe on campus, and perceived stress. *Addictive Behaviors, 35,* 168–171.

Renn, K. A. (2000). Including all voices in the classroom. *College Teaching, 48*(4), 129–135.

Scott, D. A., Belke, S. L., & Barfield, H. G. (2011). Career development with transgendered college students: Implications for career and employment counselors. *Journal of Employment Counseling, 48,* 105–113.

Sherry, M., Thomas, P., & Chui, W. H. (2010). International students: A vulnerable student population. *Higher Education, 60*(1), 33–46. doi:10.1007/s10734-009-9284-z

Smith, S. S., & Jones, J. A. M. (2011). Intraracial harassment on campus: Explaining between- and within-group differences. *Ethnic and Racial Studies, 34,* 1567–1593.

Steele, C. M. (2010). *Whistling Vivaldi and other clues to how stereotypes affect us.* New York, NY: W. W. Norton & Company.

Taylor, K. B. (2008). Mapping the intricacies of young adults' developmental journey from socially prescribed to internally defined identities, relationships, and beliefs. *Journal of College Student Development, 49*(3), 215–234.

Thomas, S. B. (2000). College students and disability law. *The Journal of Special Education, 33*(4), 248–257.

Tinto, V. (2006). Research and practice of student retention: What next? *Journal of College Student Retention: Research, Theory and Practice, 8*(1), 1–19.

United States Government Accountability Office. (2009). *Higher education and disability: Education needs a coordinated approach to improve its assistance to schools in supporting students.* Retrieved October 21, 2012, from http://www.gao.gov/new.items/d1033.pdf

Waldo, R. C. (1998). Out on campus: Sexual orientation and academic climate in a university context. *American Journal of Community Psychology, 26*(5), 745–774.

Walpole, M. (2003). Socioeconomic status and college: How SES affects college experiences and outcomes. *Review of Higher Education, 27*(1), 45–73.

Weiner, E., & Weiner, J. (1996). Concerns and needs of university students with psychiatric disabilities. *Journal of Postsecondary Education and Disability, 12,* 2–9.

6

Social Involvement: Helping Students Find Their Place in Campus Life

NATHAN R. BOOTH, STERLING P. TRAVIS,
CHRISTINE BORZUMATO-GAINEY, AND
SUZANNE DEGGES-WHITE

Universities are becoming increasingly appreciative of the importance of students' college experiences outside of the classroom. Though some opponents claim these activities conflict with academic work, the overarching belief is that extracurricular engagement is positive and growth oriented; thus, such offerings to students are numerous and varied. Accordingly, a large number of students are involved in multiple activities in addition to their academic endeavors. The benefits of these extracurricular experiences are broad, ranging from enhancing students' personal and professional development, advancing feelings of social connectedness, to improving university retention rates and postgraduation financial donations.

Increased campus involvement meets numerous student needs that are uncovered during the counseling process. Clearly, students lacking social connection would benefit from concrete information that addresses campus social groups and campus resources. In addition to providing a list of clubs and organizations, counselors should have knowledge of and experience with these organizations in order to help refine the list of options to best fit the student's personality, interests, and needs. Furthermore, helping students process their interests and the many membership possibilities may protect them from potential problems with organizational involvement such as overcommitting their time or facing a hazardous disconnect between their own values and an organization's values.

SOCIAL INVOLVEMENT AND STUDENT
WELL-BEING IN COLLEGE

Several major theorists have built their concepts of human wellness upon the importance of interpersonal connection and feelings of belonging. Alfred Adler proposed that social interest is inborn and should be nurtured for the well-being of the individual as well as for all humanity. In Maslow's (1943) hierarchy of needs, social bonds must be developed in order for an individual to have sufficient self-esteem. During the young adult stage of psychosocial development, Erikson (1968) described the tension between developing healthy intimate relationships with others versus isolation. Felicia Huppert (2008) from Cambridge University stated there are five things each person needs to achieve positive well-being. These are to (a) connect with others, (b) be active with others, (c) take notice of the things around us (mindfulness), (d) keep learning, and (e) give to others (acts of kindness). If we are able to achieve all of these, her research suggested that our mental well-being would increase. By becoming involved in the world around us and with other people, it appears that our life satisfaction will also increase. Yet involvement is more complex than simply living in a dorm or joining an organization on campus.

Without healthy intimate relationships, students are likely to experience a feeling of isolation, rejection, and unwanted solitude. Specifically, if individuals are unable to feel a sense of community with others or a feeling of belonging, they may become socially avoidant, experience low self-esteem, and suffer health problems, among other negative consequences. Gere and MacDonald (2010) found that loneliness predicted physical changes (e.g., enhanced sympathetic activity in the nervous system and higher levels of total peripheral resistance), generated higher stress and threat ratings, and predicted lower levels of positivity and higher levels of negativity for college students. Their findings underscore the importance of helping students connect and become involved in their university and geographical communities. Indeed, on a daily basis across the country, college students present for counseling due to feeling out of place and lonely.

According to Braxton and Hirschy (2005), becoming involved is not as simple as joining the mainstream culture. It is more important that an individual find a group of close friends, regardless of the size of the group, rather than seeking membership in diffuse social groups. Therefore, it is of primary importance to focus on helping students find a solid friend or build a friendship network, whether this is done by building social skills or guiding the student toward a campus organization that would provide an opportunity for a good "fit" for the student's personality or interests. In other words, it is better to find a group that shares a student's interests rather than have the student adapting to fit into a poorly matched group.

Students need to find ways to balance the need to be a valued part of a group and the need to maintain their uniqueness as an individual within a group. Compromising aspects of individuality and identity may lead to compromised well-being rather than enhancing self-worth and character (Hornsey & Jetten, 2004). Each of these tasks is important for healthy development and it is essential that students find a way to balance successfully these two juxtaposed needs.

Social life can be a significant and substantial component of the college experience. Many students experience seismic shifts in their social self-concept from high school to college as well as throughout their college career (Pascarella & Terenzini, 1991). Some students carry negative baggage from high school friendship fiascos while others bring confidence that they have the social aplomb to navigate smoothly the college social environment. These self-concepts greatly influence the student upon entering college, the time when most students need to create a new social network. Colleges often attempt to help students make these early connections through transition programs or even online web pages where students can chat with other incoming freshmen. A best-case scenario would include a student befriending her suitemates, including her roommate, as well as building relationships outside the suite. Students' levels of social self-concept tend to rise over the course of their college experience as they make friends and find appropriate niches.

ASSESSING STUDENT INVOLVEMENT

College counselors can better assist students seeking to find their place on campus through an effective understanding of the level of a student's involvement in campus activities and an understanding of any barriers preventing them from becoming involved. The most basic method of gathering this information is through an intake session in which students are queried about their campus involvement. It is also helpful to explore a student's interests and aspirations to begin to identify possible avenues for engagement. Another useful way to assess student involvement is the Cooperative Institutional Research Program's Your First College Year survey. This survey has been found to be helpful in assessing student social and academic involvement (Sharkness & DeAngelo, 2010) and can be a means through which counselors can assess the relationship between these two aspects of campus engagement.

Social Anxiety

Social anxiety is one of the most common presenting concerns in a college counseling setting. Though this topic is covered in a later chapter, it is worth noting at this point since it is a major factor in social integration. Students who manifest symptoms of social anxiety may have difficulty becoming socially integrated. Possibly saddled with feelings of self-consciousness, they are often slower to meet new people and to develop friendship networks. For these students, simply going into the crowded cafeteria and not being able to locate a familiar face to join for lunch may cause a high level of anxiety. The "easy solution" to this type of anxiety-provoking situation is often to simply avoid the situation altogether. While this helps in the short run, it lessens the opportunities for the student to meet new friends and build a support system, which can further negatively influence the student's feeling of belonging on campus. As Mellings and Alden (2000) noted, social anxiety is a product of the negative thoughts that occur before, during, and after a social event. Further, self-focus and postevent rumination lead to biased judgment and memory. Not only do those with social anxiety seek to determine what they did wrong and why it was wrong, they tend to forget anything positive that occurred. This results in additional negative rumination during the anticipatory process before the next social event.

In thinking about the cyclical nature of these processes and the importance that is placed on social interaction during college years, social anxiety can be a tremendous hurdle for college students. A student going through fraternity rush may go into the first event feeling nervous because he remembers only the times he felt rejected by a group or embarrassed. He would focus only on himself and would analyze his own behavior rather than that of the people he was meeting. He would then go home and think about the instances that night where he said or did the wrong thing. As this cycle repeats itself, he would likely become even more nervous in social situations, and possibly withdrawn. Buckner, Eggleston, and Schmidt (2006) noted that another unfortunate outcome of social anxiety may include self-medication—a student might turn to alcohol to increase positive affect or to ease anxiety and gain a sense of control. An even more productive method of treatment, however, can be provided by the college counselor.

Cognitive-behavioral techniques in individual therapy are the standard methods taken by therapists to combat social anxiety. Damer, Latimer, and Porter (2010), however, suggest cognitive-behavioral group therapy as another option. The group setting, in itself, provides numerous advantages for students, such as support, evidence that they are not alone in their fears, and the opportunity to practice speaking in a group setting. The primary method used in this approach is structured role-play, which exposes students to anxiety-provoking situations and allows them to rehearse how they would like to respond. In one session, for example, the group topic is "Assertiveness and Interacting With Authority Figures" where the group acts out aggressive, passive, passive-aggressive, and assertive styles of interacting with professors or employers (Damer et al., 2010, p. 16). Following is a brief discussion of some specific areas in which student social involvement can be facilitated.

CAMPUS GROUPS AND RESOURCES

Athletics

Both attending and participating in varsity and intramural sports offer opportunities for a wide variety of levels of involvement. Regardless of the size of the school or athletic division, varsity athletics are often a large part of the college culture. The college counseling center is typically not the first stop for athletes who are dealing with poor grades, overwhelming schedules, or broken hearts since athletic programs have programmatic structures in place to help prevent significant emotional distress. Intramural and club sports offer a sense of belonging and camaraderie that can be very effective in forging important social bonds. Former high school athletes who are unable to make the college team or who do not have the interest in committing the time and energy required by the team may find intramurals a good choice.

Athletic events can also be the focus of much informal social interaction prior to, during, and postgame. Athletic events on many college campuses are a hub for social interaction, although alcohol consumption and overconsumption can be an unfortunate activity choice connected with this aspect of college life. It can be helpful for college counseling center personnel to be aware of the risks of underage drinking and overconsumption, and prepare psychoeducational programs that encourage students to be mindful of the temptations that are present during "football weekends" and "game days." Many campus organizations and clubs may be hosting game-related activities during athletics seasons, so it can be wise to encourage health-promoting activities or alternative activities to students, including such programs as "Be Green" initiatives where students promote recycling during tailgating parties. Although pregame festivities, game attendance, victory celebrations, and defeat grumbling all provide opportunities for communal experiences, it is important to recognize that these activities do not hold equal appeal for all students.

Community Service

Community service organizations offer students the opportunity to give back to their college, the surrounding community, and even larger regions through their "hands-on" endeavors. Through helping others, students are able to develop a more deeply rooted and personally satisfying connection with their fellow students and their community. Through service trips, students are offered the opportunity to be exposed to diverse geographical regions, lifestyles, and belief systems that can help expand their worldviews. Moreover, community service projects may be a great way for some students to build friendships. The structured service activity offers a focus for conversation and may alleviate anxiety for shy or socially anxious students. Students with Asperger's or autism may find service-oriented groups to be more understanding and emotionally generous as well as benefiting from the structure. Students also can connect and build relationships with others who share their values and commitment to helping make the world a better place. Many colleges around the country have developed a specialized on-campus department for service learning or community involvement; college counselors should have a list of resources of organizations and local institutions that focus on diverse areas of service including building projects (such as Habitat for Humanity), the environment, food delivery (such as Meals on Wheels), food pantries, international service groups, community children's tutoring teams, and so forth.

Greek Letter Organizations (Social Fraternities and Sororities)

While Greek involvement may be subject to criticism and ridicule on campus and in the media, it plays a very big role in the lives of many students. Sometimes joining a Greek organization emboldens fun times and feelings of camaraderie for a student. Greek membership often inspires greater involvement in campus activities as well as opportunities for student to gain leadership experience by serving as officers and in leadership roles in the organization (McClure, 2006). However, due to the differences in prestige and reputation, some fraternities and sororities attract far more students than they can initiate; the membership process may be quite selective and can be a cause for a great deal of personal distress. Students who do not get accepted into the "right" fraternity or sorority may feel painfully rejected. Built on the concepts of brotherhood and sisterhood, these organizations may be perceived as offering the intimacy desired by young adults, especially students already suffering from feeling outcast. Aggrieved students have been known to have full-blown tantrums, numerous tearful phone calls to family and friends, and even taken costly emergency flights home to be with supportive (or angry) parents. Even more troubling, being refused acceptance into the Greek organization of one's choice may be experienced as confirmation of feelings of social failure at an academic institution or the final blow to one's self-esteem.

It is important for mental health professionals to be knowledgeable of the Greek population on their campus. They should know the percentage of students who are members of the Greek system so they are able to help students gain perspective. Even at colleges where half the student body is Greek, half the student body is not Greek. The very real possibility of choosing to not be part of a Greek organization may be important to discuss with students who do not find a home in a fraternity or sorority. In fact, three general areas may be useful to touch upon when working with a student who was blocked when he or she tried to "go Greek": (a) What are the perceived benefits to the student? (b) Could these benefits be found in another organization? (c) What is the reality of Greek membership? In fairness, it is useful to point out the positive and negative aspects of these social organizations. One positive is that they do work well for some students. They offer leadership opportunities within the organization as well as numerous socializing opportunities. In addition, Greek organizations may be very active in their philanthropies. On the negative side, there is the expense as well as a strong sense of exclusion. McClure (2006) summarized research that described the negative aspects of fraternity membership, including less flexible attitudes among Greeks, lower levels of moral and cognitive development, less interest in social issues, very high levels of alcohol-related problems (use and abuse), as well as problems related to sexual abuse and rape. In fact, Bleecker and Murnen (2005) found that fraternity house residents had a larger number of degrading images of women visible in their living quarters than other male campus residents and, even more distressing, the fraternity residents displayed a higher level of rape-supportive attitudes than non-members did. Perhaps these fraternity men's negative attitudes toward women contribute to the higher incidence of eating disorders among sorority members that was reported by Basow, Foran, and Bookwala (2007). Whereas many single-sex institutions are likely to enhance the relative self-esteem and self-confidence of their members, it appears that the gender role stereotypes that denigrate women may be supported through the Greek system.

When addressing the dangers of Greek organizations, it is important to address pledging. Pledging is the process in which the individual invited to join a Greek organization is put through a trial membership period. During this potentially difficult period, pledges demonstrate how well they might fit into the organization and are able to determine whether the organization is the right fit for them. During this time, strong relationships can be created between fraternity members and fellow pledges, and pledges can learn a great deal about the functioning and culture of the fraternity as they decide whether to cement their decision to join. However, through the development of extreme hazing, pledging has become something quite different for many organizations. Some Greek letter organizations strive to "break down" a pledge in order to bring the pledge back up in the image of what the fraternity wishes its members to be. When pledging is done with temperance and meaning, it can instill a strong sense of brotherhood or sisterhood; however, all too frequently, pledges must set aside personal values to become another copy of what the organization expects its members to be. Pledging also creates the environment in which superiority and inferiority complexes frequently develop. Active upperclass members may believe they have power over pledges and choose to abuse that power; in some settings, pledges may come to believe that they are less than human and take on the sole role of obedient lackey. However, during the past two decades, media attention has galvanized institutions to take action to regulate and limit hazing in order to protect the physical and emotional safety of pledges. In fact, some Greek organizations have gone as far as to abolish their pledging periods completely in order to ensure student safety. If a student seeks counseling related to the decision to join a Greek organization, the student should be encouraged to research the organization and reflect on his or her own college goals, self-image, and self-esteem. Understanding the negative and positive influence of Greek life prior to making the decision on membership can help prevent potential problems.

Honors Societies, Professional Organizations, and Academic Interest Groups

Honors societies, professional organizations, and academic groups are worthwhile ways for students to become involved and engage their minds outside of the classroom. Many universities offer a huge range of student organizations from the Society of Human Resource Management to literature and debate groups, to engineering robotic clubs. Special interest academic groups allow students to expand on their academic interests, gain opportunities to attend conferences, network, add to resumes, and meet others with similar interests or career aspirations. Becoming involved in extracurricular, academically oriented groups is a great way for individuals to explore an area outside their major or expand their major interest. For instance, a science student may enjoy attending philosophy club meetings to fulfill an interest in the subject and to be exposed to students who like to think deeply about themselves and the world. College counselors should make themselves aware of the various professional societies/organizations available at their campus to be able to help students connect with those who share their interests, as well as to help students begin the transition from student to professional.

Religious Organizations

Religious and faith-based organizations can play significant roles in the lives of many college students. Some students actively seek involvement in faith-based groups as soon as they arrive on campus. When students are able to become involved with others who share their beliefs, it eases the transitions they are experiencing in college.

Faith-based campus groups may also be safe havens for students who may have social difficulties fitting in with the campus mainstream. For instance, if alcohol use is prevalent on campus, faith-based groups may use less alcohol or at least hold occasional alcohol-free social events. For many students, these groups can provide a strong emotional support system; shared belief systems and faith-based practices can help a student feel a strong sense of belonging.

Multicultural and Minority Groups

Many campuses have special organizations to foster connectedness for students who are at risk for feeling marginalized on campus. While a separate chapter addresses campus diversity, it is also important to note that organizations that support these students may be helpful in helping diverse students develop a sense of belonging and connection. Most campuses offer organizations that address the interests of groups such as those of different ethnicities or races, first-generation students, low-income students, and lesbian–gay–bisexual–transgendered students. However, while these groups may provide a welcome social connection based on a student's unique differences, it is important to encourage students to also seek out connections with a varied group of peers on campus.

CONCLUSION

Social involvement is directly related to self-esteem among college students. On one hand, social involvement fosters self-esteem. Having friends boosts self-esteem and helps a student feel a sense of belonging (Bean, 2005). Students do not need to interact with large groups to reap the benefits of social interaction; a small group of close friends is preferable to most students than a large group of more distant friends. Those who lack friendships, however, will be more prone to developing low self-esteem and feeling like an outsider. That being said, the equation also might be reversed in that low self-esteem is responsible for a lack of social involvement. Feelings of low self-esteem may be linked to a variety of causes, including social anxiety, feeling out of place, identity confusion, or perceived discrimination. Because it may be difficult to determine whether a lack of social activity is causing low self-esteem or vice versa, counselors are better served by both encouraging social involvement and confronting issues related to self-esteem in therapy sessions.

Just as there is an almost endless variety of paths to social involvement, there are exponentially more varieties of students. Understanding the range of outlets at the college at which the counselor works is essential in being ready to help students "plug in" to campus life.

REFERENCES

Basow, A. A., Foran, K. A., & Bookwala, J. (2007). Body objectification, social pressure, and disordered eating behavior in college women: The role of sorority membership. *Psychology of Women Quarterly, 31*, 394–400.

Bean, J. P. (2005). Nine themes of college student retention. In A. Seidman (Ed.), *College student retention: Formula for student success* (pp. 215–244). Westport, CT: Praeger.

Bleecker, E. T., & Murnen, S. K. (2005). Fraternity membership, the display of degrading sexual images of women, and rape myth acceptance. *Sex Roles, 53*, 487–493.

Braxton, J. M., & Hirschy A. S. (2005). Theoretical developments in the study of college student departure. In A Seidman (Ed.), *College student retention: Formula for student success* (pp. 61–87). Westport, CT: Praeger.

Buckner, J. D., Eggleston, A., & Schmidt, N. B. (2006). Social anxiety and problematic alcohol consumption: The mediating role of drinking motives and situations. *Behavior Therapy, 37*, 381–391.

Damer, D., Latimer, K., & Porter, S. (2010). "Build your social confidence": A social anxiety group for college students. *Journal for Specialists in Group Work, 35*, 7–22.

Erikson, E. H. (1968). *Identity youth and crisis*. New York, NY: Norton.

Gere, J., & MacDonald, G. (2010). An update of the empirical case for the need to belong. *Journal of Individual Psychology, 66*(1), 93–115.

Hornsey, M. J., & Jetten, J. (2004). The individual within the group: Balancing the need to belong with the need to be different. *Personality and Social Psychology Review, 8*(3), 248–264.

Huppert, F. (2008). *State of science review: Psychological wellbeing: Evidence regarding its causes and consequences.* Office of Science and Innovation: Foresight Mental Capital and Wellbeing Project. Retrieved from http://www.foresight.gov.uk/Mental%20Capital/SR-X2_MCWv2.pdf

Maslow, A. H. (1943). A theory of human motivation. *Psychological Review, 50*(4), 370–396.

McClure, S. M. (2006). Voluntary association membership: Black Greek men on a predominantly white campus. *The Journal of Higher Education, 77,* 1036–1055.

Mellings, T. B., & Alden, L. E. (2000). Cognitive processes in social anxiety: The effects of self-focus, rumination and anticipatory processing. *Behaviour Research & Therapy, 38,* 243. doi:10.1080/01933920903463510

Pascarella, E. T., & Terenzini, P. T. (1991). *How college affects students: Findings and insights from twenty years of research.* San Francisco, CA: Jossey-Bass.

Sharkness, J., & DeAngelo, L. (2011). Measuring student involvement: A comparison of classical test theory and item response theory in the construction of scales from student surveys. *Research in Higher Education, 52,* 480–507.

7

The Journey of Grief and Loss for College Students: Clinical Interventions

CHRISTINE BORZUMATO-GAINEY
AND ELISE NOYES

While grief is a natural reaction to a loss, it can feel anything *but* natural to the person who experienced the loss. When the door to a possibility is closed or someone we love is taken from us, our hearts may fill with pain and longing. Regarding the college student population, statistics show that from 22% to 30% of college students will experience the death of someone close to them in any given year (Cooley, Toray, & Roscoe, 2010). And when non–death-related losses are included, the figure jumps to 79% of students reporting a significant loss during a 2-year period. Thus, college counselors may find themselves working with students who are suffering grief-related symptoms from a variety of causes. Non–death-related causes span the gamut from grave personal illness to the disintegration of a formerly close relationship.

Grief is a highly personal experience or transition process, and while the focus of this chapter is meeting the needs of students dealing with death-related loss, the information provided is useful for many different grief-related concerns. To open a discussion of the manifestation of grief in college students, it seems highly valuable to consider two differentiating components: the developmental shift to emerging adulthood and the context of the college environment.

BEREAVEMENT IN COLLEGE

The earlier chapters of this book described the enormous developmental challenges and personal growth that college students typically experience. However, many students have yet to face the death of someone

81

close or to have fully experienced the grief process prior to arrival on campus and when these challenges are met, students are seldom prepared for the forceful blow they may deal. These students are often *first-time grievers* and as these years are a time of continued identity exploration, career development, and relationship development, bereavement may greatly influence these processes. Furthermore, a first-semester freshman may have a very different reaction to loss than a second-semester junior. Students who have settled into college should have a stronger support network to help them cope with their grief, whereas a brand-new freshman may feel overwhelmed by a loss and strongly desire to return home to an existing support system.

With their entrance to college, students may be leaving behind old friends and a structured daily routine. Now on campus, they must establish new friendships, continue building their identity as young adults, be independently responsible for themselves on a daily basis, as well as excel academically. Already facing the loss of all that was familiar, the death of someone close to them may be an event that feels like a "tipping point" in an already overwhelming year. This is clearly illustrated by the words of a grieving first-year student, *"I'm not like other freshmen looking for friends; I'm looking for a support group. And I hate it."*

One of the most common themes presented by underclassmen that have lost a parent can be summed up by the question, *"Who will take care of me?"* Because they are still learning to be responsible for themselves, the need to handle academic, physical, social, and emotional adjustments while suffering the loss of a loved one can seem debilitating. Grieving students may need additional support as they adjust to college life. This support might take the form of guidance on where and how to seek out potential friends on campus, and encouragement and acknowledgment of responsible decisions. Although it should go without being said, it is important to note that counselors should be careful to not unconsciously step into a parental (or grandparental) role with younger students, although this may seem a natural response to a student's grief. Upperclassmen typically have a more mature repertoire of coping skills developed during their additional years of independence and life experience. Their campus community-based support networks are also typically more secure and so they have a larger support system on which they can rely.

The availability and attitude of bereaved students' support networks play a significant role in their well-being. Students may openly share their initial feelings of despair with friends, but friends are seldom any more equipped to help with the process than the bereaved students themselves. Clients, including upperclassmen, frequently report that their friends don't know what to say or else may try to help them feel better in ways that unintentionally belittle the loss; students tend to report these encounters once their shock has subsided and they are experiencing the arrival of more complex bereavement-related feelings. Given the college climate, many clients feel isolated from other students and feel as if their friends are wanting them to "hurry up and get over" the loss. Counselors may need to reassure students that their feelings of isolation are a normal part of the grief process and that even mature adults have difficulty responding to those who are in bereavement. This can provide students with a more realistic understanding of what they are going through and what their peers are experiencing in their efforts to help.

The College Climate

Few aspects of college life are conducive to helping students process their grief. Heavy and frequent partying, hooking up, and substance use, common to the college scene, are counter to the bereaved students' best interests. While friends are talking about last weekend's events or the upcoming party, grieving students may feel out of place and alone as they contemplate existential issues regarding meaning, life, and death. These students may chastise themselves for focusing on such heavy topics, but may just as frequently pass judgment on their friends for their superficial interests. They may envy other students as they engage in the seemingly carefree, fun-filled life of "typical" college students.

Depending on the size and locale of the college, the physical environment of the school may present barriers to students finding space to process their emotions. The provision of adequate private spaces both indoors and out can provide space for grieving students to retreat and reflect on their loss as well as journal, talk aloud to the deceased, and cry. The constant presence of roommates and suitemates can inhibit these activities for many students, as they fear displaying vulnerability or weakness to others. Without an opportunity to find emotional and physical space to work through their feelings, some students may pass from normal grief into prolonged or unresolved grief.

Contrary to the common perception of college as an idyllic place without significant stress, students face numerous challenges that can overwhelm them (Kadison & DiGeronimo, 2004). The increasingly competitive atmosphere requires students to give intense focus to their academic obligations on a daily basis; grief symptoms, however, significantly interfere with concentration and focus. Grieving students frequently experience a drop in their grades, which could result in losing scholarships, being placed on academic probation, or failing out of school, in the worst-case scenarios. The cumulative impact of these events, coupled with feelings that friends don't understand, can be the engenderment of a sense of shame for grieving students on their healing journeys, where no shame should exist.

THE GRIEVING PROCESS

Students often bring presenting issues, such as troubling social situations or psychological or physical symptoms, to counseling that they do not necessarily attribute to grief. However, as the counselor draws out the client's story, the student may reveal that these issues began or intensified correspondingly with a loss. Although there is a spectrum of "normal" grief reactions, uniqueness is a hallmark of grief; so, too, is complexity.

Emotional Responses to Grief

As much as our student clients would like to know the timeline or endpoint of grief, as they would with any distress, there is no clear timeline or single linear progression of grief and bereavement. Many clients may have knowledge of and ask about Elisabeth Kübler-Ross's (1969) Five Stages of Grief. These stages include denial (this didn't happen), anger (this shouldn't have happened), bargaining (I promise to do x if ...), depression (sad and hopeless), and acceptance (finding a sense of peace). However, it is important to share with clients that these stages were based on the emotional processes experienced by individuals coping with the diagnosis of terminal illness, not the experience of grieving survivors, and so these stages may not be as relevant and predictive as they might like. And most counselors will discover a much broader array of client emotions than these five stages would suggest. Emotions such as guilt, anxiety, loneliness, relief, and longing for the deceased are common. A strong sense of longing, in fact, distinguishes grief from other presenting disorders. Like depression, grief commonly brings low energy and a sense of meaninglessness. Or akin to anxiety, grief brings fearful rumination and even panic attacks.

Symptoms of grief exist on an intensity continuum and clients can experience swings in the symptom intensity from day to day and even moment to moment. In assessing a client's well-being, counselors should explore the degree of disruption of daily functioning from mild to severe as well as the temporal domain of these symptoms ranging from brief and transient to sustained and persistent. Counselors should also assure clients that these fluctuations are entirely normal. Typically, the acuity of symptoms is strongest shortly after a loss and subsides gradually over a year, with intensification around anniversaries or special dates. It can be helpful to explore "grief triggers" with clients so that they can be prepared and not caught off-guard by a strong emotional response in such locations as classrooms or social situations. However, the ebbing of intense emotions can be a cause of concern for some clients who might feel that they are "betraying" the memory of the deceased or lost relationship.

Clients should also be reminded that counseling cannot "fix" their grief or remove the loss, but it can help them cope with bereavement as they move through a process that can take both a psychological and physical toll.

Physiological Reactions to Grief

Grief can be an extremely painful experience and the emotional pain is often transformed into physical pain in the body. When confronted with a deep emotional loss, the body reacts immediately. The high level of stress induced by the loss has a cumulative effect over time and there can be significant physiological fallout (Hardison, Neimeyer, & Lichstein, 2005). A brief list of physical symptoms includes loss of appetite, lack of energy, heart palpitations, headaches, and gastrointestinal problems. Ailments initially inflamed by mourning could result in hospitalization of the bereaved.

Sleep disruption may be one of the most commonly reported symptoms of bereavement. Sleep is compromised primarily through two means: (a) rumination about the deceased that keeps students from falling asleep; and (b) disturbing dreams. Lack of sleep exacerbates other grief symptoms such as loss of motivation and concentration difficulties *and* co-occurs so frequently with prolonged grief it appears that insomnia and complicated grief may actually mutually reinforce the other (Hardison et al., 2005). Thus, insomnia potentially inhibits the resolution of grief. Counselors should address the sleep hygiene of grieving students, as healthy and adequate rest is essential in coping with grief and with keeping up with other responsibilities. While many of the physical symptoms of grief may often be managed with cognitive-behavioral interventions, it is not unusual for clients to seek medical referral, particularly when it may help someone get the necessary sleep.

INFLUENTIAL FACTORS IN THE GRIEF PROCESS

The grief response varies based on a number of factors. These include sociocultural upbringing, the current environment, the circumstances surrounding the death, the relationship with the deceased, and a host of individual factors related to the bereaved.

Cultural Beliefs

People of different cultures and faiths hold culturally unique, powerful, and overarching beliefs about death, dying, and possibilities for an afterlife. These beliefs often describe expectations around accepted bereavement behavior, rituals, and customs, which in turn influence the manifestation of individual grief reactions. For instance, Mexican Americans reported an overall greater intensity of response to death and were more likely to express emotions at funerals than their Caucasian counterparts (Oltjenbruns, 1998). It was expected that mourners would vocalize their anguish over a loss. When working with grieving students, counselors may want to explore their clients' cultural identification and their cultural beliefs about grief and mourning. This may be an especially significant exploration when working with clients whose cultural identification is divergent from the campus norm as is the exploration of a client's level of acculturation. An example of the relevance of these areas of assessment were underscored by the following example: *A Mexican American female, age 19, came to the counseling center depressed and suffering prolonged intense grief from the loss of a parent several years prior; her grief was compounded by the student's guilt and shame at having disregarded the bereavement customs of her family culture in favor of the White American culture she had longed to fit into at the time of the loss.* In this case, the counselor recognized that an important area of focus in the work with this client would be working through a reconciliation of cultural conflicts to allow the client to grieve in such a way that she felt was best for her own mourning process.

Though most of the grief literature explores and describes the experiences of Caucasians, there are a number of studies that have focused on other diverse populations. Laurie and Neimeyer (2008) found that African American and Caucasian college students have significant differences in most aspects related to death, including the means of death, intensity of grief, coping methods, and support infrastructure. Further, African American students were more likely to be grieving a death by homicide (11%) than their Caucasian peers (2%), but less likely to be grieving a suicide. African American students also reported more acute grief but had a broader support system; they also did not seek professional help as frequently as Caucasian students. It might be surprising, but demographics also play a role in a student's grief reactions. For instance, out-of-state African American students will need more support than students whose families are local; however, they may feel more comfortable in a nonclinical group environment. To best meet these students' needs, the counselor should ask about the students' cultural and familial beliefs about death, dying, and mourning.

Death-Related Factors

Circumstances surrounding the actual death influence the responses of clients to loss; therefore, it is beneficial for counselors to understand how the death occurred. Depending on the individual event, clients may focus on years of illness or struggle leading up to a death or the immediate circumstances of the death. It can be painful at times for counselors as they first begin to work with grieving students, but it is clinically important for students to relate these experiences.

On occasion, many seek counseling due to anticipatory grief, which is grief related to an impending loss; this usually occurs related to the anticipated loss of an immediate family member or close friend. The range of emotions of students facing these crises can vary from a sense of anguish and shock of having just learned of an imminent death to depression and fatigue from being involved in a struggle of a significant other's battle with a terminal illness.

The prospective death of a loved one may impact a client in some of the same ways of an actual loss. Fear of the looming loss may threaten the client's sense of self and hinder daily functioning. Anticipatory grief can make it hard for students to behave as if everything is "normal" or that their family is "just like everyone else's family," when, in reality, the everyday thoughts and feelings experienced and the challenges faced may differ dramatically from their peers. These students may be shouldering their own concerns as well as the worries of their parents. Students may be privy to their parents' financial stressors, as health care costs, tuition expenses, and routine bills can topple many families' financial equilibrium. College students may feel guilty accepting family funds that are already strained. For students attending college far away from home, breaks from school may mean taking shifts in the caretaking of a terminally ill family member. And being away at college may mean not being present to support or gain support from the rest of the family, not spending time with the terminally ill loved one, and not being present when death comes.

Students with intense anticipatory grief will often consider staying at college or leaving school to be with the terminally ill. Counselors should be supportive to students who need to process this type of decision and help students make the best choice for their individual situations. Counselors may want to encourage students to weigh several aspects in decisions of this magnitude, including such issues as the imminence of the death, living one's life without regret, the variety of ways of staying connected and supportive, the desires of the terminally ill, to name a few common considerations. Whether a client decides to remain at school or return home or whether there are days or months of life expectancy, counselors may want to share with students the suggestions of Ira Byock (2004), a palliative care physician, regarding the five essential statements to tell loved ones: I'm sorry, I forgive you, thank you, I love you, and goodbye.

While some students have been anticipating an impending loss, other students present to counseling completely shocked by the death of a loved one. It is very important to recognize that violent or unexpected deaths have been found to prolong and complicate the grieving process (Mathews & Servaty-Seib, 2007). Some of the more surprising and unanticipated losses are the result of car accidents, murders, strokes, and heart attacks. Suicide is a pernicious form of death that can provoke intense and complicated grief responses from the survivors. The survivors of suicide frequently experience intense, prolonged anger, as well as experience more difficulty moving forward in life. Students whose parents have committed suicide often struggle to differentiate themselves from the deceased parent and from the mental illness behind the suicide. Suicide survivors may struggle to reconcile attachment and abandonment issues, both with the deceased and within their current relationships.

Death-related variables to investigate include age of deceased at time of death, perceived preventability of the death, experiences in the hospital and the funeral, as well as experiences with other professionals such as doctors and clergy. Unfortunately, the behavior of helpers may sometimes exacerbate the client's sorrow and these students may need remedial support from a college counselor to help them process this experience.

As part of the initial contact with a bereaved client, counselors should pay attention to the quality of the relationship the student had with the deceased. Explore the multiple meanings this loss may hold for the client. For instance, the loss of a brother may mean a complete restructuring of the family system as a surviving younger brother may need to step up into the responsibilities and role of a deceased older brother. For many students, the loss of a sibling often means a concurrent emotional loss of a parent who slips into the mourning process or depression. The unique constellation of positive and negative aspects of the relationship and any "collateral damage" should be examined. In fact, in close relations, relationship conflict has been found to increase the risk for psychological problems following the loss (Jerga, Shaver, & Wilkinson, 2011).

Individual Factors and Resilience

Counter to the conventional belief that the death of a loved one causes significant impairment in the functioning of the bereaved, research contends that greater than 50% of bereaved are "resilient" in that they remain stable and continue to psychologically and physically fully function, as well as experience positive emotion after a death of a loved one (Bonanno & Mancini, 2008). Bonanno, a contemporary researcher whose findings on resiliency are shaping the extant literature on the grief response, postulated four grief trajectories: resilient, delayed, chronic, and recovery. The most common trajectory is the resilient trajectory, as described above, in which there is little change in the daily functioning of the bereaved. Bonanno attributed the internal factors associated with resilience to mostly pragmatic coping and flexible adaptation with a nod to personality type; he coined the term *cope ugly* to describe a person who can do "whatever needs to be done." Interestingly, the personality types he described as more likely to be resilient were narcissists and avoiders of unpleasant emotions. Bonanno debunked the existence of delayed grief, attributing these symptoms instead to an intensifying posttraumatic stress disorder. The recovery trajectory is most similar to what has been considered the typical grief response; the chronic trajectory described what has been traditionally considered complicated grief but is now termed *prolonged grief*. In prolonged grief, individuals are unable to integrate the loss into a coherent sense of meaning after a reasonable period of time, taking into consideration the relationship with the deceased. They continue to be unsettled by the emotional symptoms or feel unable to move on with their lives as they continue to experience a debilitating sense of sadness and loss.

Some of the individual factors that influence the grief process can be addressed in counseling, such as emotional hardiness. The construct of hardiness, which includes a sense of control or influence over one's life and commitment to activities in one's life, contributes to individual grief reactions (Mathews & Servaty-Seib, 2007). Counselors are in an excellent position to help student clients develop this quality. Frequently, successful counseling entails helping clients recognize the control they do have (e.g., choices that can be made, areas of influence, etc.) as well as facilitating the letting-go process for the parts of life they do not control. Moreover, the pursuit of meaningful commitments in life is central in several types of counseling such as career counseling, as well being an integral component of counseling theories such as logotherapy. Certainly on a regular basis, a counselor will facilitate the values prioritization and decision-making process of a client in order for the client to pursue what is most personally meaningful. Grief, the certainty of future death and loss, and awareness of the brevity of one's mortal life can actually be used to help clients shift focus from unsatisfying activities and relationships onto the present, meaningful activities, and the fortification of valuable relationships.

Throughout the grief literature, other individual factors have been found to influence grief's trajectory. Age and gender are factors counselors should consider. Another frequently mentioned factor is an individual's previous experience with loss (cumulative grief) with a greater volume or more problematic losses contributing to intensified or prolonged grief reactions. High self-esteem has also been an individual attribute that seems to help people heal from a loss. Moreover, the presence or absence of adaptive coping strategies is a particularly important factor as these skills are relevant goals in counseling. For many individuals, the reliance on faith is potential coping mechanism (Walsh, King, Jones, Tookman, & Blizard, 2002).

Faith and Loss

Although emerging adulthood is a time when individuals question their belief systems and religious views, the majority of college freshmen are actively attending faith-based services and profess a belief in God (Higher Educational Research Institute, 2005). However, researchers have found that college students' levels of religiosity do diminish during the first couple of years of school, suggesting that the role faith plays in coping with loss may be reflective of a student's class year. Thus, the loss of a loved one frequently generates spiritual and religious questioning about the meaning of life, the existence of a higher power, and whether there is an afterlife. Some people question their relationship to God, religion, or their spiritual community. College counselors may find themselves working with clients whose grief sends them into a spiritual crisis. Some students may express anger at their God for allowing a loved one to be taken from them. Conversely, other students may share their sense of comfort and support from their faith and their faith communities. Counselors should invite students to discuss their thoughts about what they believe happens at death and the meaning of death they hold. Helping students explore the beliefs they "inherited" from their upbringing as well as beliefs they currently hold can allow them to try and make sense of what has happened or can result in a shifting of beliefs. Changing one's worldview, either religious- or secular-based, can require a change in one's underlying foundation, a shift in the core of one's faith in oneself, others, and the world. This can be a difficult experience as students work to process the loss of a loved one as they also let go of no longer valued beliefs. Counselors should have on hand a list of campus religious organizations and community resources for students who would like to discuss these issues with a member of the faith community.

ASSESSMENT AND INTERVENTION

As noted previously in the chapter, students do not always recognize that they are grieving. Grief symptomology overlaps both depression and anxiety symptoms; thus, the first step in an assessment is to differentiate the diagnosis. To determine any need for a medical referral, counselors should assess the student's physiological symptoms giving particular attention to sleep quality; as noted, poor sleep is associated with an inability to move effectively through grief as well as with exacerbation of other associated problems. Once the precipitating loss is fully addressed, the next step is facilitating the student's processing of the loss.

Discussion of the loss should be simultaneously investigative and healing. It is important to inquire about the student's relationship with the deceased, including the nature of the attachment (e.g., conflictual, secure) and the multiple losses the student has incurred as a result of this individual's death (e.g., loss of a confidant, loss of a fun person, etc.). The details and factors surrounding the death can be important for students to share with their counselors. Counselors should expect students to relate information about topics such as the mode of death, the dying process, the actual death, and the funeral or memorial service. People sometimes suffer from perceived deficits in the deceased's medical care or even the response of the clergy. Counselors will need to be open to hearing about events that may in some ways seem peripheral but are actually central to the loss in the client's mind. Moreover, we need to help the client voice his or her most disconcerting thoughts and feelings.

Several other factors already discussed are important to consider, such as the student's personality, previous experiences with loss, the student's support system, and sense of meaningfulness in life. Finally, William Worden (2009) developed a model quite useful to practitioners. Counter to a stage model, Worden proposes there are certain "tasks of mourning" that grievers must achieve in order to move through the grieving process.

Tasks of Mourning

Grief can be immobilizing, thus, counselors should help students understand that the goal of grief work is helping them construct a "new normal" without their loved one (Servaty-Seib, 2004). In her comparative analysis of mourning and counseling theory, Servaty-Seib (2004) describes Worden's (2009) four tasks of mourning—accepting the reality of loss, working through pain, adjusting to a reality without the loved one, and moving on emotionally—in precisely this manner. These tasks capitalize on the Western cultural paradigm of productivity as conducive to well-being and allow the individual to hold a sense of agency in what feels like a situation of powerlessness in the face of a significant loss. Approaching grief as a series of tasks can provide students with an opportunity to create meaning from loss and this can also provide feelings of peace or comfort. These tasks, however, should not be interpreted as necessarily linear or final; rather, they could be readdressed as students face new experiences and life stages. The tasks may be completed "out of order" or they may be occurring simultaneously. Perhaps counselors should view themselves as facilitators of their students' journey through grief. They can provide individual support and direct clients to others undergoing similar experiences to make the tasks personal, as well as connect students to others who are traveling on a similar journey.

College students especially benefit from a structured approach due to their current state of individuation and development. Grief can turn a student's world upside down while they are already functioning in the typical college world of chaos and busy-ness. Being provided with a sense of structure and intentionality regarding the grieving process creates a beneficial framework. One client who returned to college soon after losing one of her parents commented on how difficult it was initially to accept the reality of the loss and work through the pain. This was then followed by a description of her journey from coming out of the initial shock and relative numbness to an overwhelming surge of emotions. Being back at college, according to her, helped with the task of adjusting to a reality without her parent. She was able to gain external stability through not only participating in "normal" college student life, but also by participating in counseling sessions focused on coping with her grief. She was then prepared to revisit the tasks of accepting the loss and the pain that came with it that before it felt too crushing to bear. Counselors can encourage grieving students to view their grief work as part of a process that they can take one step at a time. For the client described above, as it is for many students who have suffered a loss, external stability functions as a necessary prerequisite for healthy coping with and accepting of the loss, although those two stages may be discussed as parts of the process when counselors first review the experience of grief with their clients.

Counselors should be particularly mindful about how they discuss and approach the task of "moving on" emotionally. Broached too soon, this sends the wrong message to the client. The client may not be able to comprehend what it would be like to "move on" or think that such a progression would somehow betray the one lost. This can be especially troublesome for students who may already feel a sense of guilt for returning to school (or taking time off, depending on their decision and what is best for them) and, in a sense, believe that they have not grieved "properly." One client noted, *"My first semester back was so hard because I felt like I was not only abandoning my dad and my brother, but also like I was betraying my mom—shouldn't I still be at home crying all the time? I actually felt guilty that I wasn't."* Thus, counselors should be careful about implying any sort of "timeline" regarding grief; allowing students to move at their own pace will allow them to acknowledge that they are beginning to move forward when they actually are emotionally ready.

Grief Groups
The tasks of mourning do not just occur within the confines of a counseling office or in the privacy of the home. Particularly for college students, these tasks are negotiated within an interpersonal context. College students are expected to be social and surrounded by friends, but what happens when many peers do not understand what it means to lose a loved one? Student grief support groups are helpful in meeting the social support needs of students while providing a space where they do not have

to hold their emotions at bay (Students of AMF, 2013). Citing important findings in the field related to college students and grief, the National Students of AMF (2013) stated that group work has been shown to be an effective way for individuals to cope with grief, particularly as a resource for those who will not seek or attend individual counseling. Grief groups also reduce the likelihood of students using unhealthy or dangerous behaviors to cope; they provide emotional support and a place of understanding; and potentially relieve or alleviate grief symptoms that may interfere with student academic performance.

At one university, participants in a student-run grief support group found that they were a comfort to each other in ways that their close friends and even other family members could not be. *"I have the best friends in the world,"* one participant said, *"but I can't talk to them about losing my mom. They just don't get it. It's nice to go to the grief support group because even if I can't articulate or express what I'm trying to say well, they get it."* Participants frequently discussed feeling frustrated with or alienated from their peers and how they got annoyed at people who took their loved ones for granted. One participant said, *"It's not like you can go up to someone who is yelling at their dad for forgetting to put something in the mail and say, 'At least you have a dad!' even though that's definitely what you want to say."* They cited the grief support group as a place where they felt their feelings were heard, affirmed, and at least released if not resolved. One participant noted, *"When words fail you, at least you have someone to cry with. They don't try to stop it or make it better; they just cry with you."*

The Arts and Grief Processing

Grief often brings up emotions that students may not be able to articulate through words. As Earl Rogers (2007), an artist, clinical consultant, and thanatologist, noted, "Grief often lies beyond words, beyond the simple explanation of our conscious minds. It is in the unconscious, in the mystery of life, that expression of the deep wounds and tragedy of loss is found" (p. 3). The use of the arts in grief support groups has provided members the opportunity to express their complicated emotions.

One example of using the arts as a medium of expression is the Heart Box, an activity that was successfully implemented in the grief support group described above. Participants were each provided with a heart-shaped box and then given strips of tissue paper to use to papier-mâché the box. Through applying the strips of paper with their fingers, they were able to use this as a medium to get "in touch" with their feelings, as well as visually and symbolically engage with their emotions as they created a safe space for their feelings. Once they had completed the papier-mâché process, participants were asked to write a signed note to each other that read, *"Your heart is safe with me."* Even those who typically do not think of themselves as artistic may feel drawn to some form of creative expression. A student who lost a parent took up drawing despite describing herself as "not artistic"; others paint, scrapbook, make photo collages, and so forth.

Art activities geared toward remembering lost loved ones may be particularly healing. At a local hospice, grief group participants made memory boxes. They were decorated to remind the mourning individuals of their lost loved one and constructed to hold fond keepsakes such as cards, possessions of their loved ones, or pictures. By tapping into potentially heightened creativity due to the affective intensity of grief, bereaved college students can find outlets for feelings previously unarticulated or unknown, while creating ways to remember and honor their loved one and to keep a part of this person with them as they move forward in their adult life.

CONCLUSION

Unlike many presenting issues, student grief is not "fixable," but counselors can help it become manageable. Students can be assisted through their mourning and helped to preserve a sense of identity as they learn ways to better cope with their loss while facing the demands of college. Counselors should bear in mind, too, that while grief can seem overwhelming for students, it can also be a period of great personal development for students. Through their mourning, students may also experience a great deal of personal growth, develop a heightened sense of appreciation for loved ones, and dedicate themselves to a life of meaningful endeavors and relationships.

REFERENCES

Bonanno, G. A., & Mancini, A. D. (2008). The human capacity to thrive in the face of trauma. *Pediatrics, 121,* 369–375.

Byock, I. (2004). *The four things that matter most.* New York, NY: Simon & Schuster.

Cooley, E., Toray, T., & Roscoe, L. (2010). Reactions to loss scale: Assessing grief in college students. *Omega, 61,* 25–51.

Hardison, H. G., Neimeyer, R. A., & Lichstein, K. L. (2005). Insomnia and complicated grief symptoms in bereaved college students. *Behavioral Sleep Medicine, 3*(2), 99–111.

Higher Educational Research Institute. (2005). *The spiritual life of college students: A national study of students' search for meaning and purpose.* Los Angeles, CA: University of California, Los Angeles.

Jerga, A. M., Shaver, P. R., & Wilkinson, R. B. (2011). Attachment insecurities and identification of at-risk individuals following the death of a loved one. *Journal of Social and Personal Relationships, 28,* 891–914.

Kadison, R., & DiGeronimo, T. F. (2004). *College of the overwhelmed: The campus mental health crisis and what to do about it.* San Francisco, CA: Jossey-Bass.

Kübler-Ross, E. (1969). *On death and dying.* New York, NY: Routledge.

Laurie, A., & Neimeyer, R. A. (2008). African Americans in bereavement: Grief as a function of ethnicity. *Omega, 57,* 173–193.

Mathews, L., & Servaty-Seib, H. (2007). Hardiness and grief in a sample of bereaved college students. *Death Studies, 31,* 183–204.

Oltjenbruns, K. (1998). Ethnicity and the grief response: Mexican American versus Anglo American college students. *Death Studies, 22,* 141–155.

Rogers, J. E. (2007). Introduction. In J. E. Rogers (Ed.), *The art of grief: The use of expressive arts in a grief support group* (pp. 3–8). New York, NY: Routledge.

Servaty-Seib, H. L. (2004). Connections between counseling theories and current theories of grief and mourning. *Journal of Mental Health Counseling, 26,* 125–145.

Students of AMF. (2013). *College grief information.* Retrieved from http://www.studentsofamf.org/grief-support-resources/college-grief-statistics

Walsh, K., King, M., Jones, L., Tookman, A., & Blizard, R. (2002). Spiritual beliefs may affect outcome of bereavement: Prospective study. *British Medical Journal, 324,* 1551–1554.

Worden, J. W. (2009). *Grief counseling and grief therapy: A handbook for the mental health practitioner* (4th ed.). New York, NY: Springer Publishing Company.

8

The "Beauty Pageant Effect" on Campus: Consequences and Clinical Implications

MEGHAN LYNWOOD REPPERT, CATHERINE B. ROLAND, AND MARCELA KEPICOVA

Women are very familiar with the experience of being evaluated by their physical attractiveness. This socialization intersects across all stages of a woman's development beginning in early childhood. Thus, women often give significant weight to their physical appearance. Too often, college women's beliefs about their own attractiveness influence their self-worth (Darlow & Lobel, 2010). This chapter addresses the consequences that college women experience due to an emphasis on their physical appearance. In order to explore this topic, developmental and sociocultural factors are discussed.

SOCIAL COMPARISON

Social comparison is a key component in the developmental trajectory of college women's self-image and self-esteem. It plays an especially integral role because of the value and investment women give to their relationships and the weight they give to others' opinions of them. The imaginary audience factor, which is the person's assumption that others are observing them, plays a central role in this stage of development (Elkind, 1967). Adolescents and young adults operate under the belief that they are acting out their lives on an imaginary stage, which reflects their tendency to assume that others are as focused on their appearance and flaws as they are themselves. Thus, they feel extremely self-conscious, which contributes to ongoing comparisons with others around them and with others from social media.

Social comparison theory states that humans frequently and continuously assess their behaviors. In order to do so, they need to find standards against which to compare themselves (Festinger, 1954). When a student has not created a set of secure personal standards, she will tend to look to the social environment and engage in comparison with peers. College females often measure their weight and size against those of their classmates and determine what is acceptable for them based on the behavior or appearance of others. When a discrepancy is perceived between the self and idealized others, the individual adjusts his or her behavior to reduce the perceived discrepancy. Comparisons are made in multiple aspects of a person's self-concept, and for women, competition often surrounds their physical appearance. Research consistently indicates that women feel worse about their own appearance directly after comparing themselves with peers, images in the media, or other women in general (Barnett, 2010; Darlow & Lobel, 2010). Thus, even a brilliant young woman who excels academically may use beauty as her measure of self-worth and allow herself to feel unworthy of others' esteem when appearance seems to be valued the most highly of all feminine attributes.

Young women seek accurate self-perceptions and will often compare themselves to others in order to gain insight in instances in which they are unsure of how to evaluate themselves (Loya, Cowan, & Walters, 2006). Social behaviors are motivated by a desire to feel good about oneself and, because college women are functioning within the decidedly patriarchal culture of higher education, they must compensate for occupying an already "one-down" position in relation to the campus males. Therefore, a woman often is more likely to denigrate the appearance and behaviors of other women as they are "safe" targets for projections of her own inadequacy, which allows her to find a level of self-acceptance, although at the cost of another. This may be an especially effective strategy when the woman chosen as a scapegoat is the member of an already marginalized group (Loya et al., 2006). Some women may use upward social comparison, which is looking to groups that she views as superior to her own level of worth. In contrast, downward social comparison occurs when women compare themselves to a group that they perceive to be inferior. The goal of upward social comparison is the identification of similarities and the goal of downward comparison is the identification of differences.

Gibbson and Buunk (1999) found that those who compare themselves frequently to others are generally more unsure of themselves. They might exhibit higher levels of social anxiety, public consciousness, and neuroticism, and they are more likely to have lower self-esteem. They tend to be more sensitive and reactive to others' behaviors, which can be especially unfortunate due to the need others might feel to establish their own high self-appraisal at the cost of peers. Furthermore, research investigating social comparison in women with and without eating disorder symptoms found that the greater tendency to engage in everyday social comparison predicted the presence of eating disorder symptoms (Corning, Krumm, & Smitham, 2006). Studies testing the links among media exposure to women's body dissatisfaction, internalization of the thin ideal, and eating disorders support the notion that exposure to media images depicting the thin-ideal body is related to body image concerns for women (Grabe, Ward, & Hyde, 2008).

The Socialization of Women and Its Manifestation in Female College Students

Literature indicates that college women may not have significant advantages over their preceding counterparts (Schrick, Sharp, Zvonkovic, & Reifman, 2012) in terms of liberation from patriarchal values. Beginning at a young age, women are taught to be caregivers, meaning they are often encouraged to put the needs and emotions of others above their own. This type of relational pattern is not only encouraged in society, but is often taught in the family as well (Epstein & Ward, 2011). The United States adheres to the values and expectations of a patriarchal society, which means that women receive mixed messages about femininity, desirableness, and success. For instance, young girls and women are told that they are naturally good at certain things such as listening and caring for others, but these behaviors are not valued highly by society. Therefore, in order to succeed in this society, women must be able to conform to conventions that are associated with masculinity as well as adhere to behaviors and qualities that are considered feminine. In college, these warring ideals can lead to increased insecurity and therefore harsher standards for self-acceptance and acceptance of others.

Women often receive mixed messages about goals for college. Research suggests that while young men consider their future, their fantasies are more uniformly career oriented; young women vary in their degree of aspirations to be careerists, homemakers, and some combination of both (Li & Kerpelman, 2007). Furthermore, many women enter college with the intentions of finding a husband or engaging in a long-term romantic relationship (Schrick et al., 2012). When a young woman is having little success in the romantic realm, these aspirations may grow in their intensity or imagined importance. This can lead college students to obsess about ways to attract the right partner, which can also lead to unsafe and unwise choices regarding social situations. Young women may sacrifice their beliefs about sexual boundaries, alcohol or other drug use, and standards for companions in an effort to fulfill the desire for a romantic partner.

Given the perceived importance of being desirable to men in order to find a romantic partner, college women are experiencing fierce competition in multiple realms, from the classroom to the library to the dating scene. However, competition among women can negatively affect their ability to form meaningful, supportive relationships, as well as negatively affect self-esteem. Fears that a friend may be interested in the same romantic partner or fare better on a high-stakes exam may lead to intense feelings of jealousy, anxiety over one's adequacy, and potentially the shifting of goals to avoid conflicts. In fact, women who show stronger tendencies toward focusing on others also exhibit lower academic engagement and higher levels of distress than those who were more cognizant and responsive to their own opinions, needs, and desires (Schrick et al., 2012). Often, women will develop harmful behavioral patterns in order to maintain a balance between putting others first and meeting their own needs. Sometimes it is valuable to ask a client how much she is willing to sacrifice to please others.

Rumination

There are many ways in which these conflicts can lead to maladaptive behaviors and harmful consequences; these include rumination on her romantic status, development of eating disorders, and self-silencing behaviors. Some women may engage in rumination in their attempts to work through challenges they experience in college. Rumination (Morrow & Nolen-Hoeksema, 1990; Nolen-Hoeksema & Girgus, 1994) encompasses a multitude of coping mechanisms that increase the risk of depression. It is characterized by directing attention internally toward negative feelings and thoughts. Whereas counselors often encourage clients to "talk through" their issues, a repetitive reexamining and retelling of negative experiences without accompanying problem solving may actually result in a more negative mood. Many students present to counseling after "wearing out" their friends with their ruminations or exacerbate their problems by isolating themselves to dwell on the minutiae of their issues.

Self-Silencing

The repression of one's own thoughts feelings and needs is referred to as "self-silencing" or "silencing" (House, 2011; Schrick et al., 2012) and is an adverse coping style in which college women may engage. The relational patterns and personal characteristics that women can develop as a result of ongoing silencing become particularly relevant to traditionally aged college women. Silencing has been positively correlated with anxiety, depression, the increased desire to present as perfect, and issues with body image (Schrick et al., 2012). Focusing on other's judgments encourages young women to strive for unrealistic ideals and, therefore, intensifies competition among peers. Furthermore, women often receive the message that in order to succeed, they need to learn to be more competitive (Jordan, Kaplan, Baker Miller, Stiver, & Surrey, 1991), which goes against their natural and culturally shaped relating styles. The conflict women face can create significant internal struggles as they weigh their need to support others while maintaining a strong level of self-support.

Striving for Perfection in a Multitude of Realms

Women in college strive for perfection in different domains, including academic performance, romantic relationships, and physical appearance. Striving for perfection may actually be a protective factor in terms of the academic realm (Schrick et al., 2012) if it results in a strong academic performance and confidence in one's intelligence. However, women who are in male-dominated majors may increasingly resort to silencing in order to assimilate into the culture and project the image of a skilled and competitive peer (Schrick et al., 2012). This dynamic may lead to increased psychological stress for female college students in traditionally male-dominated majors such as science, technology, and mathematics, as well as higher rates of attrition (Morganson, Jones, & Major, 2010). While college is clearly a site for intellectual challenges, it is also the location of a significant amount of more concrete, body image challenges as well. Research indicates that a significant number of college women struggle with body image issues, disordered eating, self-doubt, and inequality in romantic relationships (Piran & Cormier, 2005; Swim, Eyssell, Murdoch, & Ferguson, 2010). Regardless of major, body image concerns seem to crop up across the board.

The Unrealistic Pursuit of Body Image Perfectionism

In exploring the manner in which silencing and perfectionist tendencies influence college women's experience in the domain of physical appearance, it is important to examine how self-concept is impacted by the recognition, or lack of recognition, by others (Poran, 2006). It is not uncommon for women to hold themselves to unrealistic standards of beauty that can have adverse psychological and physiological consequences. Some have termed this phenomenon as women having *normative discontent* with their bodies (Snapp, Hensley-Choate, & Ryu, 2012). In a society that touts a thin woman with large breasts as the standard of beauty, women's negative perceptions of their bodies are mirrored by the messages they receive by media and others in society (Poran, 2006; Schrick et al., 2012; Snapp et al., 2012).

Women in college are evaluated based on their physical appearance, both by themselves and by their peers (Darlow & Lobel, 2010). Women who experience normative discontent with their bodies are at higher risk for maladaptive eating practices (Snapp et al., 2012). There is a chapter devoted to this topic as it holds significant concern for this population.

Risk Factors Associated With Body Image Dissatisfaction

An array of risk factors for body image dissatisfaction and eating disorders has been clearly identified. Some of the most prevalent are exposure to thin ideals in family or community, social anxiety, higher socioeconomic status, having a history of eating disorders in the family, racial background, and body dissatisfaction. Body dissatisfaction is one of the more serious risk factors that might lead to development of eating disorders. Research shows that negative body image is a significant predictor of eating disorders in adolescent girls (Attie & Brooks-Gunn, 1989). Moreover, girls who are dissatisfied with their bodies in their early 20s continue to engage in disordered dieting throughout their adulthood (Heatherton, Mahamedi, Striepe, Field, & Keel, 1997). Body dissatisfaction can lead to emotional, cognitive, and behavioral disturbances that are highly prevalent in young women. Attention needs to be given to this risk factor and improving body satisfaction needs to be one of the goals of counseling in order to improve or prevent significant psychopathology.

What "They" Say Behind Our Backs

Women in college face a double-edged sword in terms of attractiveness. While contemporary Western culture places unrealistic physical and beauty standards on women, there also can be negative perceptions associated with being attractive. For instance, Schrick et al. (2012), suggested that attractive women are assumed to be more promiscuous, date more often, and are more likely to demand a divorce. Interestingly, when a woman is considered to be attractive she is considered more likely to cheat, as well as being valued as a more desirable choice for a long-term partner. Research indicates that regardless of a woman's physical characteristics, if she dresses in a sexually provocative manner she will be viewed negatively by her peers. Similarly, women who are perceived by other women as "sexy" can be the recipients of negative reactions that serve to isolate and admonish them. Thus, women who are attempting to compete successfully for their chosen romantic partner run a very real risk of compromising their social support networks. Women are designed to function in a relational world, but the sexual competition for a suitable mate can create conflicting situations as she is forced to weigh one relationship over another.

Spreading rumors, the silent treatment, and passive-aggressive behavior are ways in which women are reprimanded by peers for dressing in a sexually provocative manner. The purpose of this manner of social reprimand is to discourage competition, and more broadly, to deter other women from making sex too readily available to men to ensure the best selection among mates. Vaillancourt (2011) found that clothing choices of other women are especially scrutinized by peers. In fact, it was found that regardless of body size and weight, women who dress in a sexually provocative manner are likely to receive disapproving reactions from other women.

How do college women know that they are being judged by their peers? Typically, college women express their negative evaluation of another through nonverbal behavior, such as eye rolling and disapproving looks, as well as dismissive and avoidant behavior, which Vallencourt (2001) described as "once-overs/death stares," body posture, back biting or a mocking, sarcastic tone of voice, and fake smiles. Relational aggression is a form of aggression in which social manipulations, such as excluding or gossiping, have the aim of hurting relationships or another person's social status. Unfortunately, students may experience the most unkind remarks from close friends or suitemates, potentially making their housing situation a painfully uncomfortable one.

In sum of the aforementioned research, college women in the United States are living in a culture in which they need to be caring, empathic, independent but effective at making and maintaining relationships, competitive but not hurt others' feelings, and attractive but not sexy. If they are unsuccessful in meeting these goals, there are social consequences. One of the consequences of this relationship among culture, socialization, and individual characteristics is the competition in which college women engage. Following the tenets of evolutionary theory, men and women become aggressive when competing for resources (Greskevicus, 2009). The collegiate experience can serve as a conduit to rich relationships and connections that college women crave. If we accept the premise that the establishment of personal connection is a vital component to female development, it would be possible to assume that positive self-esteem and self-acceptance would follow (Balkin & Roland, 2005). However, the college years have the potential to create sadness and frustration as women feel motivated to seek a life partner and measure their own success against that of friends who have found long-term romantic partners. Ideally, young women will be able to build support networks in which honesty about personal insecurities is accepted and friends provide honest but helpful and supportive feedback. Unfortunately, a college campus may create an atmosphere where competition and self-appraisal can be stiff and the fallout can be damaging.

Diversity as a Factor in Self-Appraisal

Social concerns, including the presence or lack of a social support network, get more complex once diversity issues are present. Not only are adolescents dealing with identity development, those of diverse background might experience another layer of concern pertaining to their racial, ethnic, gender, sexual orientation, or religious status. Although the relationship between sexual orientation and body image needs to be further explored, research does suggest differences exist among groups (Struble, Lindley, Montgomery, Hardin, & Burcin, 2010). Additionally, differences have been found in self-appraisals based on such factors as ethnicity, socioeconomic status, and peer approval (Paxton, Eisenberg, & Neumark-Sztainer, 2006).

Many minority groups are being marginalized, which complicates and often negatively influences their development. When the tall, blond, willowy White girl is the prototype of culturally accepted beauty, it can be very difficult for those who do not fit the stereotype to feel valued. Theories suggest that those who are discriminated against or marginalized might immerse themselves in their racial or cultural group, thereby rejecting the dominant cultures, which eventually can lead to isolation and depression (Broderick & Blewitt, 2010). Thus, it is important for counselors to acknowledge differences during sessions and allow young women to feel comfortable discussing these concerns.

CLIENT ASSESSMENT AND TREATMENT

College women who are wrestling with self-image and social comparison struggles may best be assessed via detailed biopsychosocial interviews in which clients are invited to share their experiences in terms of their personal cultural history. For freshmen clients, it can be especially important to ensure that they are making successful social connections with peer groups. It is important for counselors to be cognizant of their own campus culture when helping young women develop ways in which they can find appropriate groups with whom to connect. Ideas for working with new students can be found in earlier chapters in which social connections and transitions are more fully addressed.

Another aspect of biopsychosocial assessment that needs to be identified is the size, intimacy, and reliability of a social network. Research continues to show that the smaller the peer group, the more cohesive and intimate the group may become (Finn, Pannozzo, & Achilles, 2003; Forsyth, 2010). Therefore, it is crucial to assess the size and quality of friendships based on the information gathered in the initial stages of the counseling relationship. As with all assessment, this should be an ongoing process throughout the counseling relationship.

Finally, in terms of social support, clients should be assessed for the presence of social anxiety. This can be present in various sectors of a client's functioning, for example, academic situations, informal social settings, or large groups. This disorder can be a by-product of a young woman's unsuccessful social comparison to others, and attention to interventions addressing self-esteem and self-confidence may be beneficial. Further attention is given to this disorder in the chapter on anxiety.

In addition to biopsychosocial assessment, some standardized assessment tools might be helpful in determining the severity and intensity of specific challenges or already-exhibited symptoms. The Body Shape Questionnaire, Body Image Avoidance Questionnaire, Physical Appearance Comparison Scale, and Sociocultural Attitudes Toward Appearance Scale—which includes an internalization subscale, measure of appearance importance, cognitive reappraisal, and self-care—might be helpful in determining the degrees of body dissatisfaction and appearance acceptance (Wade, George, & Atkinson, 2009). There are also assessments related to an eating disorder diagnosis in the chapter on eating disorders.

As a counselor gains a better understanding of the client's history and her current difficulties related to self-acceptance, the client and counselor can co-construct goals and determine which interventions will be most useful.

Treatment Strategies

After many years of socialization in a male-dominated society with ambiguous societal messages, young women grow up believing that to be successful, they must be submissive, please others, and hold back their own thoughts and wishes, sometimes to the point of self-destruction. Frequently young college females participating in the "beauty pageant" would benefit from a more solid sense of identity where one's appearance and partnerships with males are relatively small parts of a healthy whole. In order to navigate through ongoing psychosocial developmental challenges and environmental demands, young females might benefit from foci such as boosting self-esteem and confidence and learning self-care and assertiveness.

Embracing Ourselves and Embracing Difference

Because of the constant societal pressure for individualism and competitiveness, interventions chosen for this population should demonstrate a healthy balance between individualism and collectivism, between competitiveness and cooperation, and modeling assertiveness in a nonaggressive manner. Clients may be encouraged to develop lists of their favorite qualities about themselves and what they value most in their friends and their role models. Helping clients to connect their own strengths to their own goals may allow them to recognize the role they play in achieving their dreams. Allowing them to see how their own qualities are present in important others will help them recognize the connections and similarities between people. However, by comparing dissimilar traits between themselves and significant others may help them begin to see how valuable differences can be in keeping a system flowing, whether it is within the personal, familial, or academic realm. In the event that clients find that there are individuals with whom they believe they have close relationships, but lack affinity or complementary traits, they may need to reevaluate the value of the relationship. In friendships that are out of balance, clients can be encouraged to invite honest discussions about these issues with their friends and, if appropriate, provide support if they choose to break off a friendship.

A Focus on the Body—Letting Go of Discontent

One of the main goals of treatment will be the development of self-acceptance regarding appearance and body image, as research suggests that appearance acceptance is one of the protective factors against the negative repercussion of body discontent (Webster & Tiggemann, 2003). Besides the cognitive-behavioral approaches to treatment of body-related dissatisfactions, literature further suggests that finding time for self-care (e.g., relaxation, massage, and exercise) is an additional but crucial component of many treatment interventions. The "Love Your Body" campaign materials include the suggestion that campus centers host exercise classes and relaxation type trainings. A self-massage brochure or the idea of "stress relief" massage breaks during anxious times of the academic year (i.e., final exams) can also be introduced to the campus as well as encouraging clients to participate in these activities on their own. By actively involving themselves in the care and support, as well as maintenance, of their bodies, young women can grow in their appreciation of their physical self and be taught to value and care for their bodies regardless of their reflection of the culturally promoted, but unrealistic, standards of perfection. Accepting themselves in the bodies they possess will free up energy that young women can more effectively use as they work to attain their dreams.

Releasing Rumination

Specific interventions that have been proven effective for young women struggling with these issues include rumination attention control, challenging cognitive dissonance, distraction, expressive writing, and yoga, just to mention a few (Mitchell, Mazzeo, Rausch, & Cooke, 2007; Stice & Shaw, 2004; Stice, Shaw, Burton, & Wade, 2006). Rumination, as mentioned earlier, can keep clients from moving forward as they become caught up in cyclical, spiraling negative thoughts. Allowing the negative messages to interfere in pursuit of goals can easily happen on a college campus where status is achieved through appearance. However, there is a useful intervention that can help young women challenge the negative ruminations and the cognitive dissonance that block them from seeing the value and worth they embody. A counselor can invite a client to focus on the parts of her body, face, or self that she does like. Next, she can be asked to write down a detailed list of the things she likes about her appearance and she should be reminded that an empty list is not acceptable. After the list is complete, the counselor should let the client know that what she should now focus on is not the parts of herself that she deems inadequate or dislikes, but she should focus on the parts that she does find attractive and likes. She should be encouraged to focus on this list when she is in situations that are typically stressful regarding self-appraisal and self-judgment, such as at the gym or at social events. For instance, if a client notes that she likes her eyes, she could be told, "When you are in the gym, how would things be different if you keep telling yourself that you have beautiful eyes and that eyes are beautiful forever. ..." Counselors should use the session as a rehearsal hall for new positive self-statements and for replacement cognitive beliefs to help clients grow comfortable with these newly developed, esteem-building statements.

Speaking Up and Staying Cool

Students could also benefit from social skills building, such as practicing assertiveness. By encouraging clients to role play anxiety-producing, confidence-defeating situations from campus life, the counselor can help the client build a new repertoire of responses to these situations. The client can then be encouraged to practice these on campus, in the dorms, during class meetings, and during formal and informal student gatherings.

Another way to prevent the negative consequences of unhealthy competition could be through developing and practicing a repertoire of effective verbal and behavioral approaches to handle situations in which a student feels that someone is the recipient of relational aggression and harmful actions. Once a student is more confident in her ability to address harmful relational and competition behaviors, she will be able to more effectively address such behaviors as they arise.

The Company You Keep

Counselors may want to encourage students to seek out positive environmental surroundings according to students' interests or temperaments. After working with students to develop the lists of personal qualities and strengths they appreciate in themselves, the counselor can encourage clients to brainstorm ways in which these traits may be best utilized through group activities. Finding supportive and relevant organizations and environments would provide opportunities for students to become involved beyond their social/academic circles and potentially provide opportunities to develop leadership skills and build new relationships.

Knowing Your Boundaries

Lastly, an important area to address is the development and respect of personal boundaries. Using a visual of a circle on a page, the counselor can ask the client to create a set of "friendship" limits, "intimacy" limits, and "what 'they' say" limits. On each page, the client can list the topics and acceptable behaviors that she lets into her "inner circle," and around the exterior of the circle the client can list those things that she does not want to allow into her life. In terms of friendship limits, the client may exclude "jealousy," "back stabbing," and so forth and the counselor should ask the client to provide specific examples of what the behavior would look like as well as responses the client could use if such a situation occurs. By developing her own limits, the client is being encouraged to move beyond self-acceptance into self-assertion and calculated risk-taking.

PREVENTION

Prevention work needs to target all women on campus and especially any at-risk populations, such as women with a history of mood disorder, socially isolated students, and those with a personal or family history of eating disorders. Preventive interventions should include student mentor programs; encouragement to join major-related clubs, student government, and student leaders; and encouragement to form meaningful, supportive relationships. The need to connect with others of like mind and values is essential for all students and finding paths to social support beyond the academic world is necessary. Ideas for assisting clients in this endeavor are found in the chapter addressing social transitions.

The National Organization for Women (NOW) sponsors an annual "Love Your Body" campaign. The focus of this event is self-acceptance and appreciation for one's own physical appearance. The website is found at loveyourbody.nowfoundation.org, and there are links to publications, promotional materials, blogs, and so forth available to individuals and groups.

Media Literacy

Media literacy must also be incorporated into prevention efforts, since the messages, images, and resulting social comparison are heavily influenced by the media (Stice & Shaw, 2004; Stice et al., 2006). Finally, prevention efforts need to be incorporated systemically; for example, legislative efforts have included the introduction of laws prohibiting false advertising by the diet industry. Advocacy and outreach efforts also can be supported and promoted by counseling centers and student affairs offices.

CONCLUSION

This chapter provided an overview of the "beauty pageant effect," a phenomenon in which college women compete against one another based on their physical appearance. In addition, exploration of the beauty pageant effect suggests that social comparison theory, evolutionary psychology, and realistic comparison theory play a significant role in the interactions of college women. The negative impacts of this type of competition and a brief overview of clinical implications were discussed.

REFERENCES

Balkin, R. S., & Roland, C. B. (2005). Identification of differences in gender for adolescents in crisis residence. *Journal of Mental Health, 14*, 637–646.

Broderick, P. C., & Blewitt, P. (2010). *The life span: Human development for helping professionals.* Upper Saddle River, NJ: Pearson Education.

Corning, A. F., Krumm, A. J., & Smitham, L. A. (2006). Differential social comparison processes in women with and without eating disorder symptoms. *Journal of Counseling Psychology, 53*, 338–349.

Darlow, S., & Lobel, M. (2010). Who is beholding my beauty? Thinness ideals, weight, and women's responses to appearance evaluation. *Sex Roles, 63*, 833–843.

Elkind, D. (1967). Egocentrism in adolescence. *Child Development, 38*, 1025–1031.

Epstein, M., & Ward, L. L. (2011). Exploring parent-adolescent communication about gender: Results from adolescent and emerging adult samples. *Sex Roles, 65*, 108–118.

Festinger, L. (1954). A theory of social comparison. *Human Relations, 7*, 117–140.

Finn, J. D., Pannozzo, G. M., & Achilles, C. M. (2003). The "why" of class size: Student behavior in small classes. *Review of Educational Research, 73*, 321–368.

Forsyth, D. R. (2010). *Group dynamics.* Belmont, CA: Wadsworth Cengage Learning.

Gibbson, F. X., & Buunk, B. P. (1999). Individual differences in social comparison: The development of a scale of social comparison orientation. *Journal of Personality and Social Psychology, 76*, 129–142.

Grabe, S., Ward, L. M., & Hyde, J. S. (2008). The role of the media in body image concerns among women: A meta-analysis of experimental and correlational studies. *Psychological Bulletin, 134,* 460–476.

Heatherton, T. F., Mahamedi, F., Striepe, M., Field, A. E., & Keel, P. (1997). A 10-year longitudinal study of body weight, dieting, and eating disorder symptoms. *Journal of Abnormal Psychology, 106,* 117–125.

Jordan, J. V., Kaplan, A. G., Baker Miller, J., Stiver, I. P., & Surrey, J. L. (1991). *Women's growth in connection: Writings from the stone center.* New York, NY: The Guilford Press.

Li, C., & Kerpelman, J. (2007). Parental influences on young women's certainty about their career aspirations. *Sex Roles, 56,* 105–115.

Loya, B., Cowan, G., & Walters, C. (2006). The role of social comparison and body consciousness in women's hostility toward women. *Sex Roles, 54,* 575–583.

Mitchell, K. S., Mazzeo, S. E., Rausch, S. M., & Cooke, K. L. (2007). Innovative interventions for disordered eating: Evaluating dissonance-based and yoga interventions. *International Journal of Eating Disorders, 40,* 120–128.

Morganson, V. J., Jones, M. P., & Major, D. A. (2010). Understanding women's underrepresentation in science, technology, engineering, and mathematics: The role of social coping. *Career Development Quarterly, 59,* 169–179.

Morrow, J., & Nolen-Hoeksema, S. (1990). Effects of responses to depression on the remediation of depressive affect. *Journal of Personality and Social Psychology, 58,* 519–527.

Nolen-Hoeksema, S., & Girgus, J. S. (1994). The emergence of gender differences in depression during adolescence. *Psychological Bulletin, 115,* 424–443.

Paxton, S. J., Eisenberg, M. E., & Neumark-Sztainer, D. (2006). Prospective predictors of body dissatisfaction in adolescent girls and boys: A five-year longitudinal study. *Developmental Psychology, 42,* 888–899.

Piran, N., & Cormier, H. C. (2005). The social construction of women and disordered eating patterns. *Journal of Counseling Psychology, 52,* 549–558.

Poran, M. A. (2006). The politics of protection: Body image, social pressures, and the misrepresentation of young black women. *Sex Roles, 55,* 739–755.

Schrick, B., Sharp, E., Zvonkovic, A., & Reifman, A. (2012). Never let them see you sweat: Silencing and striving to appear perfect among U.S. college women. *Sex Roles, 67,* 591–604.

Snapp, S., Hensley-Choate, L., & Ryu, E. (2012). A body image resilience model for first-year college women. *Sex Roles, 67,* 211–221.

Stice, E., Shaw, H., Burton, E., & Wade, E. (2006). Dissonance and healthy weight eating disorder prevention programs: A randomized efficacy trial. *Journal of Consulting and Clinical Psychology, 74,* 263–275.

Stice, E., & Shaw, H. E. (2004). Eating disorder prevention programs: A meta-analytic review. *Psychological Bulletin, 130,* 206–227.

Struble, C., Lindley, L. L., Montgomery, K., Hardin, J., & Burcin, M. (2010). Overweight and obesity in lesbian and bisexual college women. *Journal of American College Health, 59,* 51–56.

Swim, J. K., Eyssell, K. M., Murdoch, E. Q., & Ferguson, M. J. (2010). Self-silencing to sexism. *Journal of Social Issues, 66,* 493–507.

Vaillancourt, T., & Sharma, A. (2011). Intolerance of sexy peers: Intrasexual competition among women. *Aggressive Behavior, 37,* 569–577.

Wade, T., George, W. M., & Atkinson, M. A. (2009). Randomized controlled trial of brief interventions for body dissatisfaction. *Journal of Consulting and Clinical Psychology, 77,* 845–854.

Webster, J., & Tiggemann, M. (2003). The relationship between women's body satisfaction and self-image across the lifespan: The role of cognitive control. *Journal of Genetic Psychology, 164,* 241–252.

9

Hook-Up or Healthy Relationship? Counseling Student Partnering Through the College Years

REBECCA EARHART MICHEL AND NICOLE M. RANDICK

Most campus cultures encourage intellectual, personal, and social development, while students are also exploring the development of adult intimate relationships. A student's vocational future is often sought through a relatively linear path of coursework and internships; however, the path to relationship success is not as straightforward. Counselors can help college students establish and navigate healthy romantic relationships and learn lessons that may last a lifetime. In this chapter, we provide an overview of romantic relationships within the college setting, including the ways relationships develop, benefit, and challenge students. The college culture and influence of technology are explored, including the decision students face to "officially" define a relationship in the digital world. Finally, suggestions are provided for counselors working with college couples.

BECOMING ATTACHED: FACTORS INFLUENCING COLLEGE ROMANTIC RELATIONSHIPS

The college years fall during a critical period of an individual's identity and relational development. According to Erikson (1950, 1968), adolescence is a time of self-discovery and identity formation, in which an individual develops his or her sense of self in preparation for the establishment of romantic relationships. Traditional students—that is, those who enroll in college directly after graduating from high school—progress from adolescence to "emerging adulthood" during college (Arnett, 2000). This developmental

113

stage includes significant benchmark events, including moving away from home, friends, and family for the first time (Moller, Rauladi, McCarthy, & Hatch, 2003). As students leave all that is familiar, the transition to college presents new freedoms, discoveries, and relationships (Stevens & Morris, 2007). Regardless of the new setting, an individual's existing attachment patterns will influence the development and quality of these new relationships launched in college (Madey & Jilek, 2012).

Attachment Styles

An understanding of attachment theory is helpful in conceptualizing the formation of romantic relationships between emerging adults (Fraley & Shaver, 2000; Hazan & Shaver, 1987). A comprehensive review of attachment theory is beyond the scope of this chapter (see Bowlby, 1969; Pistole & Vocoturo, 1999); however, in essence, attachment patterns (e.g., secure, anxious, ambivalent, avoidant) affect and shape the way individuals form and maintain relationships. Individuals with a secure attachment typically exhibit high levels of commitment, intimacy, and passion (Madey & Rodgers, 2009). Conversely, individuals with avoidant attachment styles strive to maintain independence within relationships, which often results in a fear of dependence, self-disclosure, and intimacy (Brennan, Clark, & Shaver, 1998). Children grow up witnessing and learning from the attachment patterns of their parents and their parents' partners, which serve to shape their attitudes and beliefs about relationships.

The Opinions of Friends and Family

College student opinions and attitudes about romantic relationships are shaped through interactions and influence of family members, friends, and social networks. The value of parental approval of romantic relationships differs by culture (MacDonald, Marshall, Gere, Shimotomai, & Lies, 2012). While a majority of college students will have been romantically involved with someone from another culture by the time they exit college, many believe at least one parent would respond negatively or, at best, neutrally to this information (Reiter, Krause, & Stirlen, 2005). Similarly, findings suggest interracial relationships receive less support from family members (Wang, Kao, & Joyner, 2006). While many emerging adults long for their independence from parents' support and influence, research suggests that when parents support their children's romantic relationships, there is a greater likelihood of relationship stability, satisfaction, and commitment (Felmlee, 2001).

In many cases, friends influence the romantic choices of college students more than parents (Wright & Sinclair, 2012). Young adults rely on their friends for relationship advice and matchmaking (Parks, 2007). In fact, the opinions of friends and social network members are good predictors of romantic partner choice and romantic relationship quality (Felmlee, 2001; Wright & Sinclair, 2012). When friends perceive a student to be enjoying high relationship satisfaction with a partner, they are more likely to approve of the relationship (Etcheverry, Le, & Hoffman, 2012). In general, there is a direct correlation between the support from a student's social network and the quality of a relationship (Jin & Oh, 2010). Conversely, disapproval of a partner choice by a friend can often lead to a breakup (Felmlee, 2001).

DEFINING THE ROMANTIC RELATIONSHIP

As mentioned, college student romantic relationships do not follow a linear path. There are no longer clear stages of relationship development that were pro forma a generation or two ago. College students do not "go steady" and many couples prefer not to label anything about their experiences together (Owen, Rhoades, Stanley, & Fincham, 2010). Even a decade ago, college students might have expressed romantic interest by asking someone on a date. In the current college environment, many students explore relationship potential by "hooking up," or engaging in physically intimate behavior with an individual who may be of interest (Owen et al., 2010). When individuals hook-up, there are "no strings attached." Hooking up, as a description of personal interaction, is ambiguous, and allows individuals to take their time to determine whether to pursue or avoid a romantic relationship (Bogle, 2008; Glenn & Marquardt, 2001). If in hooking up, participants become interested in the establishment of a more serious relationship, they may anxiously initiate "the talk" to determine if their partner feels the same (Nelms, Knox, & Easterling, 2012). If a college couple eventually decides to define their relationship, they will often make it official through technology. In doing so, they will notify others through social networking sites (Papp, Danielewicz, & Cayemberg, 2012) with an update to everyone in their social networks that they are now "in a relationship."

TECHNOLOGY AND COLLEGE ROMANTIC RELATIONSHIPS

Today, individuals use technology to initiate, explore, and sustain relationships; in fact, most young adults navigate the majority of their social relationships via technology (Drouin & Landgraff, 2012). College students use social networking sites, such as Facebook, LinkedIn, and Twitter, to construct a personal profile, connect with others, and communicate with users who share a common interest (Boyd & Ellison, 2007; Jencius & Rainey, 2009). Facebook, in particular, has changed the way people enter into relationships (Fox, Warber, & Makstaller, 2013).

Social Networking

On college campuses today, Facebook plays an important role, as individuals gain information about potential or current romantic partners by viewing their profiles (Muise, Christofides, & Desmarais, 2009). Facebook is also used to express a relationship identity, as users can list their romantic relationship status (e.g., single, dating, or married) and link to their partner in their profile (Pempek, Yermolayeva, & Calvert, 2009). Although young adults may prefer not to label their partnership, the social pressure to update one's relationship status online forces students to directly discuss the status of their romantic relationship with their partners (Fox et al., 2013). In this way, social networking sites can become a burden to users and may very well illuminate problems in romantic relationships. In fact, Facebook use has been shown to promote jealousy among romantic partners and is linked with both relationship satisfaction and dissatisfaction among users (Muise, Christofides, & Desmarais, 2009; Sheldon, Abad, & Hinsch, 2011).

While social networking sites provide an opportunity to express individuality, they also make public one's personal relationships and behaviors. When one partner in a relationship is hesitant to communicate commitment via a status update, it may lead to resentment by partners as well as a fear of lack of commitment. In the past, an individual who dated many partners might have been able to keep relationships separate; however, the desire of a partner to see a pledge of online commitment to the relationship may create tension in the relationship. Working with couples who are at diverse stages of commitment to a relationship may be required of counselors as the public aspect of relationships may reveal hidden hesitance to commit.

Text Me, Maybe

In addition to connecting through social networking sites, text messaging is a popular method of communication among emerging adults. Almost all college students use text messaging to stay connected with romantic partners (Drouin & Landgraff, 2012). It is interesting to note that one study found that of the overwhelming two thirds of college students who snoop or check-up on their partners, 88% of them read their partners' text messages as a way to find out about their partners' behaviors (Derby, Knox, & Easterling, 2012). While many standard text message abbreviations and memes exist, couples often develop a set of "personal codes." Cell phones allow virtually constant contact, yet their presence and availability may create relationship conflicts as many romantic partners develop unwritten rules about cell phone use, such as when it is appropriate to call or text. College students in romantic relationships are expected to follow these norms in order to avoid conflicts regarding communication (Yang, Brown, & Braun, 2013).

Technology provides the means for both connection and autonomy and this conflict can create tension for partners (Duran, Kelly, & Rotaru, 2011). The most tension-producing areas for couples are generally related to a partner who doesn't call or text frequently enough. When couples are involved in separate activities, texting is a lifeline that keeps them connected; when a partner forgets to text at scheduled times, it has the potential to create rifts in the relationship as well as encourage worries about the partner's level of commitment or faithfulness. When a student has prior experience with an unfaithful partner, he or she may place even more intense expectations on a partner's immediate response to a text. No longer do students sit by the phone, waiting for it to ring. Instead, they are frequently texting their partners to check in and, if a partner is slow to respond, the student's emotional response may be at a level that obstructs him or her from focusing on class or schoolwork. For some couples, counselors may need to help couples understand the other partner's level of need for autonomy and independence as well as help them mediate what is reasonable versus unreasonable expectations for technological connectivity.

So Far Away—Long-Distance Relationships

The accessibility and ease of technology also facilitate the management of long-distance romantic relationships (LDRRs). During the past decade, students have witnessed the growing prevalence of cell phone and text capabilities as well as social networking sites and video telecommunications (e.g., Facetime, Skype). It has become even easier to stay connected to long-distance romantic partners. While Stafford (2005) suggested the majority of college students will engage in a LDRR at some point during their education, other research suggests romantic partner separation often ends a relationship or decreases the quality of the relationship (Knox, Zusman, Daniels, & Brantley, 2002). However, Stafford (2005) actually found LDRRs to be more stable than college proximal romantic relationships. With regard to LDRR satisfaction, Roberts and Pistole (2009) found attachment style was a key antecedent to LDRR satisfaction.

As an example, partners with low attachment avoidance tend to feel secure about their relationship and, thus, more successfully manage the unique demands of a LDRR (e.g., increased phone calls, coordinating free time). In sum, research strongly suggests technology can contribute to the success or demise of college romantic relationships.

BENEFITS AND CHALLENGES WITHIN
ROMANTIC RELATIONSHIPS

Ideally, relationships provide companionship, love, and intimacy to emerging adults, which allow them to successfully navigate the psychosocial crisis of intimacy versus isolation. College students engaged in romantic relationships experience numerous psychological and social benefits. Romantic partners enjoy social support and the relationship provides a buffer against stress (Tolpin, Cohen, Gunthert, & Farrehi, 2006). The majority of young adults report romantic relationship satisfaction (Cramer, 2004), most notably when they experience more positive events (e.g., socializing with the romantic partner) and fewer stressors (e.g., argument with the romantic partner) in their relationship (Tolpin et al., 2006). Intimate relationships are associated with increased emotional well-being (Simon & Barrett, 2010), as well as higher self-esteem and body esteem than non-partnered peers (Pettijohn, Naples, & McDermott, 2010). Additionally, some research suggests college students in committed relationships experience fewer mental health problems than uncommitted or single peers (Braithwaite, Delevi, & Fincham, 2010).

In essence, when college students are satisfied in their relationship, they experience greater happiness, well-being, and positive feelings. As they become emotionally involved, they generally seek ways to spend increasing amounts of time with one another, which may conflict with work and school (Zusman & Knox, 1998). As such, romantic partners can be a source of positive and/or negative influence, encouraging or drawing the partner away from career or educational pursuits (Manning, Giordano, Longmore, & Hocevar, 2011).

College students can also experience numerous challenges within their romantic relationships, including issues with communication, lack of commitment, jealousy, lack of time for the relationship, different values, unhealthy relationships, and termination of a relationship (Darling, McWey, Howard, & Olmstead, 2007; Zusman & Knox, 1998). Romantic relationships may be challenging for young adults because they require skills to cope with conflict, negotiate intimacy and support, and navigate feelings of rejection after a breakup (Davila, 2011). Jealousy is one of the most frequently reported concerns among college couples, and the use of social media can intensify the feelings of jealousy when individuals who have communicated with old flames or potential new interests are discovered by their romantic partner. Our culturally ingrained belief is that women are more upset by emotional infidelity than physical cheating, and men are assumed to feel the exact opposite. However, Varga, Gee, and Munro (2011) found that when it comes to actual experience with either type of cheating, college students of both genders did not display any gender differences based on the means of infidelity. Thus, college counselors should expect to work with both men and women who have unresolved feelings toward their cheating partners, regardless of whether it was a meeting of the hearts or a meeting of a more physical nature. Relationship stressors can be even more difficult when compounded with the unique demands of the college environment.

Eating Disorders

Although this book includes a chapter addressing the incidence and treatment of eating disorders, it is important to note here that body image distortions are a prevalent issue among highly stressed college students. The culture of college may contribute to eating disorders among students (Kashubeck, Walsh, & Crowl, 1994). While college students in committed relationships are less likely to be overweight (Braithwaite, Delevi, & Fincham, 2010), approximately a third of college students have been told by their romantic partners to lose or gain weight (Sheets & Ajmere, 2005). Additionally, women who do not feel supported by their romantic partners tend to be concerned with body image, weight gain, and dieting (Weller & Dziegielewski, 2004). Negative body image is often associated with other destructive behaviors, such as relationship violence.

Relationship Violence

Relationship violence includes the infliction or threat of infliction of psychological, physical, or sexual abuse to establish control over a romantic partner. Relationship violence is estimated to be present in as many as one in three college romantic relationships (Lewis & Fremouw, 2001), which is a sobering statistic. Increased academic strain (e.g., pressure to meet deadlines, time spent studying, worrying about exam results) may contribute to high instances of relationship violence on the college campus (Mason & Smithy, 2012). Additional risk factors include family history, peer influences, beliefs, and psychological well-being (Murray & Kardatzke, 2007). Often, romantic partners are involved in a mutually violent intimate relationship in which both individuals exhibit perpetration and victimization behaviors (Kaukinen, Gover, & Hartman, 2012).

Relationship violence impacts both men and women and occurs within heterosexual and lesbian, gay, bisexual (LGB) relationships (Calhoun, Mouilso, & Edwards, 2012). College relationship violence victimization rates vary based on numerous factors, including abuse type, gender, race, and sexual orientation (Fincham, Cui, Braithwaite & Pasley, 2008; Luthra & Gidycz, 2006). It is estimated that as many as 80% to 90% of college students experience psychological victimization or perpetration, including verbal aggression or controlling or coercive behaviors (Katz, Arias, & Beach, 2000; White & Koss, 1991). Approximately 17% to 45% of college students worldwide experience physical abuse victimization (e.g., hitting, biting, pushing); these abusive interactions are characterized by greater violence than the abuse that occurs in marital relationships (Straus, 2004).

Sexual assault victimization (e.g., sexual activities obtained through coercion or force) rates on college campuses are "alarmingly high," with estimates between 2.8% and 55% (Calhoun, Mouilso, & Edwards, 2012, p. 264). Racial and ethnic minorities and LGB college students are at higher risk for sexual abuse (Porter & McQuiller Williams, 2011). Women experience the greatest risk of sexual assault during college than any other stage of life, with the greatest risk occurring during their freshman year (Kimble, Neacsiu, Flack, & Horner, 2008). Additionally, college men self-report sexually aggressive perpetration rates between 10% and 35% (Gidycz, Warkentin, & Orchowski, 2007; White & Smith, 2004).

The Far Reach of Relationship Violence

Relationship violence is related to decreased relationship satisfaction and increased mental health problems among college students (Kaura & Lohman, 2007). Long-term mental health consequences include depression, suicidal ideation, eating disorders, lower self-esteem, and posttraumatic stress disorder (Amar & Gennaro, 2005; Murray, Wester & Paladina, 2008). Many survivors of relationship violence engage in risky behaviors and experience poor academic performance (Hanson, 2002), which can negatively impact their college experience.

College students involved in violent romantic relationships are likely to remain in those relationships or engage in future unhealthy partnerships (Murray & Kardatzke, 2007; Smith, White, & Holland, 2003). However, research indicates that when survivors receive positive responses from support systems, they may experience a healthier adjustment and break cycles of relationship abuse perpetration (Borja, Callahan, & Long, 2006;

Murray & Kardatzke, 2007). Many college students would benefit from a college counseling intervention to end unhealthy relationships before they become violent.

RELATIONSHIP DISSOLUTION

Most students will experience relationships and breakups throughout their college years. According to practitioners, relationship dissolution is a common presenting issue in college counseling centers. There are many reasons college students end romantic relationships. Students cite issues of intimacy (e.g., poor communication, distrust), affiliation (e.g., boredom, diminishing fun), sexuality (e.g., diminishing physical attraction or affection), and autonomy (e.g., control, loss of identity) as justification for a breakup (Field, Diego, Pelaez, Deeds, & Delgado, 2010). Often, relationship dissolution is a result of low commitment, poor communication, high conflict, cheating, aggression, and/or low relationship satisfaction (Rodrigues, Hall, & Fincham, 2006).

Young adults who have experienced a recent breakup often report an increase in psychological distress (e.g., depression, sleep disturbance) and a decrease in life satisfaction (Rhoades, Kamp Dush, Atkins, Stanley, & Markman, 2011). The attachment style of each individual impacts the experience of relationship dissolution, including feelings of hopelessness, stress, loneliness, and general adjustment following a breakup (Moller et al., 2003). College students with secure attachments are less likely to get back into former relationships and are more willing to explore other relationship options (Madey & Jilek, 2012). College students experiencing high breakup distress often experienced an unexpected breakup that they did not initiate, which left them feeling rejected and betrayed (Field et al., 2010).

While many college students experience negative emotions following a romantic breakup, others feel positive emotions, such as joy and relief (Sprecher, 1994). Some college students experience growth as a result of the relationship breakup. For example, Tashiro and Frazier (2003) found college students who had been through a recent romantic relationship dissolution were able to note numerous ways in which they felt their future relationships would be better due to self-perceived personal growth they attributed to their recent breakup. In response to an open-ended question about self-perceived growth, students were generally able to describe at least five different types of growth. Once single, students learned ways to improve themselves (e.g., learning to admit when they are wrong) and incorporated more positive environmental factors (e.g., increased academic achievement) into their lives (Tashiro & Frazier, 2003). College counselors can assist students to process the experience of initiating, sustaining, and ending romantic relationships in order to achieve higher levels of personal and relational growth.

COUNSELING COLLEGE STUDENTS ABOUT ROMANTIC RELATIONSHIPS

College counselors are in a unique position to help students learn positive attitudes and behaviors that will allow them to form and navigate healthy romantic relationships throughout adulthood. According to the Association for University and College Counseling Center Directors national survey, relationship issues rank only third in terms of most common presenting issues trailing behind anxiety and depression, respectively (Gallagher, 2011); however, there is great likelihood that relationship issues are a part of other student issues. For instance, romantically involved students trying to balance personal well-being, time spent with a partner, and academic workload may present to counseling for anxiety (Zusman & Knox, 1998; Zvonkovic, Pennington, & Schmiege, 1994) but frequently benefit in all aspects of life from learning assertiveness skills. Furthermore, since positive relationships and strong relationship skills are protective factors, understanding the intricacies of college student romantic relationships is an important task for college counselors (Abowitz, Knox, Zusman, & McNeely, 2009).

ASSESSMENTS AND INTERVENTIONS

College students experience a multitude of challenges that can interfere with the development of healthy romantic relationships. There are a number of culturally and developmentally appropriate assessments and interventions that college counselors can use to effectively engage the college student population (Sharkin, 2012). College counselors must also possess a thorough understanding of attachment theory to guide their interventions with students.

Assessment Possibilities

There are many assessments available for use with college students. Counselors can measure problem-solving abilities with the Problem Resolution Outcome Survey (Heppner, Cooper, Mulholland, & Wei, 2001). Reiter, Richmond, Stirlen, and Kompel (2009) recommend students in intercultural relationships would benefit from exploring intimacy and relational issues using the Personal Assessment of Intimacy in Relationships (Schaefer & Olson, 1981). The Intimate Partner Violence Attitude Scale–Revised (Fincham, Cui, Braithwaite, & Pasley, 2008) serves to identify beliefs regarding relationship violence so that college counselors can intervene accordingly. The Breakup Distress Scale allows counselors to develop appropriate interventions for students who have experienced a relationship breakup (Field et al., 2010). The use of family genograms may also help both counselors and clients understand the deeper patterns of attachment and relating within each partner's family system.

Understanding Clients' Attachment Styles

A comprehensive understanding of attachment theory can help guide appropriate interventions. The counseling relationship itself is reflective of one's style of attachment, thus offering an opportunity for clients to explore, understand, and change their ineffective attachment functioning within a safe space (Pistole & Watkins, 1995). Counselors are also advised to use specific assessments and interventions to help a person explore his or her attachment style. Providing an attachment assessment at intake, such as the Attachment Style Questionnaire (Feeney, Noller, & Hanrahan, 1994) or Experiences in Close Relationships (Brennan et al., 1998), can provide useful information and guide interventions. According to Moller et al. (2003), counselors can reexamine familial relationships and the meaning placed on childhood experiences to discover how past attachments affect current relationship patterns. Clients may gain perspective through exploration of current relationship expectations as well as the impact of previous relationship history. Counselors might also explore the impact of technology on college student attachment and relationship functioning.

Proactive Use of Technology

Counselors can assess the emergence, maintenance, and decline of romantic relationship development through a client's use of technology (e.g., texting, social networking sites). Together counselors and students can explore how the use of technology may be linked to attachment style (e.g., avoidant, anxious), and how technology is used to initiate or avoid proximity (Drouin & Landgraff, 2012; Pempek et al., 2009). Fox et al. (2013) suggest using Knapp's (1978) relational model to help conceptualize a couple's current relational development stage (i.e., initiating, experimenting, intensifying, integrating, and bonding) and to what extent technology parallels this development. For example, during the intensifying stage, a relationship grows stronger as more information is shared within the couple (e.g., Facebook pictures, defining the relationship). On the other hand, during a breakup a couple can use this information against one another as communication becomes threatening and exploitive (e.g., de-friending the person on Facebook, changing relationship status). Technology has fundamentally changed the way in which relationship information is disseminated and interpreted by others, setting up "new norms, expectations, and behaviors" of relationship communication (Fox et al., 2013, p. 4).

Helping Couples Stay Connected

Technology allows for college students to engage in LDRRs. Separation and lack of intimacy and commitment are common challenges among college students in LDRRs. These stressors contribute to communication and intimacy issues between partners (Mietzner & Lin, 2005). By targeting specific concerns (e.g., attachment distress and proximity), counselors can address relational issues among partners and help students develop skills associated with healthy LDRR attachment. Through counseling, college students will establish realistic relationship goals, develop proximity responses (i.e., behaviors that influence contact with partners), utilize time management techniques, and develop a sense of independence and connectedness with peers (Mietzner & Lin, 2005). College students regulate contact with romantic partners by clarifying specific and realistic times to communicate via telephone and/or Internet and by sharing intimate responses with one another, such as "I love you" and/or "I miss you" (Roberts & Pistole, 2009). These strategies help foster healthier relationships among students in LDRRs.

COPING WITH ROMANTIC CHALLENGES

There are several additional strategies for college counselors working with students experiencing problems in their romantic relationships. Many college students feel torn between spending time on academics, friendships, or their romantic relationships. Couples counseling would allow students to voice concerns about their career development and relationship issues (e.g., communication concerns, jealousy) in a safe and supportive environment (Gibbons & Shurts, 2010). College students could also use time within couples or individual counseling to discuss their own challenges within the college culture (e.g., hook-ups, body image issues). These problems could serve as a starting point to illuminate the complexities of romantic relationships within the college environment.

Encouraging Mindful Partnership

Nontraditional counseling techniques may also be beneficial for college students. Mindfulness is an emerging intervention that enhances relationship satisfaction and provides a greater capacity to respond constructively to relationship stress (Barnes, Brown, Krusemark, Campbell, & Rogge, 2007). College students can learn mindfulness strategies to become more aware of their "in the moment" thoughts, feelings, and behaviors. Counselors using this approach help couples enhance their relationship quality through in-session mindfulness training (i.e., breath awareness, guided meditation), designed to increase self-control and emotional regulation (Barnes et al., 2007). College counselors who incorporate mindfulness-based interventions in their counseling practice promote the well-being of college students experiencing stress when attempting to balance their social, academic, and romantic lives (Lynch, Gander, Kohls, Kudielka, & Walach, 2010).

Interventions Beyond the Counseling Office

Interventions with college students are not restricted to the counseling office. Student groups and workshops can support healthy relationship development. Groups that address symptoms prevalent in students experiencing breakup distress (e.g., loss, hopelessness, and isolation) are appropriate for college students (Roberts & Pistole, 2009; Tashiro & Frazier, 2003). Counselors can also implement relationship education programs (Hays, Michel, Smith, Bayne, & Neuer Colburn, in press; Olmstead et al., 2011) to increase knowledge and awareness of healthy relationships. Additionally, violence bystander intervention programs can assist students, particularly men (Gidycz, Orchowski, & Berkowitz, 2011) and individuals within the lesbian, gay, bisexual, or transgender community (Potter, Fountain, & Stapleton, 2012) to intervene when witnessing relationship violence among college students.

CONCLUSION

Students spend their formative college years preparing for their careers, developing new friendships, and evaluating possible romantic relationships. Initiating and maintaining romantic partnerships can be difficult in college; where relationships are ambiguous, unwritten rules guide behavior, and students struggle to balance relationships and academics. Counselors can provide culturally and developmentally appropriate assessments and interventions with students struggling to navigate their romantic relationships within the culture of college.

REFERENCES

Abowitz, D. A., Knox, D., Zusman, M., & McNeely, A. (2009). Beliefs about romantic relationships: Gender differences among undergraduates. *College Student Journal*, *43*, 276–284.

Amar, A. F., & Gennaro, S. (2005). Dating violence in college women: Associated physical injury, health care usage, and mental health symptoms. *Nursing Research*, *54*(5), 235–242.

Arnett, J. J. (2000). Emerging adulthood: A theory of development from the late teens through the twenties. *American Psychologist*, *55*, 469–480.

Barnes, S., Brown, K., Krusemark, E., Campbell, W., & Rogge, R. D. (2007). The role of mindfulness in romantic relationship satisfaction and responses to relationship stress. *Journal of Marital and Family Therapy*, *33*(4), 482–500. doi:10.1111/j.1752-0606.2007.00033.x

Bogle, K. A. (2008). *Hooking up: Sex, dating, and relationships on campus*. New York, NY: New York University Press.

Borja, S. E., Callahan, J. L., & Long, P. J. (2006). Positive and negative adjustment and social support of sexual assault survivors. *Journal of Traumatic Stress*, *19*(6), 905–914.

Bowlby, J. (1969). *Attachment and loss: Vol. 1. Attachment*. New York, NY: Basic Books.

Boyd, D. M., & Ellison, N. B. (2007). Social network sites: Definition, history, and scholarship. *Journal of Computer-Mediated Communication*, *13*, 210–230.

Braithwaite, S. R., Delevi, R., & Fincham, F. D. (2010). Romantic relationships and the physical and mental health of college students. *Personal Relationships*, *17*, 1–12.

Brennan, K. A., Clark, C. L., & Shaver, P. R. (1998). Self-report measures of adult attachment: An integrative overview. In J. A. Simpson & W. S. Rholes (Eds.), *Attachment theory and close relationships* (pp. 46–76). New York, NY: Guilford.

Calhoun, K. S., Mouilso, E. R., & Edwards, K. M. (2012). Sexual assault among college students. In R. McAnulty (Ed.), *Sex in college: The things they don't write home about* (pp. 263–288). Santa Barbara, CA: ABC-CLIO.

Cramer, D. (2004). Satisfaction with a romantic relationship, depression, support and conflict. *Psychology Psychotherapy*, *77*, 449–461.

Darling, C. A., McWey, L. M., Howard, S. N., & Olmstead, S. B. (2007). College student stress: The influence of interpersonal relationships on sense of coherence. *Stress and Health*, *23*, 215–229.

Davila, J. (2011). Romantic relationships and mental health in emerging adulthood. In F. D. Fincham & M. Cui (Eds.), *Romantic relationships in emerging adulthood* (pp. 275–292). New York, NY: Cambridge University Press.

Derby, K., Knox, D., & Easterling, B. (2012). Snooping in romantic relationships. *College Student Journal*, *46*, 333–343.

Drouin, M., & Landgraff, C. (2012). Texting, sexting, and attachment in college students' romantic relationships. *Computers in Human Behavior*, *28*, 444–449.

Duran, R. L., Kelly, L., & Rotaru, T. (2011). Mobile phones in romantic relationships and the dialectic of autonomy versus connection. *Communication Quarterly*, *59*, 19–36.

Erikson, E. H. (1950). *Childhood and society*. New York, NY: Norton

Erikson, E. H. (1968). *Identity: Youth and crisis*. New York, NY: Norton.

Etcheverry, P. E., Le, B., & Hoffman, N. G. (2012). Predictors of friend approval for romantic relationships. *Personal Relationships.* doi: 10.1111/j.1475-6811.2012.01397.x

Feeney, J. A., Noller, P., & Hanrahan, M. (1994). Assessing adult attachment. In M. B. Sperling & W. H. Berman (Eds.), *Attachment in adults: Clinical and developmental perspectives* (pp. 128–152). New York, NY: Guilford.

Felmlee, D. (2001). No couple is an island: A social network perspective on dyadic stability. *Social Forces, 79*(4), 1259–1287.

Field, T., Diego, M., Pelaez, M., Deeds, O., & Delgado, J. (2010). Breakup distress and loss of intimacy in university students. *Psychology, 1,* 173–177.

Fincham, F. D., Cui, M., Braithwaite, S., & Pasley, K. (2008). Attitudes toward intimate partner violence in dating relationships. *Psychological Assessment, 20*(3), 260–269. doi: 10.1037/1040-3590.20.3.260

Fox, J., Warber, K. M., & Makstaller, D. C. (2013). The role of Facebook in romantic relationship development: An exploration of Knapp's relational stage model. *Journal of Social and Personal Relationships.* Retrieved from http://spr.sagepub.com/content/early/2013/01/06/0265407512468370

Fraley, R., & Shaver, P. R. (2000). Adult romantic attachment: Theoretical developments, emerging controversies, and unanswered questions. *Review of General Psychology, 4*(2), 132–154. doi:10.1037/1089-2680.4.2.132

Gallagher, R. P. (2011). *National survey of counseling center directors, 2011.* Alexandria, VA: International Association of Counseling Services.

Gibbons, M. M., & Shurts, W. M. (2010). Combining career and couples counseling for college students: A narrative approach. *Journal of College Counseling, 13,* 169–181.

Gidycz, C. A., Orchowski, L. M., & Berkowitz, A. D. (2011). Preventing sexual aggression among college men: An evaluation of a social norms and bystander intervention program. *Violence Against Women, 17*(6), 720–742. doi: 10.1177/1077801211409727

Gidycz, C. A., Warkentin, J. B., & Orchowski, L. M. (2007). Predictors of perpetration of verbal, physical, and sexual violence: A prospective analysis of college men. *Psychology of Men & Masculinity, 8,* 79–94. doi:10.1037/1524-9220.8.2.79

Glenn, N., & Marquardt, E. (2001). *Hooking up, hanging out, and hoping for Mr. Right: College women on dating and mating today.* New York, NY: Institute for American Values.

Hanson, R. F. (2002). Adolescent dating violence: Prevalence and psychological outcomes. *Child Abuse & Neglect, 26,* 447–451.

Hays, D. G., Michel, R. E., Smith, J., Bayne, H., & Neuer Colburn, A. A. (in press). Counseling with HEART: A college student dating violence prevention program. *Journal of College Counseling.*

Hazan, C., & Shaver, P. (1987). Romantic love conceptualized as an attachment process. *Journal of Personality and Social Psychology, 52*(3), 511–524.

Heppner, P. P., Cooper, C., Mulholland, A., & Wei, M. (2001). A brief, multidimensional, problem-solving psychotherapy outcome measure. *Journal of Counseling Psychology, 48,* 330–343.

Jencius, M., & Rainey, S. (2009). Current online career counseling practices and future trends. *Career Planning and Adult Development Journal, 25,* 17–28.

Jin, B., & Oh, S. (2010). Cultural differences of social network influence on romantic relationships: A comparison of the United States and South Korea. *Communication Studies, 61*(2), 156–171.

Kashubeck, S., Walsh, B., & Crowl, A. (1994). College atmosphere and eating disorders. *Journal of Counseling and Development, 72,* 640–645.

Katz, J., Arias, I., & Beach, S. (2000). Psychological abuse, self-esteem, and women: Dating relationship outcomes. *Psychology of Women Quarterly, 24*(4), 349–357.

Kaukinen, C., Gover, A. R., & Hartman, J. L. (2012). College women's experiences of dating violence in casual and exclusive relationships. *American Journal of Criminal Justice, 37,* 146–162. doi 10.1007/s12103-011-9113-7

Kimble, M., Neacsiu, A. D., Flack, W. F., & Horner, J. (2008). Risk of unwanted sex for college women: Evidence for a red zone. *Journal of American College Health, 57*(3), 331–337.

Knapp, M. L. (1978). *Social intercourse: From greeting to goodbye.* Needham Heights, MA: Allyn & Bacon.

Knox, D., Zusman, M. E., Daniels, V., & Brantley, A. (2002). Absence makes the heart grow fonder? Long distance dating relationships among college students. *College Student Journal, 36*(3), 365–367.

Lewis, S. F., & Fremouw, W. (2001). Dating violence: A critical review of the literature. *Clinical Psychology Review, 21,* 105–127.

Luthra, R., & Gidycz, C. A. (2006). Dating violence among college men and women: Evaluation of a theoretical model. *Journal of Interpersonal Violence, 21,* 717–731.

Lynch, S., Gander, M., Kohls, N., Kudielka, B., & Walach, H. (2011). Mindfulness-based coping with university life: A non-randomized wait-list-controlled pilot evaluation. *Stress and Health: Journal of the International Society for the Investigation of Stress, 27*(5), 365–375. doi:10.1002/smi.1382

MacDonald, G., Marshall, T. C., Gere, J., Shimotomai, A., & Lies, J. (2012). Valuing romantic relationships: The role of family approval across cultures. *Cross-Cultural Research, 46*(4), 366–393.

Madey, S. F., & Jilek, L. (2012). Attachment style and dissolution of romantic relationships: Breaking up is hard to do, or is it? *Individual Differences Research, 10*(4), 202–210.

Madey, S. F., & Rodgers, L. (2009). The effect of attachment and Sternberg's Triangular Theory of Love on relationship satisfaction. *Individual Differences Research, 7,* 76–84.

Manning, W. D., Giordano, P. C., Longmore, M. A., & Hocevar, A. (2011). Romantic relationships and academic/career trajectories in emerging adulthood. In F. D. Fincham & M. Cui (Eds.), *Romantic relationships in emerging adulthood* (pp. 317–333). New York, NY: Cambridge University Press.

Mason, B., & Smithy, M. (2012). The effects of academic and interpersonal stress on dating violence among college students: A test of classical strain theory. *Journal of Interpersonal Violence, 27*(5), 974–986. doi: 10.1177/0886260511423257

Mietzner, S., & Lin, L. (2005). Would you do it again? Relationship skills gained in a long-distance relationship. *College Student Journal, 39*(1), 192–200.

Moller, N. P., Rauladi, R. T., McCarthy, C. J., & Hatch, K. D. (2003). Relationship of attachment and social support to college students' adjustment following a relationship breakup. *Journal of Counseling and Development, 81,* 354–369.

Muise, A., Christofides, E., & Desmarais, S. (2009). More information than you ever wanted: Does Facebook bring out the green-eyed monster of jealousy? *CyberPsychology & Behavior, 12,* 441–444.

Murray, C., & Kardatzke, K. (2007). Dating violence among college students: Key issues for college counselors. *Journal of College Counseling, 10*(1), 79–89.

Murray, C. E., Wester, K. L., & Paladina, D. A. (2008). Dating violence and self-injury among undergraduate college students: Attitudes and experiences. *Journal of College Counseling, 11*, 42–57.

Nelms, B. J., Knox, D., & Easterling, B. (2012). The relationship talk: Assessing partner commitment. *College Student Journal, 46*, 178–182.

Olmstead, S. B., Pasley, K., Meyer, A. S., Stanford, P. S., Fincham, F. D., & Delevi, R. (2011). Implementing relationship education for emerging adult college students: Insights from the field. *Journal of Couple & Relationship Therapy, 10*, 215–228. doi: 10.1080/15332691.2011.588093

Owen, J. J., Rhoades, G. K., Stanley, S. M., & Fincham, F. D. (2010). "Hooking up" among college students: Demographic and psychosocial correlates. *Archives of Sexual Behavior, 39*(3), 653–663. doi: 10.1007/s10508-008-9414-1

Papp, L. M., Danielewicz, J., & Cayemberg, C. (2012). "Are we Facebook official?" Implications of dating partners' Facebook use and profiles for intimate relationship satisfaction. *Cyberpsychology, Behavior, and Social Networking, 15*(2), 85–90. doi: 10.1089/cyber.2011.0291

Parks, M. R. (2007). *Personal relationships and personal networks.* Mahwah, NJ: Erlbaum.

Pempek, T. A., Yermolayeva, Y. A., & Calvert, S. L. (2009). College students' social networking experiences on Facebook. *Journal of Applied Developmental Psychology, 30*, 227–238.

Pettijohn, T. F., Naples, G. M., & McDermott, L. A. (2010). Gender, college year, and romantic relationship status differences in embarrassment and self attitudes of college students. *Individual Differences Research, 8*(3), 164–170.

Pistole, M., & Vocaturo, L. C. (1999). Attachment and commitment in college students' romantic relationships. *Journal of College Student Development, 40*(6), 710–720.

Pistole, M., & Watkins, C. (1995). Attachment theory, counseling process, and supervision. *The Counseling Psychologist, 23*(3), 457–478. doi:10.1177/0011000095233004

Porter, J., & McQuiller Williams, L. (2011). Intimate violence among underrepresented groups on a college campus. *Journal of Interpersonal Violence, 26*, 3210–3224.

Potter, S. J., Fountain, K., & Stapleton, J. G. (2012). Addressing sexual and relationship violence in the LGBT community using a bystander framework. *Harvard Review of Psychiatry, 20*(4), 201–208.

Reiter, M. D., Krause, J. M., & Stirlen, A. (2005). Intercouple dating on a college campus. *College Student Journal, 39*(3), 449–454.

Reiter, M. D., Richmond, K., Stirlen, A., & Kompel, N. (2009). Exploration of intimacy in intercultural and intracultural romantic relationships in college students. *College Student Journal, 43*(4), 1080–1083.

Rhoades, G. K., Kamp Dush, C. M., Atkins, D. C., Stanley, S. M., & Markman, H. J. (2011). Breaking up is hard to do: The impact of unmarried relationship dissolution on mental health and life satisfaction. *Journal of Family Psychology, 25*(3), 366–374.

Roberts, A., & Pistole, M. C. (2009). Long-distance and proximal romantic relationship satisfaction: Attachment and closeness predictors. *Journal of College Counseling, 12*, 5–17.

Rodrigues, A. E., Hall, J. H., & Fincham, F. D. (2006). What predicts divorce and relationship dissolution? In M. A. Fine & J. H. Harvey (Eds.), *Handbook of divorce and relationship dissolution* (pp. 85–112). Mahwah, NJ: Erlbaum.

Schaefer, M. T., & Olson, D. H. (1981). Assessing intimacy: The PAIR inventory. *Journal of Marital and Family Therapy, 7,* 47–60.

Sharkin, B. S. (2012). *Being a college counselor on today's campus: Roles, contributions, and special challenges.* New York, NY: Routledge.

Sheets, V., & Ajmere, K. (2005). Are romantic partners a source of college students' weight concern? *Eating Behaviors, 6*(1), 1–9.

Sheldon, K. M., Abad, N., & Hinsch, C. (2011). A two-process view of Facebook use and relatedness need-satisfaction: Disconnection drives use, and connection rewards it. *Psychology of Popular Media Culture, 1*(5), 2–15.

Simon, R. W., & Barrett, A. E. (2010). Nonmarital romantic relationships and mental health in early adulthood: Does the association differ for women and men? *Journal of Health and Social Behavior, 51*(2), 168–182. doi: 10.1177/0022146510372343

Smith, P. H., White, J. W., & Holland, L. J. (2003). A longitudinal perspective on dating violence among adolescent and college-age women. *American Journal of Public Health, 93,* 1104–1109.

Sprecher, S. (1994). Two sides to the breakup of dating relationships. *Personal Relationships, 1,* 199–222.

Stafford, L. (2005). *Maintaining long-distance and cross-residential relationships.* Mahwah, NJ: Erlbaum.

Stevens, S. B., & Morris, T. L. (2007). College dating and social anxiety: Using the Internet as a means of connecting to others. *Cyberpsychology & Behavior, 10*(5), 680–688. doi:10.1089/cpb.2007.9970

Straus, M. (2004). Prevalence of violence against dating partners by male and female university students worldwide. *Violence Against Women, 10*(7), 790–811. doi:10.1177/1077801204265552

Tashiro, T., & Frazier, P. (2003). "I'll never be in a relationship like that again": Personal growth following romantic relationship breakups. *Personal Relationships, 10,* 113–128.

Tolpin, L. H., Cohen, L. H., Gunthert, K. C., & Farrehi, A. (2006). Unique effects of depressive symptoms and relationship satisfaction on exposure and reactivity to daily romantic relationship stress. *Journal of Social and Clinical Psychology, 25*(5), 565–583.

Varga, C., Gee, C., & Munro, G. (2011). The effects of sample characteristics and experience with infidelity or romantic jealousy. *Sex Roles, 65,* 854–866.

Wang, H. Y., Kao, G., & Joyner, K. (2006). Stability of interracial and intraracial romantic relationships among adolescents. *Social Science Research, 35,* 435–453.

Weller, J. E., & Dziegielewski, S. F. (2004). The relationship between romantic partner support styles and body image disturbance. *Journal of Human Behavior in the Social Environment, 10,* 71–92.

White, J. W., & Koss, M. P. (1991). Courtship violence: Incidence in a national sample of higher education students. *Violence and Victims, 6,* 247–256.

White, J. W., & Smith, P. H. (2004). Sexual assault perpetration and reperpetration: From adolescence to young adulthood. *Criminal Justice and Behavior, 31,* 182–202. doi:10.1177/0093854803261342

Wright, B. L., & Sinclair, H. C. (2012). Pulling the strings: Effects of friend and parent opinions on dating choices. *Personal Relationships, 19*, 743–758.

Yang, C., Brown, B. B., & Braun, M. T. (2013). From Facebook to cell calls: Layers of electronic intimacy in college students' interpersonal relationships. *New Media Society, 0*, 1–19.

Zusman, M. E., & Knox, D. (1998). Relationship problems of casual and involved university students. *College Student Journal, 32*(4), 606.

Zvonkovic, A. M., Pennington, D. C., & Schmiege, C. J. (1994). Work and courtship: How college workload and perceptions of work environment relate to romantic relationships among men and women. *Journal of Social and Personal Relationships, 11*(1), 63–76. doi:10.1177/0265407594111004

10

Counseling College Students About Sexuality and Sexual Activity

CARRIE V. SMITH, EMILY FRANKLIN,
CHRISTINE BORZUMATO-GAINEY,
AND SUZANNE DEGGES-WHITE

Long before most college students arrive on campus, they have been exposed to a great deal of sexual content that conveys cultural messages about sex, sexuality, and attraction. Some of this sexual content may include healthy messages about sex but almost inevitably, some of it is misinformation, laden with unhealthy ideas. College students must make sexual choices; more clearly define their sexual identity; and consistently consider sexual health in order to maintain a strong and positive holistic sense of self. When their knowledge base or support system is lacking, healthy decisions are harder to make. College counselors should be able to provide accurate information on a wide variety of sexual issues as well as a safe environment for students to determine what is best.

Most young people tend to become sexually active during their teen years. In fact, results from a recent research study indicated that by the age of 19, 70% of teenagers have engaged in sexual intercourse (Abma et al., 2010). Thus, counseling is not typically around the decision to become sexually active, but rather helping students better understand themselves as sexual beings and help them make healthier sexual choices. Educating students about everything from vocabulary to communicating with partners about topics such as sexual concerns and safe sexual practices are the areas in which clients will most likely need assistance.

LEARNING TO SPEAK THE CLIENTS' LANGUAGE

In order for the counselor to address adequately the needs of university students in the area of sexual issues and interactions, counselors need to become fluent in their clients' sexual vocabularies (Trotter & Alderson, 2007). Counselors should be aware that students are likely to define terms differently and should seek to confirm mutual understanding when using sexual terminology. Most students in Trotter and Alderson's study identified sexual situations according to the behaviors present, such as penile–vaginal intercourse regardless of orgasm (76%–99%). However, many students considered an encounter to be "sex" if any type of genital touching produced an orgasm. In fact, virginity may be defined differently by different individuals. Most students in the Trotter and Alderson study agreed that if penile–vaginal penetration took place, virginity would be lost. Women tended to narrow their own definitions of virginity to such a degree that they had guidelines that would allow them to maintain their status as "technical" virgins. Gay and lesbian individuals might also have differing perspectives on what constitutes being sexually active and what constitutes virginity.

In addition to clarifying language pertaining to sexual behavior, counselors should also note possible differences in client definitions of a sexual partner. It appears that the more nuanced the situation, casualness of the relationship, different gender relationship versus same sex, and lack of orgasm, the more variability there was in the individual's appraisal of the relationship. While clients might be engaging in sexual activities with others, not only may they not consider it to be sex but they may not consider that the "other" is a sexual partner based on the fluidity or casualness of the relationship. If the client does not consider an activity sexual in nature, they might not consider the situation to be one of risk requiring forethought and consideration; thus, a client may be less sexually responsible regarding safe-sex behaviors.

The Pressure to Have Sex

College settings often have highly sexualized social environments, thus students sometimes experience a great deal of pressure to engage in sex. Experts and students alike refer to the contemporary college setting as a "hook-up" culture (Owen, Rhoades, Stanley, & Fincham, 2010). Students can feel pressured by their romantic partners or by friends who may encourage them, overtly or inadvertently, to either lose their virginity or "keep up" with their more sexually active peers. Students who seek out sexual contact at parties have been known to expect their peers to do likewise. This type of pressure from intimate people in their lives can be hard to resist. Other factors such as substance use may also affect student resolve.

Drug and alcohol use may be the largest predictor of risky sexual behaviors for both genders (Cooper, 2002; Turchik, Garske, Probst, & Irwin, 2010). The use of alcohol and other substances leads to weaker inhibitions, poorer decision making, and greater risk-taking behaviors (Turchik et al., 2010) such as casual sex, multiple sex partners, and unprotected sex. With the high level of binge drinking that occurs on college campuses each weekend, many college students are at high risk for negative repercussions of risky behaviors.

Unplanned Consequences of Sexual Activity

When two people are either relative strangers or otherwise do not feel a sense of caring toward one another, there is a decreased sense of responsibility. With casual sex or hook-ups between uninvested partners, there is an increased likelihood for unprotected sex, the transmission of sexually transmitted infections (STIs), and unintended pregnancies. And with the increased sense of sexual freedom among emerging adults, it makes sense that women between the ages of 18 and 24 exhibit the highest rate of unwanted pregnancies (Finer & Henshaw, 2006) and people aged 15 to 24 account for half the STIs in the United States. In a recent study, it was found that young adults are likely to dismiss the risk of unprotected sex, as if that happens only to other people (O'Sullivan, Udell, Montrose, Antoniello, & Hoffman, 2009).

Who Are the Sexual Risk Takers?

There are personality traits that have also been found to increase the likelihood of engagement in high-risk sexual behaviors. Men often feel pressure from their male friends to prove their sexual potency and success and then transfer that pressure to their female partners to "give in." In empirical research studies, men who exhibited higher extraversion and lower agreeableness were more likely to engage in sexually risky behaviors (Turchik et al., 2010), and it was also noted that men with low agreeableness were also more likely to cheat on their partners and have multiple sexual partners. With a lower level of agreeableness, these men seemingly lack concern for others and would be more likely to use persuasion to manipulate women into having sex. For women, higher sexual excitation and lower inhibition created greater risk taking, which was further heightened by increased substance use. Turchik et al. (2010) suggested that women who seek novel experiences, such as the altered states achieved through use of alcohol or drugs, may be more likely to experiment sexually as well. The level of conscientiousness in a college student is actually a better predictor of whether or not a condom is used during sex; in fact, Hagger-Johnson, Conner, O'Connor, and Shickle (2011) found this trait to be a better predictor of safe-sex behaviors than the absence of alcohol use. Thus, good habits instilled early may help college students make the choice to use contraception and make the effort to protect themselves against STIs.

Alcohol not only lowers inhibitions, but research shows that when alcohol is introduced into an event, the perceptions of the involved individuals' behaviors become more sexually tinged (Abbey, 2000). These perceptions may color expectations of both genders. Patrick and her colleagues' (2011) study brought into focus the "friendly agreements" that diverge based on gender. Women tend to develop understandings with their friends prior to partying in which they ask friends to help them stick to preset limits to avoid getting too drunk and engaging in sex or other sexually risky behaviors. Men, on the other hand, often form agreements with other men promoting the opposite; namely, agreements to get drunk and to pursue sexual conquests before an evening's end. This gives evidence that the societal double standard for sexual activity is still very much a part of our culture. Men are encouraged to plan for sexual encounters; women, on the other hand, usually plan to limit their sexual activities and behavior. Thus, for men, friendship goals emerged as a risk factor, while for women, they represented a protective factor.

Greeks and Athletes and Sexual Activity

Two specific campus groups are generally found to be more likely to display and respond to peer norms regarding sexual aggression and alcohol use; these are fraternity members and student-athletes (Adams-Curtis & Forbes, 2004; Humphrey & Kahn, 2000). With an emphasis on brotherhood and exclusivity, both groups enjoy the experience of being known by their bond. However, most likely due to the strong level of homophobia among males, their need to show their own affection toward one another is sublimated and expressed through strongly male-associated behaviors such as heavy drinking and sexual exploits. The greater the number of "conquests," the more manly—and revered—a member of the group will seem.

Greek-affiliated students do seem to engage in more at-risk behaviors, but many of the sex-related behaviors were found to be no different based on membership (Scott-Sheldon, Carey, & Carey, 2008). While Greek students are indeed more likely to use alcohol and smoke both tobacco and marijuana, they are also experiencing sex with a larger number of partners as well as engaging in sexual activity while under the influence of drugs or alcohol. Bartoli and Clark (2006) found that while Greek members endorse the consumption of alcohol in dating situations more so than non-Greeks, Greek men also have higher expectations of sexual intercourse occurring in a dating situation. However, education on taking steps to protect one's health crosses Greek lines—members are no less or more likely than non-Greeks to use condoms or have unprotected sex (Scott-Sheldon et al., 2008). Thus, those looking for opportunities to "party hard" might be more inclined to pursue membership in Greek organizations due to their tolerance and, frequently, encouragement of heavy alcohol use (Park, Sher, Wood, & Krull, 2009), but Greek membership does not predict taking chances with sexual health.

The Hook-Up

The belief that sexual activities are reserved for romantic partners is no longer relevant to college students or most high school students. Young adults of both genders engage in "hook-ups" in which sexual behavior is enjoyed between individuals who have no interest in developing a romantic relationship with one another. Although the behavior can range from kissing to intercourse, the overarching principle of these liaisons is that they provide a means to enjoy sexual gratification with no strings or expectations of a relationship being attached (Kelly, 2012). Although this topic is also addressed in the chapter on romantic relationships, it is important to recognize that this activity speaks to the greater freedom women now experience regarding sexual promiscuity. Though women may no longer be as tightly bound as generations past by a cultural double standard regarding sexuality, family culture may still play a strong role in a woman's level of comfort in exercising sexual freedom and choice. Counselors should be prepared to help these young women weigh their personal choices and beliefs against family perspectives and expectations if they experience confusion or distress at their behavioral choices. There may also be young men and women who feel pressured to engage in "hook-ups," but are still virgins or sexually inexperienced. These clients may need to fully explore their value systems, personal expectations, and sexuality within the safe space of the counseling office.

Making the Decision to Have Sex

Though many students have engaged in intercourse prior to college, ideally one would make a conscious decision to engage in intercourse with each partner. In fact, every sexual interaction, even kissing it could be argued, would be best considered as a conscious decision. Counselors working with students who wrestle with decisions to move further along the sexual continuum with others should encourage students to reflect on their motivation and their hesitance to do so. In session, it is helpful to encourage a student to process what is desired to happen in a relationship prior to deepening the level of sexual activity with a partner. Discussing potential levels of intimacy with the student, including examples of levels along the sexual continuum, will help the student gain an understanding of possible factors to consider.

Planning for Sexual Activities

Depending on the geographical location of the campus, the knowledge and access to contraception may vary. And although the counseling center is not the optimal site for providing this information, some counselors may need to provide impromptu "sex ed" briefings. Awareness of which safe-sex products are offered at which campus sites is essential knowledge for counselors to possess. In some schools, contraceptives are made available in very public places such as the student union, the library, or the cafeteria. Schools ahead of the curve are letting students order contraception online and be mailed to their campus boxes. By leaving students free to pick up the items they need without the embarrassment of having to request them or purchase them, the school is investing in their student body's health as well.

Assertiveness and Boundary Setting

Though sometimes students acknowledge their own lack of concern that relationships reach the highest degree of sexual intimacy, they do generally want a moderate degree of intimacy such as emotional and intellectual understanding of each other. Many students express a desire to meet their partners' needs or expectations and, in fact, researchers have found that as many as a third of college students in relationships will consent to sexual activities that they would prefer not to experience (O'Sullivan & Allgeier, 1998). When invited to share the reasons for allowing themselves to be engaged in unwanted sexual activity, responses focused on meeting their partners' needs, a desire to promote intimacy in the relationship, and to avoid tension in the relationship. The need to protect the relationship over protecting self-boundaries was clear.

Speaking Up

Counselors may be of great assistance to their clients by helping them develop and practice communication skills. Encouraging clients to explore their own preferences and ideal limits before they are tested or inhibitions lowered by alcohol or a persuasive partner can help them be stronger in their own "in-the-moment" limit setting. As noted earlier, many individuals who were found to be engaging in sex even while drinking still remembered to use condoms. Clients who have been able to explore and articulate their sexual boundaries with a counselor are also probably much more likely to honor them when faced with opportunities to break them. Our culture has promulgated the belief that "sometimes a woman's 'no' means 'yes,'" but by helping our students—both male and female—understand their right to create boundaries regarding their bodies, we are giving them transferable skills that may help them in many other aspects of their lives. Encouraging clients to speak to their partners about limits before being tested can prevent misunderstandings and foster necessary communication.

Counselors must be prepared to offer both information and relevant resources to these students. Young adults fluent in the digital means of communication may be most comfortable accessing information regarding sexual behavior and health issues on the Internet (Judson, Goldsack, & Sonnad, 2010). It is notable that even at schools in which great efforts were made to supply health information to their students, the resources are likely to be underused. When working with clients who are struggling with decisions related to sexual activity, it is essential that counselors stress safety and health as well as provide students with opportunities to explore and set personal boundaries and feel comfortable discussing sexual concerns within the counseling office.

SEXUAL EDUCATION

As of March 2012, only 21 states in America actually required public high schools to teach sex education (NCSL, 2012). As a result, many college students lack the critical knowledge necessary to safely navigate their way through what can be a time of extreme sexual awakening (King, 2012). This lack of information can lead to risky sexual behaviors and negative outcomes often affecting the rest of a person's life (Feigenbaum & Weinstein, 1995; Kirby, Lavis & Rolleri, 2007; Synovitz, Hebert, Carson, & Kelley, 2005). In one study, approximately half of the students reported that they were not adequately educated in subjects related to sex, even after enrolling in college. The specific deficits were noted in the areas of contraception, abortion, and sexual orientation in general (Synovitz et al., 2005).

Despite the lack of knowledge, the majority of colleges and universities do not require or even offer sexual education classes in their standard curricula; thus, most college students gain knowledge about sex through nonacademic means while enrolled at the university (Feigenbaum & Weinstein, 1995; Franklin & Dotger, 2011). Unfortunately, some students graduating at 22 years of age may still possess limited accurate sexual knowledge. Perhaps more troubling is the fact that although some students may have an increased knowledge of certain sexual topics, they frequently have difficulty seeing the connection between this knowledge and their own personal sexual risk-taking behaviors (Ratliff-Crain, Donald, & Dalton, 1999; Synovitz et al., 2005). Thus, counselors working with clients who bring in issues related to sexuality or romantic relationships may want to do a quick "check-in" regarding safe-sex knowledge and practices. Offering courses in human sexuality within the curricula as well as providing workshops, easy access to contraceptives, and confidential resources and referrals are all potentially successful methods for assisting students to attend to and maintain their sexual health.

RAPE, DATE RAPE, AND SEXUAL ASSAULT

According to the Sexual Victimization of College Women Report conducted by the United States Department of Justice in 2000, rape is the most common crime committed at United States colleges and universities. It reported that a college with 10,000 women may have as many as 350 rapes a year, but because less than 5% of rapes are reported to the police, experts consider this a conservative estimate. Experts have conducted many studies on the topic of rape among college students and it appeared that about 50% of college women reveal that they have been sexually assaulted at some time and more than 25% reported that they were victims of rape or attempted rape (Abbey, Zawacki, Buck, Clinton, & McAuslan, 2004). Rape is a word that often carries stereotypes of a man forcing himself sexually on a woman by threatening her with a weapon, but the crime of rape can take many other forms (Talbott, Neill, & Rankin, 2010). On college campuses, "date rape" is the type of sexual assault in which the victim has been in the company of the perpetrator prior to the assault (Fisher et al., 2000). Victims reported that their attackers are often acquaintances, classmates, intimate partners, or declared significant others (Angelone, Mitchell & Lucente, 2012; Fisher et al., 2000; Kimble, Neacsiu, Flack, & Horner 2008; Talbot et al., 2010).

CASE STUDY: ANGELA

Consider the case of Angela, a freshman at a large public university in the southeastern United States. Angela has been on one date with Tim, an upperclassman at the same university. Mutual friends had introduced the couple and so they had knowledge about each other's backgrounds. For their second date, they went to a local bar where Tim and Angela each consumed three alcoholic drinks.

After the date, Angela invited Tim back to her dorm where they began to kiss. Angela told Tim that she did not want to go further sexually, but Tim was persistent and they had sexual intercourse. Angela believed that Tim has violated her and, in essence, raped her. Because she had no visible marks of abuse or coercion, she felt as though she could not tell anyone about what has happened even though she felt strongly that Tim breached her communicated limit of acceptable sexual behavior. Angela began to feel strong feelings of social isolation because of her desire to avoid Tim, as they had a large group of mutual friends. Her strong sense of shame led to falling grades and symptoms of depression as she began spending more time alone and feeling that she had no one whom she could trust enough to reveal her experience. Angela felt unable to speak to the authorities about the incident because of the underage drinking in which she was engaged at the time of the sexual assault and she, therefore, felt partially responsible for what occurred.

Implications and Interpretations

As noted, only about 5% of rapes are reported. Often attributed to concerns about consequences of embarrassment or social isolation should the occurrence be reported (Cole, 2006; Fisher et al., 2000), studies provide evidence that these feelings are not unfounded. There are many factors that may affect the ways in which an alleged sexual assault or rape are perceived by college students. This includes who paid for the date, who invited whom into their home, or even the victim and perpetrator's styles of clothing (Angelone, Mitchell, & Lucente, 2012; Basow & Minieri, 2011; McMahon, 2010). In the case of Angela, she invited Tim back to her dorm room, which some college students would argue indicated that Angela was aware that some sort of sexual act would occur (Basow & Minieri, 2011; Talbot et al., 2010). However, many young women who have only recently begun to live away from home may lack the experience necessary to comprehend the potential threat of sexual pressure by a date. Younger and less sexually sophisticated students may lack knowledge about common expectations or sexual scenarios, as well as knowledge of how to respond appropriately to an unwanted sexual advance (King, 2012). This has been referred to as "the red zone," or "a period early in a female's first year at college during which she may be at a higher risk for unwanted sexual experiences" (Kimble, Neacsiu, Flack, & Horner, 2008, p. 331). Angela's shame may also stem from her inability to accept or admit this lack of education or in ability to protect herself sufficiently in such a situation. Counselors suspecting that a client may have been the victim of a sexual assault should assess for sexual abuse or trauma and maintain awareness of the difficulty victims might have in revealing these experiences. Patience and support are essential elements of creating an environment in which the client can open up about past trauma. While Angela may mistakenly believe she is potentially responsible for the assault, the college culture often promulgates this belief among both male and female students.

In one study, college students responded to a series of date rape scenarios in which various parts of the rape were changed (Basow & Minieri, 2011). More than their female counterparts, male students believed that if the date was expensive, then the woman on the date should expect that the man would insist on sexual intercourse. Furthermore, additional research must be conducted in order to learn more about this idea of "rape-accepting attitudes," most commonly reported by males who believe in traditional gender roles (Talbott et al., 2010). Even female college students see scenarios from different perspectives including sometimes failing to intervene in a situation that may appear harmful (McMahon, 2010).

Alcohol often plays a role in sexual assault and rape on college campuses in both the specifics of a sexual encounter and the perception of those external to the incident. In essence, the level of intoxication by the victim or the perpetrator greatly influences how an encounter is interpreted (Abbey et al., 2004; Angelone, Mitchell, & Lucente, 2012; Fisher et al., 2000). One of the most difficult challenges to investigating a date rape occurs when both parties are consuming alcohol, which is most often the case for college students (Abbey et al., 2004). Experts can have a difficult time discerning which individual's behaviors deviated from the norm when alcohol is involved. Many times, younger college students begin drinking at the start of freshman year and do not realize the effects that any quantity of alcohol may have on their actions and reactions (Fisher et al., 2000; Talbot et al., 2010). Angela is underage and therefore she may feel guilt for breaking a law or she may even believe that by breaking a law, she forfeits her right to report a rape (Cole, 2006). Though being careful not to further victimize Angela through blaming language, it may be empowering to help her determine aspects of the night that were within her control so that she does not have to feel completely out of control or fear future assaults. But a vital part of working with a victim of assault is to affirm that the behavior of her date was his responsibility, beyond her control.

Potential Campus Outreach Programming

More research is needed to determine the most effective types of programs in decreasing the number of sexual assaults and attempted assaults on campus. Traditionally, the focus has been on working with the victims or the perpetrators after the incident, but to address the problem, administrators and counselors may be able to team up to establish preventive programming and campus climate shifts. Some of the more frequently integrated program efforts include the Clothesline Project, an event in which a clothesline hung with shirts representing assault victims is hung in a public traffic zone on campus; the White Ribbon Campaign, which was begun by a group of men protesting violence against women and includes the dissemination of white ribbons to be worn; and the Purple Ribbon Project, which is a campaign protesting all types of violence against women and men. Incorporating education on what consent is and is not through orientation programming can occur. Research indicates that an opportunity to engage with the knowledge and its meaning is more beneficial than simple exposure to information. In a study by Rothman and Silverman (2007), first-year undergraduate students participated in a mandatory sexual assault prevention program with a two-pronged approach. First, students attended a seminar that focused on sexual issues, including sexual assault and preventing risky dating behavior, as part of their orientation programming. Upon the completion of this portion of the training, students worked in small groups for 2 hours to discuss current issues, potential scenarios, and myths about sexual behavior. After implementation, the prevalence of sexual assaults decreased across demographics, except for those people identified as having been victimized prior to the orientation.

Another, more cost- and time-effective program is bibiliotherapy (Yeater, Naugle, O'Donohue, & Bradley, 2004). This has taken the form of the distribution of self-help books to incoming female students. The books cover dating issues in general, with multiple chapters dedicated to the prevention of sexual assault, including tips on how to avoid risk-taking behaviors. Currently, studies about bibiliotherapy in this area have focused on women who report that it is a very useful and informative program, but again, researchers are unable to draw exact connections between the decrease in reported victimization and the use of the books. Books need to be adapted to various ethnicities, cultures, and sexual orientations in order to meet the needs of a diverse campus. Other programs aim to educate those who may be potential perpetrators of assault (Garrity, 2011). While this type of educational literature may show progress in areas such as debunking rape myths and educating men as to what constitutes sexual assault, it is difficult to gather analyzable or generalizable data. Tailoring a program to fit the needs of each college campus, while laborious, seems to be the best option. Campus climates can vary considerably, so counselors should be willing to develop programming based on their unique community.

SEXUAL ORIENTATION

Adolescents transitioning to college encounter a variety of new experiences socially, academically, and emotionally. Lesbian, gay, bisexual, and transgender (LGBT) college students have additional factors, their sexual identity and orientation, that can greatly influence their college experiences. Although statistics that pinpoint the prevalence of primary attraction to same-sex partners are impossible to calculate, Haas, Eliason, and Mays (2010) reviewed the literature and noted that approximately 3% of the population identifies as gay, lesbian, or bisexual. Data regarding the percentage of the population that is transgender are even harder to assess, but they noted that 0.2% of the population may identify as the opposite biological sex. It is essential that counselors recognize that transgendered individuals are not necessarily straight or gay; they may show either primary attraction to same-sex or opposite-sex partners. Due to the limited acceptance of anyone showing sex-related deviance from the straight majority, transgendered individuals are traditionally viewed as members of the lesbian, gay, and bisexual community.

For many, college is a time during which they strengthen or begin to develop their identity as LGBT. Therefore, counselors must be aware that in addition to the average stressors and nuances of college life, LGBT college students must also attempt to function in an environment that may be homophobic, heterosexist, or generally uneducated about minority sexual orientations (Stevens, 2004). Although there is a surprisingly significant amount of research concerning various aspects of LGBT life on college campuses, adequate sample sizes are often hard to obtain because of the hesitance of some students to identify themselves as LGBT (Longerbeam, Inkelas, Johnson, & Lee, 2007). Well-known theorists like Cass and D'Augelli might attribute this type of hesitance to the stage of identity formation that the students are navigating (1984, 1994). Because identified stages of development are not limited to any particular age group, an entering college freshman or a graduating college senior may be at the same point in the understanding and tolerance of his or her sexual orientation (Cass, 1984). Thus, counselors should be aware that sexual identity development is a process and that the trajectory varies from student to student.

Some students fail to identify themselves as having a nonheterosexual orientation based on the fear of how their classmates will receive the information. In a report funded by the National Gay and Lesbian Task Force Policy Institute, researchers found that approximately 74% of those surveyed considered their campus homophobic, and 60% surveyed said they concealed their orientation at some point in their college career in order to avoid discrimination (Rankin, 2003). However, depending on the campus culture and the proximity to family or active LGBT cultural centers, there is a great variability in a student's willingness to come out on campus. Concealing one's sexual orientation is difficult and taxing emotionally and physically (Sylva, Rieger, Linsenmeier, & Bailey, 2007). As mentioned previously, college stressors create an even larger "cognitive demand" than average life situations, and therefore those attempting to hide their sexual orientation tend to be unsuccessful in doing so, thus exposing their identity perhaps before they are ready (Sylva et al., 2007).

The amount of support or acceptance found on college campuses depends on demographics and geographical location, but even on campuses where there is a general sense of acceptance of LGBT individuals, students often are hesitant to show active support, such as speaking out publicly in favor of gay rights or student concerns (Jurgens, Schwitzer, & Middleton, 2004). Counselors should be aware that even on campuses with active Gay–Straight Alliances or other LGBT-related organizations, students may not experience peer relationships in the same way as their heterosexual counterparts. Research shows that as students progress through the years of college, they often consider themselves more accepting of those with different sexual orientations (Lambert, Ventura, Hall, & Cluse-Toler, 2006). Regardless of the degree of active heterosexual support, the campus climate is improved through education of the heterosexual students on campus (Evans & Herriott, 2004). No one is sure exactly how a shift to a more LGBT-friendly atmosphere occurs, although some believe this to be a result of interactions with LGBT self-identified faculty or students and others believe it may result through increased knowledge related to human sexuality and variance, perhaps through a course on this topic (Brown, Clarke, Gortmaker, & Robinson-Kelig, 2004; Lambert et al., 2006; Rogers, McRee, & Artiz, 2009). However, the most hostile time for a student may occur during his or her freshman year before peers have been exposed to either informal or formal education about sexual diversity and acceptance. Although in retrospective studies some students reported that their freshman year had actually presented little conflict attributed to their sexual identity, this has been hypothesized to be attributed more to students not having fully come out or fully identified as LGBT at that time (Brown et al., 2004).

SPECIFIC ISSUES PERTAINING TO THE LGBT COMMUNITY

Coming Out

The process through which an individual gains a sense of personal and public identity as gay, lesbian, or bisexual is called *coming out* and it has been viewed through many developmental stage theory lenses. The benchmark theory was developed by Cass (1984) approximately 3 decades ago, and although other theories have been developed to describe the more contemporary population's progress through identity development, the Cass model is still taught in many sexual education and multicultural theory classrooms. In brief, the coming-out process begins when an individual recognizes sexual attraction to same-sex individuals.

The individual may accept and integrate this aspect of identity into his or her overall self-identity and share this aspect of identity with family, friends, and others in the individual's social network. Others may compartmentalize this aspect of self and refrain from sharing their same-sex attraction with family or peers, living a double life in effect. Still others may choose to ignore their attraction to same-sex individuals and move through life choosing heterosexual or no romantic partners in an effort to live a more traditional and culturally acceptable life.

The decision to come out is a very personal choice and counselors are often the first individuals to learn of a client's minority sexual identity concerns or acknowledgment. Thus, it is essential that the campus counseling center be visibly open and supportive of their LGBT clients. Depending on a client's family demographic identity (ethnicity, faith, geographic location, etc.), the coming-out process may be first attempted once a student arrives on campus. While many students wrestling with sexual orientation identity feel a sense of freedom upon leaving their hometowns and their high school identities, others may continue to feel bound by family and social group expectations. For students who need support in their sexual identity development, counselors should be knowledgeable about their campus and community levels of acceptance and tolerance of diverse individuals. As noted, physical and psychological safety are often threatened for LGBT students and counselors should encourage students to take a realistic perspective on choosing those to whom they come out and on publicly displaying affection with same-gender partners.

Social Life

Depending on the campus climate, the social experience of LGBT students can vary widely. At a campus with an active LGBT student organization, there may be accompanying advocacy efforts that have created a welcoming and supportive environment for sexual minority students. Faculty and staff training also may be in place that educate heterosexual employees on ways to support and advocate for LGBT individuals. This training often provides knowledge as well as tangible evidence of the employees' support, such as decals for their office doors denoting their office as a "safe zone" or "LGBT-Ally space." These formal efforts to support these students can create a climate that provides a sense of safety. However, studies show that sexual minority students continue to face more sexual abuse than other students on campus (Porter & Williams, 2011). Helping students find a safe outlet for social activities and interaction with other LGBT students can be an important effort at helping these students gain social confidence and support. If counselors are at schools that sponsor LGBT organizations, they should make themselves aware of the resources offered by the group and build an alliance between the group and the counseling center personnel. If no organization exists, counselors may need to investigate the campus climate to determine if an "invisible network" exists for LGBT-identified faculty, staff, and students, or if they may need to spearhead efforts to establish an ally group. Being aware of the culture of the school and the local community will help the counselor develop a resource and referral list for local LGBT organizations. These may include everything from nightclubs to coffee shops to faith communities that are welcoming.

Alcohol and Substance Abuse

Alcohol and substance abuse runs rampant across most college and university campuses, and the LGBT community is certainly not immune to this trend. Many studies and surveys have indicated that LGB collegians are more likely to drink or use drugs than their heterosexual counterparts, as well as being more likely to have thoughts of suicide related to the use of illicit drugs (Reed, Prado, Matsumoto, & Amaro, 2010). However, other studies have suggested that there actually may be very little difference in the prevalence of alcohol or drugs among heterosexual, homoscxual, or bisexual men (Eisenberg & Wechsler, 2003; Ridner, Frost, & LaJoie, 2006). Clearly, there may be more factors at work in determining which particular group of LGB students is more likely to use substances than another group. Popular myth leads to alcohol use as a sign of depression or social isolation, but some studies show otherwise. Eisenberg and Wechsler (2003) conducted an extensive study that demonstrated that the presence of at least one strong LGB organization was directly related to the amount of binge drinking within that community. They concluded that the organization might have facilitated in the development of strong social ties, thus leading to an atmosphere that encouraged binge drinking, similar to stereotypical, primarily heterosexual, college organizations such as fraternities and sororities and athletic clubs. In regard to lesbian and bisexual women, studies show that this population is more likely to drink, smoke cigarettes, and smoke marijuana or use other drugs (Eisenberg & Weschler, 2003; Ridner et al., 2006). Counselors should exercise extreme caution when addressing drug and alcohol behavior among LGBT college students, making sure that they do not conclude that drinking or drug use is a *result* of one's sexual orientation. Many times, these students' behavior is no different from that of heterosexual college students and so, therefore, it should be addressed as such. When assessing substance use among clients or when concerns about substance abuse are present, counselors should follow the same method of assessment and intervention regardless of a client's sexual orientation.

Suicide

Research has long linked suicide attempts within the LGBT community, especially among the adolescent population. A recent exhaustive review of the literature indicated that while sexual identity is not linked to actual fatal suicide events, LGBT individuals are much more likely to attempt suicide than their heterosexual peers (Haas, Eliason, Mays, et al., 2011). Evidence shows that struggling with one's sexual identity in a hostile climate can have negative consequences on individuals (Lebson, 2002; Savin-Williams, 2001; Silverchanz, Cortina, Konik, & Magley, 2007). In another study that focused solely on women with same-sex attraction, or who were "questioning" their sexual orientation, about 15 of the 83 participants had admitted to attempting suicide more than once (Savin-Williams, 2001). When working with depressed students, regardless of sexual orientation, counselors assess for suicidal ideation. Being aware of the campus climate toward sexual minority individuals will allow a counselor to be more effective when working with depressed LGBT students. Understanding the relationship between social support and mental health should encourage counselors to advocate for campus acceptance of all students, regardless of sexual orientation.

While the needs and experiences of LGB college students continue to be the focus of studies, limited research exists on the experiences and needs of transgender college students. They seem to experience similar, if not more intense, discrimination than their LGB counterparts (Effrig, Bieschke, & Locke, 2011). In addition, research studies and campus organizations tend to combine transgender students' needs with those who identify as lesbian, gay, and bisexual when their needs may be distinctly different from those student communities (Dugan, Kusel, & Simounet, 2012). As noted previously, gay, lesbian, and bisexual students are different based on their affectional preference for same-sex partners. Transgendered students may identify strongly as heterosexual; however, their biological sex may be the same as their preferred partner's gender. Transgendered students may experience their first significant campus-based conflict if they choose on-campus housing and must be assigned a roommate of the same gender. The challenges may exponentially increase if they try to come out as the opposite sex while trying to maintain relationships under two different genders. Just as there are increasing levels of support of these students in public K-12 schools through such venues as locker room accommodations for gym class dress-outs, separate restrooms, and so forth, college may be a place of greater freedom for gender self-expression. As support for transgendered individuals continues to grow nationwide, as evidenced in the increasing insurance coverage of sex reassignment surgeries, college campuses should also find ways to help transgender individuals feel welcome. This may involve dormitory reassignment, locker room variances, and inclusiveness in sexual discrimination policies.

CONCLUSION

Young adulthood is a time in which freedom is increasingly given, and for many college students, this is perceived to include sexual freedom, both in terms of exploration and identification. It is vital that college counseling centers provide relevant, accessible information and materials, as well as helpful referrals, for specialized information regarding safe sex, contraception, and sexual health.

RESOURCES

Some suggested resources are listed below:

- "It's Your Life: Get Yourself Tested": www.itsyoursexlife.com/gyt/?utm_source=gytnow
  This website is sponsored by MTV and it provides candid information on STIs and sexual health.
- STI Risk Assessment Too: uhs.berkeley.edu/students/pdf/Patient%20Self-assessment.pdf
  Provides an assessment for students to determine their risk for developing STIs.
- Planned Parenthood: www.plannedparenthood.org
  Information on safer sex, birth control, emergency contraception, STIs, sexuality, and more.
- American Social Health Association: www.ashastd.org
  Fast facts and helpful information on STIs, including HIV/AIDS.
- Go Ask Alice: goaskalice.columbia.edu
  Nonjudgmental Q&A website for college students on topics including sexual health, sexuality, relationships, and much more (affiliated with Columbia University).
- Alternatives to Sex: Outercourse
  Information about "outercourse" options for sexual activity, for people who choose not to have sexual intercourse (affiliated with Planned Parenthood).
- Youth Resource: www.youthresource.com
  A website by and for gay, lesbian, bisexual, transgender, and questioning young people, with a focus on sexual health and other issues.

- Sexuality Information and Education Council of the United States: www. siecus.org
    Advocacy for accurate sexual health information, comprehensive sex education, and public policy.
- National Sexual Violence Resource Center: www.nsvrc.org
    Offers a variety of resources and advocacy information related to sexual violence.

REFERENCES

Abbey, A. (2000). Alcohol's effects on sexual perception. *Journal of Studies on Alcohol, 61,* 688–697.

Abbey, A., Zawacki, T., Buck, P., Clinton, A. M., & McAuslan, P. (2004). Sexual assault and alcohol consumption: What do we know about their relationship and what types of research are still needed? *Aggression and Violent Behavior, 9,* 271–303.

Abma, J. C., et al. (2010). Teenagers in the United States: Sexual activity, contraceptive use, and childbearing. National Survey of Family Growth 2006–2008. *Vital and Health Statistics,* Series 23, No. 30.

Adams-Curtis, L. E., & Forbes, G. B. (2004). College women's experiences of sexual coercion: A review of cultural, perpetrator, victim, and situational variables. *Trauma Violence Abuse, 5,* 91–122.

Angelone, D. J., Mitchell, D., & Lucente, L. (2012). Predicting perceptions of date rape: An examination of perpetrator motivation, relationship length, and gender role beliefs. *Journal of Interpersonal Violence, 27*(13), 2582–2602.

Bartoli, A. M., & Clark, M. D. (2006). The dating game: Similarities and differences in dating scripts among college students. *Sexuality & Culture, 10,* 54–80.

Basow, S., & Minieri, A. (2011). "You owe me": Effects of date cost, who pays, participant gender, and rape myth beliefs on perceptions of rape. *Journal of Interpersonal Violence, 26*(3), 479–497. doi: 10.1177/0886260510363421

Brown, R. D., Clarke, B., Gortmaker, V., & Robinson-Kelig, R. (2004). Assessing the campus climate for gay, lesbian, bisexual, and transgender (GLBT) students using a multiple perspective approach. *Journal of College Student Development, 45,* 8–26.

Cass, V. C. (1984). Homosexuality identity formation: Testing a theoretical model. *Journal of Sex Research, 20,* 143–167.

Cole, T. B. (2006). Rape at US colleges often fueled by alcohol. *The Journal of the American Medical Association, 296,* 504–505.

Cooper, M. (2002). Alcohol use and risky sexual behavior among college students and youth: Evaluating the evidence. *Journal of Studies on Alcohol,* Suppl. 14, 101–117.

Dugan, J. P., Kusel, M. L., & Simounet, D. M. (2012). Transgender college students: An exploratory study of perceptions, engagement, and educational outcomes. *Journal of College Student Development, 53*(5), 719–736.

Effrig, J. C., Bieschke, K. J., & Locke, B. D. (2011). Examining victimization and psychological distress in transgender college students. *Journal of College Counseling, 14*(2), 143–157.

Eisenberg, M. E., & Wechsler, H. (2003). Social influences on substance-use behaviors of gay, lesbian, and bisexual college students: Findings from a national study. *Social Science and Medicine, 57*(10), 1913–1923.

Evans, N. J., & Herriott, T. K. (2004). Freshmen impressions: How investigating the campus climate for LGBT students affected four freshmen. *Journal of College Student Development, 45*(3), 316–332.

Feigenbaum, R., & Weinstein, E. (1995). College students' sexual attitudes and behaviors: Implications for sexuality education. *Journal of American College Health, 44*(3), 112–119.

Finer, L., & Henshaw, S. (2006). Disparities in rates of unintended pregnancy in the United States, 1994 and 2001. *Perspectives on Sexual and Reproductive Health, 38*, 90–96.

Fisher, B., Cullen, F., & Turner, M. (2000). *The sexual victimization of college women.* Washington, DC: National Institute of Justice.

Franklin, R., & Dotger, S. (2011). Sex education knowledge differences between freshmen and senior college undergraduates. *College Student Journal, 45*(1), 199–214.

Garrity, S. E. (2011). Sexual assault prevention programs for college-aged men: A critical evaluation. *Forensic Nursing, 7*, 140–148.

Haas, A. P., Eliason, M., Mays, V. M., ... Clayton, P. J. (2010). Suicide and suicide risk in lesbian, gay, bisexual, and transgender populations: Review and recommendations. *Journal of Homosexuality, 58*, 10–51.

Hagger-Johnson, G., Bewick, B. M., Conner, M., O'Connor, D. B., & Shickle, D. (2011). Alcohol, conscientiousness and event-level condom use. *British Journal of Health Psychology, 16*, 828–845.

Humphrey, S. E., & Kahn, A. S. (2000). Fraternities, athletic teams, and rape: Importance of identification with a risky group. *Journal of Interpersonal Violence, 29*, 417–425.

Judson, K., Goldsack, J., & Sonnad, S. S. (2010). Availability of e-information for women's health services: Assessment of California State University student health centers. *Journal of Women's Health, 19*(12), 2219–2225.

Jurgens, J. C., Schwitzer, A. M., & Middleton, T. (2004). Examining attitudes toward college students with minority sexual orientations: Findings and suggestions. *Journal of College Student Psychotherapy, 19*(1), 57–75.

Kelly, C. (2012). Feminist ethics evaluating the hookup culture. *Journal of Feminist Studies in Religion, 28*, 27–48.

Kimble, M., Neacsiu, A. D., Flack, W. F., & Horner, J. (2008). Risk of unwanted sex for college women. *Journal of American College Health, 57*(3), 331–339.

King, B. M. (2012). The need for school-based comprehensive sexuality education: Some reflections after 32 years teaching sexuality to college students. *American Journal of Sexuality Education, 7*, 181–186.

Lambert, E., Ventura, L. A., Hall, D. E., & Cluse-Tolar, T. (2006). College students' views on gay and lesbian issues: Does education make a difference. *Journal of Homosexuality, 50*(4), 1–31.

Lebson, M. (2002). Suicide among homosexual youth. *Journal of Homosexuality, 42*(4), 107–118.

Longerbeam, S. D., Inkelas, K. K., Johnson, D. R., & Lee, Z. S. (2007). Lesbian, gay, and bisexual college student experiences: An exploratory study. *Journal of College Student Development, 48*(2), 215–230.

McMahon, S. (2010). Rape myth beliefs and bystander attitudes among incoming college students. *Journal of American College Health, 59*, 3–11.

O'Sullivan, L. F., & Allgeier, E. R. (1998). Feigning sexual desire: Consenting to unwanted sexual activity in heterosexual dating relationships. *Journal of Sex Research, 35*, 234–243.

O'Sullivan, L. F., Udell, W., Montrose, V. A., Antoniello, P., & Hoffman, S. (2009). A cognitive analysis of college students' explanations for engaging in unprotected sexual intercourse. *Archives of Sexual Behavior, 39*, 1121–1131.

Owen, J. J., Rhoades, G. K., Stanley, S. M., & Fincham, F. D. (2010). "Hooking up" among college students: Demographic and psychosocial correlates. *Archives of Sexual Behavior, 39*(3), 653–663. doi: 10.1007/s10508-008-9414-1

Park, A., Sher, K. J., Wood, P. K., & Krull, J. L. (2009). Dual mechanisms underlying accentuation of risky drinking via fraternity/sorority affiliation: The role of personality, peer norms, and alcohol availability. *Journal of Abnormal Psychology, 118*, 241–255.

Patrick, M. E., Morgan, N., Maggs, J. L., & Lefkowitz, E. S. (2011). "I got your back": Friends' understandings regarding college student spring break behavior. *Journal of Youth Adolescence, 40*, 108–120.

Porter, J., & Williams, L. M. (2011). Intimate violence among underrepresented groups on a college campus. *Journal of Interpersonal Violence, 26*, 3210–3224.

Rankin, S. R. (2003). *Campus climate for gay, lesbian, bisexual, and transgender people: A national perspective.* New York, NY: The National Gay and Lesbian Task Force Policy Institute.

Reed, E., Prado, G., Matsumoto, A., & Amaro, H. (2010). Alcohol and drug use and related consequences among gay, lesbian and bisexual college students: Role of experiencing violence, feeling safe on campus, and perceived stress. *Addictive Behaviors, 35*, 168–171.

Ridner, S. L., Frost, K., & LaJoie, A. S. (2006). Health information and risk behaviors among lesbian, gay, and bisexual college students. *Journal of the American Academy of Nurse Practitioners, 18*(8), 374–378.

Rogers, A., McRee, N., & Artiz, D. L. (2009) Using a college human sexuality course to combat homophobia. *Sex Education, 9*(3), 211–225.

Rothman, E., & Silverman, J. (2007). The effect of a college sexual assault prevention program on first-year students' victimization rates. *Journal of American College Health, 55*(5), 283–290.

Savin-Williams, R. C. (2001). Suicide attempts among sexual-minority youths: Population and measurement issues. *Journal of Consulting and Clinical Psychology, 69*(6), 983–991.

Scott-Sheldon, L. A. J., Carey, K. B., & Carey, M. P. (2008). Health behavior and college students: Does Greek affiliation matter? *Journal of Behavioral Medicine, 31*, 61–70.

Stevens, Jr., R. A. (2004). Understanding gay identity development within the college environment. *Journal of College Student Development, 45*(2), 185–206.

Sylva, D., Rieger, G., Linsenmeier, J. A. W., & Bailey, J. M. (2007). Concealment of sexual orientation. *Archives of Sexual Behavior, 39*, 141–152. doi: 10.1007/s10508-008-9466-2

Synovitz, L., Hebert, E., Carson, G., & Kelley, R. M. (2005). College students sexuality education, sexual behaviors and sexual behavior intent. *American Journal of Health Studies, 20*(2), 47–58.

Talbot, K. K., Neill, K. S., & Rankin, L. L. (2010). Rape-accepting attitudes of university undergraduate students. *Journal of Forensic Nursing, 6*(4), 170–179.

Trotter, E. C., & Alderson, K. G. (2007). University students' definitions of having sex, sexual partner, and virginity loss: The influence of participant gender, sexual experience, and contextual factors. *The Canadian Journal of Human Sexuality, 16*(1–2), 11–29.

Turchik, J. A., Garske, J. P., Probst, D. R., & Irwin, C. R. (2010). Personality, sexuality, and substance use as predictors of sexual risk taking in college students. *Journal of Sex Research, 47*(5), 411–419.

Yeater, E. A., Naugle, A. E., O'Donohue, W., & Bradley, A. R. (2004). Sexual assault prevention with college-aged women: A bibiliotherapy approach. *Violence and Victims, 19*(5), 593–611.

11

Understanding and Treating Eating Disorders With College Students

CAROLINE S. BOOTH AND GREGORY S. PHIPPS

Traditionally, college is a time of personal exploration, growth, and learning. Developmental theorists have long recognized the importance of the late-adolescent and early-adulthood periods as ones of identity development (Erikson, 1950; Huebner et al., 2006), separation-individuation (Barth, 2003), and role exploration (Erikson, 1950). This time frame can also be one of significant psychological distress with many disorders first diagnosed during these years (Carolan, Bak, Hoppe-Rooney, & Burns-Jager, 2010). College counseling centers are frequently called upon to assist students with issues ranging from developmental transition to active psychosis, but many believe that the college experience is particularly ideal for the development of eating disorders (Barth, 2003; Carolan et al., 2010).

An eating disorder is defined as an "illness that causes serious disturbance to your everyday diet" (National Institute of Mental Health [NIMH], 2011, p. 1) and these disorders are among some of the most pervasive and difficult to treat (Huebner et al., 2006). It is estimated that college students present with some of the highest prevalence rates of eating disorders (Blackmer, Searight, & Ratwick, 2011) and college counseling centers have to respond to this need. Making this task more complicated is the fact that eating disorders frequently develop in conjunction with other disorders such as depression or substance abuse (NIMH, 2011). In addition, the contemporary 21st-century campus is now filled with students from varying backgrounds, ages, and cultural beliefs who are presenting with unique eating disorder expressions (Krentz & Arthur, 2001).

This chapter discusses the issue of eating disorders on college campuses, including anorexia nervosa, bulimia nervosa, binge eating disorder, and other nonspecified eating disorders. Each section includes a thorough description of presenting symptoms, diagnostic criteria, and treatment protocols, while highlighting how the eating disorder frequently manifests. Finally, multicultural implications and best practices for assessment and prevention are shared.

PREVALENCE AND HISTORY

The National Eating Disorders Association (n.d.) reports that the incidence of new cases of eating disorders has been steadily increasing since 1950. The origin of this rise is frequently mentioned as the societal change in ideal body image that has substantially *decreased* for women and *increased* for men, with thinness and physical fitness as the current societal ideals (Hoyt & Ross, 2003; Nelson, Castonguay, & Locke, 2011). This phenomenon is explained in the sociocultural model of eating disorders that states that cultural standards of thinness are internalized resulting in body dissatisfaction and dysfunctional eating behaviors (Striegel-Moore, Silberstein, & Rodin, 1986). Nowhere is this phenomenon more apparent than on college campuses, where eating disorders and disturbed eating behaviors and attitudes are prevalent due to a social environment that emphasizes physical attractiveness and the acute influence of the peer group (Hoyt & Ross, 2003; Zalta & Keel, 2006). However, while these social pressures can be very strong, not all college students will experience an eating pathology given that the development of eating disorders is a complex and multidimensional process with individual, familial, social, and biological risk factors (Cashel, Cunningham, Landeros, Cokley, & Muhammad, 2003).

Disproportionately diagnosed in females, it is believed that 7% to 10% of female college students meet diagnostic criteria for eating disorders (Blackmer et al., 2011). It is also known that certain populations of college students, such as student-athletes, are at higher risk (Hoyt & Ross, 2003), with some estimating up to 32% of female college athletes displaying pathological eating behaviors (Rosen, McKeag, Hough, & Curley, 1986). Estimates on male college students are more difficult to ascertain but it is believed that males comprise approximately 10% of the eating disorder population (Feltman & Ferraro, 2011). Exact numbers of those suffering from eating disorders on college campuses are not known because most research data rely on self-report questionnaires, generalizations from limited research samples, and data extrapolation (Gonzalez, Huerta-Sanchez, Ortiz-Nieves, Vazquez-Alvarez, & Kribs-Zaleta, 2003).

First introduced in the *Diagnostic and Statistical Manual of Mental Disorders,* third edition (*DSM-III*) (American Psychiatric Association [APA], 1980), many believe that eating disorders exist along a continuum rather than in discrete categories (Herzog & Delinsky, 2002; Yost & Smith, 2012). This continuum can best be visualized by thinking about eating in terms of restriction to excess with normal eating behaviors in the middle. This continuum is also useful because the literature frequently categorizes eating disorders as clinical (meeting *DSM* diagnostic criteria) or subclinical (falling short of *DSM* diagnostic criteria). Subclinical eating disorder behaviors are important because they are frequently precursors to more extreme behaviors. Although understudied, research has identified disordered eating (e.g., obsessive monitoring of calories, loss of appetite control, unhealthy weight fluctuations, etc.) estimates from 20% (Blackmer et al., 2011) to 86% (Cashel et al., 2003; Hoyt & Ross, 2003) of college women and 10% of college men (Blackmer et al., 2011). Another point to consider is that eating disorders describe not only eating behaviors, as the name implies, but supplementary or compensatory behaviors designed to manipulate food intake and weight, including purging, exercising, or the use of laxatives. There can be a progression of the eating disorder and compensatory behaviors but also a change and evolution from one diagnostic category to another. Because of this and the pervasive course of these disorders, it is helpful to have a thorough understanding of how each specific eating disorder may manifest in college populations.

ANOREXIA NERVOSA

Anorexia nervosa is characterized by the relentless pursuit of weight loss and thinness (Attia & Walsh, 2009). This disorder is accompanied by body distortion whereby the client perceives him- or herself as overweight despite data or observations to the contrary. To achieve and maintain low weight, sufferers usually severely restrict their eating and may resort to purging tactics such as vomiting or laxatives to further reduce their caloric intake (Attia & Walsh, 2009). These behaviors often place the body in medical starvation, which can lead to comorbid diagnoses such as depression and insomnia and other dysfunctional behaviors such as the development of bizarre food rituals like eating foods in a predetermined order. These food rituals serve to decrease anxiety related to eating, similar to rituals associated with obsessive-compulsive disorder (Steinglass et al., 2012).

Currently, the *DSM-5* (APA, 2013) outlines three diagnostic criteria for anorexia nervosa. The first is a lower than normal body weight in regards to various factors such as age, development, sex, and health, due to the restricting of food or energy intake. The second criterion is an intense fear of gaining weight even though the individual is underweight. The third criterion is a disturbance in the way one perceives body weight, a denial of the seriousness of low weight, or overemphasis on body weight as a measure of self-worth. In the *DSM-IV-TR*

(APA, 2000a), the final criterion included amenorrhea or absence of at least three consecutive menstrual cycles. This criterion was removed from the *DSM-5* (APA, 2013) because it is now known that anorexia *can* exist in the presence of normal menses and menarchal women are not the only ones susceptible to this disorder. Finally, there are two subtypes of anorexia classified by behaviors experienced in the current episode. The first is the restricting type, which is characterized by only restrictive eating, while the binge eating/purging type is characterized by instances of binging or purging behavior.

The *DSM-5* made subtle changes to the anorexia diagnosis including modification to diagnostic wording and clarification to existing diagnostic criteria (e.g., significantly low weight). Finally, it should be noted that the *DSM-5* includes a new diagnostic category for nonanorexic restrictive eating. This category is named Avoidant/Restrictive Food Intake Disorder and is characterized by feeding and nutritional disturbances motivated by the sensory qualities of food, concern about the aversive consequences of food, or lack of interest in food. This diagnosis was formerly known as childhood feeding disorder and is separate from anorexia but shares restrictive eating as a hallmark. No longer restricted to just children and adolescents, this new diagnosis is expected to be used primarily with children and adolescents, but the diagnosis is not exclusive to this population.

As previously mentioned, the hallmark of anorexia is the relentless pursuit of thinness accompanied by distorted self-image related to body weight. The attainment of the thin ideal becomes all-consuming and these individuals can seek support and validation through the notion that they are making a lifestyle choice rather than experiencing a psychological disorder (Bardone-Cone & Cass, 2007). While the causes of anorexia are believed to be multifactorial, it has been shown that exposure to media images of thin-ideal beauty seems to increase body dissatisfaction and the pressure to be thin, which can spark disordered eating (Bardone-Cone & Cass, 2007). In recent decades, the internet has served as a supportive place for pro-anorexia or "pro-ana" individuals to share stories, photos, and "thinspiration" through websites that glamorize extreme and unhealthy thinness. Unfortunately, on college campuses, it is estimated that *most* women are affected to some degree by body image issues and a concern for thinness, suggesting an environmental risk is inherent in these settings (Murray, 2003).

Treatment

Anorexia is known to have a high mortality rate. Attia and Walsh (2009) estimated that 5.6% of sufferers will die per decade of illness, which is noted to be as high as any psychological disorder. Other medical complications include cardiac arrhythmia, renal failure, and hair loss (Attia & Walsh, 2009). According to the APA (2006) eating disorder practice guidelines, many individuals with severe forms of anorexia nervosa require residential or inpatient treatment, particularly if their weight loss has been rapid or the individual is less than 75% of their ideal body weight (Attia & Walsh, 2009). This level of treatment is necessary to restore health and manage presenting medical concerns. This inpatient treatment is very costly with one study identifying a mean stay of 18 days and a mean cost of $10,019 (Attia & Walsh, 2009). While college counseling centers would not provide this type of emergency care, it is necessary to have inpatient and residential care referral sources for students who do require this treatment.

In addition to being costly, treatment of anorexia is also known to be difficult (Steinglass et al., 2012). The secretive nature of the disorder (Hoyt & Ross, 2003) and the comorbid medical concerns that accompany severe forms, such as heart and kidney failure, reproductive problems, and electrolyte imbalances (Nelson et al., 2011), can create complications for the practitioner. Anorexia is also known to have high comorbidity with other psychological disorders, such as depression, anxiety, and obsessive-compulsive disorder (Murray, 2003). Even though therapy is a recommended component of care for less severe forms of anorexia, some college counseling centers may not have the treatment team resources (i.e., medical doctor, nutritionist) that can effectively monitor and treat these individuals without referral to outside practitioners (Huebner et al., 2006). Referral may also be warranted if students do not consent to participate in all aspects of the treatment, since coordination of services by the counselor is necessary to guarantee the health and well-being of the client. In these instances, counseling center staff facilitates this transition to outside practitioners and provides support as needed.

A common treatment modality for anorexia nervosa is family counseling (e.g., the Minuchin, Maudsley Model), which has been proven to be efficacious, particularly with younger adolescents (Keel & Haedt, 2008). These family approaches target rigid system boundaries and family rules that emphasize perfectionism and appearance (Carolan et al., 2010). Family treatment can also uncover generational influences that support the development and progression of anorexia (Murray, 2003). While family treatment is effective, older adolescents and adults may benefit more from cognitive-behavioral approaches (Keel & Haedt, 2008), which can be implemented more easily on a college campus where students are often geographically separated from their families.

Cognitive-behavioral therapy (CBT) approaches are generally recognized as the first treatment choice for all eating disorders (Albers, 2011). Individuals with anorexia are known to present with emotional awareness and regulation difficulties (Albers, 2011). A distorted sense of perfectionism and body image are also hallmarks of this disorder, which can result in a general resistance to even acknowledging the behaviors as dysfunctional (Murray, 2003). This perfectionism also leads anorexia sufferers to want to please and achieve. Anorexics also fear being out of control, which pushes them toward restrictive eating behaviors to increase their perceived self-control and decrease feelings of powerlessness (Murray, 2003). Because of these disordered cognitions and perceptions, cognitive-behavioral approaches can target each of these areas (Murray, 2003). Other areas of intervention can target mindful eating, which introduces intentionality, self-awareness, and acceptance (Albers, 2011). Decreasing anxiety associated with food is also a treatment goal whereby fear related to eating is decreased (Steinglass et al., 2012).

Other treatment approaches include a feminist paradigm, which offers treatment that emphasizes a focus on gender-based power and control. Using an egalitarian stance, a feminist approach seeks to address a woman's societally driven fragmented sense of self and integrate these parts into self-acceptance (Carolan et al., 2010). Other approaches showing efficacy through clinical trials include eye movement desensitization and reprocessing (EMDR), motivational interviewing, and dialectical behavioral therapy (DBT), particularly when these are used in conjunction with CBT or another therapeutic approach (Yager et al., 2012).

It is important to keep in mind that each person's manifestation of this disorder and comorbid issues is unique so treatment often has to be individualized (Schaffner & Buchanan, 2010). Many advocate for an integrated treatment approach that targets the individual as a whole rather than as a collection of eating disorder symptomatology (Huebner et al., 2006). Treatment can be supplemented by participation in groups that serve to ease the stigma of the disorder, improve communication skills, and decrease feelings of isolation (Huebner et al., 2006).

Regardless of the treatment approach, anorexia nervosa is difficult to treat. Those with a more recent, versus chronic, diagnosis are believed to have better outcomes. In many instances, participants will discontinue treatment or experience a relapse (Albers, 2011). Since relapse often requires hospitalization, close monitoring of those presenting with anorexic symptomatology is recommended. While there are evidence-based treatment practices, there is also a continued need for more research to highlight best practices for counselors (Steinglass et al., 2012).

BULIMIA NERVOSA

Bulimia nervosa is characterized by an obsession to be thin and a general fear of obesity. Bulimia nervosa, sometimes called bulimia, consists of episodic binge eating combined with inappropriate strategies to prevent weight gain, such as vomiting, diuretic use, or excessive exercising (Fernandez, Malacrne, Wilfley, & McQuaid, 2006). These compensatory behaviors are accompanied by a loss of control, depressed mood, and self-loathing (Pyle, Halvorson, Neuman, & Mitchell, 1986). The period of late adolescence and early adulthood is the peak time for development of bulimia nervosa (Keel, Gravener, Joiner, & Haedt, 2010) with estimates that 2% to 20% of college women meet the diagnostic criteria (Fernandez et al., 2006; Gonzalez et al., 2003). Although similar to anorexia nervosa, sufferers of bulimia typically retain a more normative body weight and experience less regimented dietary control than sufferers of anorexia (Gonzalez et al., 2003). As such, bulimics are more likely to be able to mask their disorder. These individuals also tend to have unique physical side effects including damage to dental enamel, broken blood vessels in the eyes, and other damage to the digestive tract, as well more extreme damage that can include heart and kidney failure (O'Riordan & Zamboanga, 2008). More severe cases can involve excessive shame and food compulsions to the point of stealing food, "scavenging leftovers," or eating from trash cans (Gonzalez et al., 2003). In many instances, bulimia can emerge from binge eating disorder with the onset of purging happening approximately 1 year after the onset of binging (Gonzalez et al., 2003).

The *DSM-5* (APA, 2013) characterizes bulimia as recurrent episodes of binge eating with a sense of loss of control accompanied by compensatory behavior to prevent weight gain. These compensatory behaviors can include induced vomiting, overuse of laxatives, diuretics, enemas, and other medications, or instances of fasting or excessive exercise. Episodes are marked by eating a larger amount of food than most individuals would eat in a particular period of time. These binge and purge episodes must occur at least once a week for 3 months and occur independently of any anorexia nervosa episode. Finally, there is also a marked preoccupation with body shape and weight. Similar to anorexia, there are two subtype distinctions for this disorder. The purging type is characterized by misuse of laxatives, diuretics, or enemas or self-induced vomiting, while the nonpurging type is characterized by other compensatory behaviors such as fasting or excessive exercise.

The process of bulimia is best described by Fairburn (2008) who described how the disorder often evolves from a cognitive-behavioral perspective. He states that it often begins with an internalization of the unrealistically thin and fit ideal prevalent in Western cultures. This is combined with an overemphasis on the importance of appearance as a measure of self-worth. Attempts to reach this unattainable standard stimulate a chronic dieting cycle to control weight and change shape. Over time, these constant eating transitions and acute periods of stress can trigger a binging episode, which can then stimulate a purging episode to compensate for the binge.

The resultant sense of failure reinforces the low self-worth and can create an episodic repeat of the previous behaviors, which now serve as emotional regulators to moderate negative mood states. Ironically, what began as an attempt to improve self-worth ends up actually decreasing it and causing the sufferer to experience shame and feeling out of control.

Treatment

Bulimia nervosa is known to be a long-standing illness (Keel et al., 2010). Without treatment, up to 20% of bulimia and anorexia sufferers will die (Gonzalez et al., 2003). With treatment, this number improves to 2% to 3%. Unfortunately, the secretive nature of bulimia makes the disorder more difficult to treat. This, coupled with the cost of treatment programs (up to $24,000 per month for inpatient treatment), makes recovery more difficult. One study that looked at bulimia found that 50% of women were in remission after 10 years and 25% of women were in remission after 20 years (Keel et al., 2010), reiterating the long-term nature of this disorder.

Similar to anorexia, bulimia nervosa is frequently treated in younger adolescents with a family therapy approach (Keel & Haedt, 2008). However, for older adolescents and adults, individualized CBT is most frequently used to treat bulimia (Fairburn, 2008; Safer, Telch, & Agras, 2001). This approach targets restrictive eating behaviors and cognitions related to weight and body image (Gonzalez et al., 2003). Techniques such as structured eating routines, food diaries, weighing, and cognitive restructuring are frequently cited in the CBT research (Waller, Stringer, & Meyer, 2012). This treatment is often highly individualized based on the client's unique bulimic presentation. The goal of treatment is to target the individual's beliefs related to disordered eating and self-image and create a sense of self-control (Carolan et al., 2010).

However, despite the known efficacy of CBT with bulimia, success rates are frequently reported at 50%, indicating that other treatments may also need to be considered (Safer et al., 2001). Frequently cited as a shortcoming of this approach is the lack of sufficient clinical attention to the emotional dysregulation aspects of this disorder that often serve to trigger the binging episodes (Federici, Wisniewski, & Ben-Porath, 2012). To meet this need, DBT has been used to help clients learn about how they may be using food as a way to achieve emotional regulation. Clients work to identify their personal behavioral chain that begins with emotional arousal and concludes with disordered eating and purging behavior. Sufferers are taught mindfulness related to emotions and eating, as well as "distress tolerance skills" to help with emotional management (Safer et al., 2001). This approach may be particularly useful when working with clients who have a history of treatment failure or comorbid diagnoses (Federici et al.,

2012). In addition, these DBT skills have been shown to be effective when used in both individual or group formats (Federici et al., 2012). Other models that have been implemented include an affect regulation model that seeks to regulate the emotional "out of control" feeling that precedes many binge and purge episodes (Safer et al., 2001), as well as feminist approaches that address body image and integration of self as a strategy for recovery (Carolan et al., 2010). Other considerations when addressing bulimia include an awareness of the comorbidity of substance use disorders in this population with as many as 50% of bulimics presenting with alcohol abuse disorders (Carbaugh & Sias, 2010).

It should also be noted that more severe cases of bulimia may require hospitalization or residential care. In serious to moderate cases, coordination with a medical doctor and nutritionist should be a part of the treatment protocol. If counseling center resources cannot support this format or the client does not consent to this coordination of services, then external providers may need to be utilized (Huebner et al., 2006). Part of the recommended counseling center treatment model also includes participation in group counseling to increase support and decrease shame associated with the disorder.

COMPULSIVE OVEREATING OR BINGE EATING DISORDER

Although overeating is known to be a serious problem in the 21st century for Americans, less emphasis has been placed on the psychological components of these disorders. Advances in genetic and neuroscience research are bringing new attention to this prevalent issue, as is the declaration that overeating is frequently comorbid with obesity, now recognized as a global health epidemic (World Health Organization, 2003). Some estimates place two thirds of the adult population in America as either overweight or obese with overeating or the overconsumption of calories as the main cause (Kozak & Fought, 2011). However, not all who overeat do so consistently or to the point of psychological distress. While overeating will undoubtedly occur in everyone's life at some point, certain individuals seem to develop a compulsion to overeat that becomes distressing and excessively driven (Davis & Carter, 2009). This compulsive overeating behavior is also known as binge eating disorder.

Compulsive overeating can be motivated by pleasure from food (hedonic), emotional eating (coping), or an episodic desire to binge (Zai et al., 2011). Fully understanding these motivations requires a basic understanding of the neuropsychological process of food and the resultant evolution of personal eating behaviors. Foods, particularly those high in sugar, fat, and salt, are known to induce a chemical response (dopamine) in the consumer that reinforces an unhealthy overeating behavior (Davis et al., 2011). This means that a part of the physical process of consuming food is a chemical response cycle that rewards the eater with feelings of pleasure and well-being. Many researchers believe that this process is well described as a "food addiction" (Davis & Carter, 2009) and some have even proposed the idea of a "refined food addiction" (Kozac & Fought, 2011) because refined foods are not only readily available but also high in sugar, fat, and salt. This hypothesis states that certain foods, such as fast foods, are inherently addictive in nature and have the power to induce cravings and stimulate abuse similar to other drugs (Davis & Carter, 2009). This powerful chemical process also has the power to moderate negative mood states (Wagener & Much, 2010). In this manner, food can be seen as an effective coping strategy to numb, self-soothe, or even to avoid feelings (Wagener & Much, 2010), and food can also be used to simply bring pleasure (hedonic eating; Davis et al., 2011). As described, some researchers have proposed that this disorder is well described as a "food addiction" and suggest that the addictive elements of loss of control, tolerance and withdrawal, and cravings and relapse are all present in binge eaters (Davis & Carter, 2009). It should be noted that not all binge eaters are obese, although there is a link. It has been suggested that certain person variables make an individual more predisposed to compulsive overeating than others, such as impulsivity (Guerrieri, Nederkoorn, & Jansen, 2008) and lower stress tolerance (Kozak & Fought, 2011). Interestingly, binge eating disorder is the most common eating disorder among males (Telch, Agras, & Linehan, 2001) and, like other eating disorders, typically emerges in young adulthood (Mitchell & Mazzeo, 2004).

Binge eating has been characterized as a compulsion to overeat even when faced with negative consequences such as weight gain or hypertension (Davis & Carter, 2009). These individuals frequently present with low self-esteem, an overemphasis on shape and weight, and use strict dieting paradigms (Wegner et al., 2002). Many researchers believe that binges are triggered by negative mood states, with food serving as a mood regulator and acute escape mechanism (Wegner et al., 2002). Although not diagnostically identified in the *DSM-IV-TR* (2000), individuals who suffer from binge eating disorder were previously diagnosed with an Eating Disorder Not Otherwise Specified (EDNOS). The *DSM-5* now contains specific criteria for binge eating disorder. These criteria include frequent overeating (occurring at least once a week over a course of 3 months) accompanied by any three of the following behaviors: eating more rapidly than usual, eating until uncomfortably full, eating large amounts of food when not hungry, eating alone because of embarrassment, and feeling disgusted with oneself afterward. These symptoms, combined with a feeling of distress and lack of control, indicate the presence of binge eating disorder. The inclusion of this diagnostic category should lead to a greater understanding of binge eating, for which overall prevalence is currently unknown (Wolff, Crosby, Roberts, & Wittrock, 2000).

Treatment

Because of the behavioral parallels with bulimia nervosa, many of the same treatment models are used when treating binge eating. Specifically, CBT is frequently employed to decrease dietary restraint and improve cognitions related to self and weight (Telch et al., 2001). DBT has also shown promise with binge eating by seeking to replace food behaviors initiated to regulate unwelcome emotional states with emotional regulation skills (Telch et al., 2001). This approach incorporates the concept of mindful eating discussed previously (Albers, 2011). Group approaches addressing topics such as anxiety and psychoeducation about eating disorders are also easily implemented in college counseling settings (Huebner et al., 2006). Working with a physician and a nutritionist is also advised.

OTHER SPECIFIED FEEDING OR EATING DISORDERS IN THE *DSM-5*

This diagnostic category of eating disorders is the *most common eating disorder* seen among college women who present for treatment at college counseling centers (Schwitzer et al., 2008). This category, formerly known as Eating Disorders Not Otherwise Specified in the *DSM-IV-TR*, includes disordered eating that is below the threshold for clinical anorexia or bulimia, as well as disordered eating that contains aspects of both disorders (Choate, 2010). Most commonly, diagnosed individuals experience significant psychological distress as a result of their self-image and disordered eating behaviors but have not yet crossed into a clear diagnostic category (Schwitzer, Rodriguez, Thomas, & Salimi, 2001). One study suggested that this was a transitory diagnosis for individuals who were previously diagnosed with bulimia or anorexia or those who are on their way to a full diagnosis (Agras, Crow, Mitchell, Halmi, & Bryson, 2009).

While the *DSM-5* has renamed this category Other Specified Feeding or Eating Disorders, the designation continues to be for eating disorders that do not meet any other diagnostic criteria. The manual offers examples of this disorder as atypical anorexia (anorexic criteria in the presence of adequate weight), subthreshold bulimia nervosa or binge eating disorder (with low frequency or limited duration), purging disorder (in the absence of binging), and night eating syndrome (excessive caloric consumption at night). As such, this category is more broadly defined than the other diagnostic eating disorder categories, as it is designed to encompass all remaining disordered and pathological eating and compensatory behaviors. This can make identification and treatment more difficult, as it is the most heterogeneous eating disorder diagnosis.

On college campuses, this disorder can occur as a mix of subclinical bulimic and anorexic behaviors. It is believed that these disordered eating practices also result from excessive preoccupation with body image, rumination about eating, an excessive desire to be thin, and body dissatisfaction (Choate, 2010; Schwitzer et al., 2008). Perfectionistic desires also tend to be higher in this population (Schwitzer et al., 2001). The binging components of this disorder are most often seen on college campuses, while the restrictive elements tend to present less often (Schwitzer et al., 2008). For example, a frequent student presentation can be high levels of exercise (a compensatory behavior) accompanied by binge eating, without the purging or overly restrictive eating elements (Choate, 2010). As such, it can be most similar to bulimia nervosa in nature and duration (Agras et al., 2009). While the clinical presentation of this disorder can vary, the psychological stress associated with the disordered eating does not. Most sufferers report significant emotional distress and impairment to daily functioning (Schwitzer et al., 2008). Although exact numbers are not known, studies have estimated that this is the fastest growing diagnostic eating disorder category.

Finally, it bears mentioning that the *DSM-5* (APA, 2013) has two eating disorder classifications previously located in the *DSM-IV-TR* section for disorders first diagnosed in infancy, childhood, or adolescence. These disorders have been relocated to the eating disorder section to recognize the availability of these diagnoses for individuals of any age. The first is Pica, which is characterized by the persistent eating of nonfood or nonnutritive substances. The second is Rumination Disorder, which is characterized by repeated regurgitation of food. This food is then rechewed, reswallowed, or discarded. There is also a new diagnostic category labeled Unspecified Feeding or Eating Disorders designed for instances when a clinician does not have enough, or chooses not to disclose, information related to the specificity of the eating disturbance.

Treatment

Because of the similarities with bulimia, a CBT approach is believed to be the most effective treatment (Choate, 2010). As with any eating disorder, careful monitoring of weight should be an integral part of treatment to ensure that health is maintained. The goal of outpatient CBT is to normalize eating and decrease the emphasis on weight and shape. Choate (2010) outlines a detailed therapeutic approach for treating EDNOS on college campuses that includes a multistep, four-phase approach. Phase one emphasizes the importance of creating a safe and trusting environment and allowing the client to address fears related to eating and behavior changes. This, along with generating a list of pros and cons related to change, is believed to increase the readiness and motivation for change.

Next, reeducating the client related to nondieting eating practices and creating a pattern for eating are also important as they show that normative eating does not cause weight gain. To reinforce this, weekly weighing in the counselor's office is recommended with an agreed upon low weight threshold. Psychoeducation related to the dangers of erratic eating and purging, nutrition, the process of CBT, and the socially constructed ideal of beauty is also recommended. Phase two is a transitional step where the counselor assesses the effectiveness of the first phase and assesses ongoing motivation. Phase three focuses on increasing self-worth through a de-emphasis on the physical, reorganizing food attitudes, and increasing coping skills. Clients can also practice intuitive eating in this phase, which is eating in response to hunger. Finally, phase four involves termination and discussion of strategies to continue the new learned behaviors after counseling. Choate further recommends that this outpatient approach can be modified to best meet the unique needs of clients.

College counseling centers may also implement a variety of counseling groups to better educate and support this population. Psychoeducation, anxiety, and DBT groups would all work well and could serve to decrease the onset of more severe symptomatology (Huebner, et al., 2006). This group approach could also provide an entry point for treatment among students not yet ready for individual counseling work.

MULTICULTURAL CONSIDERATIONS

Eating disorders have stereotypically been thought of as a disorder affecting young, White, middle to upper class, heterosexual females (Smolak & Striegel-Moore, 2001). Those who didn't fit this preconception were thought to be at lower risk as they were believed to not ascribe to traditional Western standards of beauty emphasizing thinness, therefore making them immune from these disorders (Nelson et al., 2011). However, while these beliefs may continue to prevail, researchers have examined these assumptions and challenged these inaccurate cultural stereotypes (Lester & Petrie, 1998). While a complete discussion of this literature is space prohibitive, an overview of the multicultural dimensions of gender, sexual orientation, culture, age, socioeconomic status, and ability level is included.

Gender

Historically, males were less likely to be diagnosed with an eating disorder (Blackmer et al., 2011). Best estimates indicate that males comprise 10% of the eating disorder population (Feltman & Ferraro, 2011). However, it should be noted that when binge eating disorder is included in this taxonomy, the incidence increases to 40% (Feltman & Ferraro, 2011).

While the numbers of males diagnosed with eating disorders may be small, certain populations of males may be more likely to experience these disorders, including male athletes such as distance runners, wrestlers, or rowers where leanness is more valued (Blackmer et al., 2011). Male students who pursue certain careers may also be at higher risk, such as actors or those who select female-dominated occupations such as nursing (Krentz & Arthur, 2001). Homosexual males have also been found to be at higher risk for eating disorders with incidence rates similar to those of heterosexual women (Feldman & Meyer, 2007). Bisexual males also have higher incidence rates when compared to their heterosexual counterparts (Feldman & Meyer, 2007).

Some believe that the prevalence rates for males is underdiagnosed because of the notion that the disorder is uniquely feminine (NIMH, 2011) and the different manifestations the disorder can present in males (Feltman & Ferraro, 2011). In other words, males are more likely to desire body change not necessarily affiliated with weight loss, as in traditional definitions of eating disorders. More likely, males may present with muscle dysmorphia, a type of body dysmorphia characterized by an excessive concern to become more muscular amid a misperception of actual body size (Davey & Bishop, 2006; NIMH, 2011). These individuals are more likely to see themselves as smaller than they actually are and work to gain weight and muscle mass to enhance their shape. This is in contrast to women, who are more likely to work for thinness. As a result, men are more likely to use exercise or dietary supplements as a dieting tool, rather than oral restriction or purging (Nelson et al., 2011). However, it is believed that the underlying body dissatisfaction and disordered eating are very similar to what female sufferers experience (Feltman & Ferraro, 2011) as prevalence rates for this dissatisfaction are believed to be equivalent for both genders (Olivardia, Pope, & Hudson, 2000). Unfortunately, the stigma associated with males and eating disorders prevents many from ever seeking treatment (Krentz & Arthur, 2001). The most important thing to remember is that males are not immune to the sociocultural pressures of fitness and dieting, which can easily lead to body dissatisfaction, disordered eating, and clinical or subclinical eating pathology (Krentz & Arthur, 2001).

Sexual Orientation

While there has been increased research attention on the incidence of eating disorders in sexual minority women, the findings have been conflicting, thus making conclusions related to this population difficult. Studies have demonstrated higher, lower, and equivalent rates among these populations of women when compared to heterosexual women (Nelson et al., 2011). Some have suggested that these mixed findings can be explained by the moderating effect involvement in the lesbian/bisexual community can have on the manifestation of eating disorders with those identifying more with heterosexual communities more prone to eating pathology (Nelson et al., 2011). Some have also suggested that internalized homophobia and a desire to diverge from negative stereotypes can also push lesbian and bisexual women toward more conventional standards of attractiveness and make them more at risk for eating pathology (Krentz & Arthur, 2001). Many believed that sexual minority women were less invested in conventional beauty norms, but this narrow view has not been substantiated in the literature because these women are subjected to the same ideals of beauty as every other woman. It is unclear how internalized these ideals become and it most likely varies based on individual identity. These findings seem to indicate that sexual minority women may be just as likely to present with eating disorders as heterosexual women (Feldman & Meyer, 2007).

Conversely, homosexual and bisexual men seem to be more likely to experience an eating disorder than heterosexual men (Feldman & Meyer, 2007; Krentz & Arthur, 2001). The prevalence of eating disorders in this population of men is estimated to be 10 times higher than among heterosexual men (Feldman & Meyer, 2007). These eating pathologies are also thought to directly stem from norms related to physical appearance, which are heightened in gay culture (Krentz & Arthur, 2001). It has been suggested that gay men are more likely to feel body dissatisfaction and a stronger desire to be thin, as they attempt to conform to sociocultural body ideas that are unattainable. Identification with the gay community may moderate the development of eating disorder behaviors but this relationship remains understudied (Feldman & Meyer, 2007). Similar to heterosexual men, gay and bisexual men are much less likely to acknowledge their eating disturbances or seek treatment due to beliefs related to the feminine nature of these disorders.

As with any minority group, perceived social stress and discrimination can cause increased psychological distress, which is a known correlate for disordered eating. College counselors should also be aware of the possible correlation between sexual identity confusion and disordered eating (Nelson et al., 2011), suggesting that emerging and younger sexual minorities may be more at risk for the development of eating disorders (Feldman & Meyer, 2007). In short, it is important to note that this population can experience eating disorders at *similar* or *higher* rates than heterosexual students.

Culture

Minority women were once thought to be immune from eating disorders such as bulimia and anorexia, but researchers now believe that these women are just as and, in some cases, perhaps more susceptible to them

(Gilbert, Crump, Madhere, & Schutz, 2009). When binge eating is included in the discussion, prevalence rates can become equivalent, or higher, to rates seen in Caucasian populations (Mitchell & Mazzeo, 2004). This reality is reflected when examining obesity rates, whereby certain populations, such as African Americans, have higher obesity rates, perhaps reflecting higher incidences of binge eating (Mitchell & Mazzeo, 2004).

Research examining prevalence rates of eating disorders among minority women has been conflicting, leading some to suggest that ethnic minority development may moderate the manifestation of an actual disorder (Nelson et al., 2011). For instance, some believe that those individuals belonging to a largely collectivist culture (e.g., African and Latino) may place less emphasis on their own body image versus more individualistic cultures (Fernandez et al., 2006). These non-Western cultures are more likely to have body image ideals that are more reflective of their specific ethnic group. However, it has been suggested that while these curvier body ideals might decrease the risk factors for anorexia or bulimia, they actually increase risk for binge eating, as evidenced by higher overall obesity rates in these groups (Franko, Jenkins, & Rodgers, 2012; Mitchell & Mazzeo, 2004).

Other researchers believe that much of the research of eating disorders among cultural minority groups has been too narrow in scope by comparing general populations (e.g., Black and White students) without taking into account cultural variations within these groups (Gilbert et al., 2009). A careful consideration of culture reveals unique norms related to foods, rituals, and beauty. For instance, while some cultures value weight as a sign of fertility, others value fasting as a sign of piousness (Krentz & Arthur, 2001). This broad diversity of thought and belief indicates that eating disorders in diverse cultural groups may not always be rooted in a drive for the appearance of thinness, as may be present in the majority cultural group. Therefore, analyzing these behaviors with a Western lens does a disservice to these cultural complexities. However, all multicultural individuals experience some degree of acculturation, which can often lead to a rejection of traditionally held beliefs in favor of macrocultural views and practices (Krentz & Arthur, 2001). This, along with bias and identity issues, can increase stress and the need to conform to the dominant views.

Studies examining specific populations of minority women have found widespread weight loss attempts and disordered eating behaviors such as binging, using laxatives, and restrictive eating among African American, Native American, and Mexican American women (Lester & Petrie, 1998). In fact, some researchers have reported that Latina women are at higher risk of developing some eating disorders such as bulimia (Franko et al., 2012). Unfortunately, it is also believed that these groups of women are also underdiagnosed, most often due to clinician bias even though incidence rates among these populations are believed to be rising (Gilbert et al., 2009). Globalization and increased exposure to Western ideals of beauty are thought to be responsible for these increases and now some minority women are believed to be especially vulnerable (Franko et al., 2012). Adding to this picture is the fact that many minority women hold cultural beliefs resulting in underutilization of health services (Gilbert et al., 2009). This means that minority women are less likely to seek health services and also less likely to be diagnosed with an eating disorder should they decide to seek treatment.

The college counseling center is advised to consider that the correlates for eating disorders may differ based on ethnicity (Mitchell & Mazzeo, 2004). For instance, certain minority groups may experience "racial stress" that can contribute to negative health outcomes, such as eating disorders, that the majority population does not experience (Mitchell & Mazzeo, 2004). It is also helpful to be aware that there is very limited research that exists examining eating disorders among minority males.

Age

Although less research has been conducted on populations of midlife sufferers of eating disorders, researchers know that women remain vulnerable to developing these disorders throughout adulthood (Keel et al., 2010). It has been suggested that this may be because of society's emphasis on a youthful appearance. In addition, it is known that eating disorders are some of the most pervasive pathologies, with some women developing disordered eating and continuing the pattern for decades after onset (Keel et al., 2010). This process can also be multigenerational with negative attitudes, beliefs, and practices related to food passing from mothers to children.

Midlife men are also at greater risk for the development of eating disorders than previously thought (Keel et al., 2010). This is believed to be because of body image issues stemming from weight gain in middle age and the muscular ideal for men. One longitudinal study suggested that peak times of male onset may not even be young adulthood as previously believed (Keel et al., 2010).

With record numbers of nontraditional aged students on college campuses, it is important to note that men and women of any age can present with clinical or subclinical eating disorders. Our macroculture's emphasis on youth and vitality ensures that the drive to be fit and thin can persist well through middle age. This means that college counselors cannot, formally or informally, use age as a diagnostic marker.

Socioeconomic Status

One of the most significant, yet understudied, variables related to eating disorders is socioeconomic status (SES). An interesting line of research has suggested that middle- and upper-class women are more susceptible to overly thin body ideals, with heavier women being perceived as being from a lower class (Krentz & Arthur, 2001; Nielsen, 2000). However, research examining this dimension has been inconsistent and limited (Fernandez et al., 2006). Some research has identified no relationship between SES and eating disorders, while other research has found that prevalence rates do vary based on status. It has been suggested that higher SES women are more commonly diagnosed with anorexia nervosa, while lower SES women experience higher rates of bulimia (Fernandez et al., 2006), but drawing broad conclusions on these findings is not warranted until further research is conducted.

Krentz and Arthur (2001) provide a compelling discussion of the interrelationship between food and SES. They state that poverty can actually prompt the onset of eating disorders in one of two ways. First, food is seen as a cost-effective way to offset the stress of poverty by providing a way of coping with financial pressures. Conversely, restricting food intake can be seen as one area to control in a reality that includes economic stressors and an overall feeling of lack of control. These ideas provide a rationale for further examination into how SES can be an influential component in the development of eating pathologies.

Ability Level

Although very limited research exists on disabilities and eating disorders, it is important to note that eating disorders have been measured and studied in disabled populations (Krentz & Arthur, 2001). It has been proposed that individuals with disabilities may manifest an eating disorder as a way to manage their disability and move closer to the cultural ideal (Krentz & Arthur, 2001). Others may manifest an eating disorder as an attempt to gain control in situations where their disability causes dependency (Krentz & Arthur, 2001). Counselors need to be aware that eating disorders can exist independently in this population and should also not assume that an eating pathology is necessarily related to a client's known disability.

ASSESSMENT OF EATING DISORDERS

Before discussing assessment efforts, it should be noted that there is significant stigma associated with eating disorders because these disorders are more often perceived as being person-controlled disorders. This makes the individual feel "responsible" for the dysfunctional behavior (Crisafulli, Thompson-Brenner, Franko, Eddy, & Herzog, 2010). This stigma can result in an individual's failing to seek treatment when needed due to self-blame and can create unsupportive and negative reactions from peers and colleagues (Crisafulli et al., 2010). This stigma is perhaps partially responsible for research that indicates very few individuals with diagnosable eating disorders actually seek treatment for them (White et al., 2011). The same holds true for college-aged individuals who experience some of the highest rates of maladaptive eating and body image issues, but few ever seek treatment expressly for these disorders (APA, 2006). This means that both prevention and assessment efforts should include educational components designed to lessen this stigma by educating about the biological components of the disorders as well as discussions related to the increasing prevalence on college campuses (White et al., 2011).

It has been suggested that college counseling centers frequently overlook eating disorder pathologies because counselors are not expressly looking for them. As such, it has been recommended that college counseling centers should ask students about their eating, body image, and weight control as routine procedure, even if the student is not presenting with an eating concern (Huebner et al., 2006; White et al., 2001). Integrating this simple step into counseling center procedures is hypothesized to increase detection, prevention, and subsequent treatment of eating disorders on campuses (White et al., 2001). Along with this, educating college counseling center professionals to the unique expressions of eating pathology on college campuses is also advised to help them recognize the unique presentations among the wide variety of students.

Huebner et al. (2006) conceptualized this initial screening process as the first part of a four-part protocol for college counseling centers to follow. If a student's responses to general eating and self-image questions indicate disordered eating or body image concerns, then exploratory questions (phase two) need to follow to assess whether the client sees these issues as a potential focus for counseling. The third phase is elaboration, where counselors gather more data and clients are asked for a more detailed history. The final phase is formal assessment, which can include a structured interview or a formalized pencil and paper assessment.

The secretive nature of eating disorders can make assessment more difficult, as can the self-report element. Many times, individuals may present with an alternative issue until a trusting relationship is established (APA, 2006). It is recommended that a combination of structured interview and instrumentation be used for eating disorder assessment. Choate (2010) recommends that college counseling centers utilize the Eating Disorders Examination (Fairburn, Cooper, & Shafran, 2003) and the Eating Disorder Inventory-3 (Garner, 2004). The Eating Attitudes Test (EAT-26) can also be used to screen for those at risk of an eating disorder

(Beekley et al., 2009). In addition, it is recommended that clinicians use a psychosocial inventory or interview to also uncover eating behaviors, body image attitudes, and emotional distress that could signal a subclinical eating disorder or nonspecified eating disorder diagnosis (Schwitzer et al., 2008). Clinicians need to also be reminded of the comorbidity of eating disorders and other pathologies such as depression and anxiety in their assessment (White et al., 2011).

Based on the outcome of the screening process and in accordance with APA's (2006) practice guidelines, Huebner et al. (2006) recommend classifying students by severity in order to determine treatment. This severity is measured by frequency of episodes, severity of symptoms, and diagnostic category, and students are labeled either mild, moderate, serious, or severe. Mild cases typically include those with subclinical symptoms that can be readily treated in a college counseling center. Those classified as moderate are those with either subclinical symptoms or diagnosed with EDNOS who can also be treated at the counseling center. Those who meet diagnostic criteria for anorexia or bulimia are automatically placed in the serious category and can elect to receive comprehensive treatment (i.e., counseling, medical doctor, nutritionist) either at the counseling center or through an outside provider. The final category is severe and encompasses those who require inpatient or long-term residential treatment. Huebner et al. (2006) noted that this last category of individuals might also require involuntary commitment.

PRACTICE GUIDELINES

While treatment for clients with eating disorders will vary based on the individual presentation of the eating and body image disturbance, the APA practice guidelines inform practitioners of general treatment goals for use with all eating disordered clients (APA, 2000b, 2006). Their integrated treatment model encompasses the following target areas: nutritional rehabilitation, psychosocial interventions, and psychiatric interventions to treat underlying and comorbid concerns (APA, 2000b; 2006). Goals for each of the three target areas are briefly described in the following.

Nutritional rehabilitation focuses on changing behaviors directly related to food, weight, and eating and is accomplished through nutritional counseling or participation in a psychoeducational nutritional program. This work may be done by a nutritionist or other specially trained personnel with expertise in nutrition management. Suggested goals for this dimension include:

• Restoration or maintenance of healthy target weight with client weight as outcome measure (possible hospital-based weight restoration in severe cases)

- Establishment of healthy patterns related to hunger, eating, and nutrition to replace dysfunctional and maladaptive behaviors (e.g., minimizing food restriction, increasing food variety, etc.)
- Establishment of a healthy exercise routine with a focus on fitness versus calories

In conjunction with the behavioral changes accompanying nutritional stabilization, psychosocial interventions target the underlying beliefs and attitudes that accompany disordered eating. These goals are frequently implemented using individual and group therapy; however, support groups/12-step programs, family therapy, and guided self-help programs have also been effective modalities (Yager et al., 2012). Suggested goals for this dimension include:

- Recognition of the maladaptive behaviors and attitudes of the eating disorder
- Addressing motivation for change (i.e., motivational interviewing)
- Identification, understanding, and integration of healthier attitudes related to weight, body image, and food
- Improvement of interpersonal functioning, affect regulation, and problem solving
- Addressing themes, beliefs, or developmental concerns that underlie the eating disorder (e.g., family dysfunction, gender role expectations, etc.)
- Addressing any presenting comorbid pathologies or dysfunctions

Finally, it is recommended that a psychiatric intervention also be a part of the treatment protocol for eating disorders. This is most often achieved through client consultation with a psychiatrist or other trained medical professional. Suggested goals for this dimension include:

- Evaluation for psychopharmacological intervention
- Pharmacotherapy to alleviate depressive or anxiety symptoms that may accompany disordered eating
- Implementation of hormone or vitamin supplements

While evidence for treatment efficacy is constantly emerging, these practice guidelines continue to inform practitioners of new treatments and best practices. The APA (2006) reminds counselors working with eating-disordered clients to be mindful of the importance of the relationship, as well as the need to frequently assess and monitor the eating disorder symptoms during treatment to ensure client safety. Consultation with other professionals involved with client care is also imperative to achieve best results. College counselors are encouraged to access these practice guidelines for more detailed treatment protocol information.

PREVENTION

Because of the increased incidence of eating disorders on college campuses, it is recommended that college counseling centers focus on prevention (White et al., 2011). It is known that clients with eating problems frequently fluctuate between eating disorder diagnoses (Choate, 2010), with disordered eating typically becoming more severe over time. Similarly, dieting has been shown to be the most important predictor for new eating disorders (White et al., 2011). This suggests that attempts to control weight and eating can evolve from experimental dieting to significant diagnostic eating pathology. Therefore, prevention efforts should be aimed at reducing the emergence and progression of disordered eating practices (Schwitzer et al., 2001).

Multiple prevention programs have been developed and been proven effective (Veazey Morris, Parra, & Stender, 2011). Prevention programs can focus on strengthening protective factors such as self-esteem or modifying risk factors such as body dissatisfaction (Franko et al., 2005). One such program is *The Body Project*, which is designed to reduce eating disorder risk factors (Stice, Rodhe, Shaw, & Marti, 2012). Other foci for prevention programs include educating about social influences and gender norms. Still other programs are more physical health-based with a focus on nutrition (i.e., five fruits and vegetables a day), exercise physiology, and dieting (Franko et al., 2012; Schwitzer et al., 2001). One program that has received validation in the literature is the *Healthy Weight* program that targets both eating disorder symptoms and unhealthy weight gain (Stice et al., 2012). Some college counseling centers may incorporate a variety of these programs in an "Eating Disorders Awareness Week" format. Other ideas for content dissemination include freshman orientation courses, health and fitness courses, outreach presentations to campus groups, and counseling center educational series (White et al., 2011).

Some researchers believe the most effective prevention programs are those that are interactive and include multiple sessions (Franko et al., 2005), while others report counseling centers should implement more flexible computer-based prevention programs. Advocates of computerized or internet-based prevention programs note that this modality has been found to be not only efficacious but cost effective and popular with students (Franko et al., 2005, 2012). These computerized programs can also lessen the stigma associated with help seeking (Franko et al., 2012).

Given the prevalence of eating disorders, prevention efforts should be ongoing and routine. These efforts, combined with comprehensive screening efforts, should work in tandem to educate and identify both those at risk and those presenting with eating-disordered behaviors. Incorporating these elements into the campus culture could serve to off-set the strong sociocultural forces that drive students to conform to unattainable physical ideals.

ADDITIONAL RESOURCES

There is an abundance of materials and client resources readily available that address eating disorders. Aside from academic articles and books, multiple organizations provide detailed information for both practitioners and clients. Included below is a brief listing of these sources. Practitioner sources share general information about treatment programs, etiology, symptomatology, correlates, and other useful information. Client resources include general information relating to the disorders, as well as robust listings of bibliotherapy materials.

Practitioner Resources

American Psychological Association (www.apa.org/topics/eating/index.aspx)
National Alliance on Mental Illness (www.nami.org)
U.S. Department of Health and Human Services Office of Women's Health (www.womenshealth.gov/body-image/eating-disorders)

Client Resources

Eating Disorder Hope (www.eatingdisorderhope.com)
Eating Disorders Online (www.eatingdisordersonline.com)
National Eating Disorders Association (www.nationaleatingdisorders.org)

CONCLUSION

In summary, college counseling centers are uniquely poised to provide much-needed education, assessment, and intervention to students with clinical and subclinical disordered eating behaviors. The diversity on today's college campuses guarantees that college counselors will see a wide variety of students necessitating a broader view of who may be suffering from or at risk of an eating disorder (Krentz & Arthur, 2001). Luckily, research has now informed counselors that no group of individuals seems to be immune from eating disorders, although the manifestation of symptoms and corollaries to the disorder may vary (Choate, 2010; Franko et al., 2012).

College counseling centers are best advised to train their staff related to the presentation of these disorders on campus, as well as develop a comprehensive assessment, prevention, and treatment protocol. These procedures should be implemented routinely and consistently to ensure that all students are included. It is expected that these efforts could result in increased campus awareness of eating disorder behaviors, as well as increased diagnosis and treatment. Related to this, counselors must also stay abreast of the latest diagnostic criteria (i.e., *DSM-5*), as well as current evidence-based practice in order to provide the most ethical, comprehensive, and multiculturally competent care for the growing populations presenting with eating disorders.

Finally, given the negative health consequences, mortality, and pervasiveness of eating disorders, it is hoped that research will continue to inform practice. Currently, eating disorder research funding is estimated to be $0.93 per affected individual (National Eating Disorder Association, n.d.). This is far below other disorders such as schizophrenia and autism with spending per individual at $88 and $44, respectively. Increased advocacy efforts are needed to raise awareness of this important mental health concern and to stimulate continued research activity. College counseling centers can participate in this call for research by collecting, analyzing, and publishing data on their eating disorder demographics, assessments, and treatment outcomes. This activity has the potential to benefit not only the individual college student of today, but students from around the globe for generations to come.

REFERENCES

Agras, W. S., Crow, S., Mitchell, J. E., Halmi, K. A., & Bryson, S. (2009). A 4-year study of eating disorder NOS compared with full eating disorders. *International Journal of Eating Disorders, 42*(6), 565–570. doi:10.1002/eat.20708

Albers, S. (2011). Using mindful eating to treat food restriction: A case study. *Eating Disorders: The Journal of Treatment & Prevention, 19*(1), 97–107. doi:10.1080/10640266.2011.533609

American Psychiatric Association. (1980). *Diagnostic and statistical manual of mental disorders* (3rd ed.). Washington, DC: Author.

American Psychiatric Association. (2000). *Diagnostic and statistical manual of mental disorders* (4th ed., text rev.). Washington, DC: Author.

American Psychiatric Association. (2000). Practice guideline for the treatment of patients with eating disorders (rev.). *American Journal of Psychiatry, 157*(1), 1–39.

American Psychiatric Association. (2006). *Practice guidelines for the treatment of patients with eating disorders* (3rd ed.). Washington, DC: Author.

American Psychiatric Association. (2013). *Diagnostic and statistical manual of mental disorders* (5th ed.). Washington, DC: Author.

Attia, E., & Walsh, T. B. (2009). Behavioral management for anorexia nervosa. *The New England Journal of Medicine, 360*(5), 500–506. doi:10.1056/NEJMct0805569

Bardone-Cone, A. M., & Cass, K. M. (2007). What does viewing a pro-anorexia website do? An experimental examination of website exposure and moderating effects. *International Journal of Eating Disorders, 40*(6), 537–548. doi:10.1002/eat.20396

Barth, F. D. (2003). Separate but not alone: Separation-individuation issues in college students with eating disorders. *Clinical Social Work Journal, 31*(2), 139–153. doi:10.1023/A:1022910327003

Beekley, M. D., Byrne, R., Yavorek, T., Kidd, K., Wolff, J., & Johnson, M. (2009). Incidence, prevalence, and risk of eating disorders in military academy cadets. *Military Medicine, 174*(6), 637–641.

Blackmer, V., Searight, H., & Ratwick, S. H. (2011). The relationship between eating attitudes, body image, and perceived family-of-origin climate among college athletes. *North American Journal of Psychology, 13*(3), 435–446.

Carbaugh, R. J., & Sias, S. M. (2010). Comorbidity of bulimia nervosa and substance abuse: Etiologies, treatment issues, and treatment approaches. *Journal of Mental Health Counseling, 32*(2), 125–138.

Carolan, M., Bak, J., Hoppe-Rooney, T., & Burns-Jager, K. (2010). An integrated feminist approach to disordered eating intervention in a university campus outpatient setting. *Journal of Feminist Family Therapy, 22*(1), 43–56. doi:10.1080/08952830903453612

Cashel, M. L., Cunningham, D., Landeros, C., Cokley, K. O., & Muhammad, G. (2003). Sociocultural attitudes and symptoms of bulimia: Evaluating the SATAQ with diverse college groups. *Journal of Counseling Psychology, 50*(3), 287–296. doi:10.1037/0022-0167.50.3.287

Choate, L. H. (2010). Counseling college women experiencing eating disorder not otherwise specified: A cognitive behavioral model. *Journal of College Counseling, 13*(1), 73–86. doi:10.1002/j.2161-1882.2010.tb00049.x

Crisafulli, M. A., Thompson-Brenner, H., Franko, D. L., Eddy, K. T., & Herzog, D. B. (2010). Stigmatization of anorexia nervosa: Characteristics and response to intervention. *Journal of Clinical Psychology, 29*(7), 756–770. doi:10.1521/jscp.2010.29.7.756

Davey, C. M., & Bishop, J. B. (2006). Muscle dysmorphia among college men: An emerging gender-related counseling concern. *Journal of College Counseling, 9*(2), 171–180. doi:10.1002/j.2161-1882.2006.tb00104.x

Davis, C., & Carter, J. C. (2009). Compulsive overeating as an addiction disorder. A review of theory and evidence. *Appetite, 53*(1), 1–8. doi:10.1016/j.appet.2009.05.018

Davis, C., Zai, C., Levitan, R., Kaplan, A., Carter, J., Reid-Westoby, C., ... Kennedy, J. (2011). Opiates, overeating and obesity: A psychogenetic analysis. *International Journal of Obesity, 35*(10), 1347–1354. doi:10.1038/ijo.2010.276

Erikson, E. H. (1950). *Childhood and society.* New York, NY: Norton.

Fairburn, C. G. (2008). *Cognitive behavior therapy and eating disorders.* New York, NY: Guilford Press.

Fairburn, C. G., Cooper, Z., & Shafran, R. (2003). Cognitive behavior therapy for eating disorders: A "transdiagnostic" theory treatment. *Behaviour Research and Therapy, 41*(5), 509–528. doi:10.1016/S0005-7967(02)00088-8

Federici, A., Wisniewski, L., & Ben-Porath, D., (2012). Description of an intensive dialectical behavior therapy program for multidiagnostic clients with eating disorders. *Journal of Counseling and Development, 90*(3), 330–338. doi:10.1002/j.1556-6676.2012.00041.x

Feldman, M. B., & Meyer, I. H. (2007). Eating disorders in diverse lesbian, gay, and bisexual populations. *International Journal of Eating Disorders, 40,* 218–226. doi:10.1037/0002-9432.75.4.553

Feltman, K. A., & Ferraro, F. R. (2011). Preliminary data on risk factors and disordered eating in male college students. *Current Psychology: A Journal for Diverse Perspectives on Diverse Psychological Issues, 30*(2), 194–202. doi:10.1007/s12144-011-9109-y

Fernandez, S., Malacrne, V. L, Wilfley, D. E., & McQuaid, J. (2006). Factor structure of the Bulimia Test–Revised in college women from four ethnic groups. *Cultural Diversity and Ethnic Minority Psychology, 12*(3), 403–419. doi:10.1037/1099-9809.12.3.403

Franko, D. L., Jenkins, A., & Rodgers, R. (2012). Towards reducing risk for eating disorders and obesity in Latina college women. *Journal of Counseling and Development, 90*(3), 298–307. doi:10.1002/j.1556-6676.2012.00038.x

Franko, D. L., Mintz, L., Villapiano, M., Green, T., Mianelli, D., … Follensbee, L. (2005). Food, mood, and attitude reducing risk for eating disorder in college women. *Health Psychology, 24*(6), 567–578. doi:10.1037/0278-6133.24.6.567

Garner, D. (2004). *Eating Disorder Inventory-3 (EDI-3) professional manual.* Lutz, FL: Psychological Assessment Resource.

Gilbert, S. C., Crump, S., Madhere, S., & Schutz, W. (2009). Internalization of the thin ideal as a predictor of body dissatisfaction and disordered eating in African, African-American, and Afro-Caribbean female college students. *Journal of College Student Psychology, 23*(3), 196–211. doi:10.1080/87568220902794093

Gonzalez, B., Huerta-Sanchez, E., Ortiz-Nieves, A., Vazquez-Alvarez, T., & Kribs-Zaleta, C. (2003). Am I too fat? Bulimia as an epidemic. *Journal of Mathematical Psychology, 47*(5/6), 515–526. doi: 10.1016/j.jmp.2003.08.002

Guerrieri, R., Nederkoorn, C., & Jansen, A. (2008). The effect of an impulsive personality on overeating and obesity: Current state of affairs. *Psychological Topics, 17*(2), 265–286.

Herzog, B. B., & Delinsky, S. S. (2002). Classification of eating disorders. In R. H. Striegel-Moore & I. Smolak (Eds.), *Eating disorders: Innovative directions in research and practice* (pp. 31–50). Washington, DC: American Psychological Association.

Hoyt, W. D., & Ross, S. D. (2003). Clinical and subclinical eating disorders in counseling center clients: A prevalence study. *Journal of College Student Psychotherapy, 17*(4), 39–54. doi:10.1300/J035v17n04_06

Huebner, L., Weitzman, L., Mountain, L., Nelson, K., Oakley, D., & Smith, M. (2006). Development and use of an eating disorder treatment protocol. *Journal of College Counseling, 9*(1), 72–78. doi: 10.1002/j.2161-1882.2006.tb00094.x

Keel, P. K., Gravener, J. A., Joiner Jr., T. E., & Haedt, A. A. (2010). Twenty-year follow-up of bulimia nervosa and related eating disorders not otherwise specified. *International Journal of Eating Disorders, 43,* 492–497.

Keel, P. K., & Haedt, A. (2008). Evidence-based psychosocial treatments for eating problems and eating disorders. *Journal of Clinical Child & Adolescent Psychology, 37*(1), 39–61. doi:10.1080/15374410701817832

Kozak, A. T., & Fought, A. (2011). Beyond alcohol and drug addiction. Does the negative trait of low distress tolerance have an association with overeating? *Appetite*, *57*(3), 578–581. doi:10.1016/j.appet.2011.07.008

Krentz, A., & Arthur, N. (2001). Counseling culturally diverse students with eating disorders. *Journal of College Student Psychotherapy*, *15*(4), 7–21. doi:10.1300/J035v15n04_03

Lester, R., & Petrie, T. A. (1998). Prevalence of disordered eating behaviors and bulimia nervosa in a sample of Mexican American female college students. *Journal of Multicultural Counseling and Development*, *26*(3), 157–165. doi: 10.1002/j.2161-112.1998.tb00195x

Mitchell, K. S., & Mazzeo, S. E. (2004). Binge eating and psychological distress in ethnically diverse undergraduate men and women. *Eating Behaviors*, *5*(2), 157–169. doi:10.1016/j.eatbeh.2003.07.004

Murray, T. (2003). Wait not, want not: Factors contributing to the development of anorexia nervosa and bulimia nervosa. *The Family Journal*, *11*(4), 276–280. doi: 10.1177/1066480703252470

National Eating Disorders Association. (n.d.). *Get the facts on eating disorders*. Retrieved from https://www.nationaleatingdisorders.org

National Institute of Mental Health. (2011). *Eating disorders* (NIH Publication No. 11-4901). Washington, DC: Department of Health and Human Services, National Institutes of Health.

Nelson, D. L., Castonguay, L. G., & Locke, B. D. (2011). Challenging stereotypes of eating and body image concerns among college students: Implications for diagnosis and treatment of diverse populations. *Journal of College Counseling*, *14*(2), 158–172. doi:10.1002/j.2161-1882.2011.tb00270.x

Nielsen, L. (2000). Black undergraduate and white undergraduate eating disorders and related attitudes. *College Student Journal*, *34*(3), 353–369.

Olivardia, R., Pope, H. G., & Hudson, J. I. (2000). Muscle dysmorphia in male weight-lifters: A case-control study. *American Journal of Psychiatry*, *157*(8), 1291–1296. doi:10.1176/appi.ajp.157.8.1291

O'Riordan, S. S., & Zamboanga, B. L. (2008). Aspects of the media and their relevance to bulimic attitudes and tendencies among female college students. *Eating Behaviors*, *9*(2), 247–250. doi:10.1016/j.eatbeh.2007.03.004

Pyle, R. L., Halvorson, P. A., Neuman, P. A., & Mitchell, J. E. (1986). The increasing prevalence of bulimia in freshman college students. *International Journal of Eating Disorders*, *5*(4), 631–647. doi:10.1002/1098-108X(198605)5:4<631::AID-EAT2260050404>3.0.CO;2-E

Rosen, L. W., McKeag, D. B., Hough, D. O., & Curley, V. (1986). Pathogenic weight control behavior in female athletes. *Physician and Sports Medicine*, *14*(1), 79–86.

Safer, D. L., Telch, C. F., & Agras, W. S. (2001). Dialectical behavior therapy adapted for bulimia: A case report. *International Journal of Eating Disorders*, *30*(1), 101–106.

Schaffner, A. D., & Buchanan, L. P. (2010). Evidence-based practices in outpatient treatment for eating disorders. *International Journal of Behavioral Consultation*, *6*(1), 35–44.

Schwitzer, A., Hatfield, T., Jones, A. R., Duggan, M. H., Jurgens, J., & Winninger, A. (2008). Confirmation among college women: The eating disorders not otherwise specified diagnostic profile. *Journal of American College Health, 56*(6), 607–615. doi:10.3200/JACH.56.6.607-616

Schwitzer, A. M., Rodriguez, L. E., Thomas, C., & Salimi, L. (2001). The eating disorders NOS diagnostic profile among college women. *Journal of American College Health, 49*, 157–166.

Smolak, I., & Striegel-Moore, R. H. (2001). Challenging the myth of the golden girl: Ethnicity and eating disorders. In R. H. Striegel-Moore & L. Smolak (Eds.), *Eating disorders: Innovative directions in research and practice* (pp. 111–132). Washington, DC: American Psychological Association. doi:10.1037/10403-006

Steinglass, J., Albano, A. M., Simpson, H. B., Carpenter, K., Schebendach, J., & Attia, E. (2012). Fear of food as a treatment target: Exposure and response prevention for anorexia nervosa in an open series. *International Journal of Eating Disorders, 45*(4), 615–621. doi:10.1002/eat.20936

Stice, E., Rohde, P., Shaw, H., & Marti, C. (2012). Efficacy trial of a selective prevention program targeting both eating disorder symptoms and unhealthy weight gain among female college students. *Journal of Consulting and Clinical Psychology, 80*(1), 164–170. doi:10.1037/a0026484

Striegel-Moore, R. H., Silberstein, L. R., & Rodin, J. (1986). Toward an understanding of risk factors for bulimia. *American Psychologist, 41*(3), 246–263. doi:10.1037/0003-066X.41.3.246

Telch, C. F., Agras, W. S., & Linehan, M. M. (2001). Dialectical behavior therapy for binge eating disorder. *Journal of Counseling and Clinical Psychology, 69*(6), 1061–1065. doi: 10.1037/0022-006X.69.6.1061

Veazey Morris, K. D., Parra, G. R., & Stender, S. R. S. (2011). Eating attitudes and behaviors among female college students. *Journal of College Counseling, 14*(1), 21–33.

Wagener, A. M., & Much, K. (2010). Eating disorders as coping mechanisms. *Journal of College Student Psychotherapy, 24*(3), 203–212. doi:10.1080/87568225.2010.486291

Waller, G., Stringer, H., & Meyer, C. (2012). What cognitive behavioral techniques do therapists report using when delivering cognitive behavioral therapy for eating disorders? *Journal of Counseling and Clinical Psychology, 80*(1), 171–175. doi: 10.1037/a0026559

Wegner, K. E., Smyth, J. M., Crosby, R. D., Wittrock, D., Wonderlich, S. A., & Mitchell, J. E. (2002). An evaluation of the relationship between mood and binge eating in the natural environment using ecological momentary assessment. *International Journal of Eating Disorders, 32*(3), 352–361. doi:10.1002/eat.10086

White, S., Reynolds-Malear, J. B., & Cordero, E. (2011). Disordered eating and the use of unhealthy weight control methods in college students: 1995, 2002, and 2008. *Eating Disorders: The Journal of Treatment and Prevention, 19*(4), 323–334. doi: 10.1080/10640266.2011.584805

Wolff, G. E., Crosby, R. D., Roberts, J. A., & Wittrock, D. A. (2000). Differences in daily stress, mood, coping, and eating behavior in binge eating and nonbinge eating college women. *Addictive Behaviors, 25*(2), 205–216. doi:10.1016/S0306-4603(99)00049-0

World Health Organization. (2003). *World health report: Obesity and overweight.* Geneva, Switzerland: World Health Organization.

Yager, J., Devlin, M. J., Halmi, K. A., Herzog, D. B., Mitchell III, J. E., Powers, P., & Zerbe, K. J. (2012). *Guideline watch (August 2012): Practice guideline for the treatment of patients with eating disorders* (3rd ed.). Retrieved from http://www.psych.org/practice/clinical-practice-guidelines

Zai, C. D., Levitan, R. D., Kaplan, A. S., Carter, J. C., Reid-Westoby, C., Curtis, C., ... Kennedy, J. L. (2011). Opiates, overeating and obesity: A psychogenetic analysis. *International Journal of Obesity, 35*(10), 1347–1354. doi:10.1038/ijo.2010.276

Zalta, A. K., & Keel, P. K. (2006). Peer influence on bulimic symptoms in college students. *Journal of Abnormal Psychology, 115*(1), 185–189. doi:10.1037/0021-843X.115.1.185

12

Substance Abuse and Dependence Treatment in the College Setting

EDWARD F. HUDSPETH AND KIMBERLY MATTHEWS

In this chapter, readers will find information about substance abuse and dependence. It contains an overview of the disorders as well as related individual difference factors such as age, gender, ethnicity, year in college, Greek system involvement, and housing location. Readers will also find information about diagnosis and referrals and current recommendations for individual and group counseling, evidence-based treatment goals, and interventions. The section covering substance abuse will focus on brief, harm-reduction interventions, while the section associated with substance dependence will focus on screening, referrals, interventions, and a model campus recovery program.

THE SUBSTANCE USE CONTINUUM

It is important for all counselors to gain a factual understanding of low-versus high-risk substance use. Even minimal illicit drug and, in most states, marijuana use, are high risk not only for health reasons, but also due to unwanted consequences—a student could be expelled as well as suffer legal ramifications. Any student using a substance that could bring severe negative consequences needs to reconsider his or her behaviors. In the case of low-level alcohol consumption, underage students may also need to weigh the risks. Even at low-risk levels, a counselor may want to help the student weigh the potential consequences of the substance use as a preventive measure. Yet attempts to persuade one's entire student body to be substance free is ungrounded and may, in fact, be counterproductive. Experts in substance education emphasize the use of harm-reduction or abuse-prevention paradigms with the college population rather than traditional abstinence efforts or use prevention.

For the purpose of this text, the terms *substance use, abuse,* and *dependence* will be utilized and differentiated. Currently the *Diagnostic and Statistical Manual of Mental Disorders* (*DSM-5,* American Psychiatric Association [APA], 2013) refers, in the section Substance-Related and Addictive Disorders, to Substance Use Disorders and Substance-Induced Disorders with individual diagnoses for each drug of abuse. As a whole, the terminology may be confusing; however, it is our attempt to be clear and consistent. It is also relevant to note that the *DSM-5* (APA, 2013) combines abuse and dependence into a single classification—Substance Use Disorders—and depicts severity based on the number of criteria present. However, this chapter will use the standard terminology that has been in use for many years.

To define and differentiate between substance abuse and dependence, it is helpful to conceptualize substance use via a continuum. The continuum's poles are made up of abstinence and dependence. Moving from the low end of the continuum, after abstinence, one will find social use, misuse, abuse of a substance, with the highest level termed *substance dependence.* Each progression point of the continuum is characterized by increased use and subsequent psychosocial issues. The concept of a substance use continuum is also important when considering treatment options.

When reading contemporary substance abuse research, it is evident that the college student population experiences many issues associated with substance abuse. From a life span perspective, substance abuse peaks during emerging adulthood, particularly for ages 18 to 25, although increased substance abuse at this life stage does not definitively lead to dependence at a later stage of development.

Substance abuse is recognized by the recurrence of negative consequences with repeated substance use. Negative consequences may be social, legal, behavioral, or interpersonal. Some examples are students failing to meet an academic requirement such as missing class or not doing an assignment, engaging in high-risk behaviors such as driving while intoxicated, having sex they would not choose to engage in had they been sober, involvement with the justice system due to substance use, and refusal to abstain from the preferred substance regardless of any relational or social problems connected to its use.

Substance dependence as defined by the *DSM-IV-TR* (APA, 2000, p. 197) is a "cluster of cognitive, behavioral, and physiological symptoms indicating that the individual continues use of the substance despite significant substance-related problems." Diagnosis would require that a client display multiple symptoms, often (but not always) including high tolerance of the substance, compulsive behavior with the substance, and possibly withdrawal, though there is a great deal of variability in drug withdrawal. Difficulty or failed attempts to control use, increasing amounts of time invested in its use, narrowing of social interaction as more time is devoted to use-related behaviors, and continued use of the substance even though there is awareness of the problems it is causing in the student's life are major indicators of substance dependence.

Tolerance refers to a student's need for increasing amounts of a substance to experience intoxication once reached with lower amounts, or to the diminished effect from the same amount of a substance. It is important to know and to educate clients that the development of a high tolerance for alcohol (or any intoxicating substance) is a risk factor for alcohol dependence. Some of the most detrimental beliefs on college campuses that the ability to "hold one's liquor" or "drink someone under the table" or consume an amount of alcohol that would normally result in passing out or being sick, are positive qualities worthy of high esteem. Educating students about substance abuse should include a focus on the realities of tolerance and dependence.

In the *DSM-5*, the terms *abuse* and *dependence* are replaced with Substance Use Disorders. Substance Use Disorders are defined as a "cluster of cognitive, behavioral, and physiological symptoms indicating that the individual continues using the substance despite significant substance-related problems" (APA, 2013, p. 483). The defining characteristics also include changes in brain circuitry as well as subsequent behavioral changes (APA, 2013). According to the *DSM-5* (APA, 2013, pp. 483–484), diagnostic criteria are divided into four categories encompassing 11 criteria. They are:

Impaired Control Over Substance Use
1. Taking the substance in larger amounts or over a longer period than originally intended
2. Expressing a persistent desire to cut down or regulate substance use [may report multiple unsuccessful efforts to decrease or discontinue]
3. Spending a great deal of time obtaining, using, or recovering from the use [daily activities revolve around the substance; seen in more severe substance use disorder]
4. Craving or intense desire/urge for the drug [seen more in environments of previous use]

Social Impairment
5. Recurrent use may result in failure to fulfill major role obligations
6. Continued use despite having persistent/recurrent social or interpersonal problems caused/exacerbated by the effects of the substance
7. May give up/reduce important social, occupational, or recreational activities because of substance use

Risky Use of Substance
8. Recurrent substance use in situations in which it is physically hazardous
9. Continued substance use despite knowledge of having a persistent/ recurrent physical or psychological problem that is caused/exacerbated by the substance

Pharmacological
10. Tolerance
11. Withdrawal

As noted earlier, severity of the disorders is characterized by the number of criteria displayed: 0–1, no disorder; 2–3, mild disorder; 4–5, moderate disorder; 6 or more, severe disorder. Specifiers include early or sustained remission and one for controlled environment (APA, 2013).

RATES OF SUBSTANCE ABUSE IN COLLEGE STUDENTS

As noted previously, substance abuse in college populations is common. However, according to the *Monitoring the Future Survey* (Johnston, O'Malley, Bachman, & Schulenberg, 2012), the annual prevalence rate for use of any illicit drug was higher for noncollege, similar age individuals as compared to college students (40% vs. 36%). The survey also showed higher rates of prescription drug use among noncollege, similar age, individuals when compared to college students. Conversely, the 2-week prevalence rate for binge drinking was slightly higher for college students as compared to noncollege, similar age individuals (36% vs. 32%; Johnston et al., 2012). Thus, it seems that the college environment is more supportive of weekend partying rather than daily, habitual substance abuse.

The *National Survey on Drug Use and Health* (NSDUH; Substance Abuse and Mental Health Services Administration [SAMHSA], 2012) offers other eye-opening statistics on substance use: Marijuana use for individuals 18 to 25 years of age was 19.0%. Among full-time college students, 60.8% were current drinkers, 39.1% were binge drinkers, and 13.6% were classified as heavy drinkers. This survey report breaks these rates down further into categories we could loosely identify as underclassmen (18 to 20 year olds) and upperclassmen (21 to 25 year olds). Somewhat surprisingly, current alcohol use and binge drinking rates were 46.8% and 31.2%, respectively, which is lower for those aged 18 to 20; in comparison, alcohol use and binge drinking rates were 69.7% and 45.4%, respectively, for those aged 21 to 25. Finally, one additional statistic offers evidence contrary to the popular belief that binge drinking ends after college, a belief held by many students and other adults, as well. According to *National Epidemiologic Survey on Alcohol and Related Conditions* (NESARC, 2001), the average amount of alcohol consumed, per occasion, showed a slight decrease at age 26 but it is not until age 30 that there is there a substantial decrease in consumption per drinking occasion. This fact alone may be eye opening for college students who generally believe that heavy drinking and college go hand-in-hand, and that it is easy to change one's habits after graduation.

Alcohol-related injuries, deaths, and other negative outcomes are common in all age groups. According to Yi, Chen, and Williams (2006), in 2005, there were almost 5,000 alcohol-related traffic deaths for individuals aged 16 to 24. Over half a million college students, aged 18 to 24, experienced unintentional harm as a result of being under the influence of alcohol (Hingson, Heeren, Winter, & Wechsler, 2005). In 2001, it was estimated that 2.8 million college students drove after drinking (Hingson et al., 2005). Hingson, Heeren, Zakocs, and Kopstein (2002) and Wechsler et al. (2002) estimated that more than 150,000 college students already experience health problems due to alcohol abuse. Considering all of these findings, it is not surprising that fully 25% of college students reported routinely missing class and having lower overall grades as a consequence of drinking (Wechsler et al., 2002).

EMERGING ADULTHOOD IN A CHANGING WORLD

As mentioned in other chapters, it is beneficial to conceptualize college students via an emerging adult theoretical lens. Arnett (1998, 2000, 2005) described this life stage, from age 18 to 24, as a time of vast change and exploration. He characterizes emerging adulthood as an (a) age of identity exploration, (b) age of instability, (c) age of self-focus, (d) age of feeling in-between, and (e) age of possibilities. Arnett (1997, 2000) stated that the only consistent facet of emerging adulthood is the unpredictability of the developmental stage. Today's college student is much different from those of any other period in time. News media reports reveal college students spend longer periods in college, struggle with career indecisiveness that is exacerbated by a poor employment outlook, and consequently need to return to their parental homes once graduated.

Yet despite these additional pressures, rates of risky substance use behavior have remained relatively stable over the past few generations (Johnston et al., 2012). Emerging adulthood is a time of indecisiveness as well as exploration. It is during these years that our evolutionary programming requires individuals to try on new identities, behaviors, and relationships. In fact, many researchers conclude that the high rates of substance abuse may be due in part to the high need for novelty and exploration that is a part of emerging adulthood (Arnett, 2005) and are rooted in the cultural permissiveness and availability of substances as well as individual factors (Wechsler, Dowdall, Maenner, Gledhill-Hoyt, & Lee, 1998).

Age

As a risk factor and/or predictor of substance use, age is a frequent demographic explored in large, national studies. Many studies simply compare college student drinking to high school prevalence rates as well as rates among individuals not in college or post-college age.

The NSDUH survey (SAMHSA, 2012) reported illicit drug use rates for those older than 12 with some further age-specific rates. In the survey of college and similar-age, noncollege peers, it was noted that the highest rate of illicit drug use (23.8%) was for those age 18 to 20; followed by 19.9% for those age 21 to 25. Marijuana use for individuals 18 to 25 was 19.0%. College students, age 18 to 22, reported a 22% rate of illicit drug use. The survey also reported that the current alcohol use and binge drinking rates were 46.8% and 31.2% for those age 18 to 20, and 69.7% and 45.4% for those age 21 to 25. Current alcohol use, binge drinking, and heavy drinking prevalence rates for full-time college students, ages 18 to 22, were 60.8%, 39.1%, and 13.6%, respectively. Conversely, the highest rates of binge and heavy alcohol use were for individuals age 21 to 25, with lower rates for those age 18 to 20 (SAMHSA, 2012).

Though few studies report prevalence rates for each college age, one study did report consumption rates for specific ages. Chan, Neighbors, Gilson, Larimer, and Marlatt (2007) reported significant results from the (*N* = 42,706) *National Epidemiologic Survey on Alcohol and Related Conditions* (NESARC, 2001). They reported that alcohol consumption is inconsistent throughout life or across age cohorts, namely there is increased consumption at ages 21 and 35 and decreased consumption at ages 26 and 65. The authors reported that the amount consumed, per occasion, peaks between 18 and 29, with a slight increase from ages 21 to 25. Decreases in consumption begin at age 30.

Gender

Both the *Monitoring the Future* survey (MTF; Johnston et al., 2012) and the NSDUH survey (SAMHSA, 2012) reported gender differences for both illicit drug use and alcohol use. Specifically, the MTF survey indicated that male college students are more likely to use illicit drugs in general and even more likely to use drugs daily than their female peers (Johnston et al., 2012). This trend of higher use includes marijuana and alcohol. Current marijuana use rates for full-time college students were 23.7% for males and 17.5% for females. The study reported 8.2% of college student males and 2.7% females used marijuana daily. The report also indicated that 43% of college student males as compared to 32% of females were binge drinkers and 6.2% of college student males as compared to 2.3% of females were daily drinkers (Johnston et al., 2012).

In sum, Perkins, Haines, and Rice (2005), in the largest study to date considering substance abuse in college students, noted that perceived drinking norms and gender are the two most powerful predictors of college student drinking.

Ethnicity

Of the two large national studies previously mentioned, neither reported specific differences for ethnicity in college students. However, the NSDUH survey (SAMHSA, 2012) reported that in individuals age 12 and older, illicit drug use was 8.7% in Caucasians, 10% in African Americans, 8.4% in Hispanics, 3.8% in Asians, 13.4% in American Indian and Alaskans, 11% in Native Hawaiian and Pacific Islanders, and 13.5% in multiracial individuals.

Current alcohol use rates for the same age range were 56.8% in Caucasians, 42.1% in African Americans, 42.5% in Hispanics, 40% in Asians, 44.7% in American Indian or Native Alaskans, and 46.9% in multiracial individuals (SAMHSA, 2012). Binge drinking rates for the same age range were 23.9% in Caucasians, 19.4% in African Americans, 23.4% in Hispanics, 11.6% in Asians, 24.3% in American Indian or Native Alaskans, and 18.6% in multiracial individuals (SAMHSA, 2012). Specific to ethnicity and college student binge drinking, Wechsler and Kuo (2003) indicated that college campuses with greater diversity (viz., minority students, women, and older students) typically reported lower binge drinking rates.

Greek Membership

As a subset within college student populations, members of fraternities and sororities tend to report higher rates of substance abuse (Wechsler, Kuo, Lee, & Dowdall, 2000). Numerous factors are generally associated with higher substance abuse rates in Greek organizations. Perceived social norms are implicated in this increased prevalence of substance use, but these perceptions are not based on fact. These misperceptions include (a) a perceived overestimation of frequency and quantity of alcohol use among similar others (Baer, Stacey, & Larimer, 1991), (b) a belief that there is a higher prevalence and acceptance (or possibly expectation) of alcohol use (Borsari & Carey, 1999; Scott-Sheldon, Carey, & Carey, 2008), and (c) the impact of heavy drinking through social emulation on those who are not heavy drinkers (Cashin, Presley, & Meilman, 1998).

Housing

In describing emerging adult substance use and abuse, Arnett (2000, 2005) noted that housing location is worthy of consideration. He stated that as individuals move away from their parental homes to college, a less-controlled environment, they are more likely to engage in substance use. Not only have studies supported the increased use of substances by young adults living away from their parents but those living off campus or in Greek housing report the highest rates of substance abuse. In a study of 237 students mandated to receive substance abuse counseling at a university counseling center, Hudspeth (2009) found that over half the mandated students' living arrangements were in environments under less university control, such as off-campus housing or Greek organizational housing. University alcohol policies and the degree to which they are enforced may inadvertently move substance use to off-campus housing, where there is less oversight and greater opportunity for deleterious consequences.

HARM-REDUCTION THEORY AND BENEFICIAL COMPONENTS

The utilization of harm-reduction approaches has gained momentum in colleges and universities. Harm reduction is a paradigm shift away from traditional abstinence-focused, use-prevention substance education programming; this is similar to the move from abstinence-based sex education to a safer sex emphasis. It is a public health philosophy and intervention that recognizes that a drug-free society is not a realistic expectation. It provides practical strategies for helping communities and individuals minimize the negative effects of substance use. One example of a community level harm-reduction intervention is the provision of Safe Rides, a campus-based resource that provides intoxicated students a safe trip back to their residences.

On an individual level, a harm-reduction approach might include one-on-one counseling in which a counselor and student focus on helping the student develop person-specific goals for safer substance use and associated behaviors; thus, harm associated with substance abuse can be reduced. An example of a harm-reduction intervention with a student may be to help the student devise a plan to resist mixing drugs in order to avoid the hazards of their interaction. This may seem counterintuitive and an insignificant or even unsuitable goal at first look; however, if a student is going to continue drug use, this planned behavior change may possibly reduce the risk of substance-related death. A harm-reduction approach does not require abstinence; however, shifting substance use levels downward toward abstinence on the substance use continuum and simultaneously reducing risk to substance-related problems are the overall goals.

Drinking Moderation

As noted by Martlatt and Witkiewitz (2002), as a major part of harm-reduction efforts, drinking moderation has been a common goal for over 3 decades. It emphasizes controlled drinking rather than the prevalent college behavior of "drinking to get drunk." Students often do not have a clear concept of what *moderation* means or what it would look like on a college campus. As part of harm reduction, counselors can help students develop a realistic and fact-based understanding of what it means to drink in moderation. Recognizing that students often enjoy the altered states achieved with substance use, counselors may want to discuss the concept of the "point of diminishing returns" where the "buzz" effect from alcohol occurs at low blood alcohol content (BAC) levels. A low level "buzz" may be highlighted as being preferable to the negative consequences associated with higher BAC in which physical well-being and decision making are severely compromised. By acknowledging a student's desire to alter his or her state through substance use, but encouraging a safer and less risky level of consumption, potential harm can be reduced.

The most basic and well-known guideline for drinking in moderation is the "one drink per hour plan." However, due to the nature of the college culture, many students are unable to schedule their consumption with this guideline in mind. Pregaming, prepping for activities in which there will be no alcohol available, "2 for 1 drink specials" are just a few of the temptations to over imbibe. In addition, one drink per hour may be too many for some students, especially some females. There is, however, research evidence to support educational efforts toward use of moderation as a form of harm reduction, as well as the development of a campus climate that encourages the harm-reduction paradigm, educates students about drinking moderation, and challenges attitudes that support binge drinking.

Though many students continue to drink heavily throughout college and after graduation, other students may undergo a "natural recovery." This natural recovery is termed *maturing out*, which is a self-initiated reduction in use that sometimes occurs over the course of the college experience or as individuals finish college, get married, and/or seek full-time employment. For a relevant study, see Dawson, Grant, Stinson, and Chou (2006).

Models of Change

Many students, unfortunately, do not believe substance use and high drinking levels to be problematic. Despite experiencing negative outcomes from substance use, they are often unconcerned about their behavior. Changing beliefs and attitudes is part of any behavior change. Prochaska and DiClemente's (1982) Transtheoretical Model of Change (TTM) is of foundational importance in contemporary substance abuse and harm-reduction efforts. Though it is a complex model, it is extremely helpful for counselors to be knowledgeable in the six main stages to best facilitate student movement toward healthy behaviors.

Identifying a student's stage of change will guide the appropriate intervention. The initial stage is *precontemplation*. Students in precontemplation have not yet considered making a behavior change and it is important that the counselor not push hard for change at this point in the process. The goal is to increase the *willingness* of the student to contemplate change. Counselors can verbally acknowledge that the decision to change belongs solely to the student while encouraging the client's self-exploration (not action). Counselors should state the behavior risks to the student in personalized rather than abstract terms ("You may want to consider that when you drink to that level, sometimes you blackout and don't recall all the fun you had").

When students move into the second stage, the *contemplation* stage, they are "on the fence" about changing behaviors and are usually not considering making the change in the present but somewhere in the unknown future. Students will value the counselor's acknowledgment that the decision to change is their own, but it can also be helpful to work with students in their evaluation of the pros and cons to the proposed behavior change. Counselors can highlight the identified aspects of substance use that compel the student to use, as well as aspects that the student perceives as negative effects in order for the student to weigh which factors matter most. By identifying and reinforcing new positive outcome expectations, the decisional balance scale may be tipped and guide them off the fence ("It sounds like you might enjoy better sleep and fewer calories if you do cut back on the beer").

In the *preparation* stage, students may be experimenting with changing behaviors or at least planning to begin a desired behavior change in the very near future. Counselors may assist students in problem solving perceived obstacles and building any needed skills, as well as identifying social supports. For instance, to help prepare students for substance behavior changes, counselors may need to share assertiveness or anxiety techniques with students to help them from caving in to social pressures to use.

In the *action* stage, students will need support that reinforces feelings of self-efficacy. They need to feel capable of making the needed changes. It may also be necessary to reiterate long-term benefits to the student while also acknowledging the challenge and potential feelings of loss ("This is a hard change to make even if it will keep you healthy and safe. Eventually you and your friends will adjust to a more sober you"). Alert students that they can expect to "practice" and possibly feel discomfort with the new behaviors during this adjustment period, which may last for several months.

In the *maintenance* stage, students benefit from a periodic check-in for support and continued reinforcement of the benefits. Students may enter another stage, *relapse*. This is when a student falls back into higher-risk behaviors. When this occurs, counselors should help the student evaluate the trigger that initiated the relapse and adjust the current plan to include stronger coping strategies. A relapse could indicate that an important discussion about the indicators of substance dependence may need to occur.

Self-Efficacy

Self-efficacy is best described as ones belief that he or she can control an outcome based on his or her actions and degree of motivation (Bandura, 1999; Hudspeth, 2009). Bandura also describes self-efficacy as a sense of control over internal and external factors impacting a desired action (Bandura, 1997).

DiClemente, Prochaska, and Gilbertini (1985) relate self-efficacy to confidence and temptation. If a student feels confident about the ability to make behavioral changes, both in the level of substance use and in the associated behaviors, it increases the likelihood the student will be successful in the change process. For instance, many students use alcohol to reduce social anxiety. Students who believe they are able to build alternative social anxiety management techniques are more likely to reduce their alcohol consumption. In the face of tempting situations, that is, those that increase the urge to use or use heavily, confidence becomes particularly important to prevent relapse (DiClemente et al., 1985).

Relapse Prevention

Some theories view substance abuse as a chronic disease in which relapse is seen as failure (Larimer & Palmer, 1999). Conversely, Marlatt and Gordon (1985) theorized that substance abuse is a disorder characterized by periods of lapse or relapse. Marlatt (1985) theorized that an individual's problem-solving ability and perceived self-efficacy influence an individual's ability to resist use prior to the initial lapse and during the period after a lapse. In a harm-reduction model, it is possible to utilize a relapse to increase student motivation to actually quit using or stick to a substance-reduction plan. Practitioners need to focus on the successful part of the plan. When a student makes even small reductions in risky behavior, it is important to applaud these efforts at control and label them as successes. This shifts the focus from failure and promotes problem solving as well as offers encouragement. The goal here is to reengage student efforts in the change process.

Attitudes, Norms, and Perceptions

When discussing attitudes, norms, and perceptions, Fishbein and Ajzen's (1975) book, *Belief, Attitude, Intention, and Behavior*, is often cited. Understanding student social norms around substance use within a given college environment, a college counselor may initiate a discussion that is more pertinent to the student. These norms are often the subtle factors that may motivate a client to use and/or abuse a substance.

Researchers have identified norms as one of the most important topics for study and intervention in regard to substance abuse prevention and treatment. Borsari and Carey (2003) defined perceived social norms in terms of an individual's beliefs about substance use. Perceived social norms are different than actual alcohol usage. When it comes to perceptions about college student substance use, misperceptions abound.

Some of the most problematic beliefs pertain to perceptions of substance use prevalence and levels of substance use. Students generally believe others consume more substances and that others do so more frequently than they use substances in reality. In turn, these misperceptions lead students to believe the use of a substance is not only highly acceptable but to a degree, an expectation of participation with the social group. For instance, McCabe's study (2008) of 3,639 undergraduate students indicated that the majority of students tended to overestimate marijuana use, prescription opioids, and prescription stimulants of their peers. Moreover, the students in this study who reported using marijuana and/or a prescription opioids or stimulants, had made the highest estimates of peer usage. The same has been found to be true of alcohol use; students perceive that students drink heavily and those students who drink most heavily are the most likely to greatly overestimate peer alcohol consumption.

The general beliefs that "all college students drink" and that "college is a time for drinking" are not only inaccurate but reinforce uncontrolled drinking. Similar beliefs exist for other drugs such as "college is a time for drug experimentation." These beliefs create skewed attitudes and norms that apply pressure to all students. Not only does this pressure reinforce and increase usage among heavy users, it impacts students whose substance use is at low risk levels and those who would not readily choose to use a substance without such pressure. In order to reinforce positive substance use habits, it is important to close the gap between these perceptions, and reality is a well-substantiated focus of substance education programming.

As noted earlier, harm-reduction approaches include goals for (a) drinking moderation, (b) change, (c) increasing self-efficacy, (d) relapse prevention, (e) improving attitudes, and (f) establishing accurate norms and perceptions. The majority of harm-reduction interventions contain aspects of one or more of three modalities: (a) motivational interviewing, (b) normative feedback, and/or (c) cognitive-behavioral skills.

Motivational Interviewing

Motivational interviewing (MI) techniques as a substance use intervention are intentionally used to help inspire movement through the stages of change (Miller & Rollnick, 1991). It starts by meeting the client "where he or she is" and seeking a small progression in readiness to change a behavior. For instance, in the case of a substance-abusing college student who hasn't considered a behavior change, a counselor may hope to migrate the student through the precontemplation stage and perhaps well into the contemplation stage. MI requires a collaborative spirit between the client and counselor (contrary to former models where counselors may present themselves more authoritatively and address the substance issue more confrontationally). This collaborative spirit also reinforces the autonomy of the student in all decisions relating to substance use. Finally, in order to be successful, the counselor must pull ideas from the client such as the client's perceived benefits to substance use.

Normative Feedback

As a well-researched component of harm-reduction approaches, normative feedback is a comparison of an individual's alcohol consumption compared to other college students. In fact, the more similar the demographic comparison population, the more likely a person will perceive the information as pertinent, thus the greater the potential motivational effectiveness. Gender-specific feedback is quite effective for this and other reasons (Lewis & Neighbors, 2007). As stated, many substance abusers are believed to overestimate the consumption of others; therefore, even heavy drinkers tend to believe their consumption is "average" or possibly a little above average. Normative feedback, however, will give data points that show the heavy drinker to be in a much smaller and less desirable minority. For instance, a heavy-drinking student may be surprised and troubled about being classified as a heavy drinker; thus, normative feedback promotes change through a reality-based comparison between self and the more accurate drinking level of others (Cunningham, Wild, Bondy, & Lin, 2001). Feedback offered in the MI process will include a wide variety of data points to offer an array of potentially motivating factors in the reduction of substance use and high-risk behaviors.

Research has indicated that normative feedback when delivered as part of motivational interventions (Baer, Kivlahan, Blume, McKnight, & Marlatt, 2001; Marlatt et al., 1998) mailed to participants (Collins, Carey, & Sliwinski, 2002; Walters, 2000), and as part of a media campaign (Haines & Spear, 1996), is effective at reducing alcohol consumption and changing perceptions associated with drinking norms. Computer-delivered personalized feedback has shown mixed results (Barnett, Murphy, Colby, & Monti, 2007; Neighbors, Larimer, & Lewis, 2004). Though it is more costly, individual, face-to-face feedback may be the gold standard.

Cognitive-Behavioral Skills Training

As noted earlier, one's confidence in making behavioral changes will impact efforts at substance control behaviors. On many occasions, students may need to learn certain skills, the absence of which may be the cause of heavy substance use. Saltz and DeJong (2002) noted that cognitive-behavioral skills training includes (a) teaching stress management, (b) developing coping skills, (c) utilizing risk-reduction skills, (d) making plans to resist drinking situations, and (e) completing daily alcohol consumption logs. In addition, social skills may need to be addressed in treatment. Students who are better able to manage stress and social anxiety will better maneuver potential social pressures to drink heavily.

SCREENING AND ASSESSING FOR ALCOHOL AND OTHER DRUG PROBLEMS

College counselors should consider the following issues to address substance abuse on campus:

1. Students rarely seek help for substance abuse.
   A. Campus social norms (attitudes and behaviors) are supportive of substance use and cause students to minimize the detrimental consequences that use plays in their presenting problems.
   B. Students are more likely to seek counseling services for problems that on the surface appear unrelated to substance use.
   C. There is a negative relationship between the amount of substance abuse and help seeking—the more abuse, the less likely the student is to seek services.
   D. Studies reveal that students lack faith in college counselors' effectiveness in substance abuse issues.
   E. Racial minorities and males are even less likely to seek services.
   F. College students are in the emerging adulthood phase, which is marked by a search for autonomy.

2. Proactive strategies are necessary to reduce the dangers associated with substance abuse on college campuses.
   A. Entering freshmen experience an increased sense of autonomy from parental controls and anxiety from navigating a new environment. Counselors can advocate for mandatory addiction education for entering freshmen with topics focusing on:
      a. Social norms compared to statistical data.
      b. Risk factors that contribute to addiction potential and severity (age, genetic predisposition, environment, disease progression, drugs of abuse, affective states).
      c. Related consequences of substance abuse (relational, legal, goal-achievement, physical and mental health, behavioral, emotional).
   B. Provide educational services to faculty, staff, and the community at large regarding the dangers of college substance abuse to counter the perception of normalcy that promotes or discounts the dangers regarding college students and substance abuse.
   C. Provide Greek organizations educational services that mirror those provided to entering freshman.
   D. Establish an on-campus collegiate recovery community (CRC).
   E. Make informative substance abuse literature available to students including information that addresses seeking services and community resources.
3. Develop a comprehensive screening strategy to accurately identify those students who might benefit from individual and/or group substance abuse counseling.
   A. College counselors should consider screening students who exhibit the following behaviors:
      a. Sudden drop in grades.
      b. Excessive absenteeism and tardiness.
      c. Sudden withdrawal from extracurricular activities formerly enjoyed.
      d. Erratic or bizarre behaviors and impaired motor functions.
      e. Suicidal or homicidal threats.
      f. Excessive aggressiveness or hostility.
      g. Social isolation.
      h. University or legal consequences related to substance use.
      i. Engaging in domestic violence.
   B. Students who seek counseling services for unrelated issues warrant substance use screening. Such issues include:
      a. Psychological disorders that have an interactional relationship with substance abuse and fall within the spectrum of mood, anxiety, psychotic, personality, and impulse-control disorders.

b. Less severe presentations that include disturbances in affect, mood, behaviors, cognitions, relationships, risky sexual activity, and excessive health problems.

c. Students who fall within multiple risk factor categories (socially alienated, increased stress, immaturity, traumatic experience, genetic propensity, limited social support, academic or situational stress, Greek affiliation, current or unresolved experience with grief, poor problem solving or communication skills, low self-esteem or efficacy, nonexistent connection with spirituality).

Suggested Interventions

1. Substance abuse interventions should focus on harm-reduction strategies.
   A. Utilize cognitive-behavioral strategies to set goals for drinking moderation and safer drinking across high-risk drinking situations.
   B. Provide students with normative data to modify their perception of prescriptive and injunctive norms. Normative feedback includes challenging myths, positive alcohol expectancies, and inaccurate alcohol-related beliefs.
   C. Advocate for students to keep daily alcohol consumption logs.
   D. Utilize motivational interviewing to facilitate the change in attitudes and behaviors.
   E. Teach stress-management strategies.
   F. Developing coping and problem-solving skills that build self-efficacy.
   G. Work with students to increase their positive support network and decrease the risky social supports that normalize substance use.
2. Substance dependence interventions include:
   A. A counselor's immediate focus is to establish rapport while utilizing MI strategies to counter any ambivalence or resistance the student manifests about engaging in treatment.
   B. Provide appropriate referrals to a detoxification, inpatient, or intensive outpatient treatment facility.
   C. Assist the dependent student to navigate treatment barriers.
   D. Utilize MI strategies to facilitate treatment readiness.
   E. Coordinate continuing care services for the student utilizing the relationship the counselor has built with professionals at the referral site.
3. Relapse prevention interventions include:
   A. Support the student in navigating predictable institutional, academic, housing, and social barriers at reentry into the college environment. In addition, interventions that reduce the potential for the student to feel stigmatized and isolated must be a priority.

B. It is imperative that the counselor promotes the student's engagement into the CRC, access to outside community resources, and if possible, a peer mentor.
C. Assist the student with balancing recovery with academic demands.
D. Provide the student access to continued group and/or individual counseling services that focus on the following:
   a. Encourage the student toward personal investment in the on-campus CRC to manifest empowerment, self-efficacy, a sense of safety, and social support.
   b. Build upon the student's current strengths.
   c. Utilize interventions, such as mindfulness, to teach the student emotional modulation skills to counter harmful affective states.
   d. Collaborate with the student on developing a plan that addresses triggers, relapse, and recovery maintenance.
   e. Teach the student stress-management, anxiety reduction, and self-care strategies.
   f. Other group/individual interventions include problem solving, balancing academics with recovery, boundaries, effective communication strategies, esteem building, relaxation training, developing spiritual meaning, and interventions that focus on the student's specific needs.

The research community has developed and tested numerous substance screening and assessment instruments validated with college populations. Prior to selecting prevention or treatment options, it is best to screen individuals for substance-related problems and likelihood of substance abuse or dependence, stage of change and/or readiness to change, and alcohol use behaviors. One consideration may be whether an instrument includes scales to assess for falsification, denial, defensiveness, or random answering. When choosing the assessment instruments to use, it is important to consider the ability of the measure to detect accurately the problem within the college population and the feasibility of implementation (which depends on the measure's length, format, and cost given time, personnel, and budgetary constraints). This chapter cannot include an exhaustive list of assessment options; however, there are reference guides available that may be quite helpful.

According to Larimer, Cronce, Lee, and Kilmer (2004/2005, p. 98), screening for substance use behaviors is important and should include:

1. The severity of the substance use in order to pinpoint where the usage fits on the substance use continuum. In particular, assessing for current substance use levels, multiple substance use, and tolerance levels
2. The temporal stability (i.e., transient versus chronic) of the problem being assessed

3. The existence of high-risk behaviors and negative consequences such as missing class, engaging in sex with strangers, legal problems, and relationship issues
4. Comorbidity with other disorders

Though an in-depth interview is often helpful, assessment instruments may uncover important factors to be considered in treatment or referral.

According to Larimer et al. (2004/2005), the most frequently used assessments are the (a) Young Adult Alcohol Problems Screening Test (YAAPST; Hurlbut & Sher 1992), a 27-item instrument that provides a unidimensional measure of alcohol-related problems over the previous year; (b) College Alcohol Problems Scale–revised (CAPS-r; O'Hare, 1997), an 8-item instrument that yields a personal problems subscale and social problems subscale, as well as a total score related to alcohol consumption; (c) Rutgers Alcohol Problem Index (RAPI; White & Labouvie, 1989), a 23-item instrument or a shorter 18-item version that provides a composite of drinking frequency, typical quantity, and frequency of intoxication; and (d) Alcohol Use Disorders Identification Test (AUDIT; Saunders, Aasland, Babor, de la Fuente, & Grant, 1993), a 10-item instrument that identifies hazardous or harmful alcohol consumption. The instrument's scales cover frequency of drinking, alcohol dependence, and alcohol-related problems.

Longer than the aforementioned instruments, the Substance Abuse Subtle Screening Inventory-3 (SASSI-3; Lazowski, Miller, Boye, & Miller, 1998), a 93-item instrument, and the MacAndrew Scale (MAC: MacAndrew, 1965), a 49-item instrument, contain items that are subtle or covert in that the meaning of the items may not imply substance use, abuse, or dependence and, thus, may reduce the tendency to hide or minimize substance use.

In addition to one or two of the above mentioned instruments, a counseling center may want to have an instrument that assesses a student's readiness for change. Some options for this are the University of Rhode Island Change Assessment Scale (URICA; DiClemente & Hughes, 1990), a 32-item instrument designed to assess motivation for change in substance abusers for four stages of change: precontemplation, contemplation, action, and maintenance. From URICA results, therapists may also calculate a second-order factor (viz., overall readiness-to-change score), which can be used, pretreatment, to guide the direction of the intervention.

The Stages of Change Readiness and Treatment Eagerness Scale (SOCRATES; Miller & Tonigan, 1996), a 19-item instrument, was designed to assess an individual's motivation to change drinking behaviors for three scales: problem recognition, ambivalence, and taking steps, as well as for predicting treatment outcome (Isenhart, 1997). Vik, Culberson, and Sellers (2000) have since created a 16-item version, which produced three scales similar to the original version.

BRIEF ALCOHOL SCREENING AND INTERVENTION
FOR COLLEGE STUDENTS (BASICS)

BASICS (Dimeff, Baer, Kivlahan, & Marlatt, 1999) was developed to address the substance abuse problems of college students. In its original format, it consists of two individual, face-to-face sessions; however, it has been successfully adapted to a group format. In the first session, counselors focus on building an atmosphere of comfort and safety where students can talk openly about substance issues believed to be most pertinent. During the first session, counselors also assess student drinking patterns, alcohol-related attitudes and norms, and motivation for change. In the second session, students are offered personalized feedback with the opportunity to discuss the data in a nonjudgmental, objective but compassionate climate.

BASICS counselors are trained to use motivational interviewing techniques to highlight the parts of the feedback that appear to be the most pertinent to each individual student. This personalized discussion differs greatly from other health education programs where students may be handed substance statistics that they are unable to meaningfully apply to their own experiences with substance use. Utilizing MI techniques, it is an exploratory conversation where the student is encouraged to consider accurate alcohol effects information in conjunction with personalized data points to create a personal plan that reduces risk. Even if a student remains reluctant to change drinking behaviors, studies have shown that the program does tend to shift the student's attitude toward change along the motivational spectrum toward action (Ramos & Perkins, 2006).

The efficaciousness of BASICS is well researched and is considered to be a best-practices program for use with the college population. BASICS has been shown to be effective in reducing risky behaviors with high-risk college students (Roberts, Neal, Kivlahan, Baer, & Marlatt, 2000). The authors reported that at the 2-year mark, the high-risk intervention group who had received the two-session BASICS program had maintained improvements on alcohol-related problems and, to a lesser extent, on drinking patterns than a comparable control group.

In a thorough literature review, Hudspeth (2009) summarized the results of two more notable studies. Hudspeth noted that these studies (Marlatt et al., 1998; Murphy et al., 2001) indicated not only a reduction of binge drinking, but these reductions were maintained over time. Thus, BASICS may be useful to reduce rates of relapse.

In the following section, the authors provide a description of a model CRC as well as suggestions for helping those entering college already in recovery from substance dependence. The section also includes suggestions for those identified as substance dependent once enrolled in college.

TREATING SUBSTANCE DEPENDENCE

In today's world of heavy substance use, combined with earlier detection of substance abuse/dependence, there is an increase in diagnosed substance dependence among adolescents and emerging adults. Therefore, it is essential that college counselors feel equipped to provide effective services to this population. In the United States, just over a quarter of the individuals who enter substance abuse treatment are under the age of 25 (SAMHSA, 2009). As such, college counselors may have integral roles in providing substance abuse and recovery support. First, counselors must be able to assist students who enter college already in recovery. Second, counselors have a responsibility to be able to identify, treat, and provide continuing services for students who receive a diagnosis of dependence during the college years. Third, counselors need to support or advocate for community-level interventions in the form of substance education, social norming, and substance-free programming.

The following will provide general suggestions for counselors working with students who meet or have met the *DSM-IV-TR* criteria for dependence or *DSM-5* criteria for severe substance use disorder. First, the authors address counselors' responsibility toward students who enter college in recovery from addiction and propose suggestions to improve existing services offered. Second, the authors discuss appropriate screening, referrals, and interventions for those diagnosed as substance dependent once enrolled in college.

ADDRESSING THE NEEDS OF STUDENTS ENTERING COLLEGE IN RECOVERY FROM SUBSTANCE USE

Maintaining recovery, in the best circumstances, is difficult. Entering college in recovery increases the number of challenges and stressors to sobriety. Not only do these students have to adjust to an increased sense of autonomy, a new environment, a new set of peers, and the academic demands of postsecondary education, they also have to attempt to protect their recovery by avoiding behavioral, emotional, and cognitive triggers that plague college communities. "Simply put, the college environment is abstinence hostile, and it appears to be growing more so with each passing year" (Cleveland, Harris, Baker, Herbert, & Dean, 2007, p. 13).

Unfortunately, established college recovery communities are sparse; therefore, it falls upon the college counselor to research the needs of the student body and advocate for effective services. Bell et al. (2009) posited that an apathetic public perception that experimental substance use or abuse is a normal part of growing up manifests into institutional, societal, and interpersonal barriers toward providing effective services.

Unfortunately, the researchers also noted that without these programs, recovering students tend to avoid a college education to protect their recovery, struggle maintaining abstinence while in college, or dropout. In the end, when this population does not receive needed services, they struggle to achieve academically, which potentially leads to a lifetime income reduction and lowered self-efficacy, further exacerbating sustained abstinence (Cleveland et al., 2007). The benefits of college recovery communities are that they help recovering students navigate academia, counteract the negative stereotypes associated with seeking help for substance issues, and attract student role models for effective peer support programs (Bell et al., 2009). The following will briefly describe a successful CRC model developed by the Center for the Study of Addiction and Recovery (CSAR) at Texas Tech University. CSAR generously shares information pertaining to their program on their website in order for other schools to build upon CSAR's successes.

CSAR Model at Texas Tech

According to Texas Tech University's website, "Through this holistic approach to continuing care for recovering students, the Collegiate Recovery Community is able to address the problems and issues associated with the transitions from high school to college and from active addiction into recovery" (The Center for the Study of Addiction and Recovery, 2007). The CSAR model has five key components. First, CRC members are required to attend weekly, 1-hour seminars that focus on relapse-prevention strategies, building relationships among members, and strengthening recovery on all levels. Second, CRC members are required to attend one 12-step meeting per week (Cleveland et al., 2007). The on-campus Serenity Center provides various 12-step meetings and a weekly group to discuss all issues pertaining to recovery. Third, CRC members receive academic support through peer tutoring, a safe environment to study within the center, and academic advising from CSAR staff members that are familiar with each student and his or her individual needs (Bell et al., 2009). Fourth, CRC members are involved in a student-run organization that is committed to community service work, including carrying 12-step meetings to local penal facilities. Fifth, CRC members are eligible to apply for tuition scholarships that range between $500 and $5,000 per semester. The actual amount depends upon a member's demonstration of CRC values, service work, and grade point average. In addition, CRC members have access to individual counseling services, academic advising, and counseling referrals if necessary. There is research evidence that supports the efficacy of CRC at Texas Tech. For a full description of research studies and outcomes, see Bell et al. (2009) and Cleveland et al. (2007).

ADDRESSING THE NEEDS OF STUDENTS DETERMINED TO BE SUBSTANCE DEPENDENT

Unfortunately, college students are experiencing an increase in consequences related to the abuse of substances. Some of the consequences include injury, risky sexual behaviors, death, legal problems, compromised immune systems, academic difficulties, violence (Bell et al., 2009), and relational strife (Park & Levenson, 2002). Because of the high frequency of substance use on college campuses and the related negative consequences, it is essential that college counselors are able to competently assess risk factors, accurately diagnosis dependence versus abuse, distinguish between appropriate treatment modalities, and provide effective evidence-based treatment. In addition, they must be able to recognize the symptoms and withdrawal potential of specific drugs of abuse.

WHO TO SCREEN/ASSESS FOR DEPENDENCE/ABUSE?

Essentially, large portions of college populations are viable candidates to receive drug and alcohol assessments or screenings, including those whose lives include the above-noted consequences. Since students tend to minimize risks associated with use and a stigma exists with regard to seeking services for substance use, it is likely that those who do seek services will do so for issues that on the surface appear unrelated. For instance, a student may present to counseling due to feelings of stress around roommate issues only for the counselor to discover the student abuses substances and the roommates are tired of dealing with the student's intoxication. Other potentially unrelated issues that warrant screening are erratic or bizarre behaviors, excessive absenteeism or tardiness, withdrawal from extracurricular activities, and impaired motor functions. In addition, the following mental health issues merit consideration of screening/assessing for substance disorders.

The National Institute on Drug Abuse (NIDA) reported that there is an interaction effect between drug abuse and mood/anxiety disorders, where an individual with one diagnosis is twice as likely to qualify for the comorbid diagnosis. Moreover, NIDA documented the same phenomenon for some personality disorders and conduct disorder (NIDA, 2011). Various mental health disorders that commonly co-occur with substance disorders include posttraumatic stress disorder, untreated attention deficit hyperactivity disorder, schizophrenia, and impulse-control disorders.

Mental health issues that do not qualify within a diagnostic category also increase the likelihood of substance use. Substance use is often an attempt to self-medicate negative affective states, such as dysphoria, anxiety, stress, and hostility. Park and Levenson (2002, p. 487) reported that research "indicates that students who experience more depressed affect report more alcohol consumption (Hussong, Hicks, Levy, & Curran, 2001), more use of drinking to cope (Flynn, 2000; Tyssen, Vaglum, Aasland, Gronvold, & Ekeberg, 1998) and greater alcohol consumption and alcohol-related problems (Camatta & Nagoshi, 1995)." Moreover, research on college students suggests that higher levels of hostility positively correlate to a greater risk of substance abuse and related consequences (Barthelmes, Borsari, Hustad, & Barnett, 2010). In addition, it appears that college women are more apt to self-medicate for stress and dysphoria (Barthelmes et al., 2010), while males are more prone to outward expressions of hostility.

Typically, counselors utilize screening as a first step to determine if further action is required, such as in-depth assessments, immediate interventions, and/or treatment referrals. An in-depth assessment typically involves the use of tests/measures such as the ones listed earlier in the chapter, and a comprehensive clinical interview. The clinical interview addresses the student's biopsychosocial history, current strengths and limitations, family/peer support systems, withdrawal/intoxication potential, treatment barriers, addiction severity, and stage of change. In addition, the counselor will want to determine the drugs of abuse along with the duration, frequency, and amount of use. Information gathered from the assessment guides the next steps a counselor takes.

SUBSTANCE DEPENDENCE: WHAT IS NEXT?

Because of the pro-drug culture and cognitions of normalcy concerning substance use, harm-reduction strategies to address substance abuse are efficacious. However, harm reduction supports reducing use and is not the treatment of choice for dependence since the treatment goal is abstinence (Cleveland et al., 2007) and it is unlikely that a dependent individual can safely control use. The following will explore the next steps, utilizing the assessment data gathered after a counselor determines a student is substance dependent.

Withdrawal/Intoxication Potential

Depending upon the drug, withdrawal may be hazardous to the life of the student. Withdrawal potential is the likelihood that the individual will experience withdrawal symptoms and the degree of associated risks of those symptoms. If the drug has life-threatening withdrawal symptoms, the student will need careful monitoring and hospitalization would be the safest choice. It is also important to consider the potential risk level inherent in the behaviors related to intoxication. Counselors must assess for the likelihood that the individual, if unsupervised, would become intoxicated and, while in this altered state, present a high risk of harm to self or others. Counselors who cannot accurately assess withdrawal/intoxication potential might unintentionally propagate harm and should seek supervision.

The counselor can determine the risk potential by gathering an accurate history of drug use and the consequences related to use. A good history identifies the specific or combination of drugs of abuse; typical behavioral, emotional, and cognitive consequences related to use; and the duration, frequency, method, and amount of use. If the counselor determines that the student is at high risk to harm self or others, then the counselor should follow the same safety protocols used for any client that falls within this category.

To determine withdrawal potential, the counselor utilizes the client self-report of prior withdrawal experiences via the drug history combined with the counselor's knowledge of the withdrawal potential for the specific classes of drugs. Specific drugs of abuse that might require medical withdrawal are alcohol, benzodiazepines, opioids, and barbiturates. Typically, stimulants do not require medical withdrawal. A source of excellent information on addiction and recovery, as well as providing information about acute and postacute withdrawal, is addictionsandrecovery.org/withdrawal.htm.

Support Systems

The information the counselor gathers in this portion of the interview is essential in guiding referral decisions. Understanding the relationship dynamics of the student's family and peer groups at home or on campus helps the counselor determine the best site for treatment. For example, if the student is a freshman and he or she links hometown peers with a strong negative influence combined with strained family relations, the best choice for referral might be a facility closer to the campus. Understanding the student's financial means, including the type of insurance in place, will also direct treatment options.

Addiction Severity

To determine addiction severity, the counselor utilizes the information gathered in the withdrawal/intoxication potential section, along with conceptualizing the course of the individual's addiction (i.e., began with alcohol, now shooting heroin), the duration of time between last use and the onset of withdrawal, current consequences related to addiction, and standardized assessments. This information informs the intensity and duration of treatment referral. A client in the latter stages of addiction requires high-intensity treatment occurring for an extended period, while a recently addicted client might recover in a less-restrictive environment with a shorter stay. Because the course of addiction progresses differently depending on the substance of abuse, genetic predispositions, and environmental factors, it is possible that a college counselor will assess students in the latter stages of dependence. Because addiction, if left untreated, can lead to death, the counselor becomes a lifeline for these students.

As noted earlier in this chapter, it is important to understand the student's stage of change or readiness to engage in treatment. Standardized assessments combined with the client interview help assess readiness to receive services (see earlier section for assessments). During the interview, counselors should pay attention to what clients say, listening for signs of resistance, denial, minimization, rationalization, or justification of consequences and addiction severity. Nonverbal clues that provide insight into a student's level of resistance are observations of affect, body language, and attitude. For example, is the student's quality of affect, while discussing addiction, restricted, hostile, dysphoric, anxious, or detached? Is his or her attitude open, evasive, defensive, hostile, or cooperative? Is the student's body language closed, open, aggressive, or passive? Does the student's affect, attitude, and body language change in relation to subjects being discussed? Counselors should use all verbal and nonverbal messages to determine the level of insight the student has regarding self in relation to addiction.

Counselors should bear in mind that resistance from this population is normal and that challenging resistance via confrontation is contraindicated. Instead, counselors should utilize the MI strategies (mentioned elsewhere in the chapter) to roll with resistance. The counselor's goal is to rapidly build rapport, gain the client's trust, and establish a collaborative relationship in which the student feels that the counselor understands and empathizes with his or her thoughts, feelings, behaviors, and experiences (Scholl & Schmitt, 2009). In this manner, the counselor normalizes the ambivalence felt by the client regarding the nature of the addiction and ambivalence toward engaging in treatment. If, as a result of your assessment, you determine that your client has a high level of resistance toward treatment and a low potential for harm, it is feasible to consider MI strategies to facilitate treatment readiness.

TREATMENT REFERRALS

When making referrals for treatment, competent counselors consider the client's needs, are knowledgeable about local treatment options, and are capable of locating appropriate options beyond the local community. It is also important that the counselor establishes a rapport with local treatment facilities and understands the services they provide. Through building relationships with other professionals, the counselor can consult with these professionals when in doubt and assist in bridging the gap between the client's needs and treatment restrictions.

Building a Resource List

Counselors should contact local treatment facilities to gain insight into the programs offered, treatment flexibility, duration of treatment, cost, types of insurance accepted, available support services, and therapeutic strategies. In addition, counselors should follow up with clients after discharge and ask about the services they received. A simple way to understand the therapeutic strategies is to ask your client to describe a typical day of treatment. Excessive amounts of downtime (watching TV, playing games, sleeping) or an apathetic response regarding the experience, might raise red flags. On the other hand, if the client reports attending multiple psychoeducational and/or counseling groups throughout the day, engaging in meditative practices, reading literature, spending downtime exploring self through written assignments, attending nightly meetings, and boasting that individual sessions "opened my eyes," chances are the facility is providing evidence-based treatment strategies and not just housing your client within a restrictive environment. Specific questions to address with addiction professionals at treatment facilities follow.

1. Financial concerns. What is the cost of the program and what types of insurance do they accept? Is there any funding to accommodate clients who lack financial resources?
2. Duration. Are there different levels of treatment and what are the expectations regarding length of stay at each level?
3. Flexibility. Does their program allow and adjust for individual client differences? Is there any level of treatment that allows the client to leave the facility (perhaps to attend class)?
4. Programs. Does the facility provide onsite medical detoxification, continuing services after initial treatment, family therapy, medical services, and supportive services, which address the client's needs (NIDA, 2011)?
5. Therapeutic strategies. What is the treatment center's mission and philosophy? What is the policy regarding relapse? What type of psychoeducational groups does it have? What do the professionals within the facility consider the most efficacious form of individual therapy?

COORDINATED SERVICES

While the client is in treatment, it is important to stay in contact with the facility. To do so, the counselor must secure a consent for release of information from the client prior to enrollment. Through keeping the lines of communication open between the counselor and the facility, it is easier to coordinate services, especially concerning continuing care. Working with the onsite addiction professionals facilitates a conceptualization of the client's needs after treatment completion, a coordinated relapse prevention plan, and effective treatment strategies to implement.

Relapse Prevention

Just like initial treatment, the relapse prevention plan should be specific to individual needs. In addition, counselors should recognize the risk and protective factors concerning relapse potential. High-risk environments include those that are stressful due to the demands they put on the client or because they trigger ruminations of returning to use. Protective environments support recovery and were explained in the above section of treating students who enter college already in recovery. If an established CRC exists on campus, then a counselor might consider utilizing a peer from this community to mentor the returning student who is new to recovery. Lastly, the counselor should assist the client with navigating barriers, such as safe housing, gaining transportation to meetings, and any academic issue that arose due to the student's absence.

CONCLUSION: POTENTIAL DIRECTIONS FOR ADVOCACY

Prior to creating or overhauling a university's substance abuse and/or dependency program, it is important that counselors become competent and well versed within the field of substance abuse and dependence or have access to expert consultants and university support for any recommended changes. It is strongly suggested that counselors wishing to specialize in treating addiction issues in their student population obtain formal education in addiction counseling, concepts, and treatment. By becoming an expert, institutional barriers become less of an obstacle, established programs gain credibility, and students are more likely to access those services. Yu, Evans, and Perfetti (2003) found that college students with substance use disorders were more apt to seek services from addiction professionals than typical college counseling services.

Through knowledge of the community, counselors serve the needs of students and fill gaps within the current infrastructure. Also through this service, counselor gain direction toward advocacy and program implementation.

College counselors may need to advocate at multiples levels in order to appropriately meet the treatment and prevention needs of students. Sometimes advocacy will be needed for an individual student; however, at other times, counselors may need to influence university policy as well as advocate within the broader community.

In summary, college counselors face what seems to be a monumental task: caring for individuals who are in the middle of their journey toward adulthood, responsibility, and self-actualization. The journey is complex and substance use and abuse may greatly hamper success. College counselors must be versatile and competent to ensure that they can assist when needed and advocate when called upon.

SUBSTANCE USE ESSENTIALS

Given the pervasiveness of substance use in the college population, we are presenting a few basic facts that college counselors should have at hand and share with students (even with low levels of alcohol use) as indicated:

- Standard drink sizes: 1.5 oz of 80 proof liquor or 12 oz of beer or 5 oz of wine. It never hurts to ask a student how many standard drinks he or she drinks in an evening. If a student does not know how many drinks are typical for him/her, this is a risk factor for over consumption.
- It is extremely important to eat a meal high in protein and carbohydrates prior to drinking alcohol.
- Encourage hydration when drinking.
- Due to biological differences, females are unable to safely drink nearly what a male can drink. If you have a female client trying to keep up with her male buddies, this is dangerous.
- Drinking shots and drinking games are high risk. The rapid consumption of alcohol greatly increases the risk of overconsumption and other negative consequences.
- Be able to talk with students about spacing and pacing drinks. Use one drink per hour as a general rule.
- When it comes to marijuana abuse, students are most likely to recognize that marijuana use interferes with their productivity. On occasion, students experience decreased motivation, perceive it as interfering

with school success, or causing other social issues such as a tendency to turn inward, thus becoming less social.

Resources for Students

The National Institute on Alcohol Abuse and Alcoholism (NIAAA) has two free websites that provide information on all aspects of alcohol and drinking.

1. **Rethinking drinking: Alcohol and your health. (www.rethinkingdrinking. niaaa.nih.gov)** For anyone who drinks alcohol, this website offers valuable, research-based information. Using interactive tools, it can help students take a look at their drinking habits and how they may affect the student's health. It covers everything from learning what counts as a drink to finding out whether the student's own drinking pattern may be risky.
2. **NIAAA's college drinking prevention. (www.collegedrinkingprevention. gov)** A one-stop resource for comprehensive research-based information on issues related to alcohol abuse and binge drinking among college students.

Resources for Professionals

1. **www.SAMHSA.gov** (Substance Abuse and Mental Health Services). A government website with up-to-date statistics and excellent publications pertaining to substance use, abuse, and mental health.
2. **www.drugabuse.gov**. The website for the National Institute on Drug Abuse (NIDA). Includes information on drugs of abuse.
3. **www.acha.org**. American College Health Association (ACHA) website.
4. **core.siu.edu**. The Core Institute's information and surveys about alcohol and other drugs.
5. **www.higheredcenter.org/files/product/first-year.pdf**. The Higher Education Center for Alcohol and Other Drug Abuse and Violence Prevention's recommendations for first-year college students.

Screening Instruments
Allen, J. P., & Wilson, V. B. (Eds.). (2003). *Assessing alcohol problems: A guide for clinicians and researchers* (2nd ed.). NIH Publication No. 03–3745. Retrieved from pubs.niaaa.nih.gov/publications/AssessingAlcohol

Student Recovery Program
The CSAR model; visit www.depts.ttu.edu/hs/csa/replication.php
For information on replication of the CSAR model, visit www.depts.ttu .edu/hs/csa/collegiate_recovery.php

REFERENCES

American Psychiatric Association. (2000). *Diagnostic and statistical manual of mental disorders* (4th ed., text rev.). Washington, DC: Author.

American Psychiatric Association. (2013). *Diagnostic and statistical manual of mental disorders* (5th ed.). Washington, DC: Author.

Arnett, J. J. (1997). Young peoples' conception of the transition to adulthood. *Youth and Society, 29*(1), 3–23.

Arnett, J. J. (1998). Learning to stand alone: The contemporary American transition to adulthood in cultural and historical context. *Human Development, 41*(5/6), 295–315.

Arnett, J. J. (2000). Emerging adulthood: A theory of development from late teens through the twenties. *American Psychologist, 55*(5), 469–480.

Arnett, J. J. (2005). The developmental context of substance use in emerging adulthood. *Journal of Drug Issues, 5*(2), 235–254.

Baer, J. S., Kivlahan, D. R., Blume, A. W., McKnight, P., & Marlatt, G. A. (2001). Brief intervention for heavy-drinking college students: 4-year follow-up and natural history. *American Journal of Public Health, 9*(8), 1310–1316.

Baer, J. S., Stacy, A., & Larimer, M. (1991). Biases in the perceptions of drinking norms among college students. *Journal of Studies on Alcohol, 52*(6), 580–586.

Bandura, A. (1997). *Self-efficacy: The exercise of control.* New York, NY: Freeman.

Bandura, A. (1999). A sociocognitive analysis of substance abuse: An agentic perspective. *Psychological Science, 10*(3), 214–217.

Barnett, N. P., Murphy, J. G., Colby, S. M., & Monti, P. M. (2007). Efficacy of counselor vs. computer delivered intervention with mandated college students. *Journal of Addictive Behavior, 32*(11), 2529–2548.

Barthelmes, C. K., Borsari, B., Hustad, J., & Barnett, N. P. (2010). Hostility in mandated students: Exploratory analysis and implications for treatment. *Journal of Substance Abuse Treatment, 38*, 284–291.

Bell, N. J., Kanitkar, K., Kerksiek, K. A., Watson, W., … Harris, K. (2009) "It has made college possible for me": Feedback on the impact of a university-based center for students in recovery. *Journal of American College Health, 57*(6), 650–657.

Borsari, B. E., & Carey, K. B. (1999). Understanding fraternity drinking: Five recurring themes in the literature, 1980–1998. *Journal of American College Health, 48*(1), 30–37.

Borsari, B. E., & Carey, K. B. (2003). Descriptive and injunctive norms in college drinking: A meta-analytic integration. *Journal of Studies on Alcohol, 64*(3), 331–341.

Camatta, D., & Nagoshi, C. T. (1995). Stress, depression, irrational beliefs, and alcohol use and problems in a college student sample. *Alcoholism: Clinical and Experimental Research, 19*(1), 142–146.

Cashin, J. R., Presley, C. A., & Meilman, P. W. (1998). Alcohol use in the Greek system: Follow the leader? *Journal of Studies on Alcohol, 59*(1), 63–70.

The Center for the Study of Addiction and Recovery, Texas Tech University. (2007). *Collegiate recovery community.* Texas Tech University, Lubbock, TX (Last updated January 13, 2013). Retrieved January 12, 2013, from http://www.depts.ttu.edu/hs/csa/collegiate_recovery.php

Chan, K. K., Neighbors, C., Gilson, M., Larimer, M. E., & Marlatt, G. A. (2007). Epidemiological trends in drinking by age and gender: Providing normative feedback to adults. *Addictive Behaviors, 32*(5), 967–976.

Cleveland, H. H., Harris, K. S., Baker, A. K., Herbert, R., & Dean L. R. (2007). Characteristics of a collegiate recovery community: Maintaining recovery in an abstinence-hostile environment. *Journal of Substance Abuse Treatment, 33,* 13–23.

Collins, S. E., Carey, K. B., & Sliwinski, M. J. (2002). Mailed personalized normative feedback as a brief intervention for at-risk college drinkers. *Journal of Studies on Alcohol, 63*(5), 559–567.

Cunningham, J. A., Wild, T. C., Bondy, S. J., & Lin, E. (2001). Impact of normative feedback on problem drinkers: A small-area population study. *Journal of Studies on Alcohol, 62*(2), 228–233.

Dawson, D. A., Grant, B. F., Stinson, F. S., & Chou, P. S. (2006). Maturing out of alcohol dependence: The impact of transitional life events. *Journal of Studies on Alcohol, 67*(2), 195–203.

DiClemente, C. C., & Hughes, S. O. (1990). Stages of change profiles in outpatient alcoholism treatment. *Journal of Substance Abuse, 2*(2), 217–235.

DiClemente, C. C., Prochaska, J. O., & Gilbertini, M. (1985). Self-efficacy and the stages of self-change of smoking, *Cognitive Therapy Research, 9*(2), 181–200.

Dimeff, L. A., Baer, J. S., Kivlahan, D. R., & Marlatt, G. A. (1999). *Brief alcohol screening and interventions for college students: A harm reduction approach.* New York, NY: Guilford Press.

Fishbein, M., & Ajzen, I. (1975). *Belief, attitude, intention, and behavior: An introduction to theory and research.* Reading, MA: Addison-Wesley.

Flynn, H. A. (2000). Comparison of cross-sectional and daily reports in studying the relationship between depression and use of alcohol in response to stress in college students. *Alcoholism: Clinical and Experimental Research, 24*(1), 48–52.

Haines, M., & Spear, S. F. (1996). Changing the perception of the norm: A strategy to decrease binge drinking among college students. *Journal of American College Health, 45*(3), 134–140.

Hingson, R., Heeren, T., Winter, M., & Wechsler, H. (2005). Magnitude of alcohol-related mortality and morbidity among U.S. college students ages 18–24: Changes from 1998 to 2001. *Annual Review of Public Health, 26,* 259–279.

Hingson, R. W., Heeren, T., Zakocs, R. C., Kopstein, A., & Wechsler, H. (2002). Magnitude of alcohol-related mortality and morbidity among U.S. college students ages 18–24. *Journal of Studies on Alcohol, 63*(2), 136–144.

Hudspeth, E. F. (2009). *Relationships between substance abuse related factors, counseling, and harm reduction in emerging adult college students* (Doctoral dissertation). Retrieved from ProQuest Dissertations and Theses database (UMI No. 3385893).

Hurlbut, S. C., & Sher, K. J. (1992). Assessing alcohol problems in college students. *College Health, 41,* 49–58.

Hussong, A. M., Hicks, R. E., Levy, S. A., & Curran, P. J. (2001). Specifying the relations between affect and heavy alcohol use among young adults. *Journal of Abnormal Psychology, 110,* 449–461. [PubMed: 11502088]

Isenhart, C. E. (1997). Pretreatment readiness for change in male alcohol dependent subjects: Predictors of one-year follow-up status. *Journal of Studies on Alcohol, 58*(4), 351–357.

Johnston, L. D., O'Malley, P. M., Bachman, J. G., & Schulenberg, J. E. (2012). *Monitoring the future national survey results on drug use, 1975–2011: Volume II, College students and adults ages 19*–50. Ann Arbor, MI: Institute for Social Research, The University of Michigan.

Larimer, M. E., Cronce, J. M., Lee, C. M., & Kilmer, J. R., (2004/2005). Brief interventions in college settings. *Alcohol Research and Health, 28*(2), 94–104.

Larimer, M. E., & Palmer, R. S. (1999). Relapse prevention. *Alcohol Research and Health, 23*, 151–160.

Lazowski, L. E., Miller, F. G., Boye, M. W., & Miller, G. A. (1998). Efficacy of the Substance Abuse Subtle Screening Inventory-3 (SASSI-3) in identifying substance dependence disorders in clinical settings. *Journal of Personality Assessment, 71*(1), 114–128.

Lewis, M. A., & Neighbors, C. (2007). Optimizing personalized normative feedback: The use of gender-specific referents. *Journal of Studies on Alcohol and Drugs, 68*(2), 228–237.

MacAndrew, C. (1965). The differentiation of male alcoholic outpatients from nonalcoholic psychiatric outpatients by means of the MMPI. *Quarterly Journal of Studies on Alcohol, 26*, 238–246.

Marlatt, G. A. (1985). Relapse prevention: Theoretical rationale and overview of the model. In G. A. Marlatt & J. R. Gordon (Eds.), *Relapse prevention* (Ch. 1). New York, NY: Guilford Press.

Marlatt, G. A., Baer, J. S., Kivlahan, D. R., Dimeff, L. A., Larimer, M. E., Quigley, L. A., ... Williams, J. (1998). Screening and brief intervention for high-risk college student drinkers: Results from a 2-year follow-up assessment. *Journal of Consulting and Clinical Psychology, 66*(4), 604–615.

Marlatt, G. A., & Gordon, J. R. (Eds.). (1985). *Relapse prevention*. New York, NY: Guilford Press.

Marlatt, G. A., & Witkiewitz, K. (2002). Harm reduction approaches to alcohol use: Health promotion, prevention, and treatment. *Addictive Behaviors, 27*(6), 867–886.

McCabe, S. E. (2008). Misperceptions of nonmedical prescription drug use: A web survey of college students. *Addictive Behaviors, 33*(5), 713–724.

Miller, W. R., & Rollnick, S. (1991). *Motivational interviewing: Preparing people to change addictive behavior*. New York, NY: Guilford Press.

Miller, W. R., & Tonigan, J. S. (1996). Assessing drinkers' motivation for change: The Stages of Change Readiness and Treatment Eagerness Scale (SOCRATES). *Psychology of Addictive Behaviors, 10*(2), 81–89.

Murphy, J. G., Duchnick, J. J., Vuchinich, R. E., Davison, J. W., Karg, R. S., Olson, A. M., ... Coffey, T. T. (2001). Relative efficacy of a brief motivational intervention for college student drinkers. *Psychology of Addictive Behaviors, 15*(4), 373–379.

National Epidemiologic Survey on Alcohol and Related Conditions (NESARC). (2001). [Data File]. National Institute on Alcohol Abuse and Alcoholism.

National Institute on Drug Abuse. (2011). *Seeking drug abuse treatment: Know what to ask* (NIH Publication No. 12-7764). Retrieved January 12, 2013, from http://www. drugabuse.gov/publications/seeking-drug-abuse-treatment

National Institute on Drug Abuse, Media Guide. (2009). *How to find what you need to know about drug abuse and addiction* (Rev. December 2012). Retrieved January 13, 2013, from http://www.drugabuse.gov/publications/media-guide/science-drug-abuse-addiction

National Institute on Drug Abuse, NIDA Info Facts. (2011). *Comorbidity: Addiction and other mental disorders* (pp. 1–2). Retrieved January 13, 2013, from http://www

.drugabuse.gov/publications/research-reports/comorbidity-addiction-other-mental-illnesses/how-common-are-comorbid-drug-use-other-mental-diso

Neighbors, C., Larimer, M. E., & Lewis, M. A. (2004). Targeting misperceptions of descriptive drinking norms: Efficacy of a computer-delivered personalized normative feedback intervention. *Journal of Consulting and Clinical Psychology, 73*(3), 434–447.

O'Hare, T. (1997). Measuring problem drinking in first time offenders: Development and validation of the College Alcohol Problem Scale (CAPS). *Journal of Substance Abuse Treatment, 14*(4), 383–387.

Park, C. L., & Levenson, M. R. (2002). Drinking to cope among college students: Prevalence, problems and coping processes. *Journal of Studies on Alcohol, 63*(4), 486–497.

Perkins, H. W., Haines, M. P., & Rice, R. (2005). Misperceiving the college drinking norm and related problems: A nationwide study of exposure to prevention information, perceived norms, and student school misuse. *Journal of Studies on Alcohol, 66*, 470–478.

Prochaska, J. O., & DiClemente C. C. (1982). Transtheoretical therapy: Toward a more integrative model of change. *Psychotherapy: Theory, Research and Practice, 19*(3), 276–288.

Ramos, D., & Perkins, D. F. (2006). Goodness of fit assessment of an alcohol intervention program and underlying theories of chance. *Journal of American College Health, 55*(1), 57–64.

Roberts, L. J., Neal, D. J., Kivlahan, D. R., Baer, J. S., & Marlatt, G. A. (2000). Individual drinking changes following a brief intervention among college students: Clinical significance in an indicated prevention context. *Journal of Consulting and Clinical Psychology, 68*(3), 500–505.

Saltz, R. R., & DeJong, W. (2002). *Reducing alcohol problems on campus: A guide to planning and evaluation.* Task Force of the National Advisory Council on Alcohol Abuse and Alcoholism, National Institute on Alcohol Abuse and Alcoholism (NIH Publication No. 02-5011). Washington, DC: U.S. Department of Health and Human Services.

Saunders, J. B., Aasland, O. G., Babor, T. F., de la Fuente, J. R., & Grant, M. (1993). Development of the Alcohol Use Disorders Identification Test (AUDIT). WHO collaborative project on early detection of persons with harmful alcohol consumption. II. *Addiction, 88,* 791–804.

Scholl, M. B., & Schmitt, D. M. (2009). Using motivational interviewing to address college client alcohol abuse. *Journal of College Counseling, 12*, 57–70.

Scott-Sheldon, L. A. J., Carey, K. B., & Carey, M. P. (2008). Health behavior and college students: Does Greek affiliation matter? *Journal of Behavioral Medicine, 31*(1), 61–70.

Substance Abuse and Mental Health Services Administration. (2012). *Results from the 2011 National Survey on Drug Use and Health: Summary of national findings.* NSDUH Series H-44, HHS Publication No. (SMA) 12-4713. Rockville, MD: Substance Abuse and Mental Health Services Administration.

Substance Abuse and Mental Health Services Administration, Office of Applied Studies. (2009). *Treatment episode data set (TEDS) highlights—2007 National admissions to substance abuse treatment services* (OAS Series #S-45, HHS Publication No. SMA 09-4360). Retrieved January 12, 2013, from http://www.oas.samhsa.gov/TEDS2k7highlights/TEDSHighl2k7Tbl2a.htm

Tyssen, R., Vaglum, P., Aasland, O. G., Gronvold, N. T., & Ekeberg, O. (1998). Use of alcohol to cope with tension, and its relation to gender, years in medical school and hazardous drinking: A study of two nation-wide Norwegian samples of medical students. *Addiction, 93*(9), 1341–1349.

Vik, P. W., Culbertson, K. A., & Sellers, K. (2000). Readiness to change drinking among heavy-drinking college students. *Journal of Studies on Alcohol, 61*(5), 674–680.

Walters, S. T. (2000). In praise of feedback: An effective intervention for college students who are heavy drinkers. *Journal of American College Health, 48*(5), 235–238.

Wechsler, H., Dowdall, G. W., Maenner, G., Gledhill-Hoyt, J., & Lee, H. (1998). Changes in binge drinking and related problems among American college students between 1993 and 1997: Results of the Harvard School of Public Health College Alcohol Study. *Journal of American College Health, 47*(2), 57–68.

Wechsler, H., & Kuo, M. (2003). Watering down the drinks: The moderating effects of college demographics on alcohol use of high-risk groups. *American Journal of Public Health, 93*(11), 1929–1933.

Wechsler, H., Kuo, M., Lee, H., & Dowdall, G. W. (2000). Environmental correlates of underage alcohol use and related problems of college students. *American Journal of Preventive Medicine, 19*(1), 24–29.

Wechsler, H., Lee, J. E., Kuo, M., Seibring, M., Nelson, T. F., & Lee, H. P. (2002). Trends in college binge drinking during a period of increased prevention efforts: Findings from four Harvard School of Public Health study surveys, 1993–2001. *Journal of American College Health, 50*(5), 203–217.

White, H. R., & Labouvie, E. W. (1989). Towards the assessment of adolescent problem drinking. *Journal of Studies on Alcohol, 50*, 30–37.

Yi, H., Chen, C. M., & Williams, G. D. (2006). *Surveillance Report #76: Trends in alcohol-related fatal traffic crashes, United States, 1982–2004.* Bethesda, MD: National Institute on Alcohol Abuse and Alcoholism, Division of Epidemiology and Prevention Research. Retrieved February 1, 2009, from http://www.niaaa.nih. gov/Resources/DatabaseResources/QuickFacts/TrafficCrashes/crash04.htm

Yu, J., Evans, P. C., & Perfetti, L. (2003) Attitudes toward seeking treatment among alcohol-using college students. *The American Journal of Drug and Alcohol Abuse, 29*(3), 671–690.

13

Depression in College Students: Diagnosis, Treatment, and Campus Planning

STEPHANIE C. BELL, SUSAN R. BARCLAY,
AND KEVIN B. STOLTZ

Depression, once referred to as the common cold of mental health, remains a consistent problem for young adults. According to the Substance Abuse and Mental Health Services Administration (SAMHSA; 2008), 8.7% of the United States population ages 18 to 25 suffer from depression. More specifically, 6.7% of college men and 12.5% of college women have been diagnosed with depression (American College Health Association [ACHA], 2012). The Association for University and College Counseling Center Directors (AUCCCD) reported that depression (37.18%) and anxiety (40.94%) were the two most common presenting issues at college counseling centers for the 2010–2011 academic year (Barr, Krylowicz, Reetz, Mistler, & Rando, 2011). Not surprisingly, college-age women are twice as likely to report issues of depression as their male counterparts according to the National Alliance on Mental Illness (NAMI; Gruttadaro & Crudo, 2012). Not only is depression the most commonly acknowledged mental health problem overall, as many as 30% of college students admitted having felt depression so heavy that they felt incapable of normal functioning (ACHA, 2012).

Depression can affect many key aspects of a college student's life including self-esteem, academics, sleep, and stress levels, while possibly negating important psychological resources that help stave off depression (Eisenbarth, 2012; Field, Diego, Pelaez, Deeds, & Delgado, 2012; McCarthy, Fouladi, Juncker, & Matheny, 2006). Depression and its frequent companion, anxiety, along with many other factors, can lead to mental health crises among college students (Gruttadaro & Crudo, 2012). Oftentimes, the crises go unnoticed and untreated at college. Out of 73% identifying a crisis, 35% of students did not report or seek services for these treatable mental health concerns. Raising awareness about mental health issues and the availability and success of services is an important mission for college counselors.

COMORBIDITY OF DEPRESSION AND ANXIETY

Although a separate chapter addresses the treatment of anxiety disorders, it is important to note that depression and anxiety are often linked as comorbid disorders, which further complicates and exacerbates depression. According to recent studies, anywhere from 31% to 50% of those with depression also suffered with anxiety (Almeida et al., 2012; Angst & Dobler-Mikola, 1985; Bitsika & Sharpley, 2012). According to Riggs and Han (2009), chronic anxiety may create vulnerability for depression, although there are several theories as to how these two separate disorders co-occur (e.g., Clark & Watson, 1991; Nelson, Sarapas, Robison-Andrew, Altman, Campbell, & Shankman, 2012; Paul, 1988). As such, counselors should screen for depression with those students presenting symptoms of anxiety because, as research indicates, anxiety is often noted as a precursor to the onset of depression (Angst & Dobler-Mikola, 1985).

This chapter provides information for counselors working with college students who present with symptoms of depression and, to some degree, comorbid depression and anxiety. Depression and its effect on college students are presented. Next, we present a case scenario to provide an example of the way in which depression and anxiety may combine in presentation. In addition, we discuss screening for anxiety and depression as comorbid disorders. Finally, we provide techniques for treatment planning and prevention, cultural considerations, and college and university mental health outreach programing related to depression and comorbid anxiety and depression.

SYMPTOMS AND DIAGNOSIS

Depression is characterized as a period of time when interest is lost in most everyday activities (APA, 2000). General mood is often described as discouraged, sad, hopeless, or down. Individuals may describe a lack of feelings entirely, feeling *blah*, and feeling anxious. Occasionally, the individual may report somatic complaints such as low energy, constant tiredness, and an inability to complete necessary chores or homework instead of negative or depressed feelings. Social withdrawal and loss of interest in hobbies or sports may also occur in depression (APA, 2000).

Additional signs and symptoms of depression among students may include significant appetite changes, insomnia, changes in energy levels, and possibly decreased desire for sexual activity, which should be a particularly salient red flag due to the developmental stage and interests of this population. Weight loss or gain may most often be noticed by family members. The student may also report disruption in her or his sleep or feeling tired after a normally sufficient 8 hours of deep sleep. This can include insomnia or hypersomnia. Sleep disruption in college students can be particularly problematic because of the level of energy their day-to-day activities require. Fatigue is a primary symptom of major depressive disorder and correlates highly with depression and anxiety (Ferentinos, Kontaxakis, Havaki-Kontaxaki Dikeos, & Lykouris, 2011). In fact, those participants who were diagnosed with comorbid depression and anxiety reported the highest levels of fatigue. This lethargy can manifest itself in several ways for students, such as a lack of motivation to attend class, missing extracurricular activities, and disconnecting from friends. These all are indicators that suggest a student may be slipping into a depressive episode.

While some college students might manifest psychomotor agitation and have a hard time being still, lethargy is one of the more telling signs of depression (APA, 2000). The student's energy level may plummet. Students can become consistently tired to the point that even the smallest task can seem insurmountable. Depressed students may also begin to focus on small personal deficits and express feelings of worthlessness. Concentration problems among depressed individuals are common (APA, 2000). In college students, this could manifest itself through trouble studying or focusing in class. Grades may start to slip and students may express frustration with environmental distractions once thought to be whimsical or fun. With a lack of the ability to focus, decision-making abilities may also be impaired. To make matters worse, thoughts of dying and suicide may arise as depression takes hold. As part of a normal assessment of depression and other concerns of psychological distress, counselors have a responsibility to ask questions concerning suicidal ideation and, if suicidal ideation is present, perform a thorough suicide assessment. Please see the chapter on suicide for additional information on this topic.

EFFECTS OF DEPRESSION ON COLLEGE STUDENT FUNCTIONING AND COPING STRATEGIES

Academic difficulty is a serious problematic side effect in college students who experience depression. Heiligenstein and Guenther (1996) found that 92% of college students who were depressed showed signs of significant academic impairment, which included missing classes, interpersonal problems at school, and a decrease in academic performance. Academic problems related to depression may include lack of attention in class, test-taking anxiety, frustration, lack of energy, and the inability to focus on homework. These difficulties have profound repercussions in the life of a college student. Lower academic performance may impair feelings of self-worth and sour a student's thoughts about self. As students sink deeper into depression, academic pressures are compounded with parental and social expectations that can exacerbate students' depression.

Specific Risks During the College Years

Having clear goals and a sense of purpose is highly associated with well-being (King, Hicks, Krull, & Del Gaiso, 2006); however, as Crocker, Canevello, Breines, and Flynn (2010) explained, certain types of goals can have either positive or negative effects on people. Goals related to compassion and social connection showed a positive correlation with well-being, but psychological distress was correlated with goals related to self-image and personal accomplishment (e.g., competition with others). This suggests that a balance is necessary between self-interest and social relationships. Dykman (1998) found that seeking validation from others promoted dysphoria and, conversely, feelings of positive mood were associated with goals of self-improvement (e.g., self-actualization). This research indicates that helping students to make positive goals such as helping them come together as a community to support each other (i.e., compassion goals; Crocker et al., 2010) and to establish goals of realistic self-improvement (Dykman, 1998) may reduce stress, thereby lessening the chances of experiencing a depressive episode.

Students who have goals of fitting in through self-image concerns (e.g., I must be considered popular) and validation from others (e.g., If others like me, then I am doing okay) are at higher risk of developing stress and anxiety that can lead to depression (Crocker et al., 2010; Dykman, 1998). Students who experience chronic rumination and worry are at risk of developing higher distress that can lead to anxiety and depression as well (King et al., 2006). Not only are some goals healthier than other goals, Keller and Nesse (2006) found that negative mood signals difficulty with goal attainment. Thus, students who demonstrate negative moods may benefit from opportunities to discuss their goals and brainstorm avenues for their attainment. Inquiring about social, personal, and professional goals of a student with depressed mood will help the college counselor gain insight into a student's motivation and possible avenues for intervention. Helping students connect to a campus community and develop healthy personal self-growth goals are ways to target risk factors for mood disorders and to help them become positively engaged with their social and academic environments.

For students especially, the connection between self-esteem and symptoms of depression is relevant (Goldring, 2012). Grades are how students measure their own success and, perhaps, an even more essential measure of their parents' approval level. Thus, it is not surprising that students' depression symptoms have been found to be synchronized with the rhythm of the academic calendar's workload in Goldring's study. However, some students tend to ruminate, regardless of the semester date or items due. All students have numerous worries (e.g., financial, social, romantic, academic, loneliness, family disconnection) that can lead to symptoms of depression (Dusselier, Dunn, Wang, Shelley, & Whalen, 2005). For the students who hang on to their negative thinking, the intervention of *thought stopping* (Wolpe & Lazarus, 1968) may be a good first intervention.

SCREENING FOR DEPRESSION

The U.S. Preventive Services Task Force (2009) recommends depression screening when appropriate treatment and follow-up care are available. Most colleges and universities have both student health and mental health services; thus, depression screening on campus is an appropriate endeavor with students. Klein, Ciotoli, and Chung (2011) conducted a study on depression in college students in a primary care setting. They utilized a two-tiered screening technique that demonstrated utility in a college counseling setting or campus health clinic. Using the Patient Health Questionnaire 2 (PHQ-2) first, a two-question screening measure, they identified those students who self-reported depressive symptoms by indicating a positive score on either or both of the two questions. Those students who did not score positive on either question were not referred for additional screening concerning depression. For those who did score positive, a second screening was conducted using the Patient Health Questionnaire 9 (PHQ-9). This screening tool consists of nine diagnostic questions. In the Klein et al. (2011) study protocol, any student scoring over 10 on the PHG-9 was sent for thorough assessment. A clinical interview was used to confirm the diagnosis of depression. The results demonstrate that those students who were experiencing symptoms of depression were identified with a very high degree of accuracy. Using these two instruments could be beneficial in coordinating treatment between campus health services, student residential services, and campus counseling services. Once students are screened, there becomes a need for follow-up assessment to specify mental health disorders.

ASSESSMENTS

Several assessments exist for diagnosing depression and anxiety. Assessment differs from screening in that assessment aids in rendering a clinical diagnosis. Screening is simply a tool used to alert college student personnel and clinicians that a student may need further assessment. One of the most frequently used and applicable depression assessments is the Beck Depression Inventory II (BDI-II; Beck, Steer, & Brown, 1996). The BDI-II is a self-report scale for depression with 21 items. Each item has four responses, ranging from *not present* (0) to *severe* (3). The administration time is a short 5- to 10-minute period and renders a total scale score that can be compared to category norms. The test manual provides ample scoring and norming information. Generally, the higher the score (up to 63), the greater the level of depression (Arbisi & Farmer, 1996). Once diagnosis is verified by additional clinical processes, treatment planning is in order.

AREAS FOR CONSIDERATION

In examining potentially depressed college students, counselors should consider the following issues:

1. **General Mood.** College students with depressed moods present many of the same symptoms as the general population. Diagnosing depression within the context of the college or university setting is important. Sleep deprivation, lack of motivation, and erratic appetite often accompany college students' unusual schedules and social activities. Assessing general mood is important, yet understanding the student's context is critical to an accurate diagnosis. In addition, understanding the co-occurrence of anxiety with symptoms of depression is a critical component.
2. **Social Behavior.** College students experiencing depression may socially withdraw. Assessing for withdrawal from friends, organization meetings, sports teams, and other social activities is an important step in diagnosing depression with college students. Clinicians can ask questions about changes in socializing patterns and a lack of interest in seeking social connection.
3. **Academic Behavior.** College students who are depressed may begin to experience low motivation to attend class, complete homework, and maintain interest in school. This can be accompanied by a lack of interest in activities that were once held as valuable. Student may also report difficulty with focusing attention, general irritability, and fluctuating moods that affect academic performance.
4. **Sleeping Behavior.** The amount of sleep depressed college students are getting may change drastically. They may report sleeping much

more than usual or increasingly disturbed sleep as a result of their depression. Students may also report the reverse—waking frequently accompanied by worry and anxiety. These sleep changes may be accompanied by feelings of tiredness and a lack of interest in any activity.

5. **Appetite.** Although college students may typically experience an erratic diet due to social pressures, clinicians should ask about significant changes in diet. Drastic increases or decreases in diet can accompany depression or anxiety. Again, these changes should be assessed within the context of a college student's social environment so that the social aspects of food consumption are assessed.

USEFUL QUESTIONS FOR ASSESSMENT

- How would you describe your mood most days?
- Have you noticed any changes in your behavior with friends or has your desire to socialize changed recently?
- Are you less involved in organizations/events/work than you used to be?
- How is school going? Has there been a change in your grades lately? Are you going to class? How is your level of focus in class and with homework compared to what it used to be? Using scaling techniques for these questions may help to quantify the student's experience (e.g., When it comes to being focused in class, where would you place yourself on a scale of 1 to 10, with 1 being not at all focused and 10 being very focused?)
- On a scale from 1 to 5, how much effort does it take you to get out of bed and make it to class on time? On a scale from 1 to 5, how much effort can you muster to work on academic assignments?).
- How is your sleep these days? Do you find yourself sleeping more or having trouble sleeping lately? Are you waking up during the night or early mornings? If so, what wakes you and are you able to go back to sleep?
- How is your appetite? Have you experienced any noticeable weight loss or gain in the last few months? Do you find yourself eating more or less than normal? Do you have less desire to eat and enjoy food? Do you experience food as a way to quell anxiety?

TREATMENT PLANNING

Treatment planning for depression commences with clear, disorder-specific, overarching long-term goals (Jongsma & Peterson, 2006). The foremost long-term goal of therapy is to reduce and eliminate clients' depressive symptoms and bring students back to a healthier level of overall functioning and well-being. Over the course of therapy, the student and counselor work on the student's ability to begin identifying, accepting, and coping effectively with the depressive feelings. One of the areas of primary interest may include a student's coping skills.

Enhancing Coping Skills

A college student's ability to cope with stress is an important factor to consider when treating for depression. Experiencing transition and new challenges is a part of normal development during college; however, according to Lazarus and Folkman (1984), a person's ability to cope with a challenge mediates that individual's stress experience concerning resolving the task. Mahmoud, Staten, Hall, and Lennie (2012) used this stress model in exploring college student stress, anxiety, and depression. They found that maladaptive coping (e.g., withdrawal, failure to search for solutions) was correlated to greater psychological distress, including depression, than adaptive coping. Adaptive coping skills that can be addressed with students include identifying the problem, seeking social support, searching for effective solutions, and making corrective behaviors. Adaptive coping skills can be used in conjunction with assessing for student's goal attainment strategies. It should include questions related to how students typically handle challenges. Helping students develop positive coping strategies and behaviors is a practical approach to preventing the onset of depression and treating those suffering depression symptoms.

There are three basic types of coping skills that individuals use in facing obstacles and challenges. These are appraisal-focused skills, in which a student would change the way she thinks about a problem; for instance, helping a student refrain from catastrophizing about a single grade and helping her see that this is just one aspect of her overall performance in a course. Next are problem-focused skills, in which behaviors and actions are taken to solve a particular problem. An example would be working with a student who is depressed due to feeling unable to prepare adequately for final exams and is taught additional study skills to be more effective during testing situations. Lastly are emotion-focused strategies in which a student would intentionally revise his emotional response to a trigger. For example, if a student responds with anger to earning poor grades, he may be taught stress-reducing techniques to help him learn to manage his negative reactions more productively.

Replacement Thoughts and Behaviors

As noted earlier, thought stopping can be a good first intervention as students are asked to raise their cognitive awareness of the negative thoughts that govern their feelings and behaviors. By encouraging students to become actively aware of their habitual negative thinking and to take notice of its presence in their daily lives, students can begin to take control over their depressive thoughts. Following this with other cognitive-behavioral techniques may be effective in lessening overall symptoms of depression. A useful technique is the assessment of irrational thoughts and replacement with disputing thoughts using forms such as rational emotive behavioral therapy (REBT) worksheets. Using mindfulness techniques, including relaxation scripts and present-centered awareness activities, is also useful in helping students reduce their overall stress levels and combat depression adjunctively. Using the "one thing different" technique, students can be asked to respond to a negative self-thought or rumination that keeps them feeling down to "do one thing different" next time this type of thought pattern begins again.

Relapse Prevention Measures

Relapse prevention is another long-term goal in therapy. The student and counselor will begin by discussing and setting realistic positive beliefs about the student and specific immediate environmental factors that were originally conceptualized as negative. Additionally, students will focus on building skills for developing positive relationships. By engaging in healthy relationships, clients are in a stronger position to avoid possible relapse (Dixon & Kurpius, 2008). The role of social support networks in combatting depression—in both prevention and treatment—is significant and through helping students become involved in primary relationships and campus social organizations, relapse prevention strategies are also being put in place.

Cognitive Exploration of Precursors to Current Mood State

Short-term goals are a critical aspect to achieving long-term goals with depressed students. These goals are used throughout the treatment process when appropriate (Jongsma & Peterson, 2006). First, counselors ask students to describe any past experience(s) with depression, as well as explore the current depressive episode. Helping students describe the impact depression is having on daily functioning and relationships is an important goal so that students can get a full picture of the difficulties and how these problems interrelate to cause depression. Next, the counselor will encourage students to identify and articulate the source of their depressed mood. Effective therapy interventions include helping clients to: (a) identify behavioral strategies that will impede their depression, (b) recognize and replace negative self-talk that supports their depression,

(c) identify important persons (past and present) in their lives and examine their relationships with those people, and (d) practice assertiveness skills. Learning the use of assertiveness skills in relationships is important so that students can lessen or alleviate anxiety and stress that contribute to depression (Dixon & Kurpius, 2008). Additionally, learning conflict resolution and problem-solving techniques and examining the possibility of grief issues that might be contributing to the depression can be important topics for counseling sessions with students.

LIFESTYLE EXPLORATION

Other treatment strategies may include: (a) discussing negative thoughts and feelings associated with childhood experiences that are still influencing current thought/behavior/feeling patterns, (b) examining past and present relations with parents and siblings, (c) creating an exercise routine, (d) evaluating dietary and nutritional habits, especially in cases in which students are trying to lose weight and may be nutritionally depleted or in the case of overconsumption of alcohol, which can lead to a depressive state, (e) contributing to the well-being of others through volunteerism, and (f) reading books on understanding and overcoming depression.

CASE STUDY: JOHN

John, an active member on the board of his fraternity and captain of the intramural soccer team on campus, has shown signs of withdrawal (e.g., being absent from soccer practice, missing board meetings). He is sleeping more and longer and has a loss of interest in activities that he once enjoyed with gusto (e.g., playing soccer, talking with friends). He reports to the campus counseling center when he realizes that he has failed two quizzes in his major area and cannot understand what is going on in his life.

The counselor questions John about the key areas of functioning (mood, academic behavior, social behavior, sleep habits, and appetite) and, after hearing John's monotonic replies, decides to administer the BDI-II. John's score suggests a moderate level of depression and the counselor begins treatment with cognitive-behavioral interventions. John's complaint about falling grades was accompanied by negative self-talk regarding his future career opportunities and graduate school acceptance. The counselor encouraged John to monitor his self-defeating thoughts and, when they occurred, to dispute them with more positive thoughts such as,

"I had one poor quiz grade, but I can study harder and bring up my average on the next quiz" or "One bad day will not undo years of hard work." The client was also encouraged to remember that he did not have to "listen to depression" and that he could still choose to show up for classes and extracurricular events.

After several sessions, John admitted that the replacement thoughts and sense of control were making a big difference in his mood and thoughts. He noted that he had been able to take back his life from depression and while he still wanted to continue counseling, he felt that he was back on track and would use the counseling sessions as insurance against another severe bout of depression as he addressed some of the underlying issues that he believed contributed to his unexpected drop into the depressive state.

MULTICULTURAL CONSIDERATIONS

Hudson, Towey, and Shinar (2008) studied a sample of nontraditional college students to produce data on racial and ethnic variations of depression. They compared depression statistics of Dominican, Puerto Rican, Central/South American, and Jamaican/Haitian against African American and European American students. These authors found that the Dominican group reported the highest rates of depression when compared to all the different racial/ethnic groups. African Americans reported the lowest incidence of depression. In accordance with previous literature, Hudson et al. found the statistics on depression in females to be much higher than males across the different cultures. According to the AUCCCD (Barr, et al., 2011), White students were most likely to seek counseling services on campus (70%), followed by African Americans (9.94%), Latinos (8.2%), Asian/Asian Americans (5.8%), Multiracial students (4.08%), Other Race/ Ethnicity (3.55%), and American Indian/Native Americans (.72%).

These statistics indicate that college campuses and counseling centers may not be providing services to populations on campus that may benefit from mental health interventions. The reasons are varied and complex. Many racial and ethnic populations experience shame in, or resistance to, seeking mental health services. Overcoming these barriers falls squarely on the shoulders of the college or university. Student success and retention are important considerations for college and university administration. Helping all students learn and be successful are common goals stated by higher learning institutions. Mental health services play an important role in these institutional goals. With this in mind, we offer ways that college counseling centers can develop outreach programing to help all students discover and use mental health services when they are suffering depression.

OUTREACH EFFORTS ON COLLEGE CAMPUSES

University administration and personnel have the responsibility and excellent opportunities to implement outreach programs on their campuses. The days of passive approaches to making information available about depression are over. With the increasing number of students who are either depressed or considering suicide, campus personnel must be active agents in developing and implementing outreach programs to the entire campus community (Fratt, 2008; Washburn & Mandrusiak, 2010). Though the scope of programs may differ from campus to campus, there are common elements in the most successful outreach efforts. Those elements include psychoeducational workshops for faculty, staff, and students; training faculty, staff, and students as gatekeepers; and reducing the stigma attached to mental health issues while providing prevention, screening, and treatment to at-risk students. With so many possibilities, many times the question for university personnel becomes, "Where do we begin?"

Fortunately, there are numerous outreach programs already in existence that appear to be making a difference for university faculty, staff, and students. One program, initiated by Suffolk University in 2006 and adopted by other universities, continues to receive favorable responses. The Action for Depression Awareness, Prevention, and Treatment (ADAPT; Field, Elliott, & Korn, 2006) program is a campus-wide collaborative effort that focuses on the prevention of depression and suicide, the reduction of the stigma associated with mental health maladies such as depression, and the early detection of depression in the college population. The first phase of the ADAPT program included disseminating information about depression and suicide, providing educational sessions concerning how to prevent and treat depression, and instituting workshops to teach individuals how to talk with, and be helpful to, at-risk students. Further efforts of the Counseling Center concentrated on creating and distributing brochures, dedicating a section of the website to information about ADAPT and depression, and collaborating with the Performing Arts department to develop and produce a short play that illustrated the story of one student's journey through depression. The play, which the Counseling Center developed into an educational video, is followed by discussion groups and relaxation techniques training for attendees.

Another excellent prevention and intervention model resides at the University of British Columbia (UBC). Based on the Jed Foundation framework, the model is a seven-prong program aimed at promoting mental health awareness and well-being and preventing suicide (Washburn & Mandrusiak, 2010). Outreach includes screening efforts, life skills development, educational programs, and crisis management. An additional important component to UBC's model is that of social network promotion. Research indicates perceived social connectedness and support are strong protective factors against depression and suicide (Armstrong & Oomen-Early, 2009; Brissette, Scheier, & Carver, 2002)

Students prove to be excellent agents of action in outreach programming. At the University of Michigan, students voiced their desire for an interactive website where they could learn more about stress and anxiety, depression, and suicide. The university counseling center staff responded by creating a student-friendly website that they tout as "a cross between Facebook and WebMD" (Fratt, 2008). Included on the website is a screening tool for various mental health areas, including depression. Students are able to read informative articles pertaining to their mental health concerns and download fact sheets. In addition, the University of Michigan counseling center has created several mental health YouTube videos and included a link to those videos on their website.

These are just a few examples of proactive efforts college personnel are taking on their campuses. Colleges and universities have many more options in providing mental health programming to their student populations. Important to remember is that outreach efforts must take into consideration the diversity represented in the student body. In addition to traditional-aged college students, many campuses include nontraditional-aged students, veterans, and international students. One size programming does not fit all. University of Michigan personnel realized this when they conducted a survey in which they discovered that international students were seeking mental health services at a much lower rate than other students (Fratt, 2008). This discovery led to a collaborative partnership between the University of Michigan counseling center and the International Services office. Together, staff from these offices are able to identify at-risk international students and provide them with services to alleviate their symptoms.

Other noted outreach efforts include:

For students:

- Mental health workshops during freshman orientation (Mount Marty College; Fratt, 2008)
- Web-based surveys/assessments (Fratt, 2008)
- Anonymous "hotline" for nonemergency matters, giving students an outlet for connecting with another human and talking about their struggles (Hartwick College; Fratt, 2008)
- Mental health extravaganzas offering freebies, such as t-shirts and hats, entice students to attend (University of Michigan; Fratt, 2008)
- Peer mentoring program for incoming or existing students (Hartwick College; Fratt, 2008; also, see Phinney, Campos, Kallemeyn, & Kim, 2011)
- Educational workshops, which teach students how to identify peers who are at risk, talk to their peers about depression, and refer peers for counseling services

- Mental health screening day held nationwide annually in October (www.mentalhealthscreening.org/programs/colleges/ndsd.aspx)
- Social network development, helping students to become engaged socially and make meaningful connections (UBC; Washburn & Mandrusiak, 2010)
- Residence assistant training (for training guidelines, see Grosz [1990])

For faculty/staff:

- Educational workshops and gatekeeper training (learning how to recognize signs/symptoms of depression; learning how to talk to students; knowing when and where to refer)
- Crisis management training
- Involvement in creative endeavors, such as plays and skits (Suffolk University; Field, Elliott, & Korn, 2006)
- Encouraging curriculum infusion as a mental health promotion strategy (Mitchell et al., 2012)
- Utilizing social networking sites (Holleran, 2010; Moreno et al., 2011)

As most of the programs above represent, a holistic approach is optimal in trying to alleviate anxiety and depression and prevent suicide in college students (Fratt, 2008). A holistic approach will involve programming that reaches and involves faculty, staff, and students (Fratt, 2008). Continual program evaluation is vital for ensuring that outreach programs are representing best practices and meeting the needs of faculty, staff, and students (Washburn & Mandrusiak, 2010). For additional information and guidelines, see The Jed Foundation (2006) and Kern (2000), two excellent resources for developing outreach programs on college campuses.

CONCLUSION

Depression remains an increasingly critical issue on college campuses. The effects of mental health issues on college students are strikingly clear. Counselors who work in higher education settings have a responsibility to be proactive in raising awareness about depression and educating students on the prevention of depression and on available treatment. Proactive approaches will follow a holistic model that not only reaches out to all campus constituents, but also involves faculty, staff, and students from across campus in becoming gatekeepers, mentors, and referrers for those who experience life-altering depression.

In this chapter, we have attempted to help college counselors understand college student depression better and how to recognize symptoms and intervene on the behalf of at-risk students. We have included information about screening, assessment, and treatment of depression. We also presented information concerning the comorbid presentation of anxiety and depression as a complicating factor in working with students. In addition, we have highlighted several existing outreach programs, provided supplemental programming ideas, and suggested resources for counselors in developing outreach programs on their campuses. Our hope is that we have provided counselors who work on college campuses with enough information to be proactive agents in implementing screenings, activities, and programming that will help reduce depression among students on their campuses.

RESOURCES

ADAPT, Suffolk University Counseling Center website: www2.suffolk.edu/offices/4421.html

PBS Resources for Understanding Depression: www.pbs.org/wgbh/take-onestep/depression/resources.html

American Psychological Resources for Depression: www.apa.org/topics/depress/index.aspx

Patient Health Screeners Website: phqscreeners.com/overview.aspx

Beck Depression Inventory II Product Page: www.pearsonassessments.com/HAIWEB/Cultures/en-us/Productdetail.htm?Pid=015-8018-370

Beck Anxiety Inventory Product Page: www.pearsonassessments.com/HAIWEB/Cultures/en-us/Productdetail.htm?Pid=015-8018-400

Apps in the Apple iTunes Store: Search "Depression" or "Anxiety"

Anxiety Treatment Resources Suggested Reading List: anxietytreatmentresources.com/?ref=Suggested_Readings

National Institute of Mental Health on Anxiety: www.nimh.nih.gov/health/topics/anxiety-disorders/index.shtml

National Institute of Mental Health on Depression: www.nimh.nih.gov/health/topics/depression/index.shtml

Anxiety and Depression Association of America Resources: www.adaa.org/living-with-anxiety/ask-and-learn/resourcs

REFERENCES

Almeida, O. P., Pirkis, J., Kerse, N., Sim, M., Flicker, L., Snowdon, J., ... Paff, J. J. (2012). A randomized trial to reduce the prevalence of depression and self harm behavior in older primary care patients. *Annals of Family Medicine, 10*(4), 347–356.

American College Health Association. (2012). *American College Health Association–National College Health Assessment II: Undergraduate reference group executive summary spring 2012.* Hanover, MD: American College Health Association.

American Psychiatric Association. (2000). *Diagnostic and statistical manual of mental disorders* (4th ed., text rev.). Washington, DC: Author.

Angst, J., & Dobler-Mikola, A. (1985). The Zurich study: VI. A continuum from depression to anxiety disorders? *European Archives of Psychiatry and Neurological Sciences, 235,* 179–186.

Armstrong, S., & Oomen-Early, J. (2009). Social connectedness, self-esteem, and depression symptomatology among collegiate athletes versus non-athletes. *Journal of American College Health, 57,* 521–526.

Barr, V., Krylowicz, B., Reetz, D., Mistler, B. J., & Rando, R. (2011). *The Association for University and College Counseling Center Directors annual report.* Retrieved from http://www.aucccd.org/support/aucccd_directors_survey_monograph_2011.pdf

Beck, A. T., & Steer, R. A. (1990). *Manual for the Beck Anxiety Inventory.* San Antonio, TX: The Psychological Corporation.

Beck, A. T., & Steer, R. A. (1993). *Beck Anxiety Inventory* [1993 edition]. San Antonio, TX: The Psychological Corporation.

Beck, A. T., Steer, R. A., & Brown, G. (1996). *Beck Depression Inventory-II.* San Antonio, TX: The Psychological Corporation.

Bitsika, V., & Sharpley, C. F. (2012). Comorbidity of anxiety-depression among Australian university students: Implications for student counselors. *British Journal of Guidance & Counselling, 40*(4), 385–394.

Brissette, I., Scheier, M. F., & Carver, C. S. (2002). The role of optimism in social network development, coping, and psychological adjustment during a life transition. *Journal of Personality and Social Psychology, 82,* 102–111.

Crocker, J., Canevello, A., Breines, J. G., & Flynn, H. (2010). Interpersonal goals and change in anxiety and dysphoria in first-semester college students. *Journal of Personality & Social Psychology, 98*(6), 1009–1024.

Dixon, S. K., & Kurpius, S. E. R. (2008). Depression and college stress among university undergraduates: Do mattering and self-esteem make a difference? *Journal of College Student Development, 49*(5), 412–424.

Dusselier, L., Dunn, B., Wang, Y., Shelley II, M. C., & Whalen, D. F. (2005). Personal, health, academic, and environmental predictors of stress for residence hall students. *Journal of American College Health, 54*(1), 15–24.

Dykman, B. M. (1998). Integrating cognitive and motivational factors in depression: Initial tests of a goal orientation approach. *Journal of Personality and Social Psychology, 74,* 139–158.

Eisenbarth, C. (2012). Does self-esteem moderate the relations among perceived stress, coping, and depression? *College Student Journal, 46*(1), 149–157.

Ferentinos, P., Kontaxakis, V., Havaki-Kontaxaki, B., Dikeos, D., & Lykouras, L. (2011). Psychometric evaluation of the Fatigue Severity Scale in patients with major depression. *Quality of Life Research, 20*(3), 457–465.

Field, L., Elliott, M. S., & Korn, P. R. (2006). A successful community-based intervention for addressing college student depression. *Journal of College Student Development, 47*(1), 105–109.

Field, T., Diego, M., Pelaez, M., Deeds, O., & Delgado, J. (2012). Depression and related problems in university students. *College Student Journal, 46*(1), 193–202.

Fratt, L. (2008). Alleviating silent suffering. *University Business Magazine, 11*(7), 39–41.

Goldring, M. A. (2012). Cycling through the blues: The impact of systemic external stressors on student mental states and symptoms of depression. *College Student Jouranl, 46,* 680–696.

Grosz, R. D. (1990). Suicide: Training the resident assistant as an interventionist. *Journal of College Student Psychotherapy, 4*(3/4), 179–194. doi: 10.1300/ J035v04n03_11

Gruttadaro, D., & Crudo, D. (2012). *College students speak: A survey report on mental health.* Arlington, VA: National Alliance on Mental Illness.

Heiligenstein, E., & Guenther, G. (1996). Depression and academic impairment in college students. *Journal of American College Health, 45*(2), 59–64.

Holleran, S. E. (2010). The early detection of depression from social networking sites. *Dissertation Abstracts International: Section B: The Sciences and Engineering, 71*(5-B), 3401.

Hudson, R., Towey, J., & Shinar, O. (2008). Depression and racial/ethnic variations within a diverse non-traditional college sample. *College Student Journal, 42*(1), 103–114.

The Jed Foundation. (2006). *Framework for developing institutional protocols for the acutely distressed or suicidal college student.* New York, NY: Author.

Jongsma, A. E., & Peterson, L. M. (2006). *The complete adult psychotherapy treatment planner.* Hoboken, NJ: Wiley & Sons.

Keller, M. C., & Nesse, R. M. (2006). The evolutionary significance of depressive symptoms: Different adverse situations lead to different depressive symptom patterns. *Journal of Personality and Social Psychology, 91*, 316–330.

Kern, C. W. (2000). Outreach programming from the college counseling center. In D. C. Davis & K. M. Humphrey (Eds.), *College counseling: Issues and strategies for a new millennium* (pp. 205–219). Alexandria, VA: American Counseling Association.

King, L. A., Hicks, J. A., Krull, J. L., & Del Gaiso, A. K. (2006). Positive affect and the experience of meaning in life. *Journal of Personality and Social Psychology, 90*, 179–196.

Klein, M. C., Ciotoli, C., & Chung, H. (2011). Primary care screening of depression and treatment engagement in a university health center: A retrospective analysis. *Journal of American College Health, 59*(4), 289–295.

Kroenke, K., Spitzer, R. L., Williams, J. B. W., & Lowe, B. (2010). The patient health questionnaire somatic, anxiety and depressive symptom scales: A systematic review. *General Hospital Psychiatry, 32*(4), 345–359.

Lazarus, R. S., & Folkman, S. (1984). *Stress, appraisal, and coping.* New York, NY: Springer Publishing Company.

Mahmoud, J. S. R., Staten, R. T., Hall, L. A., & Lennie, T. A. (2012). The relationship among young adult college students' depression, anxiety, stress, demographics, life satisfaction, and coping styles. *Issues in Mental Health Nursing, 33*(3), 149–156.

McCarthy, C. J., Fouladi, R. T., Juncker, B. D., & Matheny, K. B. (2006). Psychological resources as stress buffers: Their relationship to university students' anxiety and depression. *Journal of College Counseling, 9*, 99–110.

Mitchell, S. L., Darrow, S. A., Haggerty, M., Neill, T., Carvalho, A., & Uschold, C. (2012). Curriculum infusion as a college student mental health promotion strategy. *Journal of College Student Psychotherapy, 26*, 22–38. doi: 10.1080/87568225 .2012.633038

Moreno, M., Jelenchick, L. A., Egan, K. G., Cox, E., Young, H., Gannon, K. E., & Becker, T. (2011). Feeling bad on Facebook: Depression disclosures by college students on a social networking site. *Depression and Anxiety, 28*, 447–455.

Phinney, J. S., Campos, C. M. T., Kallemeyn, D. M. P., & Kim. C. (2011). Processes and outcomes of a mentoring program for Latino college freshmen. *Journal of Social Issues, 67,* 599–621.

Riggs, S. A., & Han, G. (2009). Predictors of anxiety and depression in emerging adulthood. *Journal of Adult Development, 16,* 39–52.

Substance Abuse and Mental Health Services Administration. (2008). *National Survey on Drug Use and Health.* Retrieved November 6, 2012, from http://www.nimh.nih.gov/statistics/1MDD_ADULT.shtml

U.S. Preventive Services Task Force. (2009). *Screening for depression: Recommendations and rationale.* Retrieved from http://www.uspreventiveservicestaskforce.org/3rduspstf/depression/depressrr.htm

Washburn, C. A., & Mandrusiak, M. (2010). Campus suicide prevention and intervention: Putting best practice policy into action. *Canadian Journal of Higher Education, 40*(1), 101–119.

Wolpe, J., & Lazarus, A. A. (1968). *Behavior therapy techniques: A guide to the treatment of neuroses* (pp. 132–133). New York, NY: Pergamon Press.

14

Anxiety Disorders and Treatment Strategies for College Students

TONY MICHAEL

While some individuals idealize the college years as a time of few worries and responsibilities, many students actually find the experience stressful and demanding. Meeting academic demands, getting along with roommates, dealing with new social pressures, questioning career choices, managing finances, and other new responsibilities of the college experience can give rise to unexpected and undesired stress and anxiety. While event-related stress does not cause anxiety disorders on its own, it can worsen symptoms of a preexisting anxiety disorder or trigger an anxiety disorder in someone who may be predisposed. The symptoms of anxiety disorders generally involve disturbances in mood, thinking, and behavior. Mild anxiety may be appropriate during the week of final exams or before a first date, but college students affected by anxiety disorders experience overwhelming feelings of fear and worry that interfere with their daily lives and ability to cope effectively. According to the Association for University and College Counseling Directors (2011), 41% of all college students who visit counseling centers struggle with anxiety, making it the most common presenting problem for college counselors. This chapter assesses the different classifications of anxiety disorders and evaluates effective treatment and intervention strategies for the college student population.

ASSESSMENT AND CLASSIFICATION OF ANXIETY DISORDERS

The Anxiety Disorders Association of America (ADAA, 2012) reports that anxiety disorders are the most common mental illnesses in the United States, affecting 40 million (18%) of the adult population age 18 and older.

Although anxiety disorders are highly treatable, only about one third of those affected receive psychotherapeutic or psychopharmacological treatment (ADAA, 2012; Kessler, Ruscio, Shear, & Wittchen, 2009; Lepine, 2002). Anxiety disorders arise with other mental or physical illnesses, including alcohol and substance abuse, both of which are common among college students. Unfortunately, these other illnesses may mask anxiety symptoms or actually make them worse. The co-occuring mental and physical illnesses need to be treated before an individual can effectively respond to treatment for an anxiety disorder (National Institute of Mental Health [NIMH], 2009). Therefore, the ability to adequately assess and distinguish anxiety disorders is essential to mental health practitioners working with college students. There are six types of anxiety disorder: generalized anxiety disorder (GAD), obsessive-compulsive disorder (OCD), panic disorder, posttraumatic stress disorder (PTSD), social anxiety disorder, and specific phobias. There is a separate chapter in this book that more fully addresses OCD, but in the following section, each of the six classifications will be examined, along with the more general concept of test anxiety.

Generalized Anxiety Disorder

GAD is characterized as excessive worry with symptoms of physiological arousal such as restlessness, insomnia, and muscle tension. These symptoms tend to evolve gradually and insidiously; college students may not realize at first that their normal attention to assignment due dates and time commitments have grown into an overly consuming sense of worry. To meet diagnostic criteria for the disorder, an individual must have excessive and difficult-to-control anxiety surrounding several different events or activities for at least 6 months (ADAA, 2012). College students affected by GAD cannot refrain from worrying, even during what should be relaxed and calming situations, such as during time with friends or in leisure activities. Symptoms that students may report include difficulty with activities such as relaxing, falling asleep, and concentrating; they or their friends are also likely to notice that they are increasingly impatient and irritable. Physical symptoms accompanying GAD include sweating, an upset stomach, diarrhea, frequent urination, cold and clammy hands, a lump in the throat, a dry mouth, shortness of breath, headaches, and dizziness. Managing the normal demands of classes, work, relationships, and everyday life can become increasingly more difficult for students with this disorder (NIMH, 2010a). A typical comment by a college student may include:

> I have a hard time sleeping. The past few months I have woken up in the middle of the night and can't go back to sleep. I also

have problems concentrating on school. There are times where I feel a little lightheaded and find my heart racing fast. I tend to overreact and imagine that the worst things are happening. For instance, I had a bug bite on my arm, and thought it was skin cancer.

GAD is relatively common; the disorder affects 6.8 million adults (3.1% of the U.S. population). Women are twice as likely to have the disorder as men, with lifetime prevalence rates of 4% to 7% (ADAA, 2012; Hoge, Ivkovic, & Fricchione, 2012). While onset is usually in adolescence or childhood, the disorder may also first appear in college or the early adult years. GAD is also associated with seriously impaired social and occupational functioning, comorbidity with other disorders, and increased risk for suicide (Nepon, Belik, Bolton, & Sareen, 2010). College counselors should be aware that GAD could go undiagnosed if a student first seeks medical help for the physiological symptoms or if the student fails to seek assistance from mental health providers due to fear of the stigma of mental illness. When identified properly, however, GAD is highly treatable (NIMH, 2010a) and guidelines for treatment will follow the descriptions of each type of anxiety disorder.

Obsessive-Compulsive Disorder

OCD is a condition involving obsessions and compulsive rituals. Obsessions are intrusive, anxiety-evoking thoughts, images, and impulses, while compulsive rituals are longings to perform behavioral or mental acts to reduce distress. The specific expression of obsessions and compulsions varies widely among individuals, and often within individuals over time. Generally, obsessions concern contamination, the fear of illness, responsibility for harm or mistakes, religion and morality, exactness, sex, and violence (Rachman & Hodgson, 1980). In response to these obsessions, college students may perform a variety of compulsions or neutralizing responses such as washing, checking, arranging, or mental rituals, and may avoid the situations that provoke the obsessions (NIMH, 2009). OCD affects 2.2 million (1.0%) of the U.S. adult population and is equally common among men and women. The median age of onset is 19 with 25% of cases occurring by age 14. Furthermore, one third of affected adults first experienced symptoms in childhood (ADAA, 2012). A student affected by OCD may make comments like:

I have a lot of routines. For instance, every morning I do the same thing. If I don't follow my routine, I get stressed and have to get dressed again. To be honest, I kind of worry that if I don't do something, my parents are going to die. I know it's not normal to have this kind of worry, but these thoughts tend to trigger more anxiety and weird ideas.

Panic Disorder

College students affected by a panic disorder experience feelings that entail an abrupt, unexplainable wave of terror that seems to come from nowhere. During these moments, an individual's body reacts with the "fight-or-flight" response as it responds to the unfounded, but extremely genuine, expectation of immediate danger. Frequently, students will state that these attacks subside as inexplicably as they occur. After experiencing more than one panic attack, individuals may develop a fear of the arrival of another attack. When this occurs, the experienced affective reaction is called a "fear of fear," and students may avoid anything reminiscent of the last attack in order to prevent having one again. This can create difficulties for students who may associate the attack with a certain building, a certain classroom, or a certain individual. This may keep students from following through on academic responsibilities such as class attendance or from continuing their studies. Panic attacks can happen with or without agoraphobia (see specific phobias). Furthermore, these attacks include symptoms such as heart palpitations, shortness of breath, chest pain, feelings of choking or smothering, nausea, dizziness, sweating, and trembling (Barlow, 2002). An afflicted college student might also be overwhelmed by a fear of dying, going crazy, or losing control. A comment by a student may include:

> Sometimes I can get these intense attacks. When one occurs, I feel like my heart is going to pound out of my chest and I can't breathe. It's almost like the world is going to collapse on top of me.

Panic disorder affects 6 million (2.7%) of the U.S. population, and women are twice as likely to be affected by panic disorder as men. Panic disorder has a very high comorbidity rate with major depression (ADAA, 2012; Andrade, Eaton, & Chilcoat, 1994). This combination may be especially difficult to handle as the co-occurring symptomatology may effectively keep the student from seeking assistance and treatment.

Posttraumatic Stress Disorder

A college student can experience symptoms of PTSD in the wake of a traumatic event that is outside of the usual human experience; a student either experiences direct injury, or threatened injury, or witnesses the serious injury or death of another. In some situations, learning of an unanticipated death or injury of a loved one can bring on symptoms of PTSD. For a diagnosis of PTSD to be made, there must be a recognizable startling event and a response of intense fear, helplessness, and horror, as well as one or more of the following characteristic symptoms:

* Reexperiencing symptoms of the event through nightmares, daytime flashbacks, and/or physical sensations that recall the feelings present during the event.
* Avoidance of symptoms through the numbing and shutting down of feelings and memory. Commonly, this occurs through feeling detached from others and dissociating from the distressing memories and feelings.
* Hyperarousal symptoms of being over-alert to danger and over-avoidant to any situation associated with the event. In particular, the individual often has difficulty shutting down the "fight-or-flight" response that was quite appropriately activated during the event (NIMH, 2009).

Furthermore, these symptoms significantly disrupt a college student's daily life, as they often lead to sleeplessness, irritability, difficulty with concentration, general restlessness, and sometimes the development of an exaggerated startle response that may negatively affect relationships with others. Depending on the type of traumatic event, students might react by distrusting others, avoiding anyone or anything that reminds them of the event, or lacking confidence in their ability to keep themselves safe (Janoff-Bulman, 1989). Students with this disorder may have faulty beliefs and misattributions, which include self-blame and guilt, and overgeneralized problems with safety, trust, control, esteem, and intimacy (McCann & Pearlman, 1990; Resick & Calhoun, 2001). In general, a student affected by PTSD could say:

> I sometimes have flashbacks of the rape. When they happen, it's like a haze comes over me and I'm reliving the experience. To be honest, it's horrifying and every second is a nightmare. My mom says I can kind of zone out because I'm not aware of anything around me.

PTSD affects 7.7 million people or 3.5% of the U.S. population. Outside of the military arena, women are more likely to be affected by PTSD than men. Rape is the most likely trigger of PTSD, as 65% of men and 45.9% of women who are raped develop the disorder. Likewise, childhood sexual abuse is a strong predictor of lifetime likelihood for developing PTSD (ADAA, 2012).

Social Anxiety Disorder

Social anxiety disorder, also known as social phobia, is a strong fear of being embarrassed or judged by others. This fear can be so strong that it gets in the way of going to work, school, or doing other everyday things that involve interaction with others (Roth, Antony, & Swinson, 2001). While everyone has felt anxious or embarrassed at one time or another (e.g., giving a class presentation), college students with social anxiety disorder worry about an event for weeks before it will happen and often play out the event in detail repeatedly prior to the event. In particular, individuals with social anxiety disorder are afraid of doing common things in front of other people. A college student might be afraid to eat or drink in front of other people, for example, or use a public restroom. Most people who have social anxiety disorder know that they shouldn't be as afraid as they are, but feel unable to control their fear. To avoid the pain of potential embarrassment, students may avoid events and activities that they would actually prefer to attend. Their unfounded fears may dictate their daily routines and interactions. For some college students, social anxiety disorder is only a problem in certain situations, while others experience symptoms in nearly every social situation (NIMH, 2010b). Unfortunately, the very social nature of much of the college experience may lead students to use alcohol or other "social drugs" to alleviate their symptoms when they are going to be in social situations likely to cause symptom flare-up of their anxiety.

One way that a counselor can determine if a college student has social anxiety disorder is if the individual has experienced symptoms for at least 6 months. Without treatment, social anxiety disorder can last for many years or a lifetime. Characteristics and symptoms of individuals with social anxiety disorder include:

- High anxiety surrounding interactions with other people and having a hard time talking to them, despite a desire to be able to socialize
- High self-consciousness in front of other people and feelings of embarrassment
- Great fear that other people will judge them
- Worry for days or weeks before an event where other people will be
- Avoid places where there are other people
- Have a hard time making friends and keeping friends
- Blushes, sweats, or trembles around other people
- Feels nauseous or sick to their stomachs when with other people (NIMH, 2010b)

In counseling, a student affected by social anxiety could state:

I turn bright red after I walk into a room full of people. It feels like everyone's eyes are placed solely on me. To be honest, I really feel humiliated and would rather stay at home where I can play video games and watch movies.

Social anxiety disorder affects 6.8% (15 million) of the U.S. population. The disorder is equally common among men and women, typically beginning around age 13 (ADAA, 2012). According to the ADAA (2012), 36% of people with social anxiety disorder reported experiencing symptoms for 10 or more years before seeking help.

Specific Phobias

Phobias are attempts to compartmentalize our fears into a few limited situations that can be successfully avoided. By attaching all the panicky feelings onto a few situations, college students can typically avoid those very specific situations and continue to lead a fairly normal life. Specific phobias are classified into five major groups:

1. Animal; Insects, snakes, dogs, and so on
2. Natural environment: Storms, earthquakes, heights, darkness, and so on
3. Situational: Enclosed spaces, flying, elevators, and the like
4. Blood-injection injury: Seeing blood, receiving shots, broken bones, and so forth
5. Other: Choking, clowns, loud sounds, and so on (Ollendick et al., 2010)

Unfortunately, phobias have the ability to take on a life of their own, and without attention and treatment, take over increasingly more of a person's life. A fear of insects can be fairly easy to manage, for instance, as individuals can avoid approaching spiders, ants, and so on, and staying away from areas where they would be likely to run across feared insects. A fear of public places, on the other hand, could severely limit a college student's social, academic, and work opportunities. The more common phobias include claustrophobia (fear of closed spaces), agoraphobia (fear of public places, sometimes related to panic attacks), and acrophobia (fear of heights). A student affected by claustrophobia may say:

I'm scared to death of elevators, and I will never take one again. It is an awful feeling being trapped in a closed space. My heart pounds, and I sweat like crazy. When the elevator starts to go up, my mind races and I think that we are all going to suffocate. It's not worth having these feelings, so I try to always take the stairs.

Specific phobias affect 19 million people or 8.7% of the U.S. population. Similar to GAD, PTSD, and panic disorder, women are twice as likely to be affected as men (ADAA, 2010).

Test Anxiety

While not a formal diagnosis, test anxiety produces emotional reactions that contribute to task intervention and lower intellectual testing performance (Sarason, 1961). College students who worry about tests are more likely to have lower self-esteem, take longer to complete tasks, spend more time studying, exhibit higher state anxiety, and expect lower levels of success (Alansari, 2004; Foos & Fisher, 1988; Hembree, 1988). In particular, state anxiety manifests as an interruption of an individual's emotional state that actually yields an unexpected subversion of a student's emotional equilibrium. This is different from trait anxiety, which is a relatively stable aspect of an individual's personality (Endler & Kocovski, 2001). In addition, fears of negative evaluation, the disliking of tests, and poor study habits have been referenced with test anxiety (Hembree, 1988).

Symptoms of test anxiety may include: (a) physical symptoms of nausea, diarrhea, headaches, rapid heartbeat, light-headedness, and shortness of breath; (b) emotional symptoms of anger, fear, helplessness, and disappointment; and (c) cognitive-behavioral symptoms of difficulty concentrating, thinking negatively, and comparing oneself to others (ADAA, 2012). A typical response by a student with test anxiety is similar to "I am exhausted by the time I finish most tests. It's like my mind freezes and I can't get out any information." High levels of test anxiety have also been negatively correlated to IQ, academic achievement, memory, and cumulative grade point average (Cassady & Johnson, 2002; Hembree, 1988). While test anxiety is experienced at differing degrees, females generally report higher levels of test anxiety than their male counterparts, though they perform equally well on cognitive measures (Hembree, 1988).

For further assistance with the determination of the level and type of anxiety a student may be experiencing, please see the list of inventories provided in Table 14.1.

TREATMENT AND INTERVENTION STRATEGIES

Research findings have shown that approximately 60% to 90% of individuals with various forms of anxiety disorders were effectively treated through the interventions of psychotherapy and psychotropic medication and psychotherapy (Craske, Brown, & Barlow, 1991; Foa, Rothbaum, Riggs, & Murdock, 1991; Heimber, Dodge, Hope, Zorro, & Becker, 1990; Pohl, Wolkow, & Clary, 1998). While counselors are not psychiatrists, it is important that they recognize the potential benefits of psychotropic medications

TABLE 14.1
Anxiety Inventories

Tool	Item	Subscales	Author
State-Trait Anxiety Inventory	20	Trait or state anxiety	Spielberger et al. (1983)
Beck Anxiety Inventory	21	Anxiety	Beck & Steer (1990)
Social-Phobia and Anxiety Inventory	45	Social phobia and agoraphobia	Turner, Beidel, & Dancu (1996)
Test Anxiety Inventory	20	Worry and emotionality	Spielberger (1980)
Brief Symptom Inventory	53	Three global indices Nine symptom dimensions including anxiety	Derogatis & Melisaratos (1983)
IPAT Anxiety Scale	40	Covert and overt anxiety	Krug, Scheier, & Cattell (1976)

for individuals. Although medication may not cure anxiety disorders, research findings suggest that they can help regulate feelings of anxiety as a person receives counseling to learn ways of controlling his or her anxiety levels (Pollack et al., 2001). The principal medications used for anxiety disorders are antidepressants, antianxiety drugs, and beta blockers to control some of the physical symptoms. College counseling centers should ideally affiliate with the campus health services center to provide team-centered care to clients who would benefit from psychotropic medication.

Among other psychotherapy approaches, cognitive-behavioral therapy (CBT), relaxation therapy (RT), and mindfulness-based stress reduction (MBSR) have received considerable empirical support in the treatment of anxiety disorders (Barlow & Craske, 1994; Goldin & Gross, 2010; Gould, Otto, & Pollack, 1995; Gould, Otto, Pollack, & Yap, 1997; Mitte, 2005a, 2005b; Vøllestad, Sivertsen, & Nielsen, 2011). The following two sections will further evaluate the approaches of CBT, RT, and MBSR in the treatment of anxiety disorders.

Cognitive-Behavioral Therapy

CBT has been referenced as a highly effective and lasting strategy for treating anxiety disorders (ADAA, 2012; NIMH, 2009). CBT focuses on identifying, understanding, and changing thinking and behavior patterns. The cognitive element in particular helps students modify the thinking patterns that support their fears. The behavioral component facilitates change by helping students respond to anxiety-provoking circumstances.

According to the cognitive model, anxiety is maintained by an individual's misperception of danger and catastrophic misinterpretations of generally benign stimuli, sometimes internal and other times external. For example, a stimulus might precipitate a physiological or cognitive reaction from an individual, which is followed by an exaggerated perception of danger or threat, which strengthens the reaction, and so forth. This creates a self-perpetuating cycle of progressively intensified anxiety. Proponents of the cognitive model propose that these thoughts are accessible to conscious consideration and intentional reevaluation (Beck, Emery, & Greenberg, 1985; Clark, 1986). Treatment practices of CBT usually entail students recording symptoms between sessions, reading and reviewing psycho-educational material on stress and anxiety, and completing homework assignments. Counseling requires that the student commit to being actively involved in the process, developing a sense of control, and learning skills that are practicable outside of therapy. The benefits of CBT are usually seen in 12 to 16 weeks, depending on the student.

Cognitive Restructuring

One specific CBT technique that is especially beneficial with anxiety disorders is cognitive restructuring. With cognitive restructuring, students are asked to challenge the irrational beliefs that perpetuate their anxiety. The technique involves: (a) restructuring the negative thought processes that contribute to the student's anxiety and exchanging them with more positive realistic beliefs, and (b) teaching the student to appraise body sensations more accurately and manage the physical symptoms of anxiety (Chen, Reich, & Chung, 2002). More specifically, a counselor helps a student acknowledge the negative thoughts, confront the negative thoughts, and replace the negative thoughts with more balanced, realistic thoughts.

The first step typically involves asking students to identify specifically what they were thinking when they started feeling anxious. For instance, individuals with test anxiety may identify paralyzing feelings associated with thoughts about taking an exam and the spiraling thoughts that arise. A student who is hoping to go to law school, for example, may run through the following spiraling list of anxiety-provoking thoughts as the student prepares for an exam: "(a) I'm going to fail this test. (b) My teacher is going to think I'm an idiot. (c) My GPA is ruined. (d) I'm never going to get into law school. (e) My career is over. (f) I'm a failure." Second, counselors teach students how to evaluate their anxiety-provoking thoughts. Students are asked to question the support for their terrifying beliefs, scrutinizing unhelpful ideas, and experimenting with the reality of negative predictions. Specific strategies in this step include conducting experiments, considering the pros and cons of worrying about or avoiding the entity they fear, and determining the realistic chances that what they are anxious about will occur in reality. Third, counselors facilitate the exchange of negative thoughts with realistic thoughts. Once college students have acknowledged the irrational predictions and negative distortions in their anxious thoughts, they are then able to replace the negative cognitions with new thoughts that are more accurate and positive. For example, counselors can encourage students to create realistic, calming statements they can say to themselves when facing or anticipating a situation that normally sends their anxiety levels soaring. In the example of the prelaw student, the more realistic thoughts might now include, "This test is just one of several this semester. I usually do well in this particular subject, so I will probably do well again. Most law schools will accept a 3.5 GPA, so I don't have to be perfect." This allows students to use their tendency to engage in self-talk to enhance their mood and behaviors through their newly learned and rehearsed responses to situations that would previously result in unproductive thoughts, feelings, and behaviors.

Relaxation Therapy

RT is a coping technique with a behavioral treatment element through which students learn to relax in the presence or anticipation of feared stimuli or anxiety (Öst, 1987). The RT model of anxiety is somewhat similar to the cognitive model, but the application in treatment is entirely different. The goal in RT is to terminate the anxiety cycle by decreasing the intensity of the physiological reaction and circumventing catastrophic or negative thoughts without addressing the cognitions directly. Although there is limited empirical evidence for particular mechanisms of change, Öst (1987) suggested that RT works by (a) diminishing general tension and anxiety and, as a result, the likelihood that any particular stressor will trigger panic; (b) improving awareness about how anxiety works, thus demystifying symptoms and reducing the impact; and (c) increasing perceived self-efficacy, so that students feel equipped to cope with an anxiety reaction. This approach is consistent with both the cognitive and behavioral models of anxiety, which perceive anxiety as primarily automatic and out of consciousness, and successful treatment as operating at that level (Marks, 1987; Ohman & Soares, 1994; Siev & Chambless, 2007).

There are two primary forms of RT used in the treatment of anxiety disorders: progressive relaxation (Bernstein & Borkovec, 1973) and applied relaxation (Öst, 1987).

In progressive relaxation, students learn to relax by practicing a systematic tensing and relaxing of various muscle groups progressively working through the body. Once they are able to achieve a state of reprieve from their feelings of anxiety in progressive relaxation, students are taught differential relaxation. Differential relaxation involves learning to generate the right degree of tension in different muscles to perform a particular movement; muscles not involved in the required movement are relaxed so that energy is not wasted. An example would be to keep the muscles of the shoulder relaxed, while using the muscles in the elbow to bend the arm. This is helpful with anxiety disorders, as individuals tend to have persistent, widespread muscle tension and thereby waste unneeded energy. Building upon this, Öst (1987) added application training to progressive relaxation, whereby students practice applying the relaxation techniques in vivo (i.e., in life) by approaching increasingly feared situations and using the relaxation techniques to manage the evoked anxiety as the student nears the fear trigger. Although applied relaxation by definition involves exposure, the goal is not to extinguish anxiety through a process of habituation, but rather to practice applying the skills in vivo, thus learning to control the anxiety symptoms. In reality, exposures are often not adequately sustained to allow for habituation (Siev & Chambless, 2007).

Breath Training

Breathing retraining is another specific strategy for working with students struggling with anxiety disorders. Also referred to as abdominal retraining, students utilize their practiced breathing retraining at the first sign of hyperventilation, anxiety, or a panic attack. The technique involves teaching students proper breathing techniques by helping them learn to take slow, deep breaths. Students are encouraged to perform abdominal (diaphragmatic) breathing instead of their usual rapid, shallow breathing. This is important as many students with anxiety disorders, such as panic disorder, describe hyperventilatory symptoms as being similar to panic attack symptoms. Encouraging students to engage in meditation and meditative physical exercises such as yoga, tai chi, and so on, can also provide relief from anxiety symptoms.

There is a wealth of self-help resources for individuals who suffer from anxiety and counselors should provide student-specific suggestions for helpful literature and relaxation tapes that reinforce relaxation, while also encouraging students to practice abdominal breathing during non-panic anxiety states (Chen, Reich, & Chung, 2002).

Mindfulness-Based Stress Reduction

Mindfulness-based exercises have gained increasing attention in the treatment for anxiety and depression disorders (Allen, Chambers, & Knight, 2006; Carmody, 2009). The concept of mindfulness can be defined as "paying attention, in a particular way: on purpose, in the present moment, with acceptance" (Kabat-Zinn, 1994, p. 4). In the United States, MBSR is the most researched form of mindfulness training (Goldin & Gross, 2010; Kabat-Zinn, 1990). Clinical trials of mindfulness-based interventions for anxiety disorders indicate that these techniques considerably reduce the severity of anxiety and comorbid symptomatology (Kim et al., 2009; Koszycki et al., 2007; Lee et al., 2007). Likewise, research has denoted that mindfulness fully mediated changes in acute anxiety symptoms, and partially mediated changes in worry and trait anxiety (Vøllestad, Sivertsen, & Nielsen, 2011).

MBSR comprises various forms of mindfulness practice, utilizing formal and informal meditation practice as well as hatha yoga (Kabat-Zinn, 1990). In terms of formal practice, MBSR employs breath-focused attention, body scan–based attention to the transient nature of sensory experience, shifting attention across sensory modalities, open monitoring of moment-to-moment experience, walking meditation, and eating meditation. Alternatively, informal practices consist of brief pauses where attention is shifted to present moment awareness. When used simultaneously, the formal and informal mindfulness practices intend to improve the aptitude to examine the immediate substance of experience, particularly the transient nature of thoughts, emotions, memories, mental images, and physical sensation (Goldin & Gross, 2010; Kabat-Zinn, 1990). This section will provide an example of both a formal and informal technique for assisting college students affected by anxiety disorders.

Finding Stillness

One formal technique of MBSR is named finding stillness, which is a meditation method that highlights the importance of sitting, relaxing the body, calming the mind, and being as still as possible (McKay & Sutker, 2007). Emphasis is therefore placed on body posture, thoughts, breathing, and nonresistance, as these features can help alleviate the physical, emotional, and mental symptoms of anxiety. Regarding body posture, counselors teach college students to sit comfortably, with their spine upright and supported while their head is balanced naturally. In order for the mind to start to calm down and experience deeper states of awareness, counselors will emphasize the importance of the body being still and remaining motionless for a period of time. Finding stillness also stresses the importance of not attempting to control thoughts; the more students try to direct their thinking, the stronger the ideas become (McKay & Sutker, 2007). Like RT, the technique emphasizes the value of breathing. Highlighting the importance of breathing naturally through the nose, breathing is the central key to mindfulness meditation within this technique. Lastly, finding stillness encourages nonresistance, whether physical or emotional, as counselors help students to refrain from reacting to tension through making efforts to relax.

Noting

An informal MBSR technique for working with college students affected by anxiety is noting (Harris, 2009). Noting involves the process of describing thoughts as the ideas arise, and this involves either verbal expression, written expression, or simple silence. In therapy, counselors can utilize noting with students by having them note their anxious thoughts and feelings. The following are three examples for how noting can be utilized with a college student: (a) Students describe their thoughts as ideas arise, such as anxious thought, sad thought, neutral thought, thought about the future, thought about the past, and so forth. (b) Students note their thoughts by category, such as judging, worrying, analyzing, remembering, and fantasizing. (c) Students specifically describe each individual feeling by name, such as stress, pressure, nervousness, uneasiness, restlessness, agitation, and impatience. Likewise, students can use a similar process to operate informally throughout the day. For instance, in a tense social situation, a student might observe a feeling of anxiety and simply note it as "I'm feeling stressed" or "I'm noticing a feeling of anxiety" (Harris, 2009).

CASE STUDY: SARAH

After moving away from home last year, 19-year-old Sarah has continued to have difficulties adjusting in her second year at college. Over the year and a half, Sarah has called home four or five times a day to check in with her mother. Sarah's reasoning was that she had a weird feeling that something bad was going to happen while she was away. Concerned over her "worrying too much," Sarah's mother encouraged her to go to counseling. During the intake, Sarah stated that she feels restless, irritable, and has difficulty concentrating in class. At one point, Sarah said, "I worry so much that I'm not always sure what I'm worrying about." She also communicated difficulties with letting her roommates leave the dorm without making them call her regularly to reassure her that they are okay. This situation apparently made her best friend grow weary and impatient with Sarah's worrying. For these reasons, Sarah recognized that she needed help and came to counseling.

After hearing Sarah's experiences and symptoms, the counselor diagnosed her with GAD. Utilizing an integrated theoretical framework of CBT and RT, Sarah's counselor helped treat Sarah's anxiety over 15 weeks. Therapy began with Sarah identifying not only the stressors, but also the intensity associated with the situations, and progressed toward methods of exposure and desensitization. In counseling sessions, Sarah would also practice muscle relaxation (e.g., progressive relaxation) and abdominal breathing exercises. Homework assignments were required after every session and some included: (a) exercising, (b) yoga and tai chi, (c) logging symptoms in a daily journal, and (d) conducting experiments, such as reducing phone calls to mother and observing the outcome. Through these techniques and a strong support system, Sarah was able to take considerable strides and live a more fulfilling life.

RESOURCES

* Anxiety Disorders Association of America: www.adaa.org
* National Institute of Mental Health: http://www.nimh.nih.gov
* ULifeline: www.ulifeline.org
* The JED Foundation: www.jedfoundation.org
* Active Minds: www.activeminds.org
* Beyond OCD: www.beyondocd.org

REFERENCES

Alansari, B. (2004). The relationship between anxiety and cognitive style measured on the Stroop test. *Social Behavior and Personality, 32*(3), 283–294.

Andrade, L., Eaton, W. W., & Chilcoat, H. (1994). Lifetime comorbidity of panic attacks and major depression in a population-based study: Symptom profiles. *British Journal of Psychiatry, 165*, 363–369.

Anxiety Disorders Association of America (ADAA). (2012). *Facts and statistics.* Retrieved from http://www.adaa.org/about-adaa/press-room/facts-statistics

Association for University and College Counseling Center Directors. (2011). *The Association for University and College Counseling Center Directors annual survey.* Retrieved from http://aucccd.org/img/pdfs/aucccd_directors_survey_monograph_2011.pdf

Barlow, D. H. (2002). *Anxiety and its disorders: The nature and treatment of anxiety and panic* (2nd ed.). New York, NY: Guilford Press.

Barlow, D. H., & Craske, M. G. (1994). *Mastery of your anxiety and panic II.* Albany, NY: Graywind Publications.

Beck, A. T., Emery, G., & Greenberg, R. L. (1985). *Anxiety disorders and phobias: A cognitive perspective.* New York, NY: Basic Books.

Beck, A. T., & Steer, R. A. (1990). *Manual for the Beck Anxiety Inventory.* San Antonio, TX: Psychological Corporation.

Bernstein, D. A., & Borkovec, T. D. (1973). *Progressive relaxation training: A manual for the helping professions.* Champaign, IL: Research Press.

Cassady, J. C., & Johnson, R. E. (2002). Cognitive test anxiety and academic performance. *Contemporary Educational Psychology, 27*, 270–295.

Chen, J., Reich, L., & Chung, H. (2002). Anxiety disorders. *The Western Journal of Medicine, 176*(4), 249–253.

Clark, D. M. (1986). A cognitive approach to panic. *Behaviour Research and Therapy, 24*, 461–470.

Craske, M., Brown, T., & Barlow, D. (1991). Behavioral treatment of panic disorders: A 2 year follow-up. *Behavior Therapy, 22*, 289–304.

Derogatis, L., & Melisaratos, N. (1983). The Brief Symptom Inventory: An introductory report. *Psychological Medicine, 13*, 595–605.

Foa, E., Rothbaum, B., Riggs, D., & Murdock, T. (1991). Treatment of posttraumatic stress disorder in rape victims: A comparison between cognitive-behavioral procedures and counseling. *Journal of Consulting and Clinical Psychology, 59*, 715–723.

Foos, P. W., & Fisher, R. P. (1988). Using tests as learning opportunities. *Journal of Educational Psychology, 80*(2), 179–183.

Gould, R. A., Otto, M. W., & Pollack, M. H. (1995). A meta-analysis of treatment outcome for panic disorder. *Clinical Psychology Review, 15*, 819–844.

Gould, R. A., Otto, M. W., Pollack, M. H., & Yap, L. (1997). Cognitive–behavioral and pharmacological treatment of generalized anxiety disorder: A preliminary meta analysis. *Behavior Therapy, 28*, 285–305.

Heimber, G. R., Dodge, C., Hope, C., Zorro, L., & Becker, R. (1990). Cognitive behavioral group treatment for social phobia: Comparison to a credible placebo control. *Cognitive Therapy and Research, 14*, 1–23.

Hembree, R. (1988). Correlates, causes, effects, and treatment of test anxiety. *Review of Educational Research, 58*(1), 47–77.

Hoge, E. A., Ivkovic, A., & Fricchione, G. L. (2012). Generalized anxiety disorder: Diagnosis and treatment. *British Medical Journal, 345*(7885), 37.

Janoff-Bulman, R. (1989). Assumptive worlds and the stress of traumatic events: Applications of the schema construct. *Social Cognition, 7*, 113–136.

Kessler, R. C., Ruscio, A. M., Shear, K., & Wittchen, H. (2009). Epidemiology of anxiety disorders. In M. M. Antony & M. B. Stein (Eds.), *Oxford handbook of anxiety and related disorders* (pp. 19–33). New York, NY: Oxford University Press.

Krug, S. E., Scheier, I. H., & Cattell, R. B. (1976). *Handbook for the IPAT anxiety scale.* Los Angeles, CA: Western Psychological Services.

Lepine, J. P. (2002). The epidemiology of anxiety disorders: Prevalence and social costs. *Journal of Clinical Psychiatry, 63*(14), 4–8.

Marks, I. M. (1987). *Fears, phobias, and rituals: Panic, anxiety, and their disorders.* New York, NY: Oxford University Press.

McCann, I. L., & Pearlman, L. A. (1990). *Psychological trauma and the adult survivor: Theory, therapy, and transformation.* Philadelphia, PA: Brunner/Mazel.

Mitte, K. (2005a). A meta-analysis of the efficacy of psycho- and pharmacotherapy in panic disorder with and without agoraphobia. *Journal of Affective Disorders, 88*, 27–45.

Mitte, K. (2005b). Meta-analysis of cognitive–behavioral treatments for generalized anxiety disorder: A comparison with pharmacotherapy. *Psychological Bulletin, 131*, 785–795.

National Institute of Mental Health. (2009). *Anxiety disorders.* NIH Publication 09-3879.

National Institute of Mental Health. (2010a). *Generalized anxiety disorder: When worry gets out of control.* NIH Publication TR 10-4677.

National Institute of Mental Health. (2010b). *Social phobia: Always embarrassed.* NIH Publication TR 10-4678.

Nepon, J., Belik, S. L., Bolton, J., & Sareen, J. (2010). The relationship between anxiety disorders and suicide attempts: Findings from the National Epidemiologic Survey on Alcohol and Related Conditions. *Depression and Anxiety, 27*, 791–798.

Ohman, A., & Soares, J. J. (1994). "Unconscious anxiety": Phobic responses to masked stimuli. *Journal of Abnormal Psychology, 103*, 231–240.

Ollendick, T. H., Raishevich, N., Davis, T. E., Sirbu, C., & Ost, L. (2010). Specific phobia in youth: Phenomenology and psychological characteristics. *Behavior Therapy, 41*(1), 133–141.

Öst, L. G. (1987). Applied relaxation: Description of a coping technique and review of controlled studies. *Behaviour Research and Therapy, 25*(5), 397–409.

Pohl, R. B., Wolkow, R. M., & Clary, C. M. (1998) Sertraline in the treatment of panic disorder: A double-blind multicenter trial. *American Journal of Psychiatry, 155*, 1189–1195.

Pollack, M. H., Zaninelli, R., Goddard, A, McCafferty, J. P., Bellew, K. M., Burnham, D. B., & Iyengar, M. K. (2001). Paroxetine in the treatment of generalized anxiety disorder: Results of a placebo-controlled, flexible-dosage trial. *Journal of Clinical Psychiatry, 62*, 350–357.

Rachman, S. J., & Hodgson, R. J. (1980). *Obsessions and compulsions.* Englewood Cliffs, NJ: Prentice Hall.

Resick, P. A., & Calhoun, K. S. (2001). Posttraumatic stress disorder. In D. H. Barlow (Ed.), *Clinical handbook of psychological disorders: A step-by-step treatment manual* (3rd ed., pp. 60–113). New York, NY: Guilford Press.

Roth, D., Anthony, M. M., & Swinson, R. P. (2001). Interpretations for anxiety symptoms in social phobia. *Behaviour Research and Therapy, 39*(2), 129–138.

Sarason, I. G. (1961). Test anxiety and the intellectual performance of college students. *Journal of Educational Psychology, 52*(4), 201–206.

Siev, J., & Chambless, D. L. (2007). Specificity of treatment effects: Cognitive therapy and relaxation for generalized anxiety and panic disorders. *Journal of Consulting and Clinical Psychology, 75*(4), 513–522.

Spielberger, C. D. (1980). *Preliminary professional manual for the Test Anxiety Inventory (TAI).* Palo Alto, CA: Consulting Psychologists Press.

Spielberger, C. D., Gorsuch, R. L., Lushene, R., Vagg, P. R., & Jacobs, G. A. (1983). *Manual for the State-Trait Anxiety Inventory.* Palo Alto, CA: Consulting Psychologists Press.

Turner, S. M., Beidel, D. C., & Dancu, C. V. (1996). *Social Phobia and Anxiety Inventory: Manual.* Toronto, ON: Multi-Health Systems Inc.

15

Nonsuicidal Self-Injury and Treatment Strategies for College Students

IAN TURNAGE-BUTTERBAUGH

STARTING AT THE BEGINNING: AN UNDERSTANDING OF SELF-INJURY

Self-injury is a perplexing, complex, and multifaceted behavior that is often misunderstood, misdiagnosed, and ineffectively treated. As a result, mental health practitioners, developmental researchers, parents, and teachers, among others, may have difficulty assessing, diagnosing, treating, and responding to those engaging in self-injurious behavior. Due to the apparent inconsistencies in the current literature, it is important to have an accurate understanding of what comprises self-injury before exploring assessment, symptom manifestation, and treatment. This will help to minimize the continuation of stereotypes and ineffective, and often inappropriate, treatment of decades past.

Although the term *self-injury* itself has been a topic of recent debate across medical and social fields, there is still a lack of agreement on the overall description of self-inflicted harm. Terms such as "self-mutilation, deliberate self-harm, nonsuicidal self-harm, parasuicide, self-wounding, wrist-cutter syndrome, self-carving, self-cutting, repetitive nonsuicidal self-injurious behavior, self-inflicted violence, and self-abuse" (Miller & Brock, 2010, p. 1) have all been used to refer to self-injurious behaviors. The variety of terms may, in part, reflect current understandings of self-injury, but more clearly illustrates the vast interest in self-injury across professional fields and diverse cultures. The numerous terms are not only confusing, but also problematic for practitioners and researchers. For example, as

Nock and Favazza (2009) pointed out, *deliberate self-harm* is commonly used to describe both nonsuicidal and suicidal self-injury; and *suicidality* often refers to both self-injurious thoughts or behaviors, without clear distinction between the two. Complicating the operationalization of self-injury even further are differences in cultural and geographical terminology. Rodham and Hawton (2009) highlighted the ambiguity of the term *deliberate self-harm*. In the United States it refers to nonsuicidal self-injury, but in the United Kingdom it refers to a much broader collection of nonlethal self-injurious acts performed with or without suicidal intent, including overdose and suicide attempts.

In an effort to maintain clarity among the confusion, throughout this chapter the term nonsuicidal self-injury (NSSI) will be used. This term has been chosen for several reasons. First, *self-injury* captures the essence and nature of these behaviors; they are deliberate and intentional self-inflicted injuries. Second, *nonsuicidal* helps clarify the frequently misunderstood intent of these behaviors. Third, NSSI reflects the current understanding of self-injurious behavior among mental health professionals, which leads to a more concise definition and more precise understanding of self-injury.

Just as the appropriate terminology for self-injury has been a source of debate, so has the definition. For example, Matson and Turygin (2012) pointed out that the field of developmental disabilities defines self-injurious behavior as a repetitive act that causes physical harm; is motivated by frustration, anxiety, or the desire to escape a particular situation; is not predetermined; and typically occurs among those with intellectual disabilities or autism. The definition used by many mental health practitioners, however, describes a different phenomenon, now referred to as NSSI. NSSI is often viewed as a "class of behaviors defined by deliberate, direct, and self-inflicted tissue damage without suicidal intent and for purposes not socially sanctioned" (Glenn & Klonsky, 2011, p. 751). Additionally, and particularly relevant to the purpose and scope of this chapter, Polk and Liss (2007) clarified that NSSI is typically conducted by individuals with a "normal" IQ and afflicts as many as 20% of college students.

Following the current understanding of self-injury within the mental health field, this chapter adopts both the terminology and definition of NSSI. NSSI, therefore, is understood as voluntary and intentional self-destructive behaviors that are carried out for purposes other than ending one's life. These include a wide variety of behaviors. Some of the most common NSSI behaviors are pinching, scratching, cutting, ripping, and carving skin, but others include banging or punching an object or oneself until the point of bleeding, interfering with the healing of wounds, and pulling out hair (Whitlock, Eckenrode, & Silverman, 2006). Within this chapter, we will explore the manifestation and understood purpose of the behaviors as well as assessment and treatment.

INFLUENCES ON AND PURPOSES OF NSSI

Pinpointing the influences that lead to NSSI is much easier said than done. In a society that emphasizes "fitting in," and where media is rife with glamourized depictions of taboo and harmful behaviors, determining the true function underlying NSSI is difficult. Research over the past 3 decades, however, has identified several influential factors that may lead to NSSI behaviors as well as unveil their direct or indirect purposes. While it makes sense to start with the specific influences that may lead to NSSI behaviors, there is a wealth of research suggesting that an understanding of the utility of those behaviors may shed even more light on their underlying etiology. Therefore, this chapter adopts a functional view of NSSI behaviors and will first consider the utilitarian purposes of those behaviors and discuss their accompanying influences later.

Purposes

The transition to college often involves monumental transitions, which may have extraordinary impacts on self-perception and psychological functioning. Struggles with identification, independence, and maturity constantly compete with the familiarity of the dependence, purity, and ease of childhood. These personal and psychological struggles, while somewhat expected in adolescence, may be particularly distressing in college. College years are typically perceived as a time to find oneself and one's place in life, but the search for identity and acceptance may create or replicate previously experienced negative emotions that are uncomfortable, isolating, and overwhelming. In the absence of adequate resources, which is the case for many college students, new coping mechanisms and strategies may be adopted to minimize their painful experiences.

The most common reason for engaging in NSSI behaviors, which underlies other purposes, is to reduce distressful thoughts and emotions. Plante (2007) pointed out that these attempts are often successful. By refocusing emotional pain into a controllable behavior, psychological discomfort is reduced and perceived control, comfort, and relief are increased. Combating pain with pain defies logic for both the perpetrator and the assessor; however, recognizing that those seemingly senseless acts have a positive goal—reducing emotional pain—helps demystify their absurdity, aids in understand their utility, and provides an avenue for exploring less destructive behaviors that are more adaptive.

NSSI behaviors serve other purposes as well, including an attempt at punishment for unacceptable qualities or characteristics that do not live up to society's strict standards; a method to increase control over self, others, and environment; and a message board for identity expression. Engaging in NSSI as a punishment may help minimize victimization of perceived inadequacies by symbolically purging oneself of or providing control over those shortcomings. NSSI can also create a powerful means of control in the face of helplessness and vulnerability. Systematically and intentionally engaging in NSSI may create a sense of internal autonomy that combats experiences of external chaos. Plante (2007) described the goal of mastery and control over one's pain as an ill-advised yet "undeniably healthy underpinning of self-injury" (p. 55). Gaining control through NSSI behaviors extends beyond feelings of internal stability. That is, those engaging in NSSI may do so in order to gain leverage over neglectful, oppressive, or punitive significant others. If those significant others yield to the threat, it is likely that needs—such as attention, affection, comfort, or the like—will be met. If the threat is ignored, however, the blame for the NSSI behaviors can be shifted to those neglecting the perpetrator's needs.

Using self-injury as a form of identity expression is particularly common in adolescence and into the college years, as adolescents and emerging adults struggle to form their own unique identities. Additionally, with the proliferation of NSSI images across the media landscape, expression of one's identity through publicly visible self-inflicted wounds has become an increasingly viable and understandable language among teens and young adults. Wearing one's individuality on their sleeve, in the form of NSSI, conveys personal messages about turmoil, trauma, and pain, as well as triumph, power, and control. Therefore, NSSI is much more than just a cry for help or an attention-seeking behavior. It is a way to overcome emotional discomfort, meet needs, create calm out of chaos, and form and express a unique identity—an identity that incorporates, rather than dissociates from, shortcomings, inadequacies, traumatic and painful life events, and the resulting negative emotions.

Influences

Many of the influences of NSSI stem from events or situations that create lasting emotional pain. Most often, these events or situations are assumed to be severe abuse and neglect. While studies have corroborated these assumptions (Boudewyn & Huser Liem, 1995; Favazza, 1989; Whitlock, Eckenrode, & Silverman, 2006), others have stressed the less iniquitous events and situations in a child's or adolescent's life that deny him or her appropriate and adequate expression of feelings (Strong, 1998). For example, well-meaning parents or guardians may hold their children to unrealistically high standards, may perpetuate their own childhood traumas in the lives of their children, or may prevent a secure attachment or sense of autonomy from forming. As a result, many individuals are left with unmet needs and are forced to find a new means of communication to demonstrate and cope with their internal chaos.

Sources of emotional pain vary widely and are influenced by early childhood experiences, personal development, and a society's resources. Among those antecedents, however, several common themes have emerged from recent literature that help with the understanding and identification of NSSI. The single most common theme, or influential factor, contributing to engaging in NSSI behaviors is childhood sexual abuse (Strong, 1998; Yip, 2005). Childhood sexual abuse can have a negative impact on emotional regulation, impulse control, attachment, and stress and tension management (Turell & Armsworth, 2000; Yip, 2005), all of which may directly or indirectly influence the adoption of NSSI behaviors later in life. In a study investigating self-injurious behaviors among college students, Whitlock, Enckenrode, and Silverman (2006) found that 20.9% of college students who had engaged in at least one NSSI behavior had experienced sexual abuse. In the same study, however, it was found that among college students who had engaged in at least one NSSI act, 44% reported experiencing emotional abuse. Therefore, while sexual abuse often plays a large role, emotional wounds may be particularly influential in the development of NSSI behaviors for college students.

Yip (2005) concisely identified several other factors that seem to directly impact the occurrence of NSSI, namely self-cutting. Other forms of abuse, neglect, and trauma, high levels of anxiety, a lack of constructive anger and frustration management, and inappropriate impulse and emotion control may all contribute to self-injurious behaviors. Each of these influences, in conjunction with the purposes of NSSI, help elucidate the functional and adaptive nature of these destructive behaviors. In order to survive in maladaptive environments, one may be required to find new ways to release tension, return to reality after trauma, establish control, create a sense of security and uniqueness, gain others' attention, and vent anger (Favazza, 1989).

PREVALENCE OF NSSI IN RELEVANT POPULATIONS

Despite inconsistent data collection methods and divergent results, recent studies have identified important patterns and characteristics that separate those engaging in NSSI from those engaging in self-injury with suicidal intent. Distinguishing between self-injury with and without suicidal intent is an important step in overcoming common misconceptions about NSSI. Additionally, understanding the prevalence rates of NSSI behaviors among various populations help clarify occurrences, manifestations, frequencies, and severity, as well as identify the availability and efficacy of appropriate treatment methods. The next section of this chapter is devoted to exploring differences in prevalence rates among various groups.

Gender

It is commonly believed that NSSI behaviors are more common among females than among males, a belief that is supported by an overwhelming majority of the literature on various forms of self-harm, with and without suicidal intent. Studies examining prevalence rates among adolescents engaging in NSSI, however, have reported that rates among males and females are much more equal, with females being only slightly more likely to engage in the behaviors (Klonsky, Oltmanns, & Turkheimer, 2003; Suyemoto, 1998; Zlotnick, Mattia, & Zimmerman, 1999). A recent study taking a more acute look at NSSI behaviors among college students has identified several important gender-specific findings. Specifically, females were found to be significantly more likely than males to repeatedly engage in self-injurious behaviors (Whitlock, Eckenrode, & Silverman, 2006). Additionally, it was found that females were more likely to pinch or scratch skin, while males were more likely to punch objects with the intention of harming themselves. Lastly, females were more likely to injure their wrists and thighs, whereas males were more likely to injure their hands.

Due to the surprisingly small number of studies reporting gender differences, as well as the inconsistent results among those studies, conclusions should be drawn with caution. Much more research is needed in this area to accurately understand gender-specific prevalence rates and differences that would be beneficial for the identification, assessment, and treatment of NSSI behaviors. For the time being, it seems safe to conclude that the assumption that NSSI is a predominantly female phenomenon may not be as accurate as was once thought, especially among college students.

Ethnicity and Culture

Very few studies have been conducted with sufficient sample sizes to determine differences in NSSI behaviors among diverse ethnicities. Among the studies that have been conducted, atypical samples are common, focusing on specific groups or only one gender among groups. Due to studies with nonrepresentative samples and the likelihood of extraneous variables, correlations and generalizations are difficult to assume. For example, one of the most recent studies examining between-group differences in self-harm behaviors examined a nonclinical sample ($n = 346$) of Caucasian and African American females that were selected from a university-affiliated obstetrics/gynecology clinic (Sansone, Sellbom, Chang, & Jewell, 2012). While

Caucasian women were found to have significantly higher prevalence rates for several NSSI behaviors, such a small and specific sample limits the ability to reliably draw conclusions that would generalize to other populations.

It is important to be aware of differences in how diverse cultures view NSSI behaviors. That is, behaviors that are socially unacceptable in one culture may be socially sanctioned in another. The presence of problematic self-injurious behaviors is largely determined by social and cultural norms. What is considered harmful in Western society (i.e., flagellation) may be considered a purifying religious or spiritual ritual in other cultures. Therefore, when assessing an individual for NSSI behaviors, it is important to be mindful of the student's ethnic heritage and the accompanying beliefs, rituals, and practices, all of which might render treatment inappropriate, harmful, and offensive.

Age

The age of onset for NSSI is typically between 12 and 14 years. In the United States, however, most individuals begin engaging in NSSI behaviors around the age of 16, with earlier incidents being quite rare. Age of onset varies from person to person and is correlated with several important risk factors. Specifically, NSSI has been associated with the timing of pubertal development, depression, alcohol abuse, and sexual activity (Patton et al., 2007). While more research is needed in this area, it is suggested that delayed pubertal development, alcohol use, and sexual activity may also delay the age of onset for NSSI behaviors.

Despite the onset of NSSI typically occurring in adolescence, young adults between the ages of 18 and 25 are among the most likely to engage in NSSI behaviors. Prevalence rates vary by study and methodology, but studies conducted in the United States report lifetime prevalence rates among college students ranging from 7% to 38% (Favazza, DeRosear, & Conterio, 1989; Whitlock, Eckenrode, & Silverman, 2006). Older adults (i.e., those over the age of 60) have been shown to have lower prevalence rates of NSSI; however, incidents among this age group are closely related to suicide. That is, the line between NSSI and self-harm with intent of suicide seems to be blurred among older adults. While self-injurious acts at any age should be taken seriously, instances among individuals over the age of 60 should receive special attention and care.

SPECIFIC CONCERNS/EFFECTS ON LIFE FOR COLLEGE STUDENTS

College students are considered at high risk for engaging in NSSI for several reasons. First, as mentioned previously, studies investigating NSSI behaviors among college students have shown that the college age group is among the most prevalent to engage in self-inflicted injuries (Favazza, DeRosear, & Conterio, 1989; Gratz, Conrad, & Roemer, 2002; White, Trepal-Wollenzier, & Nolan, 2002; Whitlock, Eckenrode, & Silverman, 2006). Second, unexpected and unfamiliar situations may elicit or recreate many of the negative emotions that are often considered antecedents to NSSI behaviors.

Students making the transition to college may be at an increased risk for engaging in NSSI behaviors. Challenges inherent in college life have the potential to evoke distressing feelings, which are often combined with a lack of social resources. As a result, students may find themselves particularly vulnerable and willing to find alternative methods to manage their distress. Recall that NSSI behaviors are often an attempt to increase stability, control, acceptance, or establish a unique identity, all of which are particularly relevant in the life of a college student. In fact, Kakhnovets et al. (2010) found that among college students, depression, anger, loss of control, and stress were the most common experiences that led to NSSI behaviors. Additionally, they reported that those who engaged in more than one NSSI act experienced emotional relief and associated self-injury with positive emotions experienced after completing the behaviors. As a viable, accessible, and effective coping mechanism, NSSI may be particularly attractive to college students experiencing increased stressors, chaotic schedules, depression, isolation, and identity confusion.

ASSESSMENT

Accurate assessment of individuals engaging in NSSI behaviors involves following several steps and consideration of several influential domains. Additionally, assessment requires the assessor or interviewer to possess specific intrapersonal awareness and interpersonal skills. A complete understanding of what comprises and leads to NSSI behaviors, an awareness of one's biases and prejudices, an appropriate demeanor, and a strategic approach are all fundamental components that help ensure thorough assessment. The following section covers the response to demeanor and goals of thorough assessment. Barriers to assessment are discussed in length later in this chapter.

Initial Response

Appropriately handling the initial response of a student engaging in NSSI behaviors is crucial for the development of a positive and therapeutic alliance. Additionally, approaching assessment appropriately helps prevent misdiagnosis, unnecessary treatment, harmful and embarrassing stigmatization, and other adverse consequences. It also helps set the stage for the trajectory and effectiveness of treatment and partially determines how the student, caregivers, and other health care providers respond to the admission or discovery of NSSI. Several factors should be considered to make sure the response is handled delicately and strategically.

Discussed in more detail in the following, the assessor's initial reaction to the discovery or disclosure of NSSI can have monumental effects on the therapeutic relationship and success of treatment. Reacting with shock, disgust, or anger is very likely to prevent rapport and trust, which will likely result in a modest or superficial assessment. Overreacting or underreacting can similarly send mixed messages that prevent the development of a therapeutic alliance, influence students' perceptions of level of care, and determine how much they are willing to divulge about their NSSI behaviors. Refraining from nonclinical intuition or normative reactions is essential. For example, while it may seem natural and appropriate to try to get students to stop engaging in their NSSI behaviors through guilt, education, or contracts, initial efforts to cease the self-injurious behaviors before thorough assessment are rarely effective and often backfire. NSSI often defies logical explanations and has an adaptive and functional purpose. Therefore, D'Onofrio (2007) warns, "When the helper imposes his or her desire for the client to get better, the ensuing power struggle creates an impasse in the relationship that ultimately diminishes the helper's leverage in helping the client" (p. 113).

Respect, Curiosity, and Compassion in Assessment

While extreme reactions to NSSI, such as anger, shock, disgust, and anxiety, have very little utility in the assessment and treatment of those engaging in NSSI behaviors, it is suggested that respect, curiosity, and compassion most certainly do. The assessor's demeanor lays the foundation for those therapeutic qualities to be built on. Therefore, Walsh (2007) urges assessors to approach assessment, and later treatment, with a "dispassionate demeanor" (p. 1066) that conveys neither intense interest in the NSSI behaviors nor lackadaisical dismissal of students' experiences. Instead, a dispassionate demeanor expresses genuine interest of the behaviors and accompanying experiences, and fosters respect and compassion without emotional entanglement.

In college, the discovery or disclosure of NSSI behaviors is likely to be in the presence of persons unqualified to assess and treat self-injury. Professors, peers, roommates, and the like may be the first responders. Without an understanding of NSSI and how to appropriately respond and assess the associated behaviors, it is likely that the injurer experiences many of the negative situations and emotions already described.

Therefore, it is imperative that assessors approach assessment with empathy and understanding. Conveying messages that acknowledge the students' private worlds, validate their experiences, and recognize their previously hidden complexities and difficulties in a nonjudgmental and respectful way can enhance trust, decrease defenses, and foster a collaborative relationship for thorough assessment. In lieu of a negative or harsh response, assessors can create a comforting atmosphere in which students may respond well to gentle invitations to reveal their deepest internal conflicts.

Domains and Goals of Assessment

As a complex and multidimensional construct, NSSI requires an equally complex and multifaceted assessment process to ensure thorough conceptualization and appropriate treatment. Therefore, identifying students' NSSI behavioral manifestations, their frequency, and their severity are necessary but not adequate for the assessment process. Several important assessment domains have been identified in order to get a complete understanding of an individual's unique history and experiences prior to and after NSSI behaviors, including level of distress, desired goals, and unfulfilled needs.

Craigen, Healey, Walley, Byrd, and Schuster (2010) have outlined a two-tiered assessment process that begins with a very narrow scope of assessment and finishes with broad environmental and contextual issues that may influence, support, or perpetuate NSSI. The first tier—formal assessment—involves the use of specific inventories to assess self-injury behaviors, suicide risk, traumatic experiences, and depression. The second tier—informal assessment—involves gathering information about the student's background, family history, social and peer support, positive/ negative influences, emotional capacity, verbal ability to express emotions, and coping strategies. The use of such an integrated assessment model allows the assessor to gain a comprehensive and holistic understanding of the student's behaviors and experiences. Focusing on peripheral, yet pertinent information may help humanize the process, conveying the assessor's interest and lessening the likelihood that the student feels scrutinized, condemned, or judged. Klonsky and Weinberg (2009) describe a similar two-domain model of assessment that includes a history of NSSI behaviors and contextual features.

It is clear that social and contextual features are particularly important aspects of NSSI assessment. Contextual features, such as peer support, social support, and positive/negative influences, as recommended by Craigen et al. (2010), may be particularly crucial and revealing for college students. Transitioning to college life often involves a major shift in social support that can leave students feeling vulnerable, isolated, and helpless. Without the familiar avenues of social support that were available before going to college, students may seek new ways to cope with the stress and chaos of collegiate demands. Therefore, exploring the student's current coping mechanisms may be pertinent as well, and can provide a springboard for further exploration, conceptualization, and treatment.

BARRIERS TO THE ASSESSMENT OF NSSI

Social Factors

Self-injury has been documented throughout much of recorded history and across cultures; however, it wasn't until the 1980s that researchers and practitioners began to formally study self-injurious behavior. Previously, self-injury had been viewed as a senseless, horrific, psychopathological, and suicidal act that occurred quite rarely (Favazza, 2009). In most cases, those beliefs contradict the current understanding of NSSI, and therefore do not accurately reflect the experiences of those engaging in self-injurious behaviors. Common misunderstandings and stereotypes of NSSI, however, have led to a very negative social view of self-injury that has presented particular challenges for assessors and poses several barriers to disclosure. As a result, assessors may be blinded by prejudice and self-injurers may refrain from disclosure in order to protect themselves from being perceived negatively. While assessor biases are discussed in detail later in this chapter, Table 15.1 identifies several common myths, along with their more accurately understood realities.

Juxtaposing the myths listed in Table 15.1, which perpetuate incorrect assumptions about NSSI and its frequency, is the media's role in normalizing NSSI. Self-injury has become a prevalent topic in modern media, most often appearing on popular television shows and in song lyrics. Several celebrities, including Johnny Depp and Princess Diana, have also disclosed their NSSI behaviors, expanding the perception of normalcy beyond clinical and nonclinical populations, to include highly regarded figures in society. While normalizing such a mystifying and negatively perceived phenomenon may seem like a step in the right direction, it poses additional barriers to accurate identification and assessment of self-injurious behaviors.

The largest of those barriers is known as the "social contagion effect" (Purington & Whitlock, 2010). Already acknowledged as an influencing factor for suicidal and aggressive behaviors, the effect occurs when individuals engage in the same taboo behaviors that they have viewed other easily identifiable persons engage in. As a result, those behaviors are perceived as accessible and effective methods for dealing with life's

TABLE 15.1

**Common Myths of Nonsuicidal Self-Injury (NSSI)
That Sustain Its Social Stigma**

Myths	Realities
Self-injury is always an attempt to kill oneself.	NSSI, as the name implies, is not an attempt to kill oneself. While those who engage in NSSI behaviors are more likely to engage in suicidal behaviors, NSSI often has an adaptive function, serving as a protection against suicide.
Self-injury is not a very common occurrence.	The prevalence rate of NSSI is estimated to be around 1,200 persons per 100,000 per year. Suicide is consistently estimated at about 13 persons per 100,000 per year.
Self-injury is always psycho-pathological in origin.	Individuals engage in NSSI for quite sensible, yet harmful, reasons. Most people engage in NSSI behaviors to achieve immediate, although temporary, relief from distressful emotions or traumatic thoughts. Others engage in NSSI in an attempt to create a sense of order or control in a seemingly chaotic world.
Someone who is smart would never engage in self-injurious behaviors.	While NSSI is associated with various psycho-logical disorders, it has not been linked to intelligence.
Self-injury is only a concern among those of certain cultures or cultural beliefs.	NSSI is defined as self-harmful behavior that is not culturally sanctioned. Therefore, what is considered NSSI in one culture may not be in another. However, NSSI has no cultural, ethnic, racial, or socioeconomic boundaries.
People who engage in self-injury are just looking for attention.	Individuals engaging in NSSI very rarely disclose their behaviors to anyone and most actively attempt to conceal the behaviors.

challenges. This phenomenon is particularly concerning because, as Purington and Whitlock point out, the consequences of such behaviors are very rarely discussed or depicted in popular media. As a result, college students may view self-injurious behaviors as normal, acceptable, and harmless, which may lead to a perception that "everybody is doing it." Therefore, individuals viewing these powerful messages in modern media may be tempted to engage in NSSI behaviors even if they had never previously thought about them, due to a "copycat" phenomenon. In an attempt to "fit in," some individuals emulating NSSI behaviors seen in the media may experience severe and unexpected consequences. This assumption seems to be corroborated by the finding that 21% of college students who have engaged in NSSI injured themselves more severely than they had anticipated (Whitlock, Eckenrode, & Silverman, 2006).

Previously accepted myths about NSSI and the media's role in normalizing self-injurious behaviors make identifying and assessing NSSI problematic for several reasons. First, and discussed in more detail in the following section, unfamiliarity with NSSI or the adoption of misguided beliefs about self-injury may cause the assessor to experience negative reactions to NSSI. Those beliefs, or myths, may also lead the assessor to approach the assessment interview with preconceived notions about the perpetrator that are inaccurate. Second, while NSSI is more common than previously thought, viewing self-injury as "normal" may reduce the likelihood that the seriousness of a particular incident is assessed. Some NSSI behaviors are more serious than others and severity is important to assess. Third, identifying the influences leading to an individual's NSSI behaviors is essential in order to provide appropriate treatment. With an increasingly complex media landscape, accurately assessing the unique influences, experiences, behaviors, frequencies, and severity of an individual's self-injurious behaviors becomes increasingly difficult.

Assessor Factors

NSSI has been a subject of confusion and disagreement across fields and throughout the literature. Due to the misunderstanding of NSSI among clinicians, as well as the nonclinical population's ignorance, biases, and prejudices regarding self-injury, accurately assessing NSSI behaviors is often not achieved. As Klonsky and Weinberg (2009) point out, "many who are unfamiliar with NSSI may experience negative reactions to the behavior, such as shock, disgust, or blame" (p. 183), which may prevent objective assessment. Unfortunately, these reactions are not limited to the general public. Starr (2004) makes this point clear in her own confession of ignorance and bias that clouded her assessment and confounded treatment:

> As a primary care nurse practitioner working with female adolescents in long-term residential care, I often became frustrated, perplexed, and angry when clients deliberately engaged in self-mutilating behaviors. My belief that self-mutilation was a manipulative way to gain attention and my lack of understanding of the behaviors greatly affected my ability to provide empathetic care to these clients. I believed individuals could stop their self-mutilating behaviors at will. (p. 34)

An awareness of one's own biases is an integral part of the assessment process. Overcoming one's biases and prejudices is often the first hurdle in thorough and accurate assessment. Approaching an assessment with preconceived notions about NSSI may result in a dismissive attitude that causes the assessor to overlook the uniqueness of that particular student. As a result, pertinent information about the history, prevalence, and severity of the student's NSSI behaviors may be disregarded. On the other hand, personal beliefs about NSSI may elicit feelings of disgust, anger, or disdain, which may lead to clouded judgment or reduced empathy. Should the student feel judged or criticized, he or she may withhold, alter, or fabricate information in an effort to reduce those shameful negative reactions (Klonsky & Weinberg, 2009). In either case, or due to an interaction between the two, it is very unlikely that the strong rapport needed to create a safe environment and conduct a thorough assessment will be built.

TREATMENT GOALS

A natural reflex of those in clinical and nonclinical populations may be to immediately focus on fixing a student's NSSI behaviors. While direct or indirect problem solving may be appropriate later in therapy, as cessation of NSSI behaviors is the ultimate goal of treatment, the initial goal should be a complete understanding of the student, his or her background, unique experiences, and inner conflicts. Plante (2007) puts it this way:

> Listening and understanding and reassuring the [student] are doing something vital; launching into desperate action is not. Efforts to demand, convince, coerce, implore, or otherwise effect an end to the [NSSI] behavior becomes the primary if not sole goal. Taking action and seeking to change, control, or stop the [student's] behavior, however, rarely can produce positive results prior to the attainment of a genuine understanding of the deeper issues involved. (p. 65)

The initial stage of treatment can be extremely difficult and may seem counterintuitive. Listening, rather than acting, increases an understanding of the student's subjective reality and gives the student control over his or her treatment process. NSSI behaviors are often, at least partially, an attempt to increase control in a chaotic world. Demanding change removes control from the injurer and increases the chances that inappropriate or premature interventions will backfire. Therefore, increasing the student's control and responsibility over his or her internal environment and behavioral responses would be an appropriate next step, which is discussed in the suggested interventions section.

Another initial goal of treatment should be to establish the expectations and boundaries of therapy. Clients approach therapy in very different ways and, just as having a holistic understanding of the student's experience is vital to the success of treatment, so is understanding their expectations for the treatment process. Respecting and adhering to their expectations, within the boundaries of ethical and appropriate treatment, also increases the student's control over the situation and conveys respect and a nonjudgmental attitude. One of the main boundaries to establish is that of suicidal intention and behavior. A common practice is to use no-suicide contracts with clients where they promise to contact the counselor if they intend to end their life. No-harm and no-suicide contracts, however, have fallen out of vogue in the counseling profession and are not necessarily advised. Rather, it is suggested that a thorough and ongoing suicide assessment be conducted with each client engaging in NSSI to assess his or her impulse control and risk of engaging in suicidal behaviors. Informing of and providing emergency procedures are essential as well, so the student always has alternative options when contemplating or accidentally engaging in severe self-harm or self-destruction. Once the goals of client safety and a thorough understanding of subjective experiences have been established and reached, formal treatment can begin.

Treatment goals can vary widely from student to student, depending on their unique experiences, backgrounds, histories, environments, and contexts; however, Plante (2007) identifies several that are common and beneficial for most students engaging in NSSI behaviors. As mentioned, increasing control over impulses and responsibility for choices and behaviors is often a goal in the treatment of NSSI. Developing alternative, adequate, and appropriate resources for relieving stress is a common, if not imperative goal. Enhancing relationships, similarly, is a goal that is common in most treatment approaches and is especially relevant to the treatment of NSSI. Lastly, addressing and healing past wounds is essential in the successful treatment of the underlying and deep-rooted sources of internal conflict and pain that drive many NSSI behaviors.

SUGGESTED APPROACHES/BEST PRACTICES WITHIN A BRIEF COUNSELING MODEL

Treatment methods and approaches vary widely from clinician to clinician, given the complexity of NSSI. The treatment of NSSI, however, is a lengthy and often difficult process that requires, above all else, trust, patience, and encouragement. While delineating the details of each approach extends the scope and purpose of this chapter, several interventions and practices will be outlined in both individual and group processes. It is important to note that the research examining the effectiveness of each modality with NSSI behaviors is very limited. Unfortunately, most treatment methods stem from the treatment of borderline personality disorder (BPD) or suicidal ideation and focus on emotional regulation. While there are a few studies demonstrating positive results with individuals engaging in NSSI behaviors, there is a clear need for additional research in this area in order to determine the most effective treatment methods.

Individual Counseling

Individual counseling is more common than group or family counseling for the treatment of NSSI, primarily due to its ability to circumvent privacy and confidentiality concerns that are inherent in group modalities. While individual treatment is common, specific individual approaches are abundant in the literature and vary widely from clinician to clinician. The following section will outline some of the aims and benefits of several individual counseling approaches.

Cognitive-Behavioral Therapy

Cognitive therapists focus on the students' maladaptive cognitions—thoughts, beliefs, and expectations—that underlie and drive their NSSI behaviors. The crux of cognitive therapy is the view that those engaging in NSSI behaviors do so as a well-intended, yet vitally maladaptive, form of coping with faulty and/or distorted internalized beliefs about self and others. Therefore, the main aim of cognitive therapy for NSSI behaviors is to empathically acknowledge the student's experiences, point out and dispute irrational beliefs, explore how those beliefs impact his or her daily life, and alter those beliefs in order to adopt more effective and adaptive behaviors.

Cognitive therapy for NSSI behaviors has several unique features that set it apart from cognitive approaches to other psychological problems. First, as Slee, Arensman, Garnefski, and Spinhoven (2007) point out, self-harm "itself is the primary target of treatment, rather than it being approached as secondary to an underlying psychiatric problem such as depression" (p. 176). In other words, thoughts, emotions, beliefs, and other cognitions, as well as behaviors, are all considered NSSI-related. Additionally, cognitive therapy for NSSI often includes a strong educational component where the counselor teaches the student new coping strategies and assists with their acquisition. As with other cognitive approaches, cognitive and behavioral homework is frequently given to help transfer the skills used in therapy to situations where the student feels distressed, vulnerable, threatened, isolated, or misunderstood outside of therapy.

Dialectical Behavioral Therapy

Originally developed for the treatment of individuals with borderline personality disorder, dialectical behavioral therapy (DBT) has been shown to be effective with individuals engaging in NSSI behaviors. The fundamental view in DBT is that pathology stems from emotional dysregulation and affects a variety of life's domains—relationships, cognitions, sense of self, and behavior. Dialectical behavioral therapists approach NSSI behaviors as a function of extreme emotional reactions and chaotic life experiences. As a result, the aim of DBT is to help individuals decrease their self-destructive behaviors and increase control and overall quality of life by breaking the restraints of rigid and automatic thinking. Jones and McDougall (2007) outline several stages in the DBT process that are applicable to NSSI treatment.

The first stage—the pretreatment stage—focuses on assessment of motivation and appropriate goal setting. The second stage focuses on behaviors that are self-destructive, may interfere with treatment, and negatively impact quality of life. The third stage deals with stress stemming from childhood traumas or maladaptive experiences. Finally, the fourth stage addresses self-esteem, validation, and problem solving, helping students move toward their individualized treatment goals. DBT also includes group dynamics that foster the acquisition of adaptive skills for increased mindfulness, interpersonal effectiveness, emotional regulation, and stress management.

Psychodynamic Approaches

There are several psychodynamic approaches that have been shown to be effective with individuals engaging in NSSI behaviors, all of which focus primarily on affectively charged attachment relationships with caregivers. While the specific and unique features and interventions of each psychodynamic approach well extends the scope of this chapter, Levy, Yeomans, and Diamond (2007) have presented a detailed and inclusive description of their respective treatment processes, as well as current research findings pertaining to their efficacy. Several similarities across psychodynamic modalities exist; however, they are distinctly set apart from other approaches to the treatment of NSSI behaviors.

Psychodynamic approaches, such as transference-focused psychotherapy (TFP), tend to focus on the here-and-now rather than on childhood experiences. Differentiation of self, identity diffusion, and reality testing are all common areas of focus during therapy to help correct disturbed personality organization and the use of primitive defenses, such as splitting or dissociation (Levy, Yeomans, & Diamond, 2007). The main goal of psychodynamic approaches is to integrate polarized affective states and dichotomous representations of self and others into a unified whole that is realistic and representative of reality. As a result, clients acquire a coherent sense of identity, interpersonal relationships are threatened less, self-destructive behaviors are engaged in less frequently, and overall functioning improves.

Group Counseling

Group counseling for individuals engaging in NSSI behaviors is less common than individual counseling. This is likely due to the fears about others' negative reactions discussed previously, vulnerability to one's own negative emotions (such as shame and guilt), and discomfort in divulging one's deepest and most sensitive internal conflicts in the presence of others. Despite the additional hurdles to overcome with group counseling, it has been shown to be highly effective and uniquely beneficial with individuals engaging in self-injurious behaviors and is becoming a more common method of treatment.

Benefits inherent in group counseling, championed by Yalom (2005), have particularly relevant implications for the treatment of NSSI that are very difficult to achieve within individually designed frameworks. One of the most powerful benefits of group counseling is the development of the universality of experiences among group members. Many students engaging in NSSI behaviors feel isolated and alienated and, as a result, may be unable to convey their internal experiences to others. Appropriately screened individuals and successfully managed groups can overcome this barrier, however, by creating a social milieu that fosters caring, respect, validation, and understanding. Such an environment may open the door for deepened personal exploration, self-awareness, and increased courage to face interpersonal conflicts that perpetuate NSSI behaviors.

Other features present in group counseling, such as consistency and structure, peer support and challenges, opportunities to support others, and expressions of insight make group counseling a particularly efficacious approach to the treatment of NSSI. For example, predetermined themes for a particular session or consistent group processes across sessions can help create a sense of familiarity and consistency that provides relief from the students' subjective experiences of chaos in daily life. Support and challenges from peers may be especially compelling, especially if others in the students' lives do not understand their experiences and react negatively to their NSSI behaviors. That is, a student may be more likely to attend to and consider support or challenges from someone who has shared similar experiences and understands underlying inner conflicts, as opposed to professional counselors or insensitive or fearful parents, peers, and teachers. Lastly, students participating in group therapy may be empowered by the opportunity to provide support, encouragement, and inspiration to others. One of the most unique qualities of group counseling is that group members have the opportunity to be of value to other group members (Yalom, 2005). As a result, self-efficacy and self-esteem may increase, which can directly combat the root of irrational beliefs or core worldviews that maintain their NSSI behaviors.

Group counseling is not appropriate for every student engaging in NSSI; however, it is apparent that the interpersonal dynamics of group counseling can offer unique experiences that can provide catharsis, empowerment, and change. With the field of mental health being pushed toward time-limited and cost-effective treatment approaches, and in consideration of the therapeutic qualities of the group dynamics themselves, group counseling may be a particularly viable approach that meets the unique needs of the counselor, clients, and affiliated institutions. While group approaches seem promising, additional research is needed in this area as well, in order to effectively create a therapeutic environment that is most conducive to positive and lasting change.

CONCLUSION

A wide variety of treatment methods have been shown to be effective in treating students engaging in NSSI behaviors. While differences in foci, dynamics, and goals exist among approaches, the similarities among them, as well as the external factors that influence them, are much more important to consider. As discussed, most of the literature on NSSI reported a nonjudgmental attitude, empathy, and trust as core conditions that foster a strong therapeutic relationship and promote positive outcomes. A review of the variance in client outcomes suggested that common factors, including the therapeutic relationship itself, account for at least 30% of client change (Lambert & Barley, 2001). Given the importance of the therapeutic relationship in the treatment of NSSI behaviors, however, it would seem that common factors that attribute to the relationship's quality should receive even more attention and consideration than might have been initially thought. As Plante (2007) pointed out, "the development of a safe, confidential, and collaborative therapeutic relationship provides the cornerstone of effective treatment" (p. 88), regardless of the individually determined treatment approach. Due to the presence of maladaptive interpersonal relationships that often underlie NSSI behaviors, as well as challenges present in a society that frequently engages in superficial and distant relationships, the importance of a genuine, trusting, and close connection cannot be overstated.

Additionally, as described in this chapter, having an awareness of personal biases and combating socially derived stereotypes and myths about NSSI are essential processes in the understanding, assessment, and treatment of self-injury. Dismissing NSSI as simply a selfish, repulsive, or senseless act that is enacted as a cry for help, for example, is a response that may deny students the care and respect they desperately need and is a gross misinterpretation of their motives. The paradox of adaptive coping through maladaptive destruction defies logic and goes against the human drive for safety and health. Making sense out of a seemingly senseless act is a primary goal for clinicians and clients, since the logical nature of NSSI often eludes even the perpetrators themselves. Overcoming biases to help the student find meaning and utility in his or her actions opens the door for self-exploration, self-understanding, and the identification and adoption of more adaptive alternatives that can result in similar outcomes.

REFERENCES

Boudewyn, A. C., & Huser Liem, J. (1995). Childhood sexual abuse as a precursor to depression and self-destructive behavior in adulthood. *Journal of Traumatic Stress, 8*, 445–459.

Craigen, L. M., Healey, A. C., Walley, C. T., Byrd, R., & Schuster, J. (2010). Assessment and self-injury: Implications for counselors. *Measurement and Evaluation in Counseling and Development, 43*(1), 3–16.

D'Onofrio, A. A. (2007). *Adolescent self injury: A comprehensive guide for counselors and health care professionals.* New York, NY: Springer Publishing Company.

Favazza, A. R. (1989). Why patients mutilate themselves. *Hospital and Community Psychiatry, 40*, 137–145.

Favazza, A. R. (2009). A cultural understanding of nonsuicidal self-injury. In M. K. Nock (Ed.), *Understanding nonsuicidal self-injury: Origins, assessment, and treatment* (pp. 19–35). Washington, DC: American Psychological Association.

Favazza, A. R., DeRosear, L., & Conterio, K. (1989). Self-mutilation and eating disorders. *Suicide and Life-Threatening Behavior, 19*, 352–361.

Glenn, C. R., & Klonsky, E. D. (2011). Prospective prediction of nonsuicidal self-injury: A 1-year longitudinal study in young adults. *Behavior Therapy, 42*, 751–762.

Jones, C., & McDougall, T. (2007). Dialectical behavioural therapy for people who self-harm: Lessons from the USA, part 1. *Mental Health Practice, 11*(1), 12–15.

Kakhnovets, R., Young, H. L., Purnell, A. L., Huebner, E., & Bishop, C. (2010). Self-reported experience of self-injurious behavior in college students. *Journal of Mental Health Counseling, 32*(4), 309–323.

Klonsky, E. D., Oltmanns, T. F., & Turkheimer, E. (2003). Deliberate self-harm in a nonclinical population: Prevalence and psychological correlates. *The American Journal of Psychiatry, 160*, 1501–1508.

Klonsky, E. D., & Weinberg, A. (2009). Assessment of nonsuicidal self-injury. In M. Nock (Ed.), *Understanding nonsuicidal self-injury: Origins, assessment, and treatment* (183–200). Washington, DC: American Psychological Association.

Lambert, M. J., & Barley, D. E. (2001). Research summary on the therapeutic relationship and psychotherapy outcome. *Psychotherapy, 38*(4), 357–361.

Matson, J. L., & Turygin, N. C. (2012). How do researchers define self-injurious behavior? *Research in Developmental Disabilities, 33,* 1021–1026.

Miller, D. N., & Brock, S. E. (Eds.). (2010). *Identifying, assessing, and treating self-injury at school.* New York, NY: Springer Publishing Company.

Nock, M. K., & Favazza, A. R. (2009). Nonsuicidal self-injury: Definition and classification. In M. K. Nock (Ed.), *Understanding nonsuicidal self-injury: Origins, assessment, and treatment* (pp. 9–18). Washington, DC: American Psychological Association.

Patton, G. C., Hemphill, S. A., Beyers, L., Bond, L., Tombourou, J. W., McMorris, B. J., & Catalano, R. F. (2007). Pubertal stage and deliberate self-harm in adolescents. *Journal of the American Academy of Child & Adolescent Psychiatry, 46,* 508–514.

Plante, L. G. (2007). *Bleeding to ease the pain: Cutting, self-injury, and the adolescent search for self.* Westport, CT: Praeger.

Polk, E., & Liss, M. (2007). Psychological characteristics of self-injurious behavior. *Personality and Individual Differences, 43,* 567–577.

Purington, A., & Whitlock, J. (2010). Non-suicidal self-injury in the media. *The Prevention Researcher, 17*(1), 11–13.

Rodham, K., & Hawton, K. (2009). Epidemiology and phenomenology of nonsuicidal self-injury. In M. K. Nock (Ed.), *Understanding nonsuicidal self-injury: Origins, assessment, and treatment* (pp. 37–62). Washington, DC: American Psychological Association.

Sansone, R. A., Sellbom, M., Chang, J., & Jewell, B. (2012). An examination of racial differences in self-harm behavior. *Psychiatry Research, 200,* 49–51.

Slee, N., Arensman, E., Garnefski, N., & Spinhoven, P. (2007). Cognitive-behavioral therapy for deliberate self-harm. *Crisis, 28*(4), 175–182.

Starr, D. L. (2004). Understanding those who self-mutilate. *Journal of Psychosocial Nursing, 42*(6), 32–40.

Strong, M. (1998). *A bright red scream: Self-mutilation and the language of pain.* New York, NY: Viking.

Suyemoto, K. L. (1998). The functions of self-mutilation. *Clinical Psychology Review, 18,* 531–554.

Turell, S. C., & Armsworth, M. W. (2000). Differentiating incest survivors who self-mutilate. *Child Abuse and Neglect, 24*(2), 237–249.

White, V. E., Trepal-Wollenzier, H., & Nolan, J. M. (2002). College students and self-injury: Intervention strategies for counselors. *Journal of College Counseling, 5,* 105–113.

Whitlock, J., Eckenrode, J., & Silverman, D. (2006). Self-injurious behaviors in a college population. *Pediatrics, 117*(6), 1939–1948.

Yalom, I. (2005). *The theory and practice of group psychotherapy* (5th ed.). New York, NY: Basic Books.

Yip, K. S. (2005). A multi-dimensional perspective of adolescents' self-cutting. *Child and Adolescent Mental Health, 10*(2), 80–86.

Zlotnick, C., Mattia, J. I., & Zimmerman, M. (1999). Clinical correlates of self-mutilation in a sample of general psychiatric patients. *The Journal of Nervous and Mental Disease, 187,* 296–301.

16

Suicidal College Students: Intervention Strategies

KEVIN B. STOLTZ, LAURA McSHANE SCHULENBERG, AND JEANE B. LEE

Although college students are less likely to commit suicide than their same-age nonstudent peers, suicide is the second leading cause of death among college students (Schwartz, 2006a). In fact, a large-scale research study found that over half of undergraduate students have had thoughts of suicide, 18% have given it serious consideration, and fully 8% have actually attempted to take their own lives (Drum, Brownson, Burton Denmark, & Smith, 2009). Unfortunately, while only 20% of students who actually die by suicide have visited their college counseling center (Gallagher, 2004; Kisch, Leino, & Silverman, 2005), research shows that for the group that did seek counseling, the suicide rate would actually be 18 times higher if they had not engaged in therapy (Schwartz, in Drum et al., 2009). Thus, there is an expectation that colleges and universities will continue to develop systems and comprehensive programs to address suicide among college students (Gutierrez, Osman, Kopper, Barrios, & Bagge, 2000; Palladino & Minton, 2008; Schwartz, 2006a). But it must be borne in mind that only 26% of students may actually be aware of mental health counseling services on campus (Westefeld et al., 2005), so outreach plans may be especially effective in addition to individual counseling services. And as Drum et al. (2009) noted, students may be hesitant to seek assistance from university-based services due to a fear of negative academic consequences.

The purpose of this chapter is to provide information on effective methods of current suicide assessment practices as well as provide suggestions for suicide prevention based on the prevalent risk factor of a feeling of meaningless of life. This chapter will include a brief review of risk factors, suicide assessment, intervention protocols, a discussion of suicide research concerning the inclusion of protective factors, a review of the literature on the relationship of meaning making and suicide, and the effective use of meaning-making strategies in the treatment and prevention of college student suicide.

RISK FACTORS FOR COLLEGE STUDENT SUICIDE

Risk factors for suicide often begin with determining how well a client meets the typical demographic profile of those who attempt suicide, although these cannot predict suicidal behaviors. Although females are more likely to engage in suicidal gestures, it is college males who are more likely to commit suicide. Other risk factors for suicide include being diagnosed with a mental disorder (usually depression), existence of current suicidal ideations, having a history of suicidal behaviors and plans, and availability of a firearm (Joiner & Rudd, 2000; Schwartz, 2006b). The existence of any prior suicide attempts is especially important to assess as that is generally the primary factor determining the likelihood of another attempt. Among college students, Drum et al. (2009) found that the following types of problems were associated with undergraduates' suicidal behaviors: family, academics, romance, and finances. Self-injury, peer problems, and losses were also common.

Beyond demographic variables, researchers have sought to develop more refined predictive models of suicidal behaviors. Depression and hopelessness are frequently linked to suicide (American Association for Suicidology, 2013) and these are often exacerbated by the existence of external expectations and pressures. Thus, it is may not be surprising that stress has been implicated in the development of suicidal thinking. In addition to major stressful events (e.g., failing a test, accumulating several absences in a class), Dixon, Rumford, Heppner, and Lips (1992) found that daily hassles (daily stress) contributed to hopelessness and suicidal ideation beyond the variance accounted for by traumatic life events. Thus, the accumulation of daily stressors that might go unrecognized by a student's family, friends, or even counselor, greatly increases the risk for suicide. In fact, although suicidal ideations may be extremely intense, they tend to be transitory, thus limiting the ability of significant others or campus personnel to realize that a student is at risk of attempting suicide (Nock & Banaji, 2007).

College counselors must be vigilant when working with clients who present with depression, a sense of overwhelming burden in any area of functioning (e.g., academic, social, emotional), hopelessness about future events, and helplessness regarding solving current challenges. Males are more likely to commit suicide, but less likely to seek help; therefore, being especially aware of the suicide-related risk factors in male clients may help prevent these clients from slipping through the net.

SUICIDE ASSESSMENT

Thorough and effective suicide assessment is the bedrock of identifying suicidal students; however, accurate suicide assessment is complex and can be challenging even for seasoned practitioners (Bryan & Rudd, 2006). It is important to recognize that accurate prediction of a client's subsequent suicide is virtually an unreachable goal due to the variability of client behaviors (Pokorny, 1993). It is also important to note that, as cited in Shea (1998), approximately 40% to 60% of individuals who committed suicide had been seen in a medical office within the prior month. While most clinicians recognize the role of depressive symptoms in those likely to commit suicide, it is also important to realize that even subclinical levels of depression may be predictors of suicide ideation (Cukrowicsz, Schlegel, et al., 2011). Therefore, careful assessment is necessary and is typically made up of three separate steps. These include (a) gathering information regarding risk and protective factors and warning signs; (b) information related to current ideation, plan, means, client behaviors, desires, and intents; and (c) determining risk for the individual client based on these factors (Reed & Shea, 2011). Of the four basic current factors assessed (ideation, plan, means, intent), having a current plan and access to the means to carry out the plan are most significant and determine the current potential for an active suicide attempt.

National Suicide Prevention Organization Guidelines

The National Suicide Prevention Organization provides a wealth of information related to suicide risk factors, protective factors, and prevention. In their publication, *Suicide Risk Assessment Standards Packet* (National Suicide Prevention Organization, 2007), they review the essential areas for immediate assessment in the case of clients affirming that they are at risk of committing suicide. These four areas are: (a) desire to commit suicide; (b) capability (which involves history of violence to others, exposure to another's suicide, availability of means, current intoxification or substance abuse, acute symptoms of mental disorder, or extreme agitation); (c) intent to commit suicide, meaning access to means and plan to use them; and (d) buffers and social connectedness, which equate to protective factors. In this training guide for workers for suicide prevention hotlines

(1-800-273-TALK), guidelines are provided for assessing risk factors, imminent danger, and directions for encouraging suicidal callers to seek help. This may be an excellent resource for college counselors to have as a guide for themselves and suicide prevention responder teams.

Chronological Assessment of Suicide Events (CASE)

One very useful method of assessment uses the acronym CASE, which stands for the chronological assessment of suicide events (Shea, 1998). It asks clinicians to assess ideations/behaviors that are currently being presented, recent ideations/behaviors, past ideations/behaviors, and immediate ideation. Through the use of intervention language phrased in such a way that a valid and honest answer is received, clinicians may be better able to address specific plans. Shea suggests the use of exploring the behavioral incident matter-of-factly, such as asking specific questions about the suicidal event, "What did your roommate do when they saw the pill bottle?" Using gentle assumption, Shea suggested clinicians ask questions under the assumption that suicidal ideation and behaviors were present as were potential predictors, such as "How many exams have you failed this semester?" Shea noted that these could be seen as leading questions, something clinicians are taught to avoid; therefore, they must be used extremely cautiously and with highly intentional purposes. Lastly, he suggested exploring the denial of the specific, which is used when clients deny specific behaviors, yet when clinicians strongly believe that there is evidence of behaviors to the contrary. An example might be, "Have you thought of using the gun to kill yourself?" or "Have you thought about hanging yourself?" He notes that clinicians must leave plenty of time after asking a question for the client to phrase a response.

Enhancing Suicide Assessment Through Coping Style Inquiries

Wang, Lightsey, Pietruska, Uruk, and Wells (2007) proposed a model of stressful life events as the beginning of a causal chain that includes three types of stress coping (task-oriented, emotion-oriented, and avoidance) that affect a person's reasons for living and depression. Task-oriented coping includes behaviors that actively address stressful situations with attempts to remedy or correct the stressful situation (Endler & Parker, 1990). Emotion-oriented coping is described as negative thinking that involves self-blame and fantasizes about the stressor going away. Avoidance is defined as engaging in behaviors that divert attention from the stressor (e.g., watching television, engaging in parties or social distractions). Emotion-oriented and avoidance coping can lead to hopelessness, and then may lead to suicidal ideation or attempts (Wang et al., 2007).

Counselors can improve assessment techniques by inquiring about stress coping and its relation to suicidal thinking and behavior. Students that engage in emotion-oriented coping (e.g., I am to blame for my problems, I am incapable of correcting this problem, I am not good at fixing problems) are more likely to spend time alone, suffer from chronic depressive episodes, and have a lower tolerance for engaging in proactive coping activities to improve stressful situations. Avoidance coping is characterized by those students that simply disregard the stressor and engage in distraction (e.g., parties, drinking). These students may display behaviors that do not signal problems or difficulties and they may appear to be enjoying the abundance of social opportunities available in a college setting. Both of these coping styles can lead to the exacerbation of the original stressors, which in turn can lead to more frustration, anger, and depression, which are often precursors to suicidal ideation.

Inquiring, in counseling sessions, about the patterns of coping can help the student better understand his or her response to life events, and assist the counselor in developing an effective treatment plan, which would include helping the student to develop both task-oriented coping behaviors overlaid with positive emotion-oriented coping (Endler & Parker, 1990). An example of task-oriented coping is to encourage the student to seek consultation with a professor of a class in which the student is not performing well. An example of positive emotion-oriented coping is to help the student to use realistic, factual self-talk, such as, "I am afraid of the professor, but he is here to help me, I can learn this material, I have overcome other learning setbacks, I just need to seek help, as opposed to catastrophizing stressful, challenging events." These active and constructive interventions have the potential for helping students to prevent unnecessary suffering, agitation, and debilitating depression, which often lead to suicidal ideation and behaviors.

Assessing a Potentially Suicidal Client's Thought Processes

When a counselor uncovers a high level of suicidal ideation, it is valuable to further investigate the student's perceptions around the level of difficulty of the suicidal behaviors as well as the perceived ramifications following the idealized act. Using the Theory of Planned Behavior (TPB; Ajzen, 1985) as a framework, Shemanski-Aldrich and Cerel (2009) described the process of assessing a client's internal messages about the act. For instance, the thought "All I need to do is raise the gun and pull the trigger, it's that easy" or "No one will hardly notice I'm gone" puts the student at great risk of a suicidal attempt. A suicidal student often ignores all other aspects of the process. Working with these unrealistic statements of suicidal ideation, a counselor can help the student to more fully understand the implications of a potential suicide and possibly experience the denied fear and reluctance to attempt suicide. Helping the student mitigate events with statements (e.g., I will die if I do this, I will leave everyone I know and love if I do this, I can find hope and meaning to go forward in my life, alive) can serve to bolster the student to think more clearly if suicidal ideation begins again. Helping the student see the outcome and working to build resistance to the suicidal ideation can help prevent suicidal behavior.

Finally, sometimes students appear highly reluctant to change their negative thoughts and emotions. Shemanski-Aldrich and Cerel (2009) proposed that students' level of perceived control over their suicidal ideation and negative emotions is an indicator of risk level and thus an important aspect of overall assessment. If a student does not perceive control over emotions, then that student would be deemed at higher risk for suicide. Helping the student to develop and experience emotional control would be a constructive intervention toward prevention. One method of doing this within counseling sessions would be to invite students to complete a rational emotive behavior therapy (REBT) worksheet in which they develop disputing beliefs and more effective emotional responses to negative events. Utilizing Solution Focused Brief Therapy would also give clients a means to reflect on exceptions to their negative self-beliefs. Because students would be required to brainstorm alternative responses and exceptions, this would also enhance their sense of self-efficacy regarding their ability to control their emotions.

Recognizing the Warning Signs Outside the Counseling Center

As noted earlier, suicidal ideation can manifest quickly and it can be difficult to determine when a depressed or hopeless client moves from a "functional and depressed" state to "suicidal." Therefore, assessing for daily stressors is an important consideration when college students are showing signs of agitation and depression. As a student moves into a depressive episode, peers, professors, residential assistants (RAs), and counselors may notice that the student's tolerance for daily annoyances has decreased. The student may complain more (emotion-oriented coping) and may begin to withdraw (avoidance coping) from class, counseling sessions, and social activities. These indicators serve to alert college personnel that the student may need assistance.

RAs and peers may be the first to notice these attitudinal and behavioral changes and are in key positions for helping the student get the assistance needed. Keeping campus RAs informed of resources and programming at the campus counseling center is necessary. Also, offering suicide prevention training programs to RAs and other interested volunteers can be very helpful in destigmatizing depression and other mental disorders associated with suicidal behaviors. Helping educate the campus population (students, faculty, and administration) about the effect of daily hassles as a component of suicidal ideation can also be very useful. Thus, if students who present as depressed, hopeless, or agitated also discuss overwhelming schedules, issues involving campus stressors, and so forth, they may be referred to the campus counseling center.

Summary of Areas Warranting Assessment

Counselors and clinicians working with college students should be cognizant of the potential symptoms of suicide ideation specific to this population found in Table 16.1.

TABLE 16.1 Potential Student Symptoms and Interventions

General Category of Stressors	Potential Symptoms Related to Suicidality	Counseling Intervention	Symptom Specific Outreach Interventions
Environmental	New and unfamiliar environment and difficulties adjusting to new/increased college demands; expressed difficulty with adjustment to college and a sense of hopelessness	Behavior therapy to address adaptation and adjustment; systematic desensitization/exposure techniques for those fearful of a new environment	Encourage students to participate in new student, housing, and campus orientations and to explore new study skills; recommend on-campus tutoring services/writing centers
Academic	Academic and social pressures	Stress management; mindfulness; relaxation training	Encourage students to talk with family and friends about the difficulties that the student is experiencing; encourage students to sit at the front of the classrooms, take advantage of office hours, consult with professors, attend library workshops

(continued)

TABLE 16.1 (continued)

General Category of Stressors	Potential Symptoms Related to Suicidality	Counseling Intervention	Symptom Specific Outreach Interventions
Emotional	Feelings of failure or decreased performance; alienation or isolation	Cognitive restructuring; thought stopping; hierarchical construction; logotherapeutic activities that explore and promote meaning in life; pet/animal assisted therapy; action planning	Encourage students to join class study groups and form relationships with instructors and teaching assistants; work with students to explore how they "spend" their time during the day. Encourage participation in dorm life; expose students to academic, extracurricular, and religious organizations, intramural athletics, and on-campus support groups; encourage students to become active outdoors
Cognitive—Internal	Thoughts of not being good enough or not fitting in anywhere; negative internal view of self	Thought stopping; cognitive restructuring combined with meaning-making activities	Suggest that students find ways to become involved in areas of interest and areas where students find a sense of universality among themselves with relation to their issues
Cognitive—External	Binging and purging/starvation; body dysmorphic disorder	Assign a daily body image diary to facilitate self-monitoring; cognitive restructuring techniques; exposure therapy	Invite students to participate in an on-campus group; refer students to campus nutritionist
Financial	Inability to maintain the same workload from high school; the cost of attending college; loss of job; debt; belief that there is no way out	Stress management techniques; relaxation training; mental imagery	Explore budgeting, student employment, and make referrals to financial aid

TABLE 16.1 (continued)

General Category of Stressors	Potential Symptoms Related to Suicidality	Counseling Intervention	Symptom Specific Outreach Interventions
Sexuality	Coming out; gender issues; double minority status; severed relationships; harassment; humiliation	Self-exploration; telling stories through narrative therapy; attachment-based family therapy; teaching coping skills	Create a healthy therapeutic alliance; exhibit cultural competence; promote lesbian, gay, bisexual, and transgender (LGBT) campus support groups; promote connectedness within current relationships; make informational resources readily available
Career	Concerns about career choice and choosing the "right" major; feeling "lost"; added pressures to make a choice	Help students to explore career options; administer career-based assessments (e.g., self-directed search, semi-structured career assessment)	Discuss personality in relation to career choices; refer students to career counseling center for further career exploration

In addition to the aforementioned risks for college students, the following signs and symptoms might also suggest suicide ideation:

• Hopelessness
• Rage and/or excessive anger
• Revenge-seeking behavior
• Recklessness
• Engaging in risky activities
• Feelings of being "trapped"
• Increase in or introduction of alcohol and drug use
• Lack of sleep
• Mood swings
• Recent/previous discharge from psychiatric facility
• Family history of suicide
• Traumatic brain injury
• Lack of meaning and/or purpose in life

It is important for the college counselor to explore changes from previous functioning, reduction in class attendance, drops in grades, increases in substance use, involvement in new romantic relationships, as well as breakups. Equally important for the college counselor is knowledge of a client's history. For example, are there any preexisting mental health diagnoses or new diagnoses since the student's entrance into college?

While this chapter focuses on meaning as a protective factor, consider the following factors that may serve to decrease the risk for suicide:

- Social support network
- Religion/spirituality
- Positive coping skills
- Positive problem-solving skills
- Positive therapeutic relationship
- A sense of responsibility to family and/or friends
- Life satisfaction

While asking questions about suicidal ideation, intent, plan, and previous attempts is rarely easy for a clinician, it is important for those assessing for suicide ideation to possess a set of appropriate screening questions, the ease and confidence to ask the questions, and the intuition to recognize when to begin exploring potential suicide with the client. The following mnemonic, provided by SAMHSA, can help college counselors identify potential suicide risks.

"IS PATH WARM"
    Ideation: Threatened or communicated
    Substance abuse: Excessive or increased
    Purposelessness: No reasons for living
    Anxiety: Agitation/insomnia
    Trapped: Feeling there is no way out
    Hopelessness
    Withdrawing: From friends, family, society
    Anger (uncontrolled): Rage, seeking revenge
    Recklessness: Risky acts, unthinking
    Mood changes (dramatic) (Whiston, 2009)

Other available suicide assessments include:

- Beck Scale for Suicidal Ideation (Psychological Corporation)
- Beck Hopelessness Scale (Psychological Corporation)
- Inventory of Suicide Orientation (National Computer Systems, Inc.)
- Suicide Probability Scale (Western Psychological Services)
- Adult Suicidal Ideation Questionnaire (Psychological Assessment Resources)

Cultural Considerations

Many times individuals receive messages from cultural norms that increase suicidal risk. Males are often reluctant to seek help and the belief that "real men handle their problems alone" only contributes to feelings of isolation and failure. Female students, on the other hand, may be more willing to seek help and accept emotional expressiveness; however, this expressivity is sometimes accompanied by dangerous, life-threatening behaviors. The cultural norm is to value grades as indicators of school success and failure in school may bring feelings of shame. Subjective cultural norms can serve to exacerbate problems around suicide. The following example illustrates how the cultural value on personal privacy may prevent a student experiencing suicidal ideation from receiving needed assistance. For example, a male student may confide suicidal ideation to another male student. The nonsuicidal student comes from a culture where people do not involve themselves in other's problems. The nonsuicidal student then ignores the statement and does not report it to college or university officials. The suffering student is left to a solitary struggle with his suicidal thoughts. College counselors can be proactive in helping to define a campus culture open to discussing hard topics; through suicidal prevention programming, counselors can educate students and fellow college employees about warning signs and the importance of reporting for student safety and well-being.

While African American students are less likely to commit suicide, Westefeld, Badura, Kiel, and Schneel (1996) found that African American college students reported lower scores on measures related to reasons to live related to suicidal behavior. The authors reasoned that this result might mirror the experience of isolation on predominantly White campuses that African American students may endure. A similar study addressed reasons for living among LGBT college students and results indicated that loneliness and depression were positively correlated and that reasons for living were negatively associated with these two variables. The results also indicated that LGBT students suffered more depression, loneliness, and scored lower on reasons for living than the control group (Westefeld, Maples, Buford, & Taylor, 2001). Like African Americans, this group often experiences prejudice, isolation, and rejection; thus, these social influences are reasoned to affect this population's reasons for living.

It is clearly important to have a thorough and detailed suicide assessment as the first step in the treatment of college students presenting with suicidal ideation. However, most traditional assessments have focused primarily on risk while recent studies emphasize that a key element in further refining models of prediction should include the assessment of protective factors for students who do not pose immediate risk for suicide attempts.

Identifying and Strengthening Protective Factors: Beyond Deficits

Commonly noted protective factors against suicide include students seeking and receiving adequate mental health care, restricted access to guns and other highly lethal methods of self-harm, a solid support network, strong skills in effective methods of problem solving and conflict resolution, and cultural beliefs about suicide. Through outreach programming, several of these factors can be addressed whether through campus-wide policies or psychoeducational group training. There are also a number of factors that may protect against suicidal behaviors that can be addressed in individual counseling.

Optimism

In addition to risk factors in the assessment process, Gutierrez et al. (2000) stated that protective factors could be effective in the treatment of suicidal thoughts and behaviors. Hirsch, Wolford, LaLonde, Brunk, and Parker-Morris (2009) found that optimism is a buffer against suicidal ideation; students who feel that things can get better are less likely to have thoughts of suicide. Helping students develop problem-solving skills for the life challenges they face and that they feel contribute to their depressed mood or sense of hopelessness may help them build an optimistic attitude. Helping them identify times in which things turned out positively for them when they once seemed hopeless can also be effective in helping them to restructure their attitudes. For example, a student may attribute failure in a class to personal characteristics (e.g., I am lazy, I am stupid), not accepting that living in the residence hall is distracting at times.

Further exploration may reveal that when the student attempts to study there are many distracting social opportunities. Helping the student to restructure personal thinking about individual abilities would be a primary intervention. Helping the student recognize strengths, engage in honest self-appraisal, and use realistic thinking would assist in mitigating erroneous self-talk. Developing assertiveness skills may also be helpful in expressing personal needs to study when confronted with social opportunities. Hirsch et al. (2009) stated the results suggest that helping clients to reshape thinking toward more optimistic futures may increase hopefulness and reduce suicidal ideation.

Balancing Risk With Protection

Rutter, Freedenthal, and Osman (2008) found that talking with clients about both risk and protective factors may deepen the clinicians ability to assess overall suicidal risk for the client. Clients may acknowledge a feeling of social support yet may lack resources to use the social network, thus limiting the effectiveness of its protective power. Furthering a discussion of protective factors to include rehearsal (how to access protective factors) is an important clinical step in assessment and treatment of suicidal ideation and behaviors. Balancing protective factors, both internal and external, could assist clinicians in risk assessment. Rutter et al. (2008) concluded that risk assessment focused on only the client's deficits might inadvertently support the client's negative self-image and increase suicidal risk.

The culmination of this more recent research on college student suicide assessment indicates that broadening more traditional suicide assessment protocols to include protective factors is an important step in working with college students. Assessing the cognitive style (realistic vs. negative thinking patterns related to self and accomplishments) of the student and reasons for living may prove to be helpful additions to suicide assessment protocols. Recognizing risk and adding strengths and resilience measures may help to strengthen the suicide assessment and provide constructive feedback to the student that personal strengths (protective factors) will assist in dealing with the current stressors.

Meaning Making in Life

Linehan, Goodstein, Nielsen, and Chiles (1983) and Westefeld, Richards, and Levy (2011) supported the study of reasons college students decide to keep living. They called this a protective factor and reasoned that it was an important element in suicide prevention and treatment. Frankl (1959/2006) discussed the quest for personal meaning and how this construct may influence suicide. The meaning construct has been associated with positive psychology, and is focused on locating personal attributes that assist clients in growing and adjusting (Deci & Ryan, 2000). Ryff (1989) called meaning in life an indicator of wellness. In essence, meaning can be seen as a tool for adapting to environmental demands and life events, including trauma, loss, and stress.

Meaning in life is intuitively connected to hopefulness about life. As noted by Lapierre, Dube, Douffard, and Alain (2007), individuals who experience hopefulness are accountable for their own well-being and can improve their situations while remaining actively devoted to personal problem solving. On the contrary, those that experience hopelessness have difficulty meeting life's challenges and feeling the self-efficacy to improve situations. Thus, instilling feelings of hopefulness is a positive goal of counseling, and has been noted as especially useful in suicide prevention with college students.

COUNSELING WITH SUICIDAL COLLEGE STUDENTS

When a student is in imminent danger of harming himself or herself, getting immediate assistance for that student is the only option. This may involve walking the client to the campus counseling center or calling for emergency services to directly intervene and transport the student to an emergency medical or mental health center, depending on need. If, however, the client is dealing with feelings related to hopelessness, helplessness, and depression, but is not in imminent danger, the counselor may benefit from focusing on strengthening relevant protective factors including working with the client to ensure that he or she is actively involved in regularly scheduled mental health care treatment, shoring up the client's support system, and incorporating meaning-making activities within the counseling work with this client.

While many interventions used to treat depression itself are also useful for clients who have expressed suicidal ideations, presented here are a few interventions and activities that may be especially useful with these clients. Bear in mind that the following tasks, as proposed by the National Resource Center for Suicide Prevention and Aftercare, are likely to be relevant to helping clients wrestling with suicidal thoughts: unconditional self-acceptance, social skills enhancement, support network development, communication skill development, accepting some outcomes as positive failures, development of skills for coping with grief, stress management, decision-making skills, developing a sense of humor, helping skills development, anger management, emotion control and management, and purpose and meaning in life exploration.

Meaning-Making Activities

As previously evidenced, a wealth of research and literature has been devoted to discovering factors that put individuals at risk for suicide; however, a more recent trend in addressing individuals who present suicidal tendencies is giving attention to protective factors, including the use of meaning. The evidence suggests that creating meaning can assist individuals in building protective factors to combat feelings of hopelessness, depression, and suicide. With the inclusion of these protective factors, professional counselors have the ability to capitalize on client strengths emphasizing that the resources clients bring to counseling can be used to assist the client in meeting the challenges of living. Following are a few techniques from the literature concerning building meaning that have been tailored to be useful with college students.

Forgiving Others and Finding Meaning

"To Forgive Is Divine" (O'Hanlon & Bertolino, 2012) is a tool used primarily for clients who are angry with someone else. Many times college students experiencing suicidal ideation are angry with a parent or family member. This technique can allow the student to express the anger and hostility in a positive and expressive manner. When using this intervention, the counselor asks the student to list a person or several people against whom he or she holds the anger. Following the listing and any mini-stories that come from the listing, the student is instructed to write a letter to any or all of those people. This letter is not to be sent, but is intended to give voice and record the student's experiences and resentments. In addition, the student declares her or his willingness to forgive that person and let go of the resentment. An exercise of this nature allows the client to express frustration while allowing for forgiveness. People sometimes find meaning in close relationships. Discussing the anger they experience in these relationships may offer some relief. This easing of the anger can be used as a way to discuss the value of forgiveness in relationships.

The Mountain Range Exercise

The Mountain Range Exercise (Frankl, 1968; Ernzen, 1990) is an activity whereby the student draws a mountain range and places people of importance to him or her (such as friends, family members, artists, actors, musicians, characters in a novel or movie) on the mountaintops. The student is asked about commonalities between himself or herself and the individuals on the mountaintops. The client is also asked whose mountains he or she would like to be part. This activity helps the student to identify positive associations in his or her life. During the discussion of the identified individuals, the counselor draws attention to the values of the student by asking what she or he likes about each of the important people. These do not have to be real people and can be fantasy or literary characters. This helps the client to unveil personal values and understand positive attributes in these relationships. Discussions about how to include people with similar values offer the student an opportunity to seek social support for personal aspirations. This activity has been used successfully in both group and individual settings with alcoholics, psychiatric inpatients, and meaningful living groups (Ernzen, 1990; Schulenberg, Hutzell, Nassif, & Rogina, 2008).

Every Life Is a Story

The Movies Exercise (Schulenberg et al., 2008) helps direct individuals to a better awareness of personal life meaning. The student is directed to develop a movie of her or his life, centered on the past, and then brought forward to the present. Additionally, the student is directed to create another movie from the present into the future. Various aspects of the film including casting, actors, titles, and genres are discussed in order to help the student identify a clear sense of what life story has brought the student to this point in time. The future movie should include the way the student wants life to unfold including how he or she plans to live through difficult experiences. By including characters, the student gets an idea of who is important and how that person plays a role in the student's life. Some of the roles models may not be positive and any negative characters can expose conflict and demonstrate how the student deals with that conflict. In these scenes of conflict, the student can script skills and strategies to navigate the difficult points in life. These struggles may help the student see that some strife can lead to hopelessness and futility, and some strife can lead to greater personal growth, helping the student to recognize that conflict in itself is not bad. From the movie, the student can build strategies to overcome the difficulties and model ways to overcome life's struggles. The exercise could include the moral or meaning of the movie story. This personal meaning can be related to the student's reasons to live and can help to create purpose and meaning in life within the student's social milieu.

Mitzvah Therapy

According to Sol Gordon, "The best way to find yourself is to lose yourself in the service of others," and that is the goal of Mitzvah Therapy (Gordon, 2004; O'Hanlon & Bertolino, 2012). This therapy is not the act of giving to charity; rather it involves the client helping someone else directly. Mitzvah Therapy is designed to connect client symptoms to social justice by helping the client to engage in helping others who have similar experiences (e.g., a client that had attempted suicide in the past may be referred to do volunteer work for a suicide prevention hotline). In addition, every time the client experiences the injustice, he or she is encouraged to contribute to the relief of another victim's suffering. Finally, the student is encouraged to try this exercise for several weeks to see what kind of difference it makes. By learning effective ways to intervene in helping others, the client begins to develop deep purpose and meaning.

Logotherapeutic Intervention

Nash and Murray (2010) suggested the use of logotherapeutic questions as an approach to meaning making for college students. Questions that address issues about a client's future vision (e.g., creating one's vision of the best way to live life; positive outcomes of not living up to others' expectations; preparing a eulogy for oneself) help the student to focus on personal accomplishments, and how these activities begin to build a sense of coherence in the student's life. The counselor and student discuss the connection of the activities and accomplishments to explore themes of coherence. Once the connections are made between the endeavors, the student and counselor work together to build themes of coherence and purpose. These themes can then help the student develop reasons for living and build a general life purpose of ultimate meaning from the array of specific individual pursuits.

Socratic Dialogue

Socratic dialogue is another technique that can be used with college students to foster a sense of meaning. In this process, a counselor asks questions of the client to promote internal exploration in an attempt to discover personal life meanings (e.g., What would give purpose to your life? How would you know when your life has purpose?), and to explore how these life meanings may be accomplished. The discussions focus on whether the student has or can develop the knowledge and understanding for reaching these goals (Schulenberg et al., 2008). By developing a list of goals with the student, the counselor is intentionally building a future focus. This future focus is designed to give the student activities and goals that bring meaningful coherence to the student's life.

In this section, several techniques for use in counseling with college students have been presented. Some techniques demonstrate relatedness and connection in the student's life, while others demonstrate how a student's contribution to others can enhance his or her own life and increase personal meaning, alongside personal pursuits. These techniques highlight meaningfulness that has been connected to well-being and reasons to live. By increasing meaningfulness, students can begin to realize coherence in their lives and articulate reasons to live, thus reducing suicidal ideation. These techniques are suggested in addition to the more traditional forms of suicide assessment and treatment.

CONCLUSION

In conclusion, although suicide rates have decreased over the past few decades, it is the second most frequent cause of death for this population. Understanding the risk factors is helpful for college counselors who may be the first line of care for students with suicidal ideations. However, it is important to note that because of the covert nature of suicide, college counseling centers should actively advocate for campus-wide awareness and intervention programming. When a student is threatening self-harm, it is essential that ideation, plan, means, and intent be assessed carefully as these factors determine the imminent risk for action. Information about counseling center services, local suicide prevention organizations, and national hotline numbers should be easily accessible and widely visible so that students at risk are able to find resource information without difficulty. Suicide can be prevented, but it may require a campus-wide initiative to effectively reach students who are at the greatest risk.

RESOURCES

Electronic Resources
- American Association of Suicidology: www.suicidology.org
- American Foundation for Suicide Prevention: www.afsp.org
- Centers for Disease Control and Prevention: www.cdc.gov/violenceprevention/suicide/resources.html
- Jed Foundation (youth suicide site): www.jedfoundation.org
- Suicide Prevention Resource Center: www.sprc.org

Print Resources
- Cukrowicz, K. C., Wingate, L. R., Driscoll, K. A., & Joiner, T. E., Jr. (2004). A standard of care for the assessment of suicide risk and associated treatment: The Florida State University Psychology Clinic as an example. *Journal of Contemporary Psychotherapy, 34*, 87–99.
- DePaulo, J. R. (2002). *Understanding depression*. Wiley Publishing.
- Jamison, K. (1996). *Night falls fast*. New York: Knopf.

Electronic Resources for Students
- Active Minds on Campus: www.activemindsoncampus.org
- Campus Blues: www.campusblues.com
- National Suicide Prevention Lifeline: www.suicidepreventionlifeline.org
- National Suicide Hotlines USA: www.suicidehotlines.com

REFERENCES

Ajzen, I. (1985). From intentions to actions: A theory of planned behavior. In J. Kuhl & J. Beckman (Eds.), *Action-control: From cognition to behavior* (pp. 11–39). Heidelberg: Springer.

American Association of Suicidology (AAS). (2013). *Youth suicide fact sheet.* Retrieved from http://www.suicidology.org/associations/1045/files/2005Youth.pdf

Deci, E. I., & Ryan, R. M. (2000). The "what" and "why" of goal pursuit: Human needs and the self-determination of behavior. *Psychological Inquiry, 11*, 227–268.

Dixon, W. A., Rumford, K. G., Heppner, P. P., & Lips, B. (1992). Use of different sources of stress to predict hopelessness and suicide ideation in a college population. *Journal of Counseling Psychology, 39*, 342–349.

Drum, D. J., Brownson, C., Burton Denmark, A., & Smith, S. E. (2009). New data on the nature of suicidal crises in college students: Shifting the paradigm. *Professional Psychology: Research and Practice, 40*, 213–222.

Ernzen, F. I. (1990). Frankl's mountain range exercise. *International Forum for Logotherapy, 13*, 133–134.

Frankl, V. (1968). *The Doctor and the soul.* New York, NY: Alfred A. Knopf.

Frankl, V. (1959/2006). *Man's search for meaning.* Boston, MA: Beacon Press.

Gordon, S. (2004). *When living hurts.* New York, NY: Dell.

Gutierrez, P. M., Osman, A., Barrios, F. X., Kopper, B. A., Baker, M. T., & Haraburda, C. M. (2002). Development of the reasons for living inventory for young adults. *Journal of Clinical Psychology, 58*(4), 339–357. doi:10.1002/jclp.1147

Gutierrez, P. M., Osman, A., Kopper, B. A., Barrios, F. X., & Bagge, C. L. (2000). Suicide risk assessment in a college student population. *Journal of Counseling Psychology, 47*, 403–413. doi:10.1037/0022

Hirsch, J. K., Webb, J. R., & Jeglic, E. L. (2011). Forgiveness, depression, and suicidal behavior among a diverse sample of college students. *Journal of Clinical Psychology, 67*, 896–906.

Hirsch, J. K., Wolford, K., LaLonde, S. M., Brunk, L., & Parker-Morris, A. (2009). Optimistic explanatory style as a moderator of the association between negative life events and suicide ideation. *Crisis, 30*, 48–53. doi. 10.1027/0227-5910.30.1.48

Joiner, T. R., & Rudd, M. (2000). Intensity and duration of suicidal crisis vary as a function of previous suicide attempts and negative life events. *Journal of Consulting and Clinical Psychology, 68*, 909–916. doi:10.1037/0022-006X.68.5.909

Lapierre, S., Dube, M., Bouffard, L., & Alain, M. (2007). Addressing suicidal ideations through the realization of meaningful personal goals. *Crisis, 28*, 16–25.

Linehan, M. M., Goodstein, J. L., Nielsen, S. L., & Chiles, J. A. (1983). Reasons for staying alive when you are thinking of killing yourself: The Reasons for Living Inventory. *Journal of Consulting and Clinical Psychology, 51*(2), 276–286. doi:10.1037/0022-006X.51.2.276

Nash, R. J., & Murray, M. C. (2010). *Helping college students find purpose: The campus guide to meaning-making.* San Francisco, CA: Jossey-Bass.

National Suicide Prevention Organization. (2007). *Suicide risk assessment standards packet.* New York, NY: National Suicide Prevention Lifeline.

Nock, M. K., & Banaji, M. R. (2007). Prediction of suicide ideation and attempts among adolescents using a brief performance-based test. *Journal of Consultation and Clinical Psychology, 75*, 707–715.

O'Hanlon, B., & Bertolino, B. (2012). *The therapist's notebook on positive psychology.* New York, NY: Routledge.

Palladino, D., & Minton, C. A. B. (2008). Comprehensive college student suicide assessment: Application of the Basic ID. *Journal of American College Health, 56,* 643–650.

Pokorny, A. D. (1993). Suicide prevention revisited. *Suicide and Life-Threatening Behavior, 23,* 1–10.

Reed, M. H., & Shea, S. C. (2011). Suicide assessment in college students: Innovations in uncovering suicidal ideation and intent. In D. A. Lamis & D. Lester (Eds.), *Understanding and preventing college student suicide* (pp. 197–222). Springfield, IL: Charles C. Thomas.

Rutter, P. A., Freedenthal, S., & Osman, A. (2008). Assessing protection from suicidal risk: Psychometric properties of the Suicide Resilience Inventory. *Death Studies, 32,* 142–153. doi. 10.1080/07481180701801295

Ryff, C. D. (1989). Happiness is everything, or is it? Explorations on the meaning of psychological well-being. *Journal of Personality and Social Psychology, 57,* 1069–1081. doi:10.1037/0022-3514.57.6.1069

Schulenberg, S. E., Hutzell, R. R., Nassif, C., & Rogina, J. M. (2008). Logotherapy for clinical practice. *Psychotherapy Theory, Research, Practice, Training, 45,* 447–463. doi: 10.1037/90014331

Schwartz, A. J. (2006a). College student suicide in the United States: 1990–1991 through 2003–2004. *Journal of American College Health, 54,* 341–352.

Schwartz, A. J. (2006b). Four eras of study of college student suicide in the United States: 1920–2004. *Journal of American College Health, 54,* 353–366.

Shea, S. C. (1998). The Chronological Assessment of Suicide Events: A practical interviewing strategy for the elicitation of suicidal ideation. *Journal of Clinical Psychiatry, 59*(Suppl. 20), 58–72.

Shemanski-Aldrich, R., & Cerel, J. (2009). The development of effective message content for suicide intervention: Theory of planned behavior. *Crisis, 30,* 174–179. doi 10.1027/0227-5910.30.4.174

Wang, M., Lightsey, O. R., Pietruszka, T., Uruk, A. C., & Wells, A. G. (2007). Purpose in life and reason for living as mediators of the relationship between stress, coping, and suicidal behavior. *Journal of Positive Psychology, 2,* 195–204. doi. 10.1080/17439760701228920

Westefeld, J. S., Badura, A., Kiel, J. T., & Schneel, K. (1996). Development of the College Student Reasons for Living Inventory with African Americans. *Journal of College Student Psychotherapy, 10,* 61–65.

Westefeld, J. S., Homaifar, B., Spotts, J., Furr, S., Range, L., & Werth, J. R. (2005). Perceptions concerning college student suicide: Data from four universities. *Suicide and Life-Threatening Behavior, 35*(6), 640–645. doi:10.1521/suli.2005.35.6.640

Westefeld, J. S., Maples, M. R., Buford, B., & Taylor, S. (2001). Gay, lesbian, and bisexual college students: The relationship between sexual orientation and depression, loneliness, and suicide. *Journal of College Student Psychotherapy, 15*(3), 71–82. doi:10.1300/J035v15n03_06

Westefeld, J. S., Richards, A. S., & Levy, L. (2011). Protective factors. In D. A. Lamis & D. Lester (Eds.), *Understanding and preventing college student suicide* (pp. 170–182). Springfield, IL: Charles C Thomas.

Whiston, S. C. (2009). *Principles and applications of assessment in counseling* (3rd ed.). Belmont, CA: Brooks/Cole, Cengage Learning.

17

Obsessive-Compulsive Disorder and Treatment Strategies for College Students

KATTRINA MILLER-ROACH AND RICARDO M. PHIPPS

A LOOK AT OBSESSIVE-COMPULSIVE DISORDER (OCD) TAKING HOLD

Trevor is a 19-year-old sophomore who has begun to find himself increasingly worried about his grades. Because of his desire to get accepted to medical school, grades and academic performance are very important to him. Always a hard worker and conscientious, he has lately been surprised at how strong his need for perfection in his assignments has become. Whereas once he was satisfied to do his best and enjoy A grades, he has begun to feel that he cannot do well enough on any assignment and that unless his work is perfect, it is not going to be good enough. This has led to him starting and restarting homework assignments, term papers, lab assignments, and exams. This has resulted in loss of sleep, outbursts of frustration in the classroom, as well as altercations with friends who tell him to "lighten up" and faculty members who are refusing to accept late work that is submitted past due dates because of his need to strive for an unattainable "perfection." He no longer has time for his girlfriend or any of his male friends as the semester gets toward the half-way mark and his roommate is losing patience living with a man who works until all hours trying to do a "perfect" job on his homework. His girlfriend and roommate finally decide that Trevor needs an intervention similar to what they have seen on cable TV and they gather all of his friends together to confront him about his obsessive behavior. Trevor does not respond well to their concern; he physically attacks his roommate, and the group decides that the campus police are needed to calm everyone down. And this final step is what it takes to get Trevor into treatment for his newly diagnosed obsessive-compulsive behaviors.

News and media platforms are saturated with information about and representations of individuals suffering from inexplicable obsessions and compulsions. While not always true stories, these portrayals do shed light on a very real and sometimes debilitating affliction clinically referred to as obsessive-compulsive disorder (OCD). This anxiety disorder causes sufferers to experience extreme levels of nervousness that are beyond their control (Tompkins, 2012). Their nervousness sparks ritualistic patterns of behavior that include physical and/or verbal routines. Often a source of distress and trauma for its sufferers, OCD has other symptomology that can include compulsions and intrusive, inappropriate thoughts. Extreme washing, extreme cleaning, intrusive sexual or violent thoughts, hoarding, and repeated checking are all possible manifestations of the disorder (Pignotti & Thyer, 2011). Because the typical onset age for OCD falls within the range of late adolescence to early adulthood, it is during the college years that individuals may first begin to notice symptoms in themselves or in others. Intrusive thoughts or repeated checking can become substantial distractions that may negatively affect the academic performance and social life of college students. For onlookers, the behaviors of those with OCD often appear paranoid or psychotic in nature; generally for the sufferers, the behavior is recognized as irrational and their recognition of their behavior changes and often becomes a source of further distress (Tompkins, 2012). Newly arising OCD-related behaviors may leave sufferers feeling frustrated and trapped in a cycle of symptoms that they recognize as irrational and counterproductive. Although unable to control their compulsions on their own, college students' lack of understanding of this disorder may leave them reluctant to seek help.

Obsessions are recurring, intrusive thoughts that persist despite conscious attempts to avoid or ignore them. In the case of Trevor, whose story opened this chapter, as much as he tried to feel satisfied with his work, he was driven to throw out his first, second, and further efforts in the belief that he could create a "perfect" product. People with OCD generally act out the preoccupying thought/behavior as a recurring act in an effort to relieve the overwhelming anxiety that builds up as a result of not completing the action (Rasmussen & Eisen, 1992). The obsessive behaviors and intrusive thoughts vary among individuals. Ranges include mild tension and a false belief that normal routine cannot proceed without correcting the "imperfection," to intense, intrusive thoughts such as being afflicted with a deadly disease or that harm will come to someone if the "imperfection" is not corrected.

Sulkowski, Mariaskin, and Starch (2011) asserted that people with OCD carry out ritualistic behaviors because they inexplicably believe that they *must* do so. Examples of compulsions include counting specific things such as stairs, counting in a specific way such as by 2s, or completing various actions in a patterned or numerical manner. Some sufferers may have compulsions that include rituals such as hand washing, clearing one's throat, checking locks, or turning off lights a specified number of times. Often, people with OCD attempt to rationalize the individual nuances of their behavior instead of the overall behavior (Swinson, Antony, Rachman, & Richer, 1998). For example, an OCD sufferer may contend that checking the lock on the door "one more time" is less stressful than having their property stolen. Thus, they ignore the reality that the ritualistic "one more check" or, in the case of Trevor, one more attempt at a perfect paper can repeat itself until the compulsion is satisfied and that this, in fact, can be much more stressful than the result the sufferer fears.

OCD can also develop without observable behavioral compulsions. In this form of OCD, the sufferer performs covert mental rituals. These individuals often feel the need to avoid situations that induce the distracting thoughts or where anxiety becomes heightened. As they become increasingly reclusive, these individuals may experience increased distress as they realize that others may not understand or accept that their need for avoidance is ever present.

EVOLUTION OF OCD

According to Berrios (1996), the history of OCD suggests that depictions of obsessions and compulsions can be found as far back as the 14th century Renaissance. He noted that an initial belief during that period involved superstitions and the notion that mental illnesses were the work of the devil. After some skepticism, this belief evolved from the supernatural framework to a more naturalistic one, thus introducing the word *scrupulosity* as a term for anxiety. It is derived from a Latin word that means uneasiness or anxiety or, literally, a small, sharp stone. Berrios went on to note that beginning in the late 1600s, clergymen began to draft formal documents on curing scrupulosity. Roman Catholics specifically prescribed strict spiritual submission as the way to overcome obsessions and compulsions. Realizing these methods were ineffective, clergymen began to defer to the aid of physicians for insight into the illness. Resources for physicians were limited during the time and they often resorted to drastic treatments such as blood draining (to filter out the responsible toxins) and celestial plotting (to physically align the afflicted person with an ideal healthy mental state). Also ineffective, these treatments were then replaced with confinement in insane asylums during the 1700s to 1800s in an effort to control the affliction. By the 19th century, progress had been made in better organizing and categorizing mental health disorders. With this, OCD sufferers were no longer viewed as *insane* but as suffering from some form of phobia. Medications were tried, but negative side effects limited their usefulness. Eventually, OCD was recognized as a form of neurosis rather than psychosis. By the early 20th century, the Freudian revolution had begun and OCD was imbued with a symbolic meaning. Berrios recounted a case of Freud's involving a college-aged woman who could not go to sleep without completing a ritual of checking her clocks and watches and arranging her pillows. Freud described this "sleep ceremony," according to Berrios (1996), as a symbol of pregnancy and sexual cipher. By the late 20th century, behaviorism emerged and its followers then questioned the tendencies of Freud to look for symbolism and sexual connotations in his patients' complaints. Systematic desensitization gained value among treatment options along with pharmaceutical advances that included the development of anti-anxiety drugs such as Anafranil, Prozac, and Zoloft. Effective treatment, however, can only begin once an accurate diagnosis is made.

DIAGNOSIS AND RELATED CHALLENGES

Understanding and accurately diagnosing OCD has proven to be a challenge due to the potential for biased or inaccurate information and reporting (Spengler & Jacobi, 1998). Specifically, challenges include limited available research and data, statistical base rate errors, failure of sufferers to report, misconceptions, and forms of reporting (typical vs. atypical) (Spengler & Jacobi, 1998). The *Diagnostic and Statistical Manual of Mental Disorders IV* (*DSM*; American Psychiatric Association [APA], 2000) classified OCD as an anxiety disorder that causes more than excessive worry over definitive problems. Sufferers recognize that the thoughts are their own and not outside stimuli. To that extent, the *DSM* (APA, 2000) noted that the illness cannot be the direct effect of substance abuse or other medical conditions. One additional specific criterion indicated that the obsessions and compulsions must occupy more than a single hour of a person's day and must cause marked distress (APA, 2000). In spite of the specificity of symptomology, there remains a wide range of obsessions and compulsions along the "symptom spectrum" that individuals with OCD exhibit. Of note, 60% of clients with OCD report multiple obsessions and 50% report engaging in one or more compulsion (Rasmussen & Eisen, 1988).

People with OCD may also be diagnosed with other conditions such as major depressive disorder, body dysmorphic disorder, and social anxiety disorder. Further, research indicated that there is a high prevalence of depression among the OCD community, believed to be attributed to feelings of being helpless and out of control (Mineka, Watson, & Clark, 1998).

Although the *DSM-5* offers slightly revised diagnostic criteria and potentially alter the traditional axis system, this chapter will reference the current manual. The Axis I diagnosis of OCD is similar to the Axis II diagnosis of Obsessive-Compulsive Personality Disorder (OCPD), but not to be confused as there are noteworthy differences. Individuals who suffer from OCPD lack the compulsive and obsessional behavior that is present in OCD. Rather, sufferers of OCPD present with a more generalized preoccupation with perfection, categorization, and domination. It is possible, however, for an individual to be diagnosed across both Axes with OCD and OCPD (Pignotti & Thyer, 2011). College students who seem obsessively focused on their academic performance may show symptoms that might reflect these disorders, yet actually they may simply be overconscientious students. If counselors suspect that a client is suffering from something more severe than garden variety test anxiety or overconcern about grades, further assessment can be required and this is addressed in a later section.

Research suggests that 80% of diagnosed OCD cases appear around age 18, just at the onset of traditional college enrollment (Swinson et al., 1998). The symptoms of OCD usually first appear somewhere between the late teen years and the mid-20s. Educational background has been shown to play a role in the onset of the illness, yet its exact relation to the disorder is still unclear. In a 1980 study of adults from several U.S. cities, OCD was lower for those who had graduated from high school than those who had not. By contrast, a lifetime prevalence of OCD is greater for those who graduate with a college degree than those who report "some" college experience. The same study suggested that OCD sufferers generally are of higher than average intelligence, as complicated thinking patterns are often involved with the illness (Swinson et al., 1998). Though symptomology typically buds during the college years, the stigma associated with disclosure results in unreported and untreated cases, which makes it critical that college counselors be aware of the symptoms and be alert to their presence in individuals who may be presenting with other complaints.

SIGNIFICANT GENDER DIFFERENCE IN OCD IN COLLEGE STUDENTS

Research findings indicate that the average onset age for college students with OCD is 19 years, however, no gender difference in age of onset has been noted (Labad et al., 2008). In addition, the *DSM* reported that OCD is equally common among males and females. However, manifesting symptoms do differ based on gender. Contamination/cleaning rituals are more prevalent for females and sexual/religious ideations are more prevalent among males (Labad et al., 2008; Mathis et al., 2011). However, gender differentials did not exist regarding the symptoms of aggression/checking behaviors, symmetry/ordering, or hoarding. Both of the gender-related dimensions also tended to show up at an earlier age. Young men who manifest OCD behaviors are more likely to be single at onset and experience a more chronic form of the illness. Females experience greater numbers of comorbid disorders, especially eating disorders and impulse control. All of these behaviors, both gender and nongender related, may affect not only sufferers of this disorder, but their roommates or house-mates as well. It is often their friends who first notice and complain about the unusual behaviors. And since sufferers are slow to seek treatment due to their fear of exposure, their friends may need to be enlisted to encourage them to seek help.

WARNING SIGNS OF OCD IN A COLLEGE STUDENT POPULATION

- Disengagement in campus activities due to excessive worry, concern about negative things happening, appearance, "to-do's," and so forth.
- Habitual tardiness to class and meetings due to the need to "feel right" about leaving the room. For example, completing certain tasks numerous times, "checking" on things (such as the lights, iron, television) to ensure that they are off or having to take a longer route to destinations before being able to arrive (such as repeating flights of stairs, walking in a certain direction, or avoidance of certain places).
- Impaired or interrupted study time before, during, and after class because of the need to perform repetitive actions or mental rituals.
- Unjustified worry about being dishonest to teacher and peers or unintentionally cheating on tests or homework.
- Continuous need for reassurance from peers and teachers.
- Withdrawal from campus life and social scenes due to incessantly cleaning the dorm room or doing laundry.
- Avoidance of peers and social groups because of worry about hurting them due to violent or unusual thoughts.
- Excessive praying (often in a particular way; i.e., uninterrupted by anyone or ending before the clocks strikes a certain point) that impairs relationships with others.
- Rituals or uncanny habits occupy a great deal of time and compromise homework completion, appropriate sleep, and study time.
- Decrease in grades and school performance due to unexplainable tasks or routines such as rereading tests and rewriting responses.
- Avoidance of or reluctance to make friends due to a fear of hurting them because thoughts of hurting them permeate.
- Strained interpersonal relationships (teachers, friends, boyfriends or girlfriends) due to uncontrollable thoughts and rituals.

- Uncontrollable worry about having missed class or a test though there is certainty that class and assignments were never missed.
- Avoidance of campus activities due to fear of death or being hurt.
- Disorganization due to inability to throw away old notes or purge unneeded paperwork.

TREATMENT OPTIONS

Two evidence-based psychotherapeutic treatments for OCD are cognitive-behavioral therapy (CBT) and exposure and response prevention (ERP; Whittal, Thordarson, & McLean, 2005).

Cognitive-Behavioral Therapy

CBT focuses on the irrational thoughts and exaggerated sense of responsibility experienced with an emphasis on healthy ways of responding to obsessive thoughts, without resorting to the compulsive behavior. For Trevor, the young man first introduced at the beginning of this chapter, CBT might be the treatment of choice as described in the following vignette.

Trevor was eventually encouraged to seek help from the University Counseling Center by his girlfriend, who had threatened to break up with him if he did not seek help. Thomas, the counselor assigned to Trevor, believed that CBT would be an effective treatment strategy and formulated the following treatment plan for him to be carried out in six sessions:

1. *Psychoeducation—The counselor would spend one 50-minute session with Trevor, helping him better understand OCD as a disordered way of processing information in his brain rather than as a sequence of bad habits. They would also discuss the risks and the benefits of treating OCD with CBT.*
2. *Relaxation Techniques—The counselor would spend the second 50-minute session teaching Trevor relaxation techniques, such as deep breathing, muscle relaxation, positive imagery, and mindfulness, to help him counteract the high level of anxiety that accompanies OCD. This is a preparation for the cognitive training they will do in the next session.*
3. *Cognitive Training—The counselor would spend the third 50-minute session leading Trevor through cognitive training. Thomas would teach Trevor to resist OCD tendencies and urges with assertive self-talk. Cognitive training is designed to help Trevor feel that he actually does have some control over OCD and that he can increase that control with practice. Thomas would help Trevor develop the self-talk statements that he*

would use when faced with the feared objects, actions, or thoughts that confront him. Trevor would utilize his earlier learning through the implementation of the previously learned relaxation techniques.

4. *Mapping OCD—The counselor would spend two 50-minute sessions helping Trevor identify the range of control and predictability he experiences with OCD. Together, they will work to determine where Trevor is completely free from OCD, where he has some limited success in controlling OCD, and where he feels completely helpless. The counselor would help Trevor focus his attention on the area where he has some limited success, sometimes known as the transition zone. Exercises would be developed to enable Trevor to use his cognitive training and self-talk in these areas first as he strengthened his ability to manage his thoughts. The goal would be to feel competent to manage the obsessive thoughts in all situations.*

5. *Termination—The counselor would spend the final 50-minute session helping Trevor explore the support systems he has in place that will help him continue his progress. A referral might be made for further counseling or he may be encouraged to join an on-campus support group to help him keep in mind that he is not alone in the journey to combat OCD.*

Exposure and Response Prevention

ERP involves repeated exposure to the source of the obsession while being monitored and supported to refrain from the normal compulsive behavior. After enduring the anxiety, the urge to engage in the compulsive behavior subsides and the individual sees that the ritual is not necessary to eliminate the associated anxiety. Using Trevor as our example again, ERP could be used in the following manner:

Trevor's counselor recognized that ERP and CBT could both be very effective when used in tandem and he added an ERP component to his treatment plan for Trevor. He introduced the following intervention:

In conjunction with the first step of the CBT treatment plan, Thomas will explain that the only way for Trevor to overcome his fear is to refrain from ritualizing and to be directly subjected to the "feared" outcome. He will place emphasis on the fact that Trevor's rituals are voluntary and he should not attempt to control the obsessions or the distress of the moment. Specifically, Thomas will encourage Trevor to confront his fear of imperfection in a graduated manner while voluntarily and simultaneously refraining from performing his rituals. The unhealthy OCD cognitions will be identified and processed as they occur.

Realizing that the length of treatment varies depending on the individual, Thomas developed a 12- to 15-session plan (weekly meetings 60–90 minutes in length) as an effective goal of symptom reduction for Trevor. The plan will be interwoven with the CBT treatment plan that he developed for Trevor and will loosely proceed as follows:

1. *Sessions 1 to 3: Assist Trevor in conducting an "inconvenience review" to outline the specific ways that his OCD currently interrupts his life; develop a fear hierarchy (to be modified as needed throughout sessions); plan various exposure exercises regarding his need for perfection; and strategize ritual-prevention practices.*
2. *Sessions 4 to 12: Discuss barriers to treatment; begin in-session, counselor-guided exposure and response prevention; assign out of session Trevor-driven exposure assignments*
3. *Sessions 13 to 15: Discuss and problem-solve treatment barriers and any occasions of noncompliance; conduct final exposure exercises; review and revise as necessary the hierarchy of fears; discuss ritual prevention strategies pros and cons; prepare for future challenges; and develop a plan for behavior reversion*

In summary, while either CBT or ERP alone are effective, Sulkowki, Mariaskin, Jordan, and Storch (2009) concluded that an intentional combination of CBT and ERP is most effective.

Psychopharmacological Treatment

Antidepressants are sometimes used in conjunction with psychotherapy as a supplement, but medication alone is typically not effective in relieving the symptoms of OCD. Relying solely on medication also results in a higher relapse rate. There are research findings that substantiate that a combination of CBT with sertraline is more effective than using CBT alone in treatment of OCD (Anonymous, 2004). CBT empowers individuals to control their obsessions and compulsions, and studies have shown that 85% of people who complete a course of CBT have eliminated or greatly reduced symptoms. University and college counseling centers generally offer CBT-based treatments, individual and group, for students experiencing OCD, with medication referrals available through university health center physicians.

Social Support

Support during treatment for OCD is critical, particularly for college students, who easily can become discouraged by feelings of isolation. Group therapy is an option many university and college counseling centers offer due both to the unique benefits of the group milieu as well as its effi-ciency in expeditiously accommodating students wait-listed for individual services (Kitzrow, 2003). Group therapy provides encouragement and support for students who might otherwise remain very secretive about their diagnosis of OCD. Important support can also be offered to students through family services. Psychoeducation for families, whether done long distance through literature and other resources or face-to-face, can help reduce family conflicts stemming from the OCD symptoms and educate family members as to how best to help their loved one. Having family and friends to talk with can help reduce anxiety in students who are undergo-ing treatment.

Psychoeducation

It is also wise for university and college counseling centers to offer psy-choeducation to students diagnosed with OCD, either in the context of therapy or otherwise, about lifestyle choices they can make to better control OCD symptoms, stress reduction through exercise or relaxing activities, healthy eating, regular sleep habits, and avoiding alcohol and nicotine. The last two areas are particularly tricky as these behaviors are often viewed as markers of adulthood and freedom from parental influ-ence. In particular, drinking alcohol is frequently perceived by students as a way to temporarily reduce anxiety and worry, but it actually ampli-fies anxiety symptoms as it wears off. Dawson, Grant, Stinson, and Chou (2005) concluded that most segments of the adult U.S. population who drink alcohol, including traditional college-age students, have increased risks for anxiety disorders, including OCD. Similarly, smoking leads to higher, not lower, levels of anxiety and OCD symptoms since nicotine is a powerful stimulant.

The Difference Between Conscientiousness and Compulsiveness

University and college counseling center clinicians should also be aware of the possible link between typical college student traits, such as per-fectionism, with OCD. Distinguishing between adaptive and maladaptive forms of perfectionism is necessary to determine whether students are compulsively and relentlessly pushing themselves to achieve impossible goals or if they are simply being extremely conscientious in meeting the academic demands of their professors. Adaptive perfectionism results in high standards, conscientiousness, and motivation to achieve, whereas maladaptive perfectionism may trap students in a self-defeating cycle from which they cannot escape. As a rule of thumb, when a student's obsession about grades and schoolwork turns into compulsions that interfere with their ability to actually complete assignments or enjoy leisure time, there may be an underlying disorder. In these situations, treatment may also involve cognitive restructuring to help students combat irrational thoughts that make anything short of absolute perfection unacceptable (Ashby & Bruner, 2005).

INTERVENTIONS IN BRIEF

- Encourage the sufferer to read about and become knowledgeable of OCD and its commonality among college students; this can be done by visiting various reputable websites, exploring resources in the campus library, or direct education from the campus counselor or other professional.
- Take advantage of all on-campus supports such as counseling centers and support groups.
- Decrease university-related stress by encouraging the sufferer to let teachers, tutors, and resident assistants know about the circumstance and assist in developing provisions.
- Seek the help of professional medical and psychological services.
- Encourage the sufferer to track the symptoms such as day, time, location, type, and triggers using a smartphone, laptop, or tablet; this provides a tangible resource on how the thoughts and rituals are impacting daily functioning; tracking will also become helpful as professional treatment is employed to assist with combating these tendencies.
- Encourage desensitization through gradual reduction in tendencies and thoughts.
- Refocus attention by encouraging light exercise, talking on the phone, internet surfing, sewing, and so forth for 15 minutes a day to delay obsessions and compulsions.
- Encourage the sufferer to make solid mental notes during the first time of execution; for example, "the iron is now turned off" or "I have washed my hands thoroughly."
- Encourage the sufferer to designate a time in each day to "worry"; during this time a list of worries and concerns can be reviewed and permission can be given to obsess over them (only for that allotted period, however).
- Encourage self-care such as relaxation techniques, healthy eating, appropriate sleep, and exercise.

- Encourage the sufferer to avoid negative self-treatment such as alcohol and drugs.
- Encourage the sufferer to identify at least one person to whom to stay connected.

IMPLICATIONS FOR COLLEGE FACULTY/ADMINISTRATION

OCD generally receives less attention on college campuses than do other anxiety disorders and many students do not seek treatment because of secrecy and shame about their symptoms (Sulkowski, Mariaskin, & Storch, 2011). Diagnoses can be difficult because symptoms often mirror the symptoms of disorders that are more prominent. Consequently, university personnel should be intentional about creating an environment where everyone—students, faculty, and staff—are aware of the signs and symptoms of OCD and of the proper channels to pursue help. Unfortunately, a tremendous stigma related to seeking mental health services continues to exist on college campuses among students. Therefore, informational campaigns should be developed to help lower the stigma as well as address the fears students have of being ostracized or ridiculed for seeking mental health care.

Students with well-documented diagnoses may be eligible for special accommodations through the Americans with Disabilities Act. These special accommodations may range from being given more time to complete reading assignments to special assistance with note taking. However, some of the accommodations commonly extended to students with other disabilities may not be helpful to students with OCD; for example, extended time to complete tests or other projects may create more opportunity for ritualizing, which exacerbates OCD (Singer, 2012). Faculty members who promote open-door policies and allow students to feel safe in discussing special needs individually might have the best luck in helping students with OCD be successful in their courses. Regular dialogue between faculty and campus mental health teams can help instructors stay abreast of current OCD-related research in order to know which accommodations are reasonable and evidence-based.

COMORBIDITY WITH OTHER DIAGNOSES

In a general population sample study, researchers found a high rate of comorbidity of OCD with other anxiety disorders (e.g., phobias, panic disorder, generalized anxiety, acute stress disorder) and major depressive disorder (Brakoulias et al., 2011). Although there is some indication that a genetic predisposition or link exists between anxiety disorders and OCD, it is believed that depression is more likely a consequence of OCD rather than a comorbid disorder already present at the onset of OCD.

A strong link between bipolar disorder and OCD has also been established, with perhaps between 10% and 35% of people with bipolar disorder also having OCD, with OCD symptoms usually presenting first (Perugi et al., 1997). One study found that OCD occurs with bipolar disorder at a much higher rate than major depressive disorder, that is, people with bipolar disorder are between two and five times more likely to have OCD than people with major depressive disorder. When bipolar disorder and OCD occur together, the symptoms of bipolar disorder tend to be much worse and more difficult to treat than bipolar conditions that occur without OCD. People with both OCD and bipolar disorder also tend to show more frequent use and abuse of substances such as drugs and alcohol, which is a critical factor for treating college students. However, because the average onset age of bipolar disorders is 20 for men and women, at which time traditional students are usually in the prime of the college experience, OCD symptoms would be much more difficult to identify and treat concurrently with bipolar disorders because of the urgency of addressing bipolar symptoms and facilitating safety for students.

OCD has long been associated with anorexia nervosa (Roberts, 2006). Obsessive behaviors of individuals with anorexia nervosa include ritualized purchase, preparation, and presentation of food. According to Halmi et al. (1991), incidence rates of concurrent OCD in persons diagnosed with anorexia nervosa may be as high as 68% for anorexia nervosa restrictive type (i.e., food intake is severely limited or eliminated) and as high as 79.1% for anorexia nervosa binge-eating-purging type (i.e., alternating periods of restricted eating and excessive eating with purging). Consequently, Roberts felt that prevention programs for eating disorders on college campuses should include some screening for and education about OCD.

Current research on OCD in college students often places OCD within a larger context of obsessive-compulsive spectrum disorders, including body dysmorphic disorder (the strong preoccupation with perceived physical defects in the individual), hypochondriasis (the presence of health anxiety and excessive worry about developing illness), trichotillomania (persistent hair pulling), and excoriation (pathological skin picking). Hollander (1993) first proposed the concept of obsessive-compulsive spectrum disorders and the list of disorders proposed to belong in this range has varied since then and into the present. Sulkowksi, Mariaskin, and Storch (2011) concluded that approximately 5% of college students may have OCD, 5% may have body dysmorphic disorder, 7% may show symptoms of hypochondriasis, 3% may have trichotillomania, and 6% may have symptoms of pathological skin picking, figures that are consistent with previous research. This same study showed strong associations between OCD and body dysmorphic disorder and hypochondriasis, suggesting high comorbidity rates between OCD and these two other obsessive-compulsive spectrum disorders. Both of these disorders can be especially relevant to college counselors, as students are quick to compare themselves with others and find themselves lacking as well as face their first experience of living on their own away from the nurturing care of their parents; thus, they may have undeveloped abilities related to monitoring their health.

CULTURAL CONSIDERATIONS

There is a virtual absence of African Americans in OCD research studies, rendering potential differences in treatment effect undetected and benefits of findings not generalizable to the population (Michalopoulou, Falzarano, & Rosenberg, 2009). African Americans tend to consult members of their informal social network, including clergy, in times of emotional stress. In addition, the stigma of mental illness and fear of being seen as "mentally ill" or "losing their minds'" may be accompanied by the belief that they will be involuntarily hospitalized or falsely arrested for their behavior. Organizations like the Historically Black Colleges and Universities (HBCU) Center for Excellence in Behavioral Health at Morehouse School of Medicine in Atlanta actively work to raise awareness about and create training opportunities for identification of mental disorders on the campuses of historically Black colleges and universities (Morehouse School of Medicine, 2012). Similarly, Latinos in the United States are underrepresented in OCD research studies in the general population. Organizers of campaigns on college campuses to increase awareness about OCD should be sensitive to negative cultural stigmas Latinos may associate with mental health care in general, different ideas about the best approach to treatment of mental illness, language barriers, and fears of reinforcing negative stereotypes about one's ethnicity (Wetterneck, 2012). Similarly, considerations should be given to other ethnically and culturally diverse groups on college campuses and potential disparities or barriers that may impede them from receiving treatment for OCD.

Beyond ethnic considerations about OCD in college students, and given that sexual obsessions are commonly experienced with OCD, attention in research should be given to the nexus of sexual orientation and OCD. Since the college years are typically a time of sexual discovery for many young people, sexual obsessions may not be an uncommon manifestation of OCD for college students. Specifically, sexual orientation OCD is defined as the fear of not knowing one's sexual orientation definitively coupled with feeling that finding a partner to whom one is genuinely attracted is impossible (Hershfield, 2010). Although sexual orientation is often considered fluid rather than an "either/or" trait, there is a form of OCD that reflects an obsessive concern with one's sexual identity. These obsessions consume the thoughts of those experiencing them and cause tremendous social impairment, as well as remain very puzzling to clinicians to whom they are presented in therapy (Williams & Farris, 2010). This form of OCD may be experienced by individuals who had previously self-identified as either lesbian, gay, bisexual, transgender, or heterosexual, but now are experiencing compulsive, intrusive doubts about their sexual orientation. Clinicians have the challenge of distinguishing between normal sexual identity questioning and obsessive and pathological questioning.

DSM-5 AND COLLEGE STUDENTS WITH OCD

The placement of OCD in the *DSM-5* is a contentious topic. There is a large amount of support for removing OCD from the anxiety disorders category in which it resides in the *DSM-IV-TR* because OCD is primarily characterized by obsessions and compulsions, rather than anxiety. However, treatments for obsessions, compulsions, and anxiety tend to be similar (Mataix-Cols, Pertusa, & Leckman, 2007).

   The *DSM-5* includes the emerging obsessive-compulsive spectrum of body dysmorphic disorder, hypochondriasis, trichotillomania, excoriation, and possibly tic disorders, but there is mixed support for including Obsessive-Compulsive Personality Disorder in the spectrum. There is considerable consensus for the inclusion of specifiers for OCD in the *DSM-5* to account for the heterogeneity of OCD (Mataix-Cols, Pertusa, & Leckman, 2007).

CONCLUSION

University and college counseling centers typically spearhead outreach programs to help raise awareness among students of the indicators of various mental health issues, yet many students still go undiagnosed and unassisted because of the tremendous stigma that still exists concerning mental health treatment on college campuses. As efforts are expanded to increasingly educate faculty and other campus personnel to understand and recognize symptoms, more students can be directed toward available resources so that their academic and social lives are not unnecessarily compromised by OCD. CBT and ERP are evidence-based treatment modes that result in a high level of success, often without the addition of medication. Special attention is needed to make sure that outreach efforts take into account the cultural considerations of students from diverse cultural backgrounds.

REFERENCES

American Psychiatric Association. (2000). *Diagnostic and statistical manual of mental disorders* (4th ed., text rev.). Washington, DC: Author.

Anonymous. (2004). Combination therapy best for obsessive disorders. *Association of Operating Room Nurses Journal, 80,* 1156–1157.

Ashby, J., & Bruner, L. (2005). Multidimensional perfectionism and obsessive-compulsive behaviors. *Journal of College Counseling, 8,* 31–40.

Berrios, G. E. (1996). *The history of mental symptoms.* New York, NY: Cambridge University Press.

Brakoulias, V., Starcevic, V., Sammut, P., Berle, D., Milicevic, D., Moses, K., & Hannan, A. (2011). Obsessive-compulsive spectrum disorders: A comorbidity and family history perspective. *Australasian Psychiatry, 19,* 151–155.

Dawson, D., Grant, B., Stinson, F., & Chou, P. (2005). Psychopathology associated with drinking and alcohol use disorders in the college and general adult populations. *Drug and Alcohol Dependence, 77,* 139–150.

Halmi, K., Eckert, E., Marchi, P., Sampugnaro, V., Apple, R., & Cohen, J. (1991). Comorbidity of psychiatric diagnosis in anorexia nervosa. *Archives of General Psychiatry, 48,* 712–718.

Hershfield, J. (2010, October 12). Gay OCD / HOCD / Sexual Orientation OCD – Part 1. Retrieved July 21, 2012, from http://www.ocdla.com/blog/sexual-orientation-hocd-gay-ocd-treatment-1010

Hollander, E. (1993). *Obsessive-compulsive related disorders.* Washington, DC: American Psychiatric Association Press.

Kitzrow, M. (2003). The mental health needs of today's college students: Challenges and recommendations. *Journal of Student Affairs Research and Practice, 41,* 167–181.

Labad, J., Menchon, J. M., Alonso, P., Segalas, C., Jimenez, S., Jaurrieta, N., ... Vallejo, J. (2008). Gender differences in obsessive-compulsive symptom dimension. *Depression and Anxiety, 25,* 832–838.

Mataix-Cols, D., Pertusa, A., & Leckman, J. (2007). Issues for *DSM-V*: How should obsessive-compulsive and related disorders be classified? *American Journal of Psychiatry, 164,* 1313.

Mathis, M. A., Alvarenga, P., Funaro, G., Torresan, R. C., Moraes, I., Torres, A. R., ... Hounie, A. G. (2011). *Gender differences in obsessive-compulsive disorder: A literature review.* Retrieved July 31, 2012, from http://www.ncbi.nlm.nih.gov/pubmed/22189930

Michalopoulou, G., Falzarano, P., & Rosenberg, D. (2009). Recruitment of African Americans for obsessive compulsive disorder treatment research. *Journal of Health Disparities Research and Practice, 3,* 71–82.

Mineka, S., Watson, D., & Clark, L. A. (1998). Comorbidity of anxiety and unipolar mood disorders. *Annual Review of Psychology, 49,* 377–412.

Morehouse School of Medicine. (2012). *HBCU Center for Excellence in Behavioral Health.* Retrieved July 21, 2012, from http://www.hbcucfe.net/about.html

Perugi, G., Akiskal, H. S., Pfanner, C., Presta, S., Gemignani, A., Milanfranchi, A., ... Cassano, G. B. (1997). The clinical impact of bipolar and unipolar affective comorbidity on obsessive-compulsive disorder. *Journal of Affective Disorders, 46,* 15–23.

Pignotti, M., & Thyer, A. B. (2011). Guidelines for the treatment of obsessive-compulsive disorders. *Best Practices in Mental Health, 2,* 84–93.

Rasmussen, S. A., & Eisen, J. L. (1988). Clinical and epidemiological findings of significance to neuropharmacologic trials in OCD. *Pyschopharmacology Bulletin, 24*(3), 27–28.

Rasmussen, S. A., & Eisen, J. L. (1992). The epidemiology and clinical features of obsessive compulsive disorder. *Psychiatric Clinics of North America, 15,* 743–758.

Roberts, M. (2006). Disordered eating and obsessive-compulsive symptoms in a sub-clinical student population. *New Zealand Journal of Psychology, 35,* 45–54.

Singer, J. (2012). OCD and college accommodations. *Psych Central.* Retrieved July 21, 2012, from http://psychcentral.com/lib/2012/ocd-and-college-accommodations

Spengler, P. M., & Jacobi, D. (1998). Assessment and treatment of obsessive compulsive disorder in college age students and adults. *Journal of Mental Health Counseling, 20,* 95–112.

Sulkowski, M., Mariaskin, A., Jordan, C., & Storch, E. (2009). Obsessive-compulsive disorder and the obsessive-compulsive disorder spectrum: A review of research. In G. Lassiter (Ed.), *Impulsivity: Causes, control and disorders* (pp. 31–58). Hauppauge, NY: Nova.

Sulkowski, M., Mariaskin, A., & Storch, E. (2011). Obsessive-compulsive spectrum disorder symptoms in college students. *Journal of American College Health, 59,* 342–348.

Swinson, R. P., Antony, M. M., Rachman, S., & Richer, M. A. (1998). *Obsessive-compulsive disorder: Theory, research, and treatment.* New York, NY: Guilford Press.

Tompkins, M. A. (2012). *OCD: A guide for the newly diagnosed.* Oakland, CA: New Harbinger.

Wetterneck, C., Little, T., Rinehart, K., Cervantes, M., Hyde, E., & Williams, M. (2012). Latinos with obsessive-compulsive disorder: Mental healthcare utilization and inclusion in clinical trials. *Journal of Obsessive-Compulsive and Related Disorders, 1,* 85–97.

Whittal, M., Thordarson, D., & McLean, P. (2005). Treatment of obsessive-compulsive disorder: Cognitive behavior therapy vs. exposure and response prevention. *Behaviour Research and Therapy, 43,* 1559–1576.

Williams, M., & Farris, S. (2010). Sexual orientation obsessions in obsessive–compulsive disorder: Prevalence and correlates. *Psychiatry Research.* doi:10.1016/j.psychres.2010.10.019. Retrieved July 20, 2012, from http://www.psychologytoday.com/files/attachments/72634/williamsfarrissexualorientationocd2010.pdf

18

Impulse-Control Disorders and Interventions for College Students

EDWARD F. HUDSPETH AND KIMBERLY MATTHEWS

When reviewing research related to Impulse-Control Disorders (ICDs), readers will find that much has changed over the last 30 years. From categories and classifications in the *Diagnostic and Statistical Manual of Mental Disorders, Third Edition* (*DSM-III*; American Psychiatric Association [APA], 1980) to changes in the *DSM-5* (APA, 2013), the classification of ICDs has changed as science adds to the understanding of the disorders. As biological, psychological, and sociological research further clarified the etiology and facets of ICDs, changes were made. Although at times the changes seem to cloud the picture, the intent is to better understand and treat. As with past editions of the *DSM*, each new edition attempts to build on success and overcome shortcomings.

Further support for changes in diagnostic categories, especially when considering ICDs, may be related to the technological advances of the 21st century. With wide availability and everyday use of the Internet, things that were once only available in person are now available at the stroke of a keyboard. At one time, communication and connection, other than in person, were delayed. Now with instant messaging, video messaging, and text messaging, there is little delay and thus a reliance on all that is immediate. From this immediate availability, it is only natural for immediate gratification to become the norm. When impulsivity controls the process and/or a need for gratification goes unmet, the potential is to lose control.

Of specific concern for this chapter is the identification and treatment of ICDs as they are displayed in college student populations. As the classification of ICDs has changed, so too has the developmental trajectory of college students. In some texts, those ages 18 to 24 are said to be in the developmental period of young adulthood or late adolescence. More recently, developmental theorists began to refer to the period as emerging adulthood (Arnett, 1998, 2000). Arnett describes this period as a time of change and exploration free of social roles and normative expectations (1998). Among other descriptors, Arnett noted that emerging adulthood is a time of instability with little concept of what adulthood means (2000). It is culturally produced and present only in highly industrialized, rapidly advancing countries (Arnett, 2000). Considering advancements in society and technology as well as changes in development, current college students may be more impulsive and at greater risk for the subsequent development of ICDs.

In the following sections, the authors present current and potential future diagnostic criteria for ICDs, as well as provide information about etiology, assessment, and treatment options specific to the college student population.

CURRENT CLASSIFICATION AND GENERAL DIAGNOSTIC CRITERIA

The *DSM-IV-TR* (APA, 2000) categorized intermittent explosive disorder (IED), kleptomania (KM), pyromania, pathological gambling (PG), and trichotillomania (TTM) as Impulse-Control Disorders (ICDs) Not Elsewhere Classified. In addition, a counselor might have diagnosed hypersexual disorder, skin picking disorder, compulsive buying, and Internet addiction under ICDs (NOS). Specific changes between the *DSM-IV-TR* and *DSM-5* will be discussed in the section *"DSM-5* Changes for ICDs."

Although each of the above disorders has specific diagnostic criteria (for *DSM-5* criteria, see pp. 247–257, 350–353, 466–469, 476–480, 585–589, 795–798), many have similar, common characteristics. According to Padhi, Mehdi, Craig, and Fineberg (2012, pp. 27–28), these include:

1. A compelling and irrepressible urge to perform an act that is potentially harmful to self or others
2. Repeated performance of the problematic behavior
3. Progressive loss of control over the behavior

Regardless of the similarities, the developmental progression, etiology, and comorbidity may be distinct and are guiding researchers to reconsider classifications. This is evident in the *DSM-5* (APA, 2013).

DSM-5 CHANGES FOR ICDs

The *DSM-5*, under the newly combined heading, Disruptive, Impulse-Control, and Conduct Disorders, recognizes Intermittent Explosive Disorder, Pyromania, Kleptomania, Other Specified Disruptive, Impulse-Control, and Conduct Disorders, and Unspecified Disruptive, Impulse-Control, and Conduct Disorders. The rationale, for changes to Pyromania and Kleptomania, is that there is not enough evidence to support that they are independent disorders but, rather, that the research suggests they are symptoms of other disorders, such as conduct disorders, ICD, or affective disorders. Trichotillomania (HPD; Hair-Pulling Disorder) was moved to the Obsessive-Compulsive and Related Disorders heading with the addition of Excoriation (SPD; Skin-Picking Disorder) and hoarding disorder (HD) (*DSM-5*, APA, 2013). Binge Eating Disorder (BED) is now under the new category of Feeding and Eating Disorders. Also, Pathological Gambling, now called Gambling Disorder (GD), is categorized as a Non-Substance-Related Disorder under the heading Substance-Related and Addictive Disorders (APA, 2013). The *DSM-5*, in Section III, Conditions for Further Study, also lists Internet Gambling Disorder.

Regardless of the changes, these disorders share similar high rates of comorbidity, genetic predisposition, underlying neurobiological mechanisms, and a diminished ability to resist urges to engage in behaviors that result in adverse consequences (Grant, Potenza, Weinstein, & Gorelick, 2010; Schreiber, Odlaug, & Grant, 2011). Despite potential consequences, the impulsive individual receives a short-term pleasure reward and a reduction of anxiety through engaging in the problematic behavior, thus making the behavior reinforcing (Dell'Osso, Altamura, Allen, Marazziti, & Hollander, 2006). However, as the behaviors escalate, the individual will typically experience dysphoria, disillusionment, and/or guilt with ensuing shame. Like chemical addiction, ICDs develop along a continuum of isolated harmful acts that offer short-term rewards. The inability to refrain from engaging in extremely harmful behaviors leads to debilitating consequences (Karim & Chaudhri, 2012).

When reading current and relevant research, it is easy to be confused because of the terminology and associated abbreviations utilized. Research written over the past 10 years about ICD may use a variety of terms to represent lesser known or potential ICDs. Add to this the changes in the *DSM-5* and comprehension may be further affected. For the purpose of this chapter, specific abbreviations will be utilized. They include diagnoses recognized in the *DSM-IV-TR* (APA, 2000), as well those that appear in the *DSM-5* (APA, 2013). This is mentioned here because much of the research published over the last 3 years refers to and makes use of diagnoses in the *DSM-5*.

PREVALENCE RATES AND GENDER DIFFERENCES IN COLLEGE STUDENTS

Odlaug and Grant (2010), from a sample of 791 college students, reported a lifetime prevalence rate of 10.4% for at least one ICD. Specifically, they noted the following prevalence rates: TTM (3.92%), CSB (3.67%), CB (1.90%), Pyromania (1.01%), PG (0.63%), IED (0.51%), and Kleptomania (0.38%). As a word of caution, Odlaug and Grant noted that other studies from the past 2 decades have reported different prevalence rates for each ICD, the point being that more research is needed utilizing consistent means of measurement.

In addition to the high frequency rate among college students, problematic ICD behaviors are first exhibited in adolescence through early adulthood (Oldlaug & Grant, 2010). This provides those working with college students an excellent opportunity to address risky behaviors before the behaviors progress to advanced or chronic criteria. Even though the frequency of ICDs among college populations is equal to or greater than the larger population (Oldlaug & Grant, 2010), there is currently a paucity of research regarding effective treatment strategies. As such, it is prudent that therapists stay abreast of the most recent research regarding screening, assessment, and evidence-based treatment strategies.

Gender Differences

Although research on the prevalence rates of ICDs in college students is limited, two studies have reported gender differences related to the prevalence of ICDs. In a project assessing for potential addictions in high school students, Pallanti, Bernardi, and Quercioli (2006) utilized the Shorter PROMIS Questionnaire and Internet Addiction Scale to measure addictive and compulsive tendencies. Results of the investigation indicated that males report higher tendencies for gambling and sex-related issues and females report higher tendencies for spending-related issues.

As mentioned, Odlaug and Grant (2010) investigated overall prevalence rates in college students as well as specific rates for gender. The project utilized the Minnesota Impulsive Disorder Interview (MIDI; Christenson et al., 1994), which is designed to assess prevalence rates for the recognized ICDs. Outcome from the study showed higher rates of compulsive sexual behavior and pathological gambling for men, as well as higher rates of compulsive buying for women (Odlaug & Grant).

ETIOLOGY FROM A BIOPSYCHOSOCIAL PERSPECTIVE

For the most part, research indicates that ICDs develop as a result of biological, psychological, and environmental or developmental factors. Where developmental perspectives differ is in the classification of ICDs. Some see ICDs as more related to obsessive-compulsive disorders or an obsessive-compulsive spectrum (Dell'Osso et al., 2006), whereas others see ICDs are similar to addictive disorders (Grant et al., 2010; Karim & Chaudhri, 2012). Although comorbidity will be covered in a following section, it is important to mention it here. Oftentimes the etiology debate leads to a discussion of comorbidities and the proverbial "chicken–egg" conundrum. Which came first? Science has explained many things, but much is left incomplete.

Biological Factors

Over the past 15 years, great strides have been made in understanding brain development and the function of each brain region. Relevant and important information related to ICDs, impulse control, and reward or punishment includes:

1. The dorsolateral prefrontal cortex and its involvement in behavioral control and self-monitoring (Adinoff et al., 2003; Royall et al., 2002).
2. The orbitofrontal cortex and its involvement in behavioral control (Adinoff et al., 2003).
3. The anterior cingulate cortex and its involvement in decision making and learning from doing (Royall et al., 2002).
4. The involvement of the ventral tegmental area, nucleus accumbens, orbitofrontal cortex, and the neurotransmitter dopamine in the reward pathway (Dagher & Robbins, 2009; Zack & Poulos, 2009).
5. The neurotransmitter serotonin and its involvement in controlling impulsivity (Dagher & Robbins, 2009; Fineberg et al., 2010; Hollander et al., 1998).

Considering the above-mentioned brain involvement, the prevailing concept is that reduced serotonin levels leads to impulsivity, alterations of dopamine levels in the rewards pathway leads to reward seeking, and impairment in the prefrontal cortex and cortex leads to problems with behavioral control.

Psychological Factors

Before the research community experienced its vast growth in brain research, much of what was conceptualized about impulsivity centered around personality and an individual's psychological ability to plan, make decisions, and cope (Barratt & Felthous, 2003; Moeller, Barratt, Dougherty, Schmitz, & Swann, 2001). Along this line, others theorized that impulsivity is one of many personality traits (Costa & McCrae, 1992, 1995). Though the psychological aspects of impulsivity may seem less concrete, they remain an important facet of the development and subsequent assessment and treatment of ICDs. Of particular usefulness are the assessment instruments, which are based on personality theory. From the standpoint of a therapist, the psychological aspects of ICDs may seem more usable. They may be more useful in the development of treatment goals or when deciding treatment options.

Social or Environmental Factors

As alluded to above, when discussing the brain, learning from environmental stimuli is an important facet of ICDs. Without citing specific research, therapists know through training and experience that making sense of the world and its subsequent impact on the human experience is the foundation for change and growth. Also, the stimuli presented by society and relationships are crucial to the foundation for learning. The brain would not develop to full capacity without stimulation (Perry, Pollard, Blakley, Baker, & Vigilant, 1995). The ability to cope would not develop if there were no need to cope. In a nonimpaired state, the individual learns from experiences and develops a variety of coping mechanisms. Related to this foundational concept is the work of Jane Loevinger, which emphasized that through growth comes an ability to control one's behaviors (Loevinger, 1979).

Another environmental and relationship issue that greatly impacts an individual's ability to self-regulate is the formation of healthy attachments (Schore, 2002). From the works of Bowlby and Ainsworth, we have all learned about the impact of healthy relationships on development throughout the lifespan. More recent research highlighted the impact of environmental stressors on the formation of dysfunctional attachment styles as well as changes in the brain (Schore, 2001, 2002; Siegel 2001). Two important things to consider about the impact of dysfunctional attachment on the developing brain are that detectible brain changes seen with attachment disturbance are similar to those seen in ICDs and that a primary symptom of a dysfunctional attachment is impulsivity.

COMORBIDITY

A simple way to understand or gauge the extent of comorbidity in ICDs would be to scan the *DSM-5* (APA, 2013). Readers will note that numerous disorders include impulsivity in their diagnostic criteria. The search, not including ICDs, would capture: (a) Eating Disorders, (b) Attention-Deficit Hyperactivity Disorder, (c) Oppositional Defiant Disorder, (d) Conduct Disorder, (e) Paraphilias, (f) Bipolar Disorder, (g) Substance Abuse Disorders, (h) Cluster B Personality Disorders, and (i) neurological disorders such as Parkinson's Disease. The mentioned disorders may or may not be present in individuals suspected of having ICD, but they may cloud the diagnostic picture.

Specific research indicates that mood disorders, substance use disorders, and affective disorders are the most common comorbid disorders seen with all ICDs. To a lesser extent, obsessive-compulsive disorder, conduct disorder, and personality disorders may be seen with some. Specific comorbidities are as follows:

1. Pathological gambling is associated with mood disorders, substance use disorders, and anxiety (Kessler et al., 2008) and personality disorders (Petry, Stinson, & Grant, 2005).
2. Kleptomania is associated with mood disorders, anxiety, and substance use disorders (Grant & Kim, 2002).
3. Trichotillomania is associated with anxiety, affective disorders, substance use disorders, and obsessive-compulsive disorder (Odlaug & Grant, 2008a).
4. Intermittent explosive disorder is associated with anxiety and substance use disorder (Kessler et al., 2006).
5. Pyromania is associated with affective disorders, anxiety, and substance use disorders (Grant & Kim, 2007).
6. Skin picking is associated with substance use disorder, affective disorders, and obsessive-compulsive disorder (Odlaug & Grant, 2008a).
7. Compulsive buying is associated with mood disorders, anxiety, and substance use disorders (Schlosser, Black, Repertinger, & Freet, 1994).
8. Compulsive sexual behavior is associated with substance use disorders, affective disorders, anxiety, and conduct disorder (Black, Kehrberg, Flumerfelt, & Schlosser, 1997)

ASSESSING IMPULSIVITY AND DANGEROUS BEHAVIORS

College counselors should consider the following issues when addressing ICDs:

1. Problematic ICDs are first exhibited during adolescence through early adulthood.

    A. Freedom from parental control provides opportunity to engage in risky behaviors.

    B. Those with a tendency for risky behavior may escalate risky behaviors during the college years.

    C. College students are in the emerging adulthood phase of development, which is marked by great change and much exploration.

    D. Males tend to engage in more pathological gambling and compulsive sexual behaviors, whereas females engage in more compulsive spending.

    E. ICDs are often comorbid with mood, substance use, and affective disorders.

    F. Individuals are more likely to seek help for negative affect states rather than an ICD.

       a. As the frequency, intensity, and duration of the ICD increases, corresponding negative affect states increase.

       b. Progressing ICDs result in increased guilt and shame.

       c. Guilt and shame may mask the ICD.

    G. Take into consideration the location of the university (i.e., proximity to casinos, adult entertainment).

2. ICDs have biological, psychological, and environmental antecedents.

    A. From a biological perspective, those who exhibit ICDs may have altered areas of the brain that are involved in behavioral control, decision making, self-monitoring, and reward seeking.

    B. From a psychological perspective, the individual's personality may reflect impulsivity and an altered ability to plan, make decisions, or cope.

    C. From an environmental perspective, individuals learn from environmental stimuli and relationships. Without proper stimulation and healthy relationships, individuals develop poor coping skills.

3. Develop a comprehensive screening strategy to identify life stressors as well as high-risk behaviors.

    A. College counselors should consider screening students who exhibit the following behaviors:

       a. Sudden drop in grades.

       b. Excessive absenteeism and tardiness.

       c. Sudden withdrawal from extracurricular activities formerly enjoyed.

       d. Erratic or bizarre behaviors and impaired motor functions.

       e. Suicidal or homicidal threats.

       f. Excessive aggressiveness or hostility.

       g. Social isolation.

       h. Students who receive university or legal consequences related to substance use.

    i. Students who engage in domestic violence.

4. For the most part, ICDs are treated with a combination of psychotherapy and medication.

Suggested Interventions

1. Prevention and psychoeducation.
   A. Offer workshops, lectures, and/or groups focusing on high-risk behaviors.
   B. Provide students with information on ICDs (i.e., general symptoms, consequences, referral information, and treatment options).
2. Treatment options.
   A. Motivational enhancement therapy or motivational interviewing for new-onset ICDs.
      a. Determine stage of change.
      b. Identify barriers to treatment.
      c. Capitalize on current strengths and skills.
      d. Encourage lifestyle changes.
   B. Multimodal treatment for progressing or advanced ICDs with a focus on social skills training, self-esteem enhancement, assertiveness training, and problem solving.
      a. Motivational interviewing.
      b. Cognitive-behavioral therapy.
      c. Family therapy.
      d. 12-step groups.
      e. Medication.
         i. Antidepressants (i.e., selective serotonin reuptake inhibitors [SSRIs], tricyclic antidepressants [TCAs]).
         ii. Mood stabilizers (i.e., lithium, atypical antipsychotics).
         iii. Opioid antagonists (i.e., naltrexone).
         iv. Glutamatergic agents (i.e., topiramate).
      f. Residential treatment.
   C. Relapse prevention interventions (for new, progressing, or advanced ICDs) include:
      a. Interventions that reduce the potential for the student to feel stigmatized and isolated must be a priority.
      b. Promote the student's engagement and access to outside community resources, and if possible, a peer mentor.
      c. Assist the student with balancing treatment with academic demands.
      d. Provide the student with access to services that focus on the following:
         i. Building upon the student's current strengths.

ii. Teaching the student emotional modulation skills to counter harmful affective states.

iii. Collaboration with the student on developing a plan that addresses triggers, relapse, and recovery maintenance.

iv. Teaching the student stress-management, anxiety reduction, and self-care strategies.

v. Other interventions include problem solving, boundaries, effective communication strategies, esteem building, relaxation training, developing spiritual meaning, and interventions that focus on the student's specific needs.

Initially, problematic behaviors produce short-term rewards that can result in individuals minimizing or failing to recognize the dangers of the behavior. As the frequency, intensity, and duration of the high-risk behaviors increase, corresponding negative affective states, such as depression, anxiety, self-loathing, guilt, and shame, also increase. At this point, the individual is more likely to seek help for his or her affective state rather than the problematic behavior. It is much easier for an individual to report that he or she feels depressed than to disclose behaviors that may be producing feelings of shame. Individuals who seek the assistance of a therapist for other life-issues or mental health concerns should be assessed for impulsivity and high-risk behaviors. Therapists can utilize standardized tests and the intake process to direct whether or not the student might benefit from ICD treatment strategies as an adjunct to receiving treatment for the primary problem. In addition, assessing the underlying factors, such as self-esteem, problem-solving skills, coping strategies, self-efficacy, negative affective states, distorted cognitions, trauma history, and the individual's genetic predisposition, are important in order to match interventions to the individual.

As mentioned in other sections of this chapter, instruments have been utilized to capture impulsive tendencies. Of those noted, the (a) Minnesota Impulse Disorder Interview (MIDI; Christenson et al., 1994) assesses for the ICDs listed in the *DSM-IV-TR* (APA, 2000) and the (b) Shorter PROMIS Questionnaire (SPQ; Christo et al., 2003) assesses addictive tendencies in 16 behavioral areas.

The above instruments assess multiple dimensions or multiple types of ICDs. For the most part, with further research, those working with college students will find other instruments assessing specific ICDs or impulsivity alone. Over the next few years, we will see new instruments developed based on *DSM-5* diagnostic criteria as well as instruments, which were previously based on *DSM-IV-TR* criteria, reworked to assess *DSM-5* criteria. Worth noting, Bohne (2010) assessed for ICDs by creating a questionnaire based on the *DSM-IV-TR* (APA, 2000) diagnostic criteria. If screening is the goal, this method may be useful.

TREATMENT OPTIONS

As discussed previously, ICDs typically have a high rate of comorbidity with other Axis I and Axis II disorders. It is important that counselors identify and treat co-occurring disorders concurrently with ICDs. Comorbid disorders have a reciprocal relationship with ICDs in that if left untreated, they exacerbate ICD symptoms and block positive treatment outcomes. In the following pages, readers will find a summary of both pharmacological as well as psychotherapeutic treatment options.

Pharmacological Options

Considering how common ICDs are, the research regarding pharmacological treatment is lacking. Currently, there are no approved medications to treat specific ICDs (Leeman & Potenza, 2012). Even though the research is limited regarding the efficacy of pharmacological options for specific ICDs, there is a great deal of research that supports the efficacy of using antidepressants for depression and anxiety, mood stabilizers for Bipolar Spectrum Disorders, opioid antagonists for addiction, and stimulants for attention deficit hyperactivity disorder (ADHD). When considering an appropriate medication, it is important that counselors assess clients individually and make appropriate psychiatric referrals. Medication options should match comorbid symptoms (Dell'Osso et al., 2006), otherwise they may exacerbate symptoms. For example, it is contraindicated to treat a client who exhibits both pathological gambling issues with bipolar symptoms with antidepressants due to the potential for the client to experience an increase in manic and gambling episodes (Dell'Osso et al., 2006). Given the limited research regarding the effectiveness of medications to treat specific ICDs, the following information regarding medications is preliminary and not a standardized pharmacological treatment approach.

Antidepressants
To date, studies on the effectiveness of SSRIs for treating ICDs are limited. However, current research suggests that some SSRIs might prove advantageous for treating ICDs. Karim and Chaudhri (2012) reported that SSRI medications reduced binge-eating episodes. One study showed that fluoxetine produced positive results in reducing aggression and irritability (Coccaro, Schmidt, Samuels, & Nestadt, 2004), which might benefit IED sufferers. Several studies report positive results regarding fluoxetine in the treatment of SPD (Simeon et al., 1997). Other studies showed mixed results when using SSRIs to treat HPD, CB, and PG (Schreiber et al., 2011). Kruesi, Fine, Valladares, Phillips, and Rapoport (1992) reported that clomipramine and desipramine decreased HSD symptoms, while Wainberg

et al. (2006) reported that citalopram decreased HSD symptoms. Other studies showed fluoxetine, sertraline, citalopram, and the combination of fluoxetine and methylphenidate reduced libido and the frequency of problematic sexual behaviors for HSD subjects (Ferraro, Gourneau, Clow, Erikson, & Anderson, 2008).

Mood Stabilizers

With the exception of PG, few studies have examined the effectiveness of mood stabilizers in treating specific ICDs. One study reported that lithium reduced gambling ruminations and behaviors for individuals with the diagnosis of PG with Bipolar Disorder (Hollander, Pallanti, Allen, Sood, & Rossi, 2005). Individual case studies have shown some positive treatment outcomes for the use of lithium with those diagnosed with HSD.

Opioid Antagonists

Like other medications, the research regarding the effectiveness of opioid antagonists in treating ICDs is limited with the exception of PG. To date, there appears to be strong support that opioid antagonists are efficacious in treating PG (Grant, Kim, & Hartman, 2008; Kim, Grant, Adson, & Shin, 2001) In addition, uncontrolled studies have found the potential for opioid antagonists to be beneficial in treating CB (Grant, 2003), HSD (Raymond & Grant, 2010; Raymond, Grant, Kim, & Coleman, 2002), IUD (Bostwick & Bucci, 2008), and SPD (Arnold, Auchenbach, & McElroy, 2001).

Glutamateric Agents

Again, the research is limited; however, preliminary findings suggest that glutamateric agents may prove efficacious in treating some individuals with specific ICDs. In open-label studies, topiramate produced positive results for the treatment of PG, CB, and SPD (Roncero, Rodrigues-Urrutia, Grau-Lopez, & Casas, 2009). In addition, Marazziti, Rossi, Baroni, Consoli, Hollander, and Catena-Dell'Osso (2011) reported that topiramate reduced the frequency of binging episodes. Two studies reported positive treatment outcomes for HPD (Grant, Odlaug, & Kim, 2009) and PG (Grant, Kim, & Odlaug, 2007) utilizing *N*-acetyl cysteine. Overall, the consensus is that effective treatment will combine pharmacological options with therapeutic interventions.

Psychotherapeutic Options

As mentioned in previous sections, research suggests that high-risk impulsive behaviors have a typical onset prior to or during college. Given the high rates of comorbidity and developmental progression of ICDs, therapists should be cognizant of individuals who present with unrelated concerns for impulsivity and high-risk behaviors. Through early identification, prevention, and psychoeducation, the therapist has an excellent opportunity to intervene and address the problematic behavior prior to the behavior escalating to advanced or chronic criteria.

Prevention and Psychoeducation

It is essential that therapists be cognizant of the unique trends occurring in his or her geographic area and/or university. Through anonymous screening of the student body, the therapist gains insight to direct effective prevention strategies. Offering psychoeducational workshops, lectures, and/or groups focused on impulsivity is a proactive strategy that will educate the student body as a whole. Psychoeducation might include information regarding the genetic predisposition, general symptoms, potential consequences, predicted outcomes, clinical course, treatment options, referral information, support groups, recognition of danger signs, and online resources that provide additional information. Through education, the student body becomes the university's greatest resource toward deterring destructive behavioral patterns, preventing future trends of destructive behaviors, and informing or encouraging student peers to seek treatment.

While the research is limited regarding efficacious treatment strategies for ICDs, there is substantial literature to support evidence-based treatment strategies for dealing with commonly occurring triggers, cognitions, and individual deficits. This will provide the therapist with direction as well as a foundation for positive treatment outcomes.

Early Treatment Focus

As with any treatment, the first objective is to establish a therapeutic relationship with the student. It is essential that the counselor establishes rapport, builds trust, and exhibits unconditional positive regard to produce a therapeutic environment in which the student feels safe to explore ICD behaviors, triggers, and cognitions. In addition, the counselor should assess a client's motivation to change early and throughout treatment to limit dropout and deliver effective counseling (Hodgins & Peden, 2008). Motivational enhancement therapy or motivational interviewing strategies can help the student who is in the precontemplation or contemplation stage of change to move toward the preparation or action stages. Identifying potential barriers, according to Hodgins and Peden (2008), provides the therapist and client with an opportunity to collaborate on strategies to remove, reduce, or circumvent barriers. In addition, a therapist can capitalize on the individual's existing strengths and skills as a framework for increasing self-efficacy and skills building.

Hodgins and Peden (2008) suggested that a counselor be flexible when developing individual treatment plans for ICDs because researchers have yet to discover which interventions lead to positive treatment outcomes. Individuals with high levels of impulsivity struggle in high-stress environments (Hodgins & Peden, 2008) and should practice impulse control. The higher education environment is often a source of stress; therefore, one strategy is to assist individuals in restructuring their environment toward reducing stress and learning new coping strategies. For example, an individual who is struggling in academics, social networking, and/or social support might benefit by receiving referrals for tutoring, peer mentoring, and/or on-campus support groups. The goal is to encourage lifestyle changes that limit exposure to high-risk situations and increase exposure to healthy activities (Grant et al., 2010). Through assessment, establishing a therapeutic alliance, and case conceptualization, the counselor is then prepared to match the intervention with the individual.

Overall, the current research suggests that treatment strategies, which mirror evidence-based treatments for addiction, are beneficial for PG, HSD, and CB (Grant et al., 2010). In general, ICDs appear to respond to a combination of treatment approaches that address the underlying individual's issues, such as motivational enhancement, cognitive-behavioral therapy (CBT), 12-step groups, relapse prevention, family therapy, brief therapy, residential treatment (Grant et al., 2010), social skills training, self-esteem enhancement, assertiveness training, problem-solving skills, functional analysis, and psychoeducation (Hodgins & Peden, 2008).

The following sections provide a brief description of promising interventions within classified ICDs. The disorder classifications reflect changes in the *DSM-5* (APA, 2013). Therapists are advised to seek additional resources that explain the theories that drive these methods and offer expansive explanations on utilizing each method.

Binge Eating Disorder (BED)

In comparison to other eating disorders and general obesity, BED tends to run in families and respond better "to specialty treatments than to generic behavioral weight loss treatments in terms of reduction of eating disorder psychopathology" (*DSM-5*, APA, 2013). One study reported positive treatment outcomes combining CBT and psychoeducation to treat BED. The clinical profile of BED is an older male with a later age of onset (*DSM-5*, APA, 2013); therefore, it is less likely that a therapist, working in a college setting, will routinely treat individuals who meet BED diagnostic criteria.

Compulsive Buying Disorder (CBD)

The *DSM-5* (APA, 2013) includes hoarding disorder but does not include compulsive buying disorder (CBD). Research suggests that CBD usually begins between 18 and 30 years of age (Karim & Chaudhri, 2012).

Regardless of whether or not CBD is classified as a disorder, it is important that therapists recognize that individuals, after leaving home for the first time, experience a new sense of autonomy from parental restrictions and an increased status in purchasing power through consumer credit. Unfortunately and often, individuals lack the ability to manage credit effectively and use buying as a means to combat emotional dysregulation, boredom, and self-loathing (Karim & Chaudhri, 2012). There are limited data regarding effective treatment strategies for CBD; however, initial findings suggest that CBT and dialectical behavioral therapy produce positive treatment outcomes (Karim & Chaudhri, 2012). Other suggested areas of clinical focus are emotional modulation, coping strategies, self-esteem, self-soothing strategies, self-care skills, and a strength-based focus to build self-efficacy (Karim & Chaudhri, 2012). Researchers note that individuals with CBD respond well to individual or group treatment modalities, which include relaxation training, guided imagery, and in vivo desensitization (where members learn to control buying urges through cognitive restructuring and anxiety reduction; Frost, Steketee, & Greene, 2003; Hodgins & Peden, 2008).

Hair Pulling Disorder (HPD) and Skin Picking Disorder (SPD)

In the *DSM-5* (APA, 2013), it is reported that the self-destructive behaviors that fall within HPD and SPD appear self-soothing in nature, are twice as likely to manifest among women, and have a strong relationship to dissociation. In addition, it is noted that individuals with HPD or SPD respond better to "habit reversal CBT instead of exposure and response prevention," which is typically used to treat OCD clients (*DSM-5*, APA, 2013). The research suggests that HPD usually begins during puberty and typically leads to social anxiety. Because of an individual's desire to keep hair pulling a secret, identification and treatment often become difficult. In addition to shame-based decisions to avoid help seeking, individuals with HPD or SPD typically experience low self-esteem, social isolation, and social anxiety (Diefenbach, Tolin, Hannan, Crocetto, & Worhunsky, 2005). Beyond CBT, it is essential that a counselor utilize strength-based, empowerment approaches that enhance the individual's self-concept and ego-strength by introducing coping strategies, life skills, social skills, healthy boundaries, and assertiveness training. As a note of caution, the clinical profile of the individual with HPD or SPD and a recent recognition that the behavior is an attempt to self-soothe indicate that it would be prudent to assess the individual's trauma history.

Hypersexual Disorder (HSD)

Currently, HSD does not appear as a disorder in the *DSM-IV-TR*; however, it was considered for inclusion in Section III of the *DSM-5* (APA 2013). unpublished). Although, in the end, HSD was not included, there is a growing body of research worth considering. Numerous trauma researchers have documented the connection between risky sexual behavior and childhood trauma. Therefore, as above, it is advised that a therapist assesses the client's trauma history if the client is exhibiting impulsive, risky sexual behaviors. Karim and Chaudri (2012) mentioned the importance of exploring "the family of origin, trauma, and underlying factors" (p. 11). Odlaug and Grant (2010) found that 3.66% of the sampled individuals reported sexual compulsivity and that risky sexual behavior increases the potential that the individual will experience harmful health, emotional, and financial consequences. Recognizing potential consequences, such as sexually transmitted diseases, unwanted pregnancies, legal issues, domestic violence, intimacy issues, and emotional dysregulation, assists the therapist in targeting his or her efforts toward segments of the student body population that present with the highest risk. Through coordinated alliances with the campus health facilities, police, support groups, and crisis lines, a therapist might receive vital information to direct assessment, treatment, and prevention efforts.

The research suggests that risky sexual behaviors are typically manifested in adolescence (Black et al., 1997); therefore, it is likely that therapists will encounter individuals engaging in high-risk behaviors and/or individuals who meet the criteria for a HSD diagnosis. Researchers hypothesize that individuals engage in risky sexual behaviors to relieve anxiety and feel pleasure (Coleman, 1992). Anxiety and mood dysregulation trigger the risky sexual behavior and, in turn, result in an increase in shame-based feelings and cognitions. As with the addiction cycle, the individual with HSD is caught in a progressive pattern of destructive behaviors that feed pathology (Schreiber et al., 2011). Effective individualized treatment focuses on breaking the cycle while providing alternative coping strategies, addressing distorted cognitions, increasing self-esteem, exploring grief, learning safety, increasing intimacy, and improving social domains. As with other ICDs and addiction, the best treatment strategy matches the individual's needs, are holistic in nature, and eclectic in methodology. An individual and/or group treatment method, along with self-help groups, provides the individual with HSD an opportunity to heal and opportunities to practice skills as they are developed. Group therapy and self-help groups allow clients to recognize that they are not alone, which reduces stigmatized shame and isolation (Kaplan & Krueger, 2010). Leading toward enhanced self-efficacy, it also provides the opportunity to practice newly developed skills within a safe environment.

Internet Use Disorder (IUD)

Like HSD, Internet use disorder (IUD) was considered for inclusion in Section III of the *DSM-5* (APA, 2013) but not included in the final product. Like other addictions, studies have shown that IUD follows a progressive course where the individual spends more time isolated in front of a computer and increasingly less time socially interacting (Weidman et al., 2012; Young, 2004). Researchers documented that there is a direct relationship between computer time, depression, and loneliness (Nie & Erbring, 2000). As a result, social support also declines. To compensate the individual fills the social void by spending more time in a virtual world (Kraut et al., 1998).

As with other ICDs, understanding the clinical profile of the afflicted guides treatment strategies. Young (2007) found that Caucasian, middle-aged men, with at least a 4-year degree, represented the largest clinical profile for an individual apt to develop IUD. In addition, individuals vulnerable to IUDs tend to exhibit low self-esteem, poor social skills, social anxiety, introversion, and impulsivity. As a result, the Internet provides a venue to compensate for perceived inadequacies (Young, 2007). Chat rooms, online gaming, and online communities offer the individual an opportunity to feel socially connected, replacing the feelings of disconnect they often feel in real-world environments. As the clinical course progresses, larger deficits occur within relational, occupational, and social domains (Young, 2007). For this population, Internet use becomes a psychological escape from painful life issues and emotional states (Greenfield, 1999).

More specifically, the current trend of massive, multiplayer, online, role-playing games (MMORPGs) provide a sense of status and accomplishment within a social arena that is especially alluring to the IUD client. Through a virtual world, where an individual creates an online persona that challenges perceived deficient self-qualities, the individual with IUD gains a boost in self-esteem and confidence. However, the positive benefits that they receive in a virtual world do not transfer to real-life settings. Additionally, the more time spent within a MMORPG environment, the less the individual is able to develop social skills within the real world. As a result, the individual is prone to return to a virtual reality with greater frequency and duration to bolster and protect the fragile ego. Ultimately, the increase in time spent on the computer reduces the likelihood that the individual will practice social skills, reduce social anxiety, or receive positive reinforcement in real-world settings (Young, 2007).

Considering the young age at which children gain access to technology and the frequency of IUDs among the U.S. population, the demand for effective treatment strategies will increase. Considering these facts, some college campuses have already begun support groups for IUD.

Research concerning the treatment of IUDs is in its infancy; therefore, it is important that therapists stay active in pursuing effective treatments. In addition, counselors can use the current profile of a gamer to direct intervention strategies. Counselors might target marginalized, isolated, shy, anxious, and socially inept individuals for assessment, prevention, and treatment.

Unlike chemical addiction and other process addictions, Young (2007) warned that the end goal of treatment in today's society could not be complete abstinence. Rather, treatment should focus on targeting problematic usage, while reinforcing appropriate use. Young explored the effectiveness of CBT for treating IUD, with an initial behavioral focus, followed by a cognitive therapy. Treatment included identifying triggers and cognitive distortions, problem solving and coping skills, modeling, support groups, and journaling. Cognitive restructuring addressed catastrophic thinking, overgeneralizations, negative core beliefs, cognitive distortions, and rationalization that supported problematic usage. Young (2007) reported that CBT was an effective treatment strategy and that treatment effects were sustained 6-months posttreatment (Young). Additionally, she suggested that effective treatment might include assertiveness training, behavioral rehearsal, coaching, desensitization, relaxations, self-management, and/or social skills training. For more information regarding IUD, a therapist may refer to the Center for Online Addictions at www.netaddiction.com, which "provides education, support, and treatment" (Young, 2007, p. 8).

Gambling Disorder or Pathological Gambling (PG)
Overwhelmingly, the majority of ICD research exists within the effective treatment of PG. Schreiber et al. (2011) reported that gambling behaviors usually begin during late adolescence into early adulthood. However, the behaviors do not typically progress into full diagnostic criteria until much later (Schreiber et al., 2011). Today's college student population is at an increased risk of exposure to gambling situations (Ferraro et al., 2008) due to advances in technology, online gambling, and the recent popularity of televised poker. Televised poker, which climaxes with one individual, oftentimes an amateur, winning millions of dollars after playing cards for a few days romanticizes the game while minimizing the potential harmful consequences. To compound the exposure issue, college-age individuals' undeveloped frontal lobes are inadequate to traverse successfully the activity of gambling, leaving them at an increased risk for harmful consequences (Neighbors, Lostutter, Cronce, & Larimer, 2002). Considering the above information, an effective therapist must understand and be capable of treating PG or risky gambling behaviors.

Like other ICDs, practitioners typically utilize chemical addiction treatments, particularly CBT, to treat PG. More specifically, treatments incorporate psychoeducation, cognitive restructuring, problem solving, social skills training, and relapse prevention. Multiple treatment modalities are effective, including individual and group counseling alongside self-help support groups. The research supports that cognitive therapy reduces gambling frequency, improves self-efficacy, and provides sustained treatment outcomes (Hodgins & Peden, 2008).

CONCLUSION

Although research on ICDs is limited, that which exists provides a better conceptualization of the disorders. Through brain research, we have a better understanding of how each disorder impacts brain regions and neurotransmitter systems. From psychological research, we are beginning to understand the motivations of individuals with an ICD as well as the faulty decision-making and coping skills utilized. For those ICDs that develop and progress similar to an addiction, researchers have adapted evidence-based practices to meet the unique needs of the individual with an ICD. Likewise, for those with ICDs that develop and progress similar to anxiety and mood disorders, researchers have applied well-researched techniques to identify efficacious, best practices. Through survey research, more is known about gender differences, prevalence rates, and comorbidities.

Considering the recent changes specific to ICD classifications, new research will begin to account for and explain the development of the disorders as well as subsequent treatments. As for the addition of new disorders that have common features with ICDs, the scientific community has already begun investigation and, as with any new frontier, there is much to left to learn. What is next? Texting Impulse Control Disorder (TICD)?

REFERENCES

Adinoff, B., Devous, M. D., Sr., Cooper, D. B., Best, S. E., Chandler, P., Harris, T., ... Cullum, C. M. (2003). Resting regional cerebral blood flow and gambling task performance in cocaine-dependent subjects and healthy comparison subjects. *American Journal of Psychiatry, 160*(10), 1892–1892.

American Psychiatric Association. (1980). *Diagnostic and statistical manual of mental disorders* (3rd ed.). Washington, DC: Author.

American Psychiatric Association. (2000). *Diagnostic and statistical manual of mental disorders* (4th ed., text rev.). Washington, DC: Author.

American Psychiatric Association. (2013). *Diagnostic and statistical manual of mental disorders* (5th ed.). Washington, DC: Author. Retrieved August 6, 2012, from www.dsm5.org

Arnett, J. J. (1998). Learning to stand alone: The contemporary American transition to adulthood in cultural and historical context. *Human Development, 41*(5/6), 295–315.

Arnett, J. J. (2000). Emerging adulthood: A theory of development from late teens through the twenties. *American Psychologist, 55*(5), 469–480.

Arnold, L. M., Auchenbach, M. B., & McElroy, S. L. (2001). Psychogenic excoriation. Clinical features, proposed diagnostic criteria, epidemiology, and approaches to treatment. *CNS Drugs, 15*(5), 351–359.

Barratt, E. S., & Felthous, A. R. (2003). Impulsive versus premeditated aggression: Implications for *Mens Rea* decisions. *Behavioral Science and the Law, 21*(5), 619–630.

Black, D. W., Kehrberg, L. L. D., Flumerfelt, D. L., & Schlosser, S. S. (1997). Characteristics of 36 subjects reporting compulsive sexual behaviors. *American Journal of Psychiatry, 154*(2), 243–249.

Bohne, A. (2010). Impulse-control disorders in college students. *Psychiatric Research, 176*(1), 91–92.

Bostwick, J. M., & Bucci, J. A. (2008). Internet sex addiction treated with naltrexone. *Mayo Clinic Proceedings, 83*(2), 226–230.

Christenson, G. A., Faber, R. J., deZwaan, M., Raymond, N. C., Specker, S. M., Eckern, M. D., ... Eckert, E. D. (1994). Compulsive buying: Descriptive characteristics and psychiatric comorbidity. *Journal of Clinical Psychiatry, 55*(1), 5–11.

Christo, G., Jones, S. L., Haylett, S., Stephenson, G. M., Lefever, R. M. H., & Lefever, R. (2003). The shorter PROMIS questionnaire: Further validation of a tool for simultaneous assessment of multiple addictive behaviors. *Addictive Behaviors, 28*, 225–248.

Coccaro, E. F., Scmidt, C. A., Samuels, J. F., & Nestadt, G. (2004). Lifetime and 1-month prevalence rates of intermittent explosive disorder in a community sample. *Journal of Clinical Psychiatry, 65*(6), 820–824.

Coleman, E. (1992). Is your patient suffering from compulsive sexual behaviors? *Psychiatric Annals, 22*(6), 320–325.

Costa, P. T. Jr., & McCrae, R. R. (1992). Normal personality assessment in clinical practice: The NEO personality inventory. *Psychological Assessments, 4*(1), 5–13.

Costa, P. T. Jr., & McCrae, R. R. (1995). Domains and facets: Hierarchical personality assessment using the revised NEO personality inventory. *Journal of Personality Assessment, 64*(1), 21–50.

Dagher, A., & Robbins, T. W. (2009). Personality, addiction, dopamine: Insights from Parkinson's disease. *Neuron, 61*(4), 502–510.

Dell'Osso, B., Altamura, A. C., Allen, A., Marazziti, D., & Hollander, E. (2006). Epidemiological and clinical updates on impulse control disorders: A critical review. *European Archives of Psychiatry and Clinical Neuroscience, 256*, 464–475.

Diefenbach, G. J., Tolin, D. F., Hannan, S., Crocetto, J., & Worhunsky, P. (2005). Trichotillomania: Impact on psychosocial functioning and quality of life. *Behaviour Research and Therapy, 43*(7), 869–884.

Ferraro, F. R., Gourneau, M., Clow, K., Erikson, S., & Anderson, L. (2008). Impulse control executive functioning, and gambling in college students. *Psychology Journal, 5*(4), 212–214.

Fineberg, N. A., Potenza, M. N., Chamberlain, S. R., Berlin, H. A., Menzies, L., Bechara, A., ... Hollander, E. (2010). Probing compulsive and impulsive behaviors, from animal models to endophenotypes: A narrative review. *Neuropsychopharmacolgy, 35*(3), 591–604.

Frost, R. O., Steketee, G., & Greene, K. A. I. (2003). Cognitive and behavioral treatment of compulsive hoarding. *Brief Treatment and Crisis Intervention, 3*(3), 323-337.

Grant, J. E. (2003). Three cases of compulsive buying treated with naltrexone. *International Journal of Psychiatry in Clinical Practice, 7,* 223–225.

Grant, J. E., & Kim, S. W. (2002). Clinical characteristics and associated psychopathology of 22 patients with kleptomania. *Comprehensive Psychiatry, 43*(5), 378–384.

Grant, J. E., & Kim, S. W. (2007). Clinical characteristics and psychiatric comorbidity of pyromania. *Journal of Clinical Psychiatry, 68*(11), 1717–1722.

Grant, J. E., Kim, S. W., & Hartman, B. K. (2008). A double-blind, placebo-controlled study of the opiate antagonist naltrexone in the treatment of pathological gambling urges. *Journal of Clinical Psychiatry, 69*(5), 783–789.

Grant, J. E., Kim, S. W., & Odlaug, B. L. (2007). *N*-acetyl cysteine, a glutamate-modulating agent, in the treatment of pathological gambling: A pilot study. *Biological Psychiatry, 62*(6), 652–657.

Grant, J. E., Odlaug, B. L., & Kim, S. W. (2009). *N*-acetyl cysteine, a glutamate modulator, in the treatment of trichotillomania: A double-blind, placebo-controlled study. *Archives of General Psychiatry, 66*(7), 756–763.

Grant, J. E., Potenza, M. N., Weinstein, A., & Gorelick, D. A. (2010). Introduction to behavioral addictions. *The American Journal of Drug and Alcohol Abuse, 36,* 233–241.

Greenfield, D. N. (1999). *Virtual addiction: Sometimes new technology can create new problems.* Paper presented at the American Psychological Association meeting. Retrieved September 4, 2012, from http.//www.virtual-addiction.com/pdf/nature_internet_addiction.pdf

Hodgins, D. C., & Peden, N. (2008). Cognitive-behavioral treatment for impulse control disorders. *Revista Brasileira de Psiquiatria, 30*(Suppl. 1), 31–40.

Hollander, E., Kwon, J., Weiller, F., Cohen, L., Stein, D. J., DeCaria, C., ... Simeon, D. (1998). Serotonergic function in social phobias: Comparison to normal control and obsessive-compulsive disorder subjects. *Psychiatry Research, 79*(3), 213–217.

Hollander, E., Pallanti, S., Allen, A., Sood, E., & Rossi, N. (2005). Does sustained-release lithium reduce impulsive gambling and affective instability versus placebo in pathological gamblers with bipolar spectrum disorder? *American Journal of Psychiatry, 162,* 137–145.

Kaplan, M. S., & Krueger, R. B. (2010). Diagnosis, assessment, and treatment of hypersexuality. *The Journal of Sex Research, 47*(2), 181–198.

Karim, R., & Chaudhri, P. (2012). Behavioral addictions: An overview. *Journal of Psychoactive Drugs, 44*(1), 5–17.

Kessler, R. C., Coccaro, E. F., Fava, M., Jaeger, S., Jin, R., & Walters, E. (2006). The prevalence and correlates of DSM-IV intermittent explosive disorder in the National Comorbidity Survey Replication. *Archives of General Psychiatry, 63*(6), 669–678.

Kessler, R. C., Hwang, I., Labrie, R., Petukhova, M., Sampson, N. A., Winters, K. C., & Shaffer, H. J. (2008). The prevalence and correlates of DSM-IV pathological gambling in the National Comorbidity Survey Replication. *Psychological Medicine, 38*(9), 1351–1360.

Kim, S. W., Grant, J. E., Adson, D. E., & Shin, Y. C. (2001). Double-blind naltrexone and placebo comparison study in the treatment of pathological gambling. *Biological Psychiatry, 49,* 914–921.

Kraut, R., Patterson, M., Lundmark, V., Kiesler, S., Mukopadhyay, T., & Scherlis, W. (1998). Internet paradox. A social technology that reduces social involvement and psychological well-being? *American Psychologist, 53*(2), 1017–1031.

Kruesi, M. J. P., Fine, S., Valladares, L., Phillips, R. A. Jr., & Rapoport, J. L. (1992). Paraphilias: A double-blind crossover comparison of clomipramine versus desipramine. *Archives of Sexual Behavior, 21*(6), 587–593.

Leeman, R. F., & Potenza, M. N. (2012). Impulse control disorders in Parkinson's disease: Clinical characteristics and implications. *Neuropsychiatry (London), 1*(2), 133–147.

Loevinger, J. (1979). Construct validity of the Sentence Completion Test of ego development. *Applied Psychological Measurement, 3*(3), 281–311.

Marazziti, D., Rossi, L., Baroni, S., Consoli, G., Hollander, E., & Catena-Dell'Osso, M. (2011). Novel treatment options of binge eating disorder. *Current Medicinal Chemistry, 18*(33), 5159–5164.

Moeller, F. G., Barratt, E. S., Dougherty, D. M., Schmitz, J. M., & Swann, A. C. (2001). Psychiatric aspects of impulsivity. *American Journal of Psychiatry, 158*(11), 1783–1793.

Neighbors, C., Lostutter, T. W., Cronce, J. M., & Larimer, M. E. (2002). Exploring college student gambling motivation. *The Journal of Gambling Studies, 18*(4), 361–370.

Odlaug, B. L., & Grant, J. E. (2008). Trichotillomania and pathological skin picking: Clinical comparison with an examination of comorbidity. *Annals of Clinical Psychiatry, 20*(2), 57–63.

Odlaug, B. L., & Grant, J. E. (2010). Impulse-control disorders in a college sample: Results from the self-administered Minnesota Impulse Disorder Interview (MIDI). *Primary Care Companion to the Journal of Clinical Psychiatry, 12*(2), 1–5.

Padhi, A. K., Mehdi, A. M., Craig, K. J., & Fineberg, N. A. (2012). Current classification of impulse control disorders: Neurocognitive and behavioral models of impulsivity and the role of personality. In J. E. Grant & M. N. Potenza (Eds.), *The Oxford handbook of impulse control disorders* (pp. 27–28). New York, NY: Oxford University Press.

Pallanti, S., Bernardi, S., & Quercioli, L. (2006). The Shorter PROMIS Questionnaire and Internet Addiction Scale in the assessment of multiple addictions in a high-school population: Prevalence and related disability. *CNS Spectrum, 11*(12), 966–974.

Perry, B. D., Pollard, R. A., Blakley, T. L., Baker, W. L., & Vigilante, D. (1995). Childhood trauma, the neurobiology of adaptation, and "use-dependent" development of the brain: How "states" become "traits." *Infant Mental Health Journal, 16*(4), 271–291.

Petry, N. M., Stinson, F. S., & Grant, J. E. (2005). Comorbidity of DSM-IV pathological gambling and other psychiatric disorders: Results from the National Epidemiological Survey on Alcohol and Related Conditions. *Journal of Clinical Psychiatry, 66*(5), 564–574.

Raymond, N. C., & Grant, J. E. (2010). Augmentation with naltrexone to treat compulsive sexual behaviors: A case series. *Annals of Clinical Psychiatry, 22*(1), 56–62.

Raymond, N. C., Grant, J. E., Kim, S. W., & Coleman, E. (2002). Treatment of compulsive sexual behaviors with naltrexone and serotonin reuptake inhibitors: Two case studies. *International Clinical Psychopharmacology, 17*(4), 201–205.

Roncero, C., Rodrigues-Urrutia, A., Grau-Lopez, L., & Casas, M. (2009). Antiepileptic drugs in the control of the impulses disorders. *Actas Españolas de Psiquiatría, 37*(4), 205–212.

Royall, D. R., Lauterbach, E. C., Cummings, J. F., Reeves, A., Rummans, T. A., Kaufer, D. I., ... Coffey, C. E. (2002). Executive control function: A review of its promise and challenges for clinical research. *Journal of Neuropsychiatry and Clinical Neurosciences, 14*(4), 377–405.

Schlosser, S., Black, D. W., Repertinger, S., & Freet, D. (1994). Compulsive buying, demography, phenomenology, and comorbidity in 46 subjects. *General Hospital Psychiatry, 16*(3), 205–212.

Schore, A. N. (2001). The effects of early relational trauma on right brain development, affect regulation, and infant mental health. *Infant Mental Health Journal, 22*(1–2), 201–269.

Schore, A. N. (2002). Dysregulation of the right brain: A fundamental mechanism of traumatic attachment and the psychopathogenesis of posttraumatic stress disorder. *Australian and New Zealand Journal of Psychiatry, 36*(1), 9–30.

Schreiber, L., Odlaug, B. L., & Grant, J. E. (2011). Impulse control disorders: Updated review of clinical characteristics and pharmacological management. *Frontiers in Psychiatry, 2*(1), 1–11.

Siegel, D. J. (2001). Toward an interpersonal neurobiology of the developing mind: Attachment relationships, "mindsight," and neural integration. *Infant Mental Health Journal, 22*(1–2), 67–94.

Simeon, D., Stein, D. J., Gross, S., Islam, N., Schmeidler, J., & Hollander, E. (1997). A double-blind trial of fluoxetine in pathological skin picking. *Journal of Clinical Psychiatry, 58*(8), 341–347.

Wainberg, M. L., Muench, F., Morgenstern, J., Hollander, E., Irwin, T. W., Parsons, J. T., ... O'Leary, A. (2006). A double-blind study of citalopram versus placebo in the treatment of compulsive sexual behaviors in gay and bisexual men. *Journal of Clinical Psychiatry, 67*(12), 1968–1973.

Weidman, A. C., Fernandez, K. C., Levinson, C. A., Augustine, A. A., Larsen, R. J., & Rodebaugh, T. L. (2012). Compensatory internet use among individuals higher in social anxiety and its implication for well-being. *Personality and Individual Differences, 53*(3), 191–195.

Young, K. S. (2004). Internet addiction: A new clinical phenomenon and its consequences. *American Behavioral Scientist, 48*(4), 402–415.

Young, K. S. (2007). Treatment outcomes with internet addicts. *Cyber Psychology and Behavior, 10*(5), 671–679.

Zack, M., & Poulos, C. X. (2009). Parallel roles for dopamine in pathological gambling and psychostimulant addiction. *Current Drug Abuse Reviews, 2*(1), 11–25.

19

Promoting Student Well-Being on Campus: It Takes a Village

LORI A. WOLFF, SUSAN R. BARCLAY, AND MEGAN M. BUNING

The purpose of this chapter is to discuss approaches to student well-being that center on collaboration between counseling center staff and other constituents associated with a college or university, particularly faculty and other staff, and also students, parents, and alumni. Although this book will be of interest to those across a wide spectrum of higher education positions, the primary audience may be those who work within a counseling center setting. Therefore, before going further, it is worthwhile to note a little about the background of the authors of this chapter as a way to set the context for the viewpoint related to the subject of the chapter.

Two of the authors currently serve as full-time faculty in higher education programs. The third recently completed her doctoral degree in higher education and is considering positions that may take her toward either the full-time faculty or administrator realm of higher education. All have full-time higher education administration or staff position experience as well, including as chief judicial officer and student affairs administrator to whom a counseling center, and various other departments, reported; associate head coach of a Division I athletic team; and counselor within a university counseling center. The one author who has served as a member of a counseling center staff has a master's degree in Community Counseling and is credentialed as a Licensed Professional Counselor, National Certified Counselor, and Approved Clinical Supervisor. In addition, her current teaching responsibilities include counseling-related courses. Thus, we bring to this chapter who we are and build on our experiences and backgrounds, as well as the collaborative relationships of which we have been a part, or those relationships in which we strived for collaboration in the promotion of student well-being.

COLLEGE STUDENT WELL-BEING

"Well-being is a multifaceted concept ... resulting from educational encounters that both guide students in the search for meaning and direction in life and help them realize their full potential" (Seifert, 2005, para. 1). Overall, well-being is essential to student success. Research indicates that students with positive well-being are more engaged in the campus community and fare better mentally, emotionally, physically, and academically (Pandolfo, 2012; Whitney, 2010). Whitney found that students who reported having five or more safe adults on whom they could rely during times of stress or difficulty experienced greater perceived positive well-being than those students reporting fewer safe adults in their lives. Safe adults were more strongly associated with a greater range of positive well-being indicators and more overall positive well-being than close friends. The type of safe adults for Whitney's study ranged from parents, relatives, and neighbors to religious leaders, teachers, employers, or others. Safe adults are most frequently defined as people who behave consistently and who will listen to the student without passing judgment, and allow the student to express autonomy when making life decisions (Horowitz, McKay, & Marshall, 2005).

Extending research on the significance of faculty members on student experiences, Pandolfo (2012) reported on results of a 10-year study conducted by Chambliss and Takacs, scheduled for release in an upcoming publication. Chambliss and Takacs found that a single positive encounter with a faculty member could have lasting influence on a student's overall well-being and success in college. Positive effects on student outcomes (e.g., college grade point average, degree aspiration, critical thinking, and communication) from student-faculty interaction is well-documented (Astin, 1984; Kim & Sax, 2009; Kuh, 1995; Kuh, Cruze, Shoup, Kinzie, 2008).

Astin (1984) contributed to the research on student involvement in relation to persistence and dropout. Astin introduced involvement as taking place along a continuum with student dropout being the ultimate form of noninvolvement, therefore anchoring the continuum at the bottom. Astin concluded that all forms of student involvement are connected to above-average changes in characteristics of entering freshmen. Some student outcomes are linked more strongly with involvement than either new freshmen characteristics or institutional characteristics. Astin reported several different types of involvement, but he specifically discussed involvement through student–faculty interaction. Student–faculty interaction had the strongest relationship with students' levels of college satisfaction in his study. This type of involvement was the strongest relationship with satisfaction over any other student or institutional characteristic or other type of involvement. Students who had frequent interaction with faculty were more likely to report satisfaction in all areas of their college experience (e.g., student friendships, variety of courses, intellectual surroundings, and administration of the institution).

The impact of adult-to-student interaction is not specific to faculty alone. As Whitney (2010) suggested, students choose several types of adults with whom to form meaningful and trusting relationships. The adults whom students choose as "safe" adults in their lives provide different types of social support and fulfill student needs in different ways. For example, Davis, Morris, and Kraus (1998) found close friends to be the strongest type of support for overall college student well-being. Whitney's (2010) findings support Astin's (1984) theory that faculty interaction is the strongest predictor of overall institutional satisfaction.

Student well-being does not occur in a vacuum or develop on its own. Human beings are social creatures who require social interaction and the support of others to thrive (Ansbacher & Ansbacher, 1956; Whitney, 2010). Knowing that someone cares for us, accepts us, and is available when we are facing difficult times is vital to the social support that promotes positive well-being (Whitney). On a college or university campus, faculty and staff are ideally positioned to promote student well-being. Faculty members in particular take on many roles with students, including confidant, advisor, and friend (Hardee, 1959). Hardee posited that students discuss "personal problems, employment, the choice of vocation, [and] the significant events of the day" (p. 2) with faculty as the students strive to find meaning in life and make decisions for the future related to those areas. Faculty, however, are not the only higher education personnel to whom students turn regarding life and well-being issues; they seek support from staff as well. For example, student athletes often seek guidance in such areas from coaches (Selby, Weinstein, & Bird, 1990). Hunt and Eisenberg (2010) advocated for collaboration across the campus community (and beyond its borders) in facilitating student well-being. Thus, both faculty and staff can optimize opportunities to promote well-being in students.

Student well-being encompasses several components. Hardee (1959) highlighted well-being domains of intellectual, social, emotional, spiritual, and physical. In their model of wellness, Myers, Sweeney, and Witmer (2000) included 17 dimensions of wellness that they believed were necessary for a holistic approach to wellness counseling. This model included spirituality as the focal point of well-being. Further research on the wheel of wellness led to an updated model that downplayed the "centrality" of spirituality and included the original 17 dimensions as factors of a third order, with five second-order factors: creative, coping, social, essential, and physical (Myers & Sweeney, 2007).

Many colleges and universities have adopted some form of a wellness wheel, incorporating the theory established by Myers and her colleagues throughout the years. One example is the University of Washington whose Department of Health and Wellness within the Division of Student Life advocates the use of a holistic wellness wheel model that contains seven dimensions: intellectual, physical, social, environmental, financial, spiritual, and emotional ("Wellness Wheel and Guide," 2010). Marquette University has a very similar wellness wheel presented by its Department of Exercise Science within the College of Health Sciences that has six dimensions: physical, emotional, occupational, spiritual, social, and intellectual ("Wellness," 2010). Five dimensions are identical to those at the University of Washington and, although Marquette University may use a similar wheel of wellness for students, Marquette University's wheel is designated as the wheel for employee wellness.

The focus of this chapter is student well-being; however, the overlapping of dimensions, as well as the new dimensions seen in some of these models, particularly environmental, financial, and occupational, are becoming key aspects in the definition of overall well-being for various constituents affiliated with a college or university campus. We believe these added dimensions lead to some of the more innovative and potentially effective outreach programs and collaborations related to student well-being that may be led by counseling center staff. We will expand the topic of programs and collaborations later in this chapter.

To show that an occupational or career dimension is not only found in employee wellness models at higher education institutions, we consider a model developed by the Gallup Organization. Following extensive research that spanned 50 years and 150 countries, the Gallup Organization, well known for its Gallup Poll division, studied wellness in those 150 countries and from that research, five general areas of wellness emerged: career, social, financial, physical, and community well-being (Rath & Harter, 2010). More recently, based on that large-scale and longitudinal study, the Gallup Campus Wellbeing Consortium (GCWC) was developed, which is focused on studying the general areas of wellness within, and applying the areas to, college and university communities ("Creating a Wellbeing Campus," 2010).

The Gallup Organization created the GCWC in 2010 to promote discussion about the well-being of students and employees in higher education environments ("Creating a Wellbeing Campus," 2010). The consortium, which began with three schools, has a goal of "quantify[ing] the impact of wellbeing over time" ("Creating a Wellbeing Campus," para. 6). Faculty, staff, and students at the member schools have access to various Gallup-designed assessment, measurement, and planning instruments to enhance the collection of data on well-being of campus constituencies ("Creating a Wellbeing Campus," 2010). In their book upon which the GCWC is based, Rath and Harter (2010) attempted to define well-being. They wrote:

> Well-being is about the combination of our love for what we do each day, the quality of our relationships, the security of our finances, the vibrancy of our physical health, and the pride we take in what we have contributed to our communities. (p. 4)

From this definition, and the multiyear and country research described above, Rath and Harter specified those five previously mentioned dimensions they believe encompass well-being: career, social, financial, physical, and community.

The GCWC is exploring these dimensions in higher education settings. The work of the GCWC is still in its infancy, however, and not much is known about the consortium beyond its plans. In addition, at the time of this writing, no data are available regarding the three inaugural members or other schools who may have completed proposals to join the consortium ("Creating a Wellbeing Campus," 2010). The call for proposals includes a statement that "[t]his announcement marks the beginning of a 5-year journey for each University to become a wellbeing campus and to help students, faculty, and staff reach thriving levels of wellbeing" ("Creating a Wellbeing Campus," para. 2). Given the wealth of support from Gallup for the GCWC, particularly related to the measurement and assessment tools referenced above, the GCWC holds promise as one of those potentially highly innovative and effective examples of collaboration that can positively affect well-being. Next, we consider other existing or prospective collaboration examples designed to enhance student well-being on a college and university campus in which counseling center staff may take a lead role in outreach and creating the collaborative relationships.

COLLABORATION AND EARLY PROGRAMMING EXAMPLES TO PROMOTE STUDENT WELL-BEING

Before continuing, we acknowledge that presenting the following examples may be seen as adding to the already busy schedules of counseling center staff. Counseling staff also should consider their individual institution's climate and culture before implementing collaboration, outreach, and programming efforts. Institutions have unique characteristics that define and shape their culture and definition of engagement (Brukardt, Holland, Percy, & Zimpher, 2004; Hirt, 2006; Kim & Sax, 2009). Not only can culture be altered from leadership style and size, but also by other characteristics, such as new freshman characteristics (Kim & Sax, 2009;

Owens & Valesky, 2010). Counseling professionals should know their institution's culture and how that culture is shaped, and should be informed and aware of the current, and sometimes ever-changing, student-body characteristics.

There may be the argument that the role of counseling center staff on a college or university campus is to provide college counseling only, which focuses on the provision of counseling to members of a higher education community by those professionals trained in counseling (Spooner, 2000). Counseling centers face challenges in the provision of such counseling services, challenges created by budgetary constraints, as well as a noted increase in number of clients seen and severity of issues presented (Terneus, 2006).

There also may be concern that creating collaborative relationships may involve turning over the individual counseling role to others (e.g., outsourcing) or allowing others to act within that role. Outsourcing psychological services can create ethical and legal issues (Webb, Widseth, & John, 1997), which is not the focus of this chapter. With respect to others on a college campus (i.e., faculty and staff), we are not advocating the creation of allied counselor roles for faculty and staff. The phrase "allied professional counselor" can have a positive connotation related to faculty and staff, often student affairs professionals, who understand student development and are able to use counseling-type skills to address student needs and issues (Dean, 2000). That term, if such a role is not defined well for noncounselor trained faculty and staff, also can lead to more harm if those without appropriate skills and ethics training are handling issues that belong only in the hands of an actual counselor. For the well-being of the counselor, clarifying the role of the counselor and level and type of services he or she is able to provide is important (Terneus, 2006). Doing so will benefit both the counselor and the client as "[t]he purpose of wellness is to maximize human potential for our clients and ourselves" (Witmer & Young, 1996, p. 152).

According to the Council on Advancement of Standards (CAS), counseling center staff members are asked to provide services that address three complementary functions: developmental, remedial, and prevention (Spooner, 2000). The role of the counselor may involve individual student counseling but increasingly involves serving the whole campus community and having an active role in areas such as assessment, budgets, and retention (Dean, 2000; Spooner, 2000). Serving the needs of the whole campus and all of its constituents is overwhelming and requires collaboration from others on campus. This fits well into one of the roles defined by the International Association of Counseling Services (IACS) whose accreditation standards describe college counselors performing "a contributive role to the campus environment that facilitates the growth and development of students" (Kiracofe et al., 1994, p. 38). This can be accomplished through outreach to the campus community, and it is those types of contributive roles and collaborative relationships on which the programs and suggestions below are based. They are presented with the following quote from Mattox (2000) in mind: "Successful college counselors recognize that positive campus relationships are essential in promoting the mission of college counseling centers and solidifying the presence of college counselors on campus" (p. 221).

University of Washington Wellness Wheel

The Department of Health and Wellness in the Division of Student Life at the University of Washington developed a "Wellness Wheel and Guide" (2010) that includes seven dimensions: intellectual, physical, social, environmental, financial, spiritual, and emotional. As noted earlier, the dimensions are similar to those developed and used in other counseling and higher education settings and also incorporate newer dimensions, including environmental and financial. What makes Washington's wellness wheel an example of the type of collaboration important to this chapter is the information presented in addition to the dimensions of wellness. Each dimension is defined, outcomes or ways in which a student could achieve thriving levels of wellness in each area are provided, and departments on campus (both within and outside of the Division of Student Life) are listed as resources for achieving wellness. The counseling center is listed specifically as a resource for three of the dimensions: social, financial, and emotional, but never listed on its own. Arguably, the counseling center could be listed as a resource within each dimension or as the center from which the spokes of other departments and resources flow.

The University of Central Florida Counseling Center

The University of Central Florida's (UCF) counseling center demonstrates multiple dynamic outreach efforts on its interactive website ("Counseling center," 2012). UCF provides students with a comprehensive site including various links specific to student mental health issues. Limited information is provided for parents and employees because the counseling center is designed for student counseling needs. The site provides easy-to-read text and links to student resources, support groups, prevention and outreach groups, and internship opportunities. UCF's counseling center is grounded by the understanding of student development theories that help counseling staff better understand where the students are in their moral and identity development. This counseling center provides an example of integrating the understanding of student development and technology into one interactive web resource. UCF counseling center provides multiple links for student resources including links to smartphone applications ranging from stress measures to women's health applications. The site provides a list of working links to all campus resources concerning academic help to general student services. A comprehensive list of self-help books with a wide variety and range is made available with the knowledge that many students may feel more comfortable accessing information on their own before seeking external help. Interactive videos, media downloads, and self-assessment tests are made available and accessible free of charge for students.

UCF provides several support group options with the intention of supporting diverse groups across campus. The prevention and outreach groups at UCF cover many of the common mental health issues students face. The counseling center offers several options in therapy style from group therapy to individual therapy sessions. UCF brings national partnerships to campus by working in collaboration with the Active Minds organization. The focus of this group is to form student-run mental health awareness, education, and advocacy groups across campus that change the way mental health and counseling are talked about by peers, faculty, and staff. The goals of this group are not only to provide mental health awareness and support, but also to counter the stigma of counseling. UCF's participation with Active Minds is part of a national effort to change the language used to describe mental health on our nation's campuses.

The UCF counseling center provides multiple support and programming for all types of students on campus. Bright Knights is group designated specifically for student athletes, and the group page provides resources for coaches and athletic trainers along with links to information on issues specific to these types of students. Many individuals may not realize the importance of a counseling group designated specifically to student athletes. Student athletes are a unique population that share similar mental health issues with the general student population, but may experience these issues in drastically different ways. Many institutions do not provide internal sports psychologist or sport-specific counseling to the athletic teams as part of the institutional experience. Student athletes often are referred to general counselors who may not be trained or familiar with the athlete's perspective and unique issues (Watson, 2003). If athletic departments do provide external sport psychology or counseling, the budget typically allows for one counselor to hundreds of athletes. By UCF including and recognizing the special counseling need of student athletes, they are reaching a needy and often overlooked population. UCF is one example of a counseling center focused on overall well-being for all types of students.

Suggestions for Counseling Staff Engagement and Outreach

Learning Communities and Early Exposure

The value of freshman learning communities has been demonstrated through research since the mid-1990s. Freshman learning communities can be instrumental to student persistence and social and academic engagement (Tinto, 1998; Tinto & Goodsell, 2004; Zhao & Kuh, 2004). The general concept of a learning community is to group students together based on common characteristics and to provide social, residential, and academic learning experiences for the intact group. The idea is that students will form relationships with each other based on common characteristics and experiences, and will use each other as resources for support, academic progress, and overall student development. Lenning and Ebbers (1999) defined four types of generic forms student communities may take: (a) curricular (students enrolled in two or more courses together), (b) classroom (cooperative learning and group processes), (c) residen tial (on-campus living arrangements), and (d) student-type (designed for target groups) learning communities. One type of student community structure that has been largely omitted by research is the student athlete community structure.

Generic student communities rely heavily on limited common experiences or characteristics of the students to be the primary source of the community and student success. The student athlete community relies not only on the common characteristics of the athletes (i.e., athletic ability and gender), but also on the support staff placed around the athletes as the facilitators of success. Up to 1 year before student athletes arrive on campus, they are provided several avenues for relationship building with staff and students on campus. Student athletes visit campuses for unofficial and official visits, and during these visits, they are exposed to their future teammates and peers, academic advisors, athletic trainers, and coaches. Some visits even include meetings with future professors and instructors. Once the student athletes leave campus after their recruiting visit, coaches and other student athletes invest time in building a relationship with the new student athlete. Some of these relationships begin long before the student athlete arrives for the official visit. After recruiting deadlines pass (NCAA, 2012), coaches and staff can correspond with the prospective student athlete through written and oral correspondence. Relationship building with prospects starts years before the athlete arrives on campus. Before the first day student athletes step on campus, they have access and relationships with more than five adults they could choose to act as "safe adults" in their college experience (Whitney, 2010). The nature of athletic teams, regardless of type of sport (i.e., individual or team) provides intact groups with common characteristics that new student athletes will join immediately.

Proactive Approaches to Exposure and Relationship Building

Although research is scarce on how early student-community development can be implemented effectively, counselors can play an active role in
helping incoming students build relationships with peers and with adults
before the traditional new-student orientation date. Counseling staff
members will not be able to reach every new student before they arrive
on campus for orientation. Therefore, before counseling centers actively
pursue early programming opportunities, there should be goals in place
that will guide the outreach efforts.

SUMMER COUNSELING. With specific goals, or target student populations in
mind, one opportunity for early exposure could be summer counseling
services open to local students or students participating in high school
to college transition programs. Some universities offer summer transition
programs to help prepare students for the rigors of freshman year including, but not limited to, financial information, academic requirements, and
necessary paperwork (Wolff-Wendel, Tuttle, & Keller-Wolff, 1999). The
counseling center could use this opportunity to collaborate with these
programs and establish an early relationship with these students and
parents. A relationship with parents should be considered with all early
programming because of the importance parents can have on student
involvement, especially in regard to financial stress (Xiao, Shim, Barber, &
Lyons, 2007). Students involved in transition programs may benefit from
personal relationships and additional support, especially first-generation
college students (Kim & Sax, 2009). Licensed counseling staff should be
the only staff members issuing counseling services and advice to students
(Terneus, 2006), but available graduate assistants and interns could participate in student interactions. Although graduate assistants and interns
are older and may not be considered incoming freshmen peers, they are
still students and may be able to connect with targeted students on a
student-to-student level.

SENIOR SEND-OFF PARTIES. Another opportunity for early exposure that is
being overlooked by many campus staff is the senior send-off parties
held during the summer. A senior send-off party is the term used to
describe social gatherings of incoming freshman in different areas of the
country. Typically, these parties are organized through the institution's
alumni or orientation office or foundation. Student parents, alumni, or
friends host the parties as a way to celebrate local students' admittance
into the same institution. Some institutions do send campus representa-
tives to these parties, but staff members are rarely active participants.
Counseling staff could use this opportunity to be more active in their
efforts to promote student well-being. Collaboration with the appropriate
institutional department could result in a semi-formal party agenda with

the intention of promoting student well-being in advance. Counseling center staff should work in collaboration with parents and alumni to present a purposeful interaction with students at the parties. Counselors should help the students at the parties become more familiar with their peers in the room and expose the students to the common characteristics they share. Counselors could help students become more aware of some of the common issues new students face and what types of help are available to them on campus. Delivery and mode of approach should be developed in ways that will show relevant value and pique student interest in the topic (Lepper & Cordova, 1992). Senior send-off parties are one opportunity to establish and build an early relationship with students and offer the counseling center and staff as one source of potentially safe adults on campus. Similar to the athletic recruiting model, counseling staff will need to cultivate relationships with these students throughout the summer and after the students arrive on campus.

ON-CAMPUS PROACTIVE EFFORTS. The most common initial exposure to counseling center staff is new student orientation. Counseling staff must remember that new students are being bombarded with relevant information throughout the course of one day. Staff members are encouraged to develop a strategy that will reach the students well before the initial orientation day. Orientation day may involve the counseling center hosting a lunch or a fun event as an opportunity to reconnect with students and issue useful information about upcoming counseling center events. Because students may not retain the material given to them during orientation because of the influx of new information, counseling center staff could use orientation day as an opportunity to provide outreach information designed for parents during the process. Parents may not be as involved in many of the orientation activities, and counseling center staff may find creative strategies to target parents and family members for additional support for the new student.

Counselors should take a proactive role and seek out group or student meetings, and use those meetings to establish a connection with the students involved. For example, athletic coaches schedule prospective student athlete visits routinely throughout the academic year and some during the summer depending on the sport. Counselors could call coaches before the start of the fall semester and request to have the prospective student athlete(s) meet with a counseling staff member during the recruiting visit on campus. Coaches want to expose recruits to the variety of resources the institution has to offer, and considering the sport-counseling situation on many campuses, coaches may welcome the thought of building a relationship with the on-campus counseling staff. Other avenues for contact with students may be early student organization meetings, cohort or departmental meetings, or yearly athletic training and compliance meetings. Counseling staff have opportunities to build relationships with other departments across campus, but more importantly, they have opportunities with students that may not otherwise engage with the counseling center. Counseling center staff will need to commit to a proactive approach that may demand time and budget adjustments, but proactive outreach will expose the center's resources and staff across campus to students who may otherwise not be aware of the benefits of mental health counseling.

BE A HOST. One proactive approach is to consider hosting functions or sponsoring an event. Depending on the type of institution, game-day cookouts are excellent opportunities to meet the students in their element. For example, universities with strong football traditions often have designated areas for pregame tailgating or cookout activities. Many of these areas allow fans to erect tents or set up chairs. The counseling center could advertise and invite students to the designated tent for free food and information about counseling services. Any social event will give the staff an opportunity to connect with students on a more personal level. Similarly, counseling centers could target specific student group functions and ask to speak or participate in a meeting. Collaboration with the alumni and foundation offices or specific alumni may be useful for this suggestion. Alumni and foundation offices hold events throughout the year that encourage alumni, donor, and student interaction. These offices could be valuable resources for access to students. Participation and programming should have a purpose and follow the goals set by the counseling center to ensure student interaction is meaningful and consistent with the center's mission.

KNOW THE TECHNOLOGY. Finally, counseling centers should make every effort to keep up to date with technology and know how students are using technology to gather information. Technology can be a powerful tool in not only cultivating relationships, but also initiating relationships with students. Proper technology use can help students understand what resources are available and which staff members are able to help in a time of need. Technology should not be the only, or even primary, source of student contact, however. Face-to-face contact can be more effective when transmitting important information (Terneus, 2006). Students like interesting concepts (Lepper & Cordova, 1992), and professionals on campus should actively pursue all ways to involve and engage students in meaningful activities (Astin, 1984). Technology can be used as a strategy to initiate and encourage face-to-face contact.

Counseling center staff have opportunities to build relationships with students who may not otherwise know about the resources the counseling center offers. Similar to athletic recruiting, counselors and other staff must find ways to cultivate relationships with students early and often. Many early opportunities exist on campuses, but counseling staff must be proactive in finding these hidden opportunities. Counseling centers should have defining goals and an established framework before implementing early programming efforts. Relationship building and promotion of resources takes commitment, effort, funding, and time. Some centers may not have the funding or staff necessary for an extensive effort. All centers should evaluate individual staffing and funding resources before setting goals for a proactive approach. Graduate assistants and interns should be used in appropriate capacities to help extend the counseling center's efforts.

REFERENCES

Ansbacher, H. L., & Ansbacher, R. R. (Eds.). (1956). *The individual psychology of Alfred Adler: A systematic presentation in selections from his writings.* New York, NY: Harper Torchbooks.

Brukardt, M. J., Holland, B., Percy, S. L., & Zimpher, N. (2004). *Calling the question: Is higher education ready to commit to community engagement? A wingspread statement.* Milwaukee, WI: Milwaukee Idea Office, University of Wisconsin Milwaukee.

Counseling Center. (2012). Retrieved from http://counseling.sdes.ucf.edu

Creating a wellbeing campus to improve lives in communities. (2010, March 23). Retrieved from http://www.gallup.com/consulting/education/146804/creating-wellbeing-campus-improve-lives-communities.aspx

Davis, M. H., Morris, M. M., & Kraus, L. A. (1998). Relationship-specific and global perceptions of social support: Associations to well-being and attachment. *Journal of Personality and Social Psychology, 74*(2), 468–481.

Dean, L. A. (2000). College counseling today: Changing roles and definitions. In D. C. Davis & K. M. Humphrey (Eds.), *College counseling: Issues and strategies for a new millennium* (pp. 41–56). Alexandria, VA: American Counseling Association.

Hardee, M. D. (1959). *The faculty in college counseling.* New York, NY: McGraw-Hill.

Hirt, J. B. (2006). *Where you work matters: Student affairs administration at different types of institutions.* Lanham, MD: University Press of America.

Horowitz, K., McKay, M., & Marshall, R. (2005). Community violence and urban families: Experiences, effects, and directions for interventions. *American Journal of Orthopsychiatry, 75*(3), 356–368.

Hunt, J., & Eisenberg, D. (2010). Mental health problems and help-seeking behavior among college students. *Journal of Adolescent Health, 46,* 3–10. doi: 10.1016/j.jadohealth.2009.08.008

Kim, Y. K., & Sax, L. J. (2009). Student-faculty interaction in research universities: Differences by student gender, race, social class, and first–generation status. *Research in Higher Education, 50*(5), 437–459.

Kiracofe, N. M., Donn, P. A., Grant, C. O., Podolnick, E. E., Bingham, R. P., Bolland, H. R., ... Yamada, K. T. (1994). Accreditation standards for university and college counseling centers. *Journal of Counseling and Development, 73,* 38–43.

Kuh, G. D. (1995). The other curriculum: Out-of-class experiences associated with student learning and personal development. *The Journal of Higher Education, 66*(2), 123–155.

Kuh, G. D., Cruce, T. M., Shoup, R., & Kinzie, J. (2008). Unmasking the effects of student engagement on first year college grades and persistence. *The Journal of Higher Education, 79*(5), 540–563.

Lenning, O., & Ebbers, L. (1999). The powerful potential of learning communities: Improving education for the future. *ASHE-ERIC Higher Education Report, 26*(6). 1–173.

Mattox, R. (2000). Building effective campus relationships. In D. C. Davis & K. M. Humphrey (Eds.), *College counseling: Issues and strategies for a new millennium* (pp. 221–237). Alexandria, VA: American Counseling Association.

Myers, J. E., & Sweeney, T. J. (2007). Wellness in counseling: An overview. *Professional Counseling Digest.* Retrieved from http://www.counselingoutfitters.com/vistas/ACAPCD/ACAPCD-09.pdf

Myers, J. E., Sweeney, T. J., & Witmer, J. M. (2000). The Wheel of Wellness counseling for wellness: A holistic model for treatment planning. *Journal of Counseling & Development, 78,* 251–266.

NCAA. (2012). *National Collegiate Athletic Association.* Retrieved from http://www.ncaa.org

Owens, R. G., & Valesky, T. C. (2010). Organizational culture and organizational climate. *Organizational behavior in education: Leadership and school reform* (10th ed., pp. 135–156). Boston, MA: Allyn and Bacon.

Pandolfo, N. (2012, May 21). Experts: College success can spring from a single conversation. *The Hechinger Report.* Retrieved from www.hechingerreport.org

Rath, T., & Harter, J. (2010). *Wellbeing: The five essential elements.* New York, NY: Gallup Press.

Seifert, T. A. (2005, Spring). *The Ryff Scales of Psychological Well-Being. Assessment notes.* Retrieved from http://www.liberalarts.wabash.edu/ryff-scales

Selby, R., Weinstien, H. M., & Bird, T. S. (1990). The health of university athletes: Attitudes, behaviors, and stressors. *Journal of American College Health, 39*(1), 11–18.

Spooner, S. E. (2000). The college counseling environment. In D. Davis & K. Humphrey (Eds.), *College counseling: Issues and strategies for a new millennium* (pp. 3–14). Alexandria, VA: American Counseling Association.

Terneus, S. K. (2006). Problematic areas of practice in college counseling. *Vista 2006 Online.* Retrieved from http://www.counselingoutfitters.com/Terneus.htm

Tinto, V. (1998). Colleges as communities: Taking research on student persistence seriously. *The Review of Higher Education, 21*(2), 167–177.

Tinto, V., & Goodsell, A. (1994). Freshman interest groups and the first year experience: Constructing student communities in a large university. *Journal of the Freshman Year Experience, 6,* 7–28.

Watson, J. C. (2003). Overcoming the challenges of counseling college student athletes. *ERIC Clearinghouse on Counseling and Student Services.* Retrieved August 28, 2012, from http:// www.ericdigests.org/2003-5/athletes.htm

Webb, R. E., Widseth, J. C., & John, K. B. (1997). Outsourcing and the role of psychological services on the college campus. *NASPA Journal, 34*(3), 186–198.

Wellness. (2012). Retrieved from http://www.marquete.edu/wellness/wheel

Wellness Wheel and Guide. (2010). Retrieved from http://www.livewell.uw.edu/students/wellnesswheel.shmtl

Whitney, C. (2010). Social supports among college students and measures of alcohol use, perceived stress, satisfaction with life, emotional intelligence and coping. *Journal of Student Wellbeing, 4*(1), 49–67.

Witmer, M. J., & Young, M. E. (1996). Preventing counselor impairment: A wellness approach. *Journal of Humanistic Education & Development, 34*(3), 141–156.

Wolff-Wendel, L. E., Tuttle, K., & Keller-Wolff, K. M. (1999). Assessment of a freshman summer transition program in an open-admissions institution. *Journal of the First Year Experience, 11*(2), 7–32.

Xiao, J. J., Shim, S., Barber, B., & Lyons, A. (2007). *Academic success and well-being of college students: Financial behaviors matter* [Monograph]. Tucson, AZ: The University of Arizona. Retrieved from http://www.cefe.illinois.edu/research/reports/Academic%20Success%20and%20Well-Being%20of%20College%20Students_112007.pdf

Zhao, C., & Kuh, G. D. (2004). Adding value: Learning communities and student engagement. *Research in Higher Education, 45*(2), 115–138.

Index